The Russian Research Center

The Russian Research Center was established February 1, 1949. It is supported by the Carnegie Corporation on a grant covering the period until July 1, 1953. The major objective of the Research Center is the study of Russian institutions and behavior in an effort to make for better understanding of the international actions and policy of the Soviet Union. The participating scholars represent all of the social sciences. In accord with the expressed wish of the Carnegie Corporation, the fields of anthropology, psychology, and sociology, which have hitherto played little part in Russian studies in this country, are strongly represented. The staff of the Center are grateful to the Carnegie Corporation not only for the opportunity to carry out their studies under favorable circumstances, but also for the moral encouragement and intellectual stimulation which have been provided by contact with individual officers and trustees of the Corporation.

RUSSIAN RESEARCH CENTER STUDIES

1. *Public Opinion in Soviet Russia; A Study in Mass Persuasion.* By Alex Inkeles
2. *Soviet Politics: The Dilemma of Power.* By Barrington Moore, Jr.
3. *The Challenge of Soviet Law.* By Harold J. Berman (in press)

Soviet Politics—

The Dilemma of Power

Soviet Politics — The Dilemma of Power

THE ROLE OF IDEAS IN SOCIAL CHANGE

By Barrington Moore Jr

HARVARD UNIVERSITY PRESS
Cambridge · Massachusetts
1950

TO **E.C.M.**

Preface

Dr. Moore's book is a distinguished contribution both to the understanding of Soviet society and to the development of a more mature social science. Although his book is remarkable for the breadth and depth of its coverage of published materials, Russian and non-Russian, most of his sources will be familiar to scholars specializing on the Soviet Union. What is new is the conceptual framework in which these data are assayed and interpreted. This framework is neither pretentious nor formalistic. But Dr. Moore draws discriminatingly upon the relevant content and ideas of history, political science, economics, psychology, sociology, and philosophy. He ranges from the classic works of Sumner, Pareto, Sorel, and Weber to the most recent studies in perceptual psychology and culture and personality. Nor is the result a watery eclecticism. No conceptual instrument is dragged in just because it is in fashion at the moment or to achieve an artificial completeness. The test is consistently: Is this idea useful in helping us to understand the concrete problems at hand? No single factor is made to explain everything, but each is utilized legitimately to explain something. The argument of the book is therefore as complex as it is cautious and poised. The reader who recognizes the intricacy of the issues and the impossibility of magic formulas will applaud the balance and sanity of the treatment and respect the modesty of the conclusions— for example, those concerning the probability of war between the United States and the Soviet Union.

The Soviet materials are employed as a highly pertinent case history bearing on one of the oldest but still most urgent problems in an over-all theory of human behavior: What is the role of ideas in action, particularly political action? Specifically: Which of the prerevolutionary Bolshevik ideas have been put into effect in the Soviet Union, which ones set aside, and why? The setting of the stage at the time of the Revolution is carefully examined, both in terms of Communist theory and in terms of the nature of Russian society at that time. The march of events, inside and outside Russia, is then scrutinized and related to constancy and change in the ideological line. Economic factors, the personalities of leaders, international pressures, historical accidents, the perduring aspects of traditional Russian culture—all are given a due examination. Especially searching and original is the study of the situational determinants of action: the dilemma of authority, the psychological dimensions and social structure of power cliques, the effects of the failure of the Communist revolution in Germany. One of Dr. Moore's most brilliant points, and an excellent example of his capacity as an integrator, is the critical analysis he makes alike of the Marxist and of the currently fashionable "culture and personality" approaches:

The weakness of these two approaches is that they take but little cognizance of the structure of the international arena in which the clash of national interests takes place. The difficulty is the same as that which beset psychology when it tried to explain human behavior by studying the individual *in vacuo*, without perceiving the society in which the individual lived. For certain purposes it is of course legitimate and desirable to study as independent entities either the balance of power or the domestic determinants of political behavior in a particular state. But to understand international politics, an approach is necessary that will combine the two areas of inquiry and assign a correct weight to the conclusions drawn from each.

This book is likewise most informative on another perennial question: To what extent is it possible to create a *new* social order? Dr. Moore skillfully analyzes the Russian case, showing how the rationally, and indeed idealistically, conceived doctrines of Marx and Lenin had to be modified as they were ground out in practice against the stubborn and irreducible facts of history, culture, and recurrent human situations. A full-bodied picture of the limitations and possibilities of directed social change emerges.

Dr. Moore makes no pretensions to a complete integration of the social sciences. He consciously avoids premature synthesis, needless abstraction, grand schematization with symmetries that are merely logical (or pseudo-logical). But he sets an admirable standard in making his assumptions and his whole modest theoretical structure explicit and hence subject to rational criticism. He draws wisely and with enormous versatility on the arsenal of contemporary social science. What he selects he binds together as tightly as is justified in the present state of our ignorance. His final theoretical product is a distinct creation which opens new roads for the study of the psychology and sociology of power, the anthropology and philosophy of ideology, and the political theory that emerges from intellectual history. The framework of this book is not bounded by arbitrary disciplinary lines. Indeed, it is difficult to point to another of which one could say with as much correctness, "Here basic social science has been achieved." In a sense, Dr. Moore's book is more than an approximation to a generalized social science, for it is informed also by the humanistic tradition. He realizes that only relatively tiny areas of human behavior can at present be treated with mechanical rigor. The broad canvas of *Soviet Politics* here receives helpful illumination generated by scrupulous workmanship, catholic scholarship, and theory which rises above common sense but yet remains intimately tied to experience.

CLYDE KLUCKHOHN

Acknowledgments

It is a pleasant custom in the community of scholars to thank those who have rendered help and to absolve them of sins committed by the author. My debts are many and cannot be repaid by a ritual obeisance here.

The Russian Research Center of Harvard University, supported by the Carnegie Corporation of New York, has provided the great boons of freedom from interruption, stimulating fellow workers, and excellent assistance in preparing the manuscript during an entire academic year. I wish to express my appreciation to Professor Clyde Kluckhohn, Director of the Center, who, in addition to writing the Preface, has ever given me generous and sustained encouragement.

Another debt I owe to the University of Chicago, which freed me from teaching duties for several months. I should like also to thank the Social Science Research Committee at the University of Chicago, which, through the generosity of the Rockefeller Foundation, gave me a grant to cover a portion of the research and clerical assistance at a certain stage of writing this study.

My colleagues at both institutions and in the wartime federal service have taught me much, and most when I have entirely disagreed with them. Professors Michael Karpovich and Merle Fainsod of Harvard, Hans Morgenthau of Chicago, Waldemar Gurian of Notre Dame, Philip Mosely of Columbia, and Isaiah Berlin of Oxford have generously given me the benefit of their specialized information, and the impact of their comments may be found in many of my interpretations. Since I have resisted their suggestions at other points, they bear no responsibility for the vagaries of this book.

To Professor Albert G. Keller of Yale I owe not only my original training in the social sciences, but also my interest in

Russian affairs. He encouraged me a decade and a half ago to begin by learning the language, and has always shown a fatherly tolerance for our differences of opinion.

Grateful acknowledgment is made to the following publishers for permission to reprint excerpts from copyrighted materials: Harper and Brothers, for use of Leon Trotsky, *Stalin* (copyright, 1941); The Macmillan Company, for use of F. S. C. Northrop, *The Meeting of East and West* (copyright, 1946); Charles Scribner's Sons, for use of Leon Trotsky, *My Life* (copyright, 1930); *The American Political Science Review,* for use of my article, "The Influence of Ideas on Policies as Shown in the Collectivization of Agriculture in Russia," August 1947 (copyright, 1947).

In the final stages of preparing this manuscript a number of persons at the Harvard University Press and the Russian Research Center have given me valuable assistance. Mrs. Helen W. Parsons, Administrative Assistant to the Director of the Center, has never failed to supply help and advice beyond the scope of her official duties. Mrs. Mildred S. Shade, Secretary to the Director of the Center, has greatly eased my task by providing an accurate typescript. Another member of the Center's staff, Mrs. Helen Constantine, has assisted at various points by typing and reading proof. The main burden of proofreading has fallen upon my wife, Elizabeth C. Moore, and Mr. Robert A. Feldmesser, Research Assistant at the Center. To all of the above my wholehearted thanks are but a scanty reward for their labors.

Throughout the entire writing of this book my wife has drawn upon an unending supply of understanding and patience to help me cope with the doubts and perplexities aroused by the apparent irreconcilables of the Soviet scene. In addition, she has cheerfully contributed her varied skills in criticizing and editing the manuscript, as well as in compiling the index. It is with the warmest affection that I acknowledge her large share in the making of this book.

BARRINGTON MOORE, JR.

Cambridge
June 1950

Contents

18 *Conclusions and Implications* **402**

Major features of ideological and social change in the
USSR, 402; Implications for modern industrial society, 405;
Are there limits to ideological change? 412; The natural
history of a successful protest movement, 418

Soviet Politics—

The Dilemma of Power

The Problem and Its Setting

Man has been concerned with the role of ideas in the shaping of human behavior ever since the first member of the species attempted to influence the behavior of another by exhortation instead of by blows. Throughout the centuries and in modern times a wide variety of views has been presented on this subject. Insofar as they concern the Soviet Union, one may note two contrasting interpretations of the relationship between Leninist doctrine and Soviet political behavior, both of which have found wide circulation.

One view holds that Stalin is a practical realist, who has un-ceremoniously tossed Marxism overboard. This view raises at once the difficult question: do not realists have ideas about the world in which they live and function so effectively? And may not these ideas have a very definite bearing on the actions taken by a so-called realist? The opposite interpretation declares that the fundamental goals of Soviet policy have remained essentially the same since their formulation by Lenin, and that all subse-quent modifications have been mere tactical detours on the road to the same goal. This view in turn raises the question of how many detours it is possible to make without getting lost, or at least without losing sight of the original goal.

The present study will attempt to provide more tenable an-swers to the problem of the interaction between Communist ideology and certain Soviet political practices. Insofar as this book is a study of a particular social system, it belongs in the familiar tradition of social morphology, along with other interpretative accounts of the social behavior and institutions of the peoples of the world. By the same token, it is an essay in applied social science, an effort to explain in systematic and general terms the relationship between various aspects of a going social system.

There is also a secondary objective. The record of the relationship between doctrine and practice in the Soviet Union provides an opportunity to test prevailing general theories concerning the role of ideas in organized human behavior. In this respect, as the subtitle indicates, this work is a case study concerned with the more general problem of the significance of ideas and ideals in social change.

It seems desirable at this point to mention some of the limitations and advantages of this approach.[1] To do so it is necessary to raise certain questions regarding the role of theory and logical methods in the study of human affairs.

Not very many years ago the student of human affairs was advised to gather the facts conscientiously and to let them speak for themselves. Much labor was expended by the followers of this advice, labor that was by no means without result. The method, however, had its limitations, a point which it is now fashionable to demonstrate. Newton certainly did not discover the law of gravitation through a carefully collected series of facts about falling apples. The procedure of letting the facts speak for themselves, it is pointed out, leads to a situation in which the investigator has no criteria except his unstated prejudices and assumptions for gathering the facts. It would be far better if the assumptions and possible prejudices were brought out into the open where they might be examined.

In a reaction against the older view, the opinion has come to prevail in certain quarters that the student of human society ought not to proceed to an examination of the facts until he has perfected a theoretical system with a chain of theorems and hypotheses, whose final links can be tested against the data. Though the critics of the older view make a valid point, these modern proponents of a strict scientific methodology sometimes overlook important matters.

In this connection it is well to remind ourselves of one general point, in the form of a logical difficulty that is passed over rather lightly by both the newer and the older schools, though it is relevant to both their claims. While one may disprove a theory by testing it against the facts, it is impossible to satisfy the requirements of logical proof by such testing. Strictly speaking, there is no such thing as verification by experiment. The agreement between the results of an experiment and one's expectations based upon theory does not exclude the possibility that the theory is wrong, and that a totally different theory is required. The behavior of the sun at sunrise and sunset may be accounted for by the theory that the earth is stationary on its axis. The hypothesis can be "verified" by repeated experiment and still be incorrect. Although some social scientists (for example, Pareto) are familiar with this elementary difficulty, it is not infrequently neglected in appeals to social scientists to follow the paths of the natural sciences.

It is pointed out correctly by the advocates of a theoretical approach that hypotheses act as searchlights, illuminating the field of inquiry to bring out the facts that are significant and that would otherwise be neglected. One may continue the figure, however, by pointing out that searchlights and hypotheses may have a blinding effect as well. The investigator who is out to prove or disprove a given hypothesis is likely to pass over unawares a number of facts that suggest an altogether different interpretation of the problem at hand. Even an undogmatic Freudian who set out to explain Soviet foreign policy might look intently for factors affecting the personality of the leaders and pay inadequate or no attention to such matters as geography and history. Someone else interested in certain economic hypotheses might neglect altogether the role of the leaders of the Soviet state. Up to a certain point such approaches are necessary and perhaps inevitable in the light of the human limitations of any single investigator. These remarks are not intended as a plea against the role of theory in the social sciences. They are a plea in favor of investigators with many and even inconsistent theories.

Another objection that may legitimately be raised against an undue preoccupation with theory at the outset of an inquiry is that it often tends to deflect the student from the task at hand.

So much time is spent on the elaboration of theory that the investigator never approaches the data. At times the German philosophical tradition has led to a situation where it appears necessary to know everything before one can know anything. The result, more often than not, is scientific sterility.

A further difficulty in the way of a precise theoretical approach is that the data of human behavior are seldom amenable to strict logical treatment, since a large portion of the most significant questions are not subject to experimental procedures. One cannot put the Roman Empire in a test tube, add a dash of Christianity, and watch to see whether it rises or falls. This well-known situation is regrettable from the point of view of theory, but it is one that has to be faced and dealt with in various ways, if we are not to leave the analysis of human behavior to the soothsayers. It does not mean that facts are totally irrelevant and unusable, that all interpretations are equally tenable, and that one man's opinion is as good as another's. It does mean that conclusions in many important fields have to be of a more tentative nature than strict logical processes might indicate. In consequence, theoretical imagination has to be directed, not so much toward the elaboration of a single system of constructs, as toward the elaboration of numberless alternative systems, some of which can actually be tested by the available data.

The previous difficulty is also related to the fact that the data of human behavior are by no means always gathered for the purpose the investigator has in mind. The existence or absence of facts is very often the result of the preservation or destruction of documents from causes that have nothing to do with the problems to be examined.

On all these counts I have come to the conclusion that it is advisable to plunge into the data with only the simplest and most flexible hypotheses, together with some ideas about the ways in which one might examine them. In practice, many investigators, even if they start with a well-developed theoretical structure, move back and forth between the facts and the theories, continually modifying the theories on the basis of new information or newly perceived relationships, and turning to the facts with fresh insight and renewed curiosity. Perhaps most students of society will agree that this is as it should be. If such is the case, more fruitful and more tenable hypotheses-conclusions should emerge at the end of a study than at the beginning.

One must recognize, in this connection, that in certain respects the tasks of applied and theoretical sciences are mutually contradictory. The applied scientist seeks to create an accurate map of a small portion of reality. If he is an engineer building a bridge, he wants to know all about the qualities of certain types of steel, the behavior of currents near the banks of a river, the possibility of high winds, and so forth. The social scientist who wishes to explain and ultimately predict the behavior of a particular social group will also want to learn a great deal about the specific economic, political, and other forces that impinge upon the behavior of this group, its organizational features and their capacity to resist certain types of strain, and similar matters. He is not necessarily concerned with mining facts for the theorist to use as evidence for or against some hypothesis. On the other hand, the theorist probably will endeavor to eliminate as many "perturbations" and "irrelevant" factors and forces as he can in order to reach as high a level of abstraction as possible. The economist who wishes to construct a logically integrated theory of economic behavior deliberately and explicitly excludes from his considerations many aspects of human activity that are not relevant for his purposes. The applied scientist must perform almost the opposite function of putting the parts back together in order to perceive the whole.

Considerations of this variety lie behind the popular distinction between a "practical" and a "theoretical" (sometimes called an academic) approach to human affairs. In many ways the emphasis on a practical or strictly empirical approach to the decisions that must be made about human affairs is probably beneficial. Disasters would probably result if philosophers became kings tomorrow. On the whole, fewer serious errors are made by persons with an intuitive and pragmatic approach to politics than by those who have a doctrinaire ax to grind. The practical man changes his behavior rapidly in response to failure, while the

doctrinaire theorist usually does not. Much sympathy can be
expressed for Pareto's dictum: let us have theoretical theories
and practical practices, for practical theories and theoretical
practices are an abomination.

Yet these considerations do not exhaust the matter. The purpose of theory is to relate as many facts as possible in a consistent
and orderly fashion. If the available theories will not do this,
that is not an argument against theories in general, but merely an
indication that the available theory or theories are inadequate.
Those who limit themselves to the practical approach to human
affairs are the ones who, in Veblen's words, are content to repeat the errors of their predecessors. If the practical attitude
had prevailed in man's approach to natural phenomena, our
knowledge would not have accumulated beyond the traditional
and stereotyped lore of the artisan, who passes a limited number
of techniques from one generation to the next. By the same token,
suspicion of theory, merely because it is theory, could effectively
prevent the development of a science of man and limit us to the
transmission of a scattered and inconsistent body of knowledge
taken from the varied insights and precepts of our ancestors.

To present a critical survey of the theories that have been
developed in the past century alone concerning the relationship
between ideas and behavior would carry us too far afield.[2] Instead, it is sufficient for the purpose of this study to point to
the two extremes that still contend for mastery as the correct
interpretation. One, represented best by Karl Marx himself, is
familiar as the materialist interpretation of history. The other extreme, which appears to be gaining favor at the moment, might
be called the "ideological" interpretation of history and finds a
definite statement in the writings of the contemporary philosopher, F. S. C. Northrop. Both these writers are, of course, cautious enough to repudiate any complete and universal causal
priority to either ideas or behavior. Yet even the briefest examination reveals the tremendous difference between these two viewpoints.

Marx regarded ideas as a sort of secondary social phenomena derived from the way in which men produced their

means of subsistence. By the latter Marx did not mean tools and machines alone; he included the types of social relationships into which men entered in order to produce goods and services.[3] "The production of ideas," Marx stated, "of conceptions, of consciousness, is at first directly interwoven with the material activity and the material intercourse of men, the language of real life. Conceiving, thinking, the mental intercourse of men, appear at this stage as the direct efflux of their material behavior." [4] There then follows the famous criticism of German idealistic philosophy, which has become axiomatic in much subsequent Marxist writing and thinking:

> In direct contrast to German philosophy which descends from heaven to earth, here we ascend from earth to heaven. That is to say, we do not set out from what men say, imagine, conceive, nor from men as narrated, thought of, imagined, conceived, in order to arrive at men in the flesh. We set out from real active men, and on the basis of their real life process we demonstrate the development of the ideological reflexes and echoes of this life-process. The phantoms formed in the human brain are also, necessarily, sublimates of their material life-process, which is empirically verifiable and bound to material premises. Morality, religion, metaphysics, all the rest of ideology and their corresponding forms of consciousness, thus no longer retain the semblance of independence.[5]

In this statement ideas are denied the significance of an independent variable among the numerous factors that make up a functioning social system. Marx did not adhere rigidly, however, to this extreme viewpoint. At times he apparently regarded this secondary role of ideas as an accurate description only for the beginning stages of social organization, as in his remark, quoted above, that thinking appears "at first" and "at this stage" as the efflux of material behavior. Elsewhere he evidently recognized the interaction of ideas with other social forces. In his comments on the writing of history Marx spoke of the need for tracing the origins and growth of religion, philosophy, and ethics, along with production, by which social development could be shown in its totality and "the reciprocal action of these various sides on one another." [6]

Nearly three and a half decades later Engels, in a letter, tried to back away from the extreme position taken in *The German Ideology*. "According to the materialist conception of history," he wrote on September 21, 1890, "the determining element in history is *ultimately* the production and reproduction in real life . . . If therefore somebody twists this into the statement that the economic element is the *only* determining one, he transforms it into a meaningless, abstract, and absurd phrase." Engels went on to say that political, legal, and philosophical theories also exercise their influence upon the course of historical struggles and in many cases determine their form. He conceded that Marx and he himself were partly to blame for the excessive stress on economic influences found in the writings of some of their followers, since in the beginning it had been necessary to "emphasize this main principle in opposition to our adversaries, who denied it, and we had not always the time, the place, or the opportunity to allow the other elements involved in the interaction to come into their rights." [7]

In the history of thought fertile theories have often been presented in their beginning stages in such a crude and definite form that their sponsors have later attempted to back away from them. Whether Northrop's views will undergo a similar modification remains to be seen. At any rate, it has some of the same qualities as the Marxist interpretation in that it is a pioneer attempt at explaining human society in terms of relatively simple principles.

Northrop's central argument is that each of the major modern civilizations is based upon a series of ideological assumptions concerning man's relationship to the universe. These assumptions are reflected in the economic, political, social, and artistic beliefs and practices that make up the content of each civilization. "This world," says Northrop, "in considerable part in its most significant manifestations is but the later reflection of the earlier technical scientific, philosophical, aesthetic and religious beliefs." [8]

Contemporary Soviet Russia is one of the civilizations examined by Northrop. Since his thesis bears directly upon the study undertaken here, it is worth-while to quote his central conclusion in full:

Russia is what it is today not because there was any necessity that it be that way, but largely because, for the reasons indicated, the leaders of the Russian revolution took the speculative philosophical theory of Marx, and by persuasive and forceful means brought others to its acceptance, and built political action and cultural institutions in terms of it . . . The Marxian philosophy as embodied in the practices and social forms of contemporary communistic Russia is one of the most spectacular examples in human history of the manner in which a philosophical theory, and a most speculative one, first formulated by a single individual—Karl Marx—has determined later social facts and institutions, and in part conditioned the character of the economic structure of society.[9]

It is well to state at the outset that I do not agree with the extremist conclusions presented either by Marx or by Northrop. Since the truth is not necessarily to be discovered by the labor-saving device of taking a position midway between two extremes, one is compelled to investigate the problem for oneself.

Stated in their simplest form, the central questions asked in this book are two: Which of the prerevolutionary Bolshevik ideas have been put into effect in the Soviet Union, which ones set aside, and why? Secondly, what can we learn from this historical experience about the role of ideas in general? Like many simple questions, these require rather complex answers, and the asking of a number of other questions. In order to limit the field of inquiry to more manageable proportions, I have concentrated upon certain political and economic ideas and their relationship to specific Soviet institutions and patterns of behavior. In particular, I have endeavored to trace the development of Bolshevik ideas and practices concerning the organization of political authority and economic institutions. What has been the Bolshevik attitude toward authority, discipline, the role of the leader and the led? How have the leaders reacted to the impact of political responsibility after a successful revolution?—in domestic affairs over which they had some measure of control?—in foreign affairs over which they had much less control? What made practice deviate from precept? What difficulties and social tensions have arisen, if any, in consequence of the contrast between promise and fulfillment?

In concentrating upon these primarily political problems it has been necessary to eliminate from any detailed consideration other important aspects of Soviet society: the institutions of the family, the school, and organized religion, as well as those surrounding the integration of ethnic minorities. However, it is believed, on the basis of a partial investigation of these fields, that developments in them to a considerable extent have reflected events in those that will be discussed in this volume. Likewise, considerations of time and space have led to the exclusion of any detailed consideration of Lenin's intellectual predecessors, Marx, Engels, and the indigenous Russian movements opposed to Tsarist autocracy. It is necessary to cut into the stream of events at some definite point, and the beginning stages of the Bolshevik movement seemed to be the best in the light of the inquiry as a whole.

The line of questioning indicated above is specific to Russian affairs. At the same time, certain broader questions are closely related to these. Does the organization of modern industrial societies have an inner logic of its own that compels these societies to adopt certain similar features whether their members wish to or not? Is organized inequality an inevitable feature of modern industrial society? What political and economic similarities and differences are possible within the framework of modern technology? It may be anticipated that an examination of the Soviet Union as an alternative form of social organization to Western capitalism may throw considerable light upon these questions. Likewise, one may hope for illumination upon the role played by a set of beliefs that are above and beyond overt rational criticism in holding together vast numbers of people in a common effort. Again, the Soviet experience may help to answer the broad question of whether or not there are a limited number of possible successors to any given current of ideas, and whether one set of ideas automatically precludes the development of other sets within the same intellectual climate zone. Through an analysis of the Soviet material one may hope to perceive some of the larger and more general forces that tend to modify any protest movement in the course of its growth and to deflect it from its goal.

Final answers to these specific and general questions cannot be expected now or in the immediate future. Perhaps they can never be found. Yet men have an insistent way of continuing to ask difficult questions throughout the ages. Some refuse to consider the stopping of their mouths with mud a satisfactory answer. Though the scholar has often ignored this minority, it is my firm and perhaps irrational belief that the scholar's best justification lies in his efforts to provide better answers for insistent questions.

In attacking a problem of contemporary significance the question of values, personal prejudices, and bias assumes great importance. There is widespread, though not universal, agreement among students of human behavior that one's personal wishes ought not to affect one's conclusions. Some may regard this as a counsel of perfection, though its difficulties are susceptible of exaggeration. Agreement on this point, it may be remarked in passing, does not preclude the possibility of making certain types of evaluations. Still retaining an objective attitude, one may conclude that one type of social system imposes more frustrations on the gratification of human desires than another, though there are many difficulties of a technical nature that have to be overcome before such a conclusion can gain even a strong semblance of probability. Or one may conclude that one social system results in a larger amount of conflict between individuals than another.

It could be maintained, of course, that such statements are not real evaluations, and that evaluation does not enter in until one adds the remark that frustrations and conflicts among individuals are "bad." That is a problem that can for the time being be left to others, since students of human society have at their command only very crude yardsticks for making such comparisons. The point is raised here chiefly to provide the opportunity for stating that it will not be raised again. Comparisons are made from time to time in the course of this book between Soviet ways and those of Western democracy, and occasionally other social systems. They are made solely for purposes of illustration. At no time is the implication intended that Western democracy is superior to the Soviet system, or vice versa. While differences, and the implications of these differences, can be observed with varying degrees of clarity, I see no scientific warrant for a crusade against political vice in the name of political virtue on either side of the so-called Iron Curtain. That such a crusade might take place in the foreseeable future is quite another matter, and one that in itself would provide a worth-while subject for dispassionate investigation.

Since even many informed people labor under the misapprehension that Russia is a mysterious land about which it is impossible to obtain accurate information, it is well to indicate briefly the nature of the sources. Changes in the official doctrine may be obtained directly from the voluminous record of official speeches, articles by prominent officials in magazines, and newspapers, as well as from changes in legislation, and other similar sources. Except for the fact that this material is not widely available in American libraries, it does not present any insuperable problems of accessibility. Since the Russian Communists have a great interest in matters of doctrine, the scholar is embarrassed by an abundance of material.

Difficulties do arise from the fact that what was accepted as official doctrine at one time may become near heresy at a later time, and vice versa. For this reason, later interpretations, made by the Soviets themselves, are generally unreliable. It is necessary to go to the original sources themselves to find out what the official theorists of the time actually meant. In general, the suppression of doctrines now considered heretical takes place through the failure to reprint the writings and speeches of men now regarded as traitors to the regime. Fortunately, a representative collection of their writings is available in American libraries either in newspaper form or in editions approved by the authors, with the consequence that it is possible to determine their positions at various times with a fair degree of accuracy.

The problem of textual reliability is not an overly severe one. For the most part, it would be preferable to depend entirely on newspapers and avoid later collections of speeches and articles gathered together in book form. However, this is practicable only for a research worker who has daily access to the New York Public Library and the Library of Congress. Furthermore, the amount of direct textual falsification is very much less than is commonly supposed.[10] The rewriting of history takes place by omissions and shifts of emphasis in the secondary accounts, rather than by direct alteration of significant texts. To be sure, occasional cases of the latter can be uncovered: the collection of Stalin's writings, currently in process of publication, omits Stalin's praise of Trotsky given in *Pravda*, November 6, 1918, which was reprinted in an English selection of Stalin's writings as late as 1934.[11] Nevertheless, no differences were noted in a comparison of several key passages in the two editions of Lenin's *Sochineniya* used in this study. One edition was published in the late twenties and early thirties; the other is now being reprinted. It is significant that Trotsky himself made frequent use of the earlier edition, even though it was edited by men who were his political opponents. Undoubtedly he would have made the most he could of any alterations or omissions.

Similarly, a comparison of several editions of the resolutions and decisions of the Communist Party, a vital record of doctrinal and behavioral changes, failed to bring out any variations. On the whole, the Soviet leaders do not appear to be sensitive to many of the changes and alterations that will be discussed, especially in the case of high doctrinal authorities such as Lenin and Stalin themselves, since various collections of their writings containing numerous mutually contradictory statements are frequently reprinted. Therefore, it is deemed reasonably safe to use such collections for the purpose of determining the viewpoints of these authorities at various stages in the history of the USSR. Even if some errors in quotation have crept in from the use of later reprints of important documents, it is believed that they are not sufficient to affect the conclusions.

The record of behavioral changes may also be found at considerable length in the Russian sources, as well as in the writings of contemporary non-Russian observers. In using such materials one has to bear in mind the ordinary cautions concerning bias and the need for corroborative evidence. Even if slanted, the information on many important matters, such as the operations of the local soviets, the trade unions, the Communist Party, the collective farms, and others, is relatively abundant. With practice one may gradually learn to disentangle from such accounts those views which represent recurring aspects of behavior. Often unintentional evidence is the best. The background of matters evidently taken for granted may reveal significant information, while the "moral" of the story may tell us nothing beyond the official viewpoint. The Russians make large-scale use of their press for the purpose of exhorting the population to adopt new patterns of behavior. The continuation of the exhortations over time may often serve as a fairly reliable indication that the new patterns have not been adopted to the desired extent. The Soviet press is also useful, since it frequently carries detailed descriptions of the situations encountered in the application and enforcement of policy.[12] While again one must exercise discrimination, such accounts provide a valuable source of data on behavior patterns.

There is a partly justifiable tradition in scholarly research that no secondary sources should be used. Obviously, if this tradition were carried to its logical conclusions, there would be no possibility of advance, since one could not build upon the conclusions of earlier research. The use of secondary sources is a matter of both discrimination and convenience. Preference has been given to those secondary sources which revealed a thorough familiarity with the original sources and which have to this extent lightened the heavy burden of research. On occasion, facts or allegations of facts have been taken from such sources and given an interpretation with which their authors might not agree. For such acts it is necessary to beg indulgence and to hope that the new interpretations will bear up under critical examination. Furthermore, I disavow any claim that I have examined all the original or secondary sources relevant to the problems investigated. Probably not even all the most important sources have been considered. Nevertheless, it is believed that a sufficient sample has been covered to provide a firm basis for the conclusions advanced. Finally, it should be pointed out that on a number of occasions translations of the original Russian texts have been utilized. Where there has been a choice, a reliable translation rather than the original Russian text has been used in order that the reader who is unfamiliar with Russian might be able to check for himself whether a given fact or statement has been correctly interpreted in the light of its context. Different editions of the same work have also been cited at different times in this book. Practical considerations have made this necessary, since this study has been written at widely scattered time intervals in Washington, New York, Chicago, and Cambridge, in which places even the most fundamental materials were seldom found in exactly the same form.

In scientific investigations it is a matter of honesty to report the way in which each fact in a chain of reasoning was obtained. In such a controversial subject as contemporary Russia, the obligation is especially great. Knowing full well that the strength of the argument does not depend on the number of footnotes, I make no apology for the numerous citations. In addition, direct quotations have been used generously in order to enable the reader to judge for himself the ideas expressed at various points in the development of Soviet ideology. It has been a chastening experience on many occasions to find my exuberant flights of fancy shattered by the exactions of strict adherence to the evidence and thus to be forced to abandon intriguing though untenable interpretations.

PART ONE

LENINIST THEORY AND PRACTICE
BEFORE THE REVOLUTION

1
How an Ideology Emerged

Russian society and the hypothesis of the inevitable revolution

In his autobiography Trotsky tells the tale of Lenin's first reaction to the Bolshevik conquest of power: "Lenin has not yet had time to change his collar, even though his face looks so tired. He looks softly at me, with that sort of awkward shyness that with him indicates intimacy. 'You know,' he says hesitatingly, 'from persecution and a life underground, to come so suddenly into power . . .' He pauses for the right word. *'Es schwindelt'* (My head spins), he concludes, changing suddenly to German, and circling his hand around his head. We look at each other and laugh a little." [1]

Lenin's astonishment was shared by most contemporary observers. Those who have attempted subsequently to answer the question of how a band of revolutionaries managed to capture the largest state in Europe disagree among themselves even when they do not share the astonishment. For the purposes of this study, this question will be given a slightly different shading. The interest here is in the problems of why a group emerged with the Leninist doctrine of revolution by a conspiratorial elite, and what factors contributed to the spread and modification of this doctrine. The search for answers to these questions is undertaken not for the sake of writing correct history, although correct history is an absolutely essential prerequisite to answering such questions, but in order to throw light on the general problem of the relationship between changing ideas and changing forms of political behavior.

Two major hypotheses concerning the origins and success of

Bolshevism provide a groundwork for any subsequent analysis. One of these holds that specific factors in Russian society prevented Russia from following the course taken by Western society in the nineteenth century toward parliamentary and democratic regimes. In general, the argument runs, the Russian middle class during the Tsarist regime was too weak to be willing or able to carry through liberal reforms similar to those which occurred in England, France, and to a lesser extent Germany, from the seventeenth century onwards. This thesis received some prominence in Trotsky's prerevolutionary writings and has become the generally accepted explanation among Marxists who hold widely varying opinions on other aspects of Russian society.[2] The acceptance of this explanation among contemporary Marxists has its curious aspects, since it involves a sharp repudiation of the prerevolutionary version of Marxism in Russia. Except for Trotsky, whose views on this topic were considered an individual aberration, most Russian Marxists before 1917 believed that a period of "bourgeois democracy" would be the inevitable result of the overthrow of Tsarism.

The thesis that the structure of Russian society in the nineteenth century ruled out the possibility of development along the lines of Western democracy has been most effectively challenged by N. S. Timasheff, a non-Marxist sociologist.[3] According to his hypothesis, Russia was proceeding along the same path of development that had taken place in Western Europe. With the passage of a few more decades, Russia might have become a constitutional monarchy, perhaps along the lines of a compromise between the British and the German models, had not the catastrophe of war intervened. To support this conclusion Professor Timasheff cites as evidence the movement toward representative institutions in the four Dumas and at the local level, the growth of industry, and the flowering of artistic and intellectual achievements in Russia of the nineteenth and early twentieth centuries. This trend was cut short, so the argument runs, by the historical accident of war and revolution.

Professor Timasheff's views represent a continuation and elaboration of the arguments presented by a number of Russian historians, who asserted in their prerevolutionary writings that Russia was following the path of social development taken by the democratic countries of Western Europe. His thesis has been criticized on the grounds that the Revolution of November 1917 did happen, and that therefore his speculations on the trend of events in Russia are fruitless. For me these criticisms fail to carry conviction. They of course have nothing to do one way or the other with the general trend of development in Russia before the November Revolution, which is a matter of recorded facts and their interpretation, difficult as the latter may be. As for the argument that hypotheses on how events might have turned out are of no use, the logical reply is that they are an essential element in any attempt to discover why they did turn out the way they did. One way to calculate the results of the Russian Revolution is to try to determine what would have happened if there had been no revolution. The "mental experiment," to be sure, is unsatisfactory in many respects, since verification can never be as certain as in the laboratory. But without such devices history is reduced to chronology.

Both the Marxist interpretation and the challenge it has received at other hands call attention to significant social forces. Perhaps the most tenable conclusion is that there were considerable, though not necessarily insurmountable, obstacles in the way of Russian development along Western democratic lines. These difficulties favored a violent resolution of domestic political tensions. Insofar as the social structure of the Russian Empire was concerned, and leaving out of account such personal factors as the political incompetence of Tsar Nicholas II, the main difficulties derived from the fact that the Tsarist regime rested upon a quasi-feudal landed nobility, and resisted—too successfully for its own good—the pressures for modernization imposed by the unavoidable advent of Western industrial civilization. The success of the Tsarist regime in resisting modernization was in turn quite largely, if not entirely, due to the weakness of those groups that pushed for modernization along moderate, constitutional, and Western democratic lines, even though these groups gained considerable strength in the closing years of the Empire.

In the West the impetus behind parliamentary democracy
had come primarily, though not exclusively, from the urban middle classes: traders, manufacturers, professional men, and intellectuals. In Russia, on the other hand, as the liberal historian
Miliukov has pointed out, proportionately few cities grew up to
furnish such a base. Those cities that did were primarily military
and administrative centers, garrison towns rather than trading
or producing centers. In the middle of the nineteenth century,
according to Miliukov's figures, Russia had only 32 cities with
more than 20,000 inhabitants, and only two with more than
150,000. The change that had begun to have an effect during the
latter part of the nineteenth century is shown by the figures for
1900, when there were nine cities with more than 150,000 inhabitants and 65 with more than 20,000.[4]

During the late nineteenth and early twentieth centuries the
relationship between the urban bourgeoisie and the Tsarist government took a form that prevented these manufacturers and
merchants from becoming a strong and effective opponent of the
autocracy. The larger industrialists became dependent upon the
autocracy as its principal customer and for subventions, while
the latter endeavored to promote industrialization for its own political and military purposes. In addition, many of the more influential members of the bourgeoisie looked to the Tsarist autocracy, especially after the abortive revolution of 1905, as the most
reliable means for keeping the industrial workers in their place.
Indeed, the Tsarist regime owed its survival in the 1905 revolution in no small measure to its success in splitting the bourgeoisie
from the industrial workers.[5]

Furthermore, until the opening of the second decade of the
twentieth century, the Russian bourgeoisie's interest in politics
was narrowly limited to the effect of political measures on the
prospects for trade and profit. It displayed little interest in liberty
for its own sake. The advantages of liberal reform from its point
of view lay in the creation of a free labor force, the promise of
an overhauling of the legal and bureaucratic machinery, and the
possibility of creating organizations to put economic pressure on
the government. Because of this, statements by leading organs of
the bourgeoisie condemned the repressions of Tsarism, such as the

closing of the universities and the pogroms against the Jews, entirely on the grounds that they were bad for business. As one writer has summarized the situation at that time, the bourgeoisie saw its politics only in its account books.[6] In part, the bourgeoisie's narrowness may have been due to the absence of widespread contact with the middle classes of Western Europe. Intellectual currents from abroad did not permeate this stratum of Russian society until very late.

Nevertheless, by about 1908 the logic of economic self-interest had begun to push the bourgeoisie in the direction of wider views and to bring about an increasing disenchantment with the Tsarist regime. It has often been observed that in the process of territorial expansion the Tsarist regime was obliged to impose a heavy economic burden upon the population, which in turn kept the masses in an impoverished state. While the autocracy was the bourgeoisie's best customer, it also prevented the growth of an internal mass market. Hence it cut the ground from under the bourgeoisie with one hand, while it helped with the other.[7] In addition, a large proportion of the state's resources went to support a bureaucratic and legal machine, staffed largely with members of the gentry who by education and training were often hostile to business, and whose rules and red tape checked the business interests at numerous points. As a consequence, influential circles among the manufacturing and trading interests came to feel by about 1908 that the expansion of their way of life in Russia could only take place in collision with the landed interests that still dominated the state.[8] For these reasons the political connections of the business world with the nobility began at this time to dissolve. As part of the same process, intellectual criticism of the status quo gained an increasingly sympathetic audience among hardheaded business men. Similarly, among the new class of managers and engineers brought into existence by the expanding economy, Marxism in its less revolutionary and "legal" forms made considerable headway. Since Russian Marxist doctrine at that time was distinguished by its insistence upon the inevitability of capitalist development, the attraction it held for members of the middle classes is understandable.

This survey of the weaknesses of the forces behind a moderate and peaceful transformation may be concluded with a brief mention of the role of the liberal gentry, or the lower ranks of the nobility. For the landed nobility was by no means a unified and cohesive group in support of the Tsarist regime. While the great landlords served in St. Petersburg or elsewhere as agents of the central government, the lesser nobility served in the *zemstvos,* local representative assemblies established in 1864, in which the landed interests predominated. A certain type of humanitarian liberalism flourished in this group, finding its reflection in extensive work for the advancement of education and health among the peasants, in resistance to the intrusions of the bureaucracy into *zemstvo* affairs, and in efforts to increase local representation in the central government.[9] Together with a portion of the less radical intellectuals, who tended to take over the actual leadership, the liberal gentry rather than the urban middle classes formed the backbone of the short-lived Constitutional Democratic Party (Cadets or Kadets, from the initials KD), founded in 1905. The political objectives of this party emphasized parliamentary government similar to the Western European pattern.[10] Nevertheless, the very composition of this group tended to prevent it from taking views that would have led to destruction of the gentry. When the peasants in 1917 came to demand the distribution of the land, long a peasant dream, the Provisional Government, in which the liberal gentry and the bourgeoisie were influential, could not bring itself either to oppose or support this movement. Despite many concrete achievements, the liberal gentry formed neither an effective brake upon revolution, nor an effective agent of Russia's modernization.

If the foregoing sections of Russian society could not effect the modification of the Tsarist regime along parliamentary lines, one may raise the question of whether or not the peasantry could or would undertake this task.

The peasants, constituting over 80 per cent of the population of Russia before the Revolution, were without question an important source of opposition to the regime. Toward the end of the nineteenth century and the beginning of the twentieth there were two major waves of peasant uprisings, one between 1881 and 1888 and another in connection with the 1905 revolution, that were a prelude to the final conflagration of 1917. Careful students have concluded that these disturbances were largely independent of the propaganda that emanated in minute quantities from urban sources, and that they represented the peasant response to economic and social hardship.[11]

The peasant uprisings were, however, primarily brief and ineffective local outbursts, *Jacqueries* in fact, that were destined to continue well into the Bolshevik regime. In the intervals between periods of concentrated unrest, peasant Russia lay quiet.[12] Though the peasants provided much of the motive force that finally overthrew the Tsarist regime in 1917, they did not succeed in developing into an organized political group with the power that their numbers might suggest. In prerevolutionary times their major political achievement appears to have been the organization of an All-Russian Peasants' Union, which met in the spring and fall of the revolutionary year 1905. In these meetings there was widespread agreement on the economic objectives of the abolition of private property in land. The peasant delegates wanted the use of the landlords' fields and those of the state domain. They also expressed desires to the effect that the state would become an impartial distributor and periodic equalizer of landholdings in the manner of the *mir* (village commune). On political objectives there was no agreement, and the union failed to become a permanent political organization, capable of providing leadership or directing discontent into effective channels.[13] As Sir John Maynard, one of the best students of Russian peasant life, points out, the peasants showed no tendency to conceive or develop a social and political organization that extended beyond their village community.[14]

The peasants' failure to develop a feasible political alternative to revolutionary Marxism can be traced to a number of conditions. One extremely important factor in the relative political passivity of the peasants was their extremely low level of education. Together with the physical isolation of peasant life, the absence of education cut them off from political and intellectual currents that swept through Russia from the cities. The main channels through which external influences reached the village were chiefly conservative ones: the church, the school, and the conscript army.[15]

Another factor was the late date at which the institutions of private property in land emerged in Russia. The Stolypin legislation, begun in 1906 and completed in 1911, aimed at the breakup of the *mir*—the village organization responsible for tax collections, for determining the dates of ploughing, harvesting, and other agricultural processes, and the periodic redistribution of land among the inhabitants. In place of the *mir* Stolypin hoped to establish a class of free farmers and thereby put an end to peasant upheavals. The result was to be achieved through three stages. The first was the affirmation by certificate of proprietary right in the peasants' strips of land as they stood at the time. The second was consolidation of the scattered strips into integral holdings. The third step involved complete separation from the *mir* and even from the village site. The man who entered this third stage turned over his original household lots for consolidation with those of other peasants, left his home on the common village site, and established himself in a new farmhouse on his own consolidated farm away from the common organization of village life.[16]

Specialists vary in their estimate of the impact of this legislation upon the Russian peasants' way of life. In any case, the proceedings were stopped during the First World War because of the large number of demobilized soldiers who were anxious concerning their rights,[17] a development which indicates that the reform may not have had as stabilizing an effect as had been hoped. Professor Robinson, after an exhaustive study, gives the following figures as an estimate of the legislation's effect. Out of a total of thirteen or fourteen million peasant allotments in the old Russian Empire, 5,000,000 remained in unchanged repartitional tenure, that is, under the sway of the *mir;* 1,300,000 holdings were covered by the law, but apparently not brought under its operation; 1,700,000 holdings were practically affected by the law, but not yet fully documented; 4,300,000 holdings had fully established hereditary titles, but were still in scattered strips; and 1,300,000 holdings had similar titles, with partly or wholly consolidated form.[18] In other words, well over half of the peasant households were affected by this administrative revolution, although only about one tenth reached its final objectives. National averages, however, conceal significant changes in certain areas. By far the greatest impact took place in the great wheat-growing areas of the southwest and the southern and southeastern steppes. In other areas the reforms had practically no effect.[19]

On balance it may be concluded that the effect of the Stolypin reforms, had not war and other disturbances intervened, would have been the encouragement of a class of free farmers and an increase in the number of town workers, drawn from peasants who were forced off the land. Both of these features would have contributed to the modernization of Russia along familiar Western lines. The changes that took place among the peasantry and the urban middle classes after 1905 indicate that Russia traveled a remarkable distance in a very short time. The social foundations for a capitalist regime and a limited monarchy, perhaps even a constitutional democracy, were being rapidly laid. But the journey was begun late and its course deflected. Sufficient social tensions had accumulated so that, when released by the disintegration of the war, the moderates would be swept from power after a few months. These social tensions Lenin and his followers would turn to their own account. In revolutions, as Miliukov observed, the appetite for change comes with eating.[20] Each concession by those in power suggests to those out of power the possibility of greater gains. This inherent dynamic of revolution often creates a tremendous advantage for extremist movements.

So far we have spoken as though some variety of democratic capitalism were the only contestant besides revolutionary Marxism in the Russian political arena before 1917. Such, of course, was by no means the case. Many volumes have been written about the colorful variety of intellectual doctrines struggling for acceptance in prerevolutionary Russia. Among these ideologies, democratic capitalism and revolutionary Marxism appeared to play relatively insignificant roles. In both reactionary and revolutionary circles faith was placed in the *mir* as a device from which a new social order might spring that would enable Russia to escape the path taken by the West. To recount or even mention the fate of the other doctrines would take us far beyond the boundaries of the problem at hand.

Nevertheless, the main alternative faced by all these groups was between a peaceable transformation of Russian society and a violent one. The Tsarist autocracy, resting upon the quasi-feudal structure of the landed nobility and the peasants, had succeeded in establishing Russia as one of the great land empires of the world. In the twentieth century this structure was an anachronism. It could either yield and be transformed, or else collapse in ruins. Since the forces for moderation in both the cities and the countryside were weak and late, and did not have the time to develop further under continuing favorable circumstances, victory went to the choice of violent transformation.

The only political group that both welcomed the impact of Western industrial institutions and promoted a revolutionary resolution of the social tensions produced or accentuated by this impact was the Marxist one, the Russian Social Democratic Labor Party, founded in 1898, and particularly its left wing, formed in 1903, the Bolsheviks. The analysis may now be focused upon this group, which retained its formal unity as a single party until 1912.

In order to perceive the various processes of ideological change at work, an account may be given of the growth of certain selected aspects of Russian Marxist, and especially Bolshevik, doctrine. The interest of this book will be primarily in the conceptions of democracy, socialism, and violent revolution, insofar as they reveal both authoritarian and anti-authoritarian trends in Bolshevik thinking and behavior.

Authoritarian and democratic trends in Bolshevik theory

The extent to which the Russian Marxists were indebted to earlier revolutionary movements and critics of the existing social order may be taken as a beginning point. The social tensions of nineteenth-century Russia had already found considerable expression among the urban intellectuals. Although there are strong reasons for doubting that the urban intellectuals represented accurately the aspirations of the groups at the bottom of the Russian social pyramid, they performed the function of providing a number of tentative solutions to the existing problems and sources of tension. Some intellectuals placed major emphasis on individualist self-affirmation and self-completion, in contrast to those who stressed reorganization of the social order. Others developed the idea of a rationalist and socialist enlightenment, a form of salvation through education. Still others, associated particularly with the name of Bakunin, founder of Russian Anarchism, put forth an emotional and mystical doctrine of revolt by the *plebs*. Finally, one may note the "Jacobin" ideal of a solution of the political problem by means of an intellectual minority—"for the people, but not through the people." [21]

Of these ideas all but the first were taken over by the Russian Marxists. In this sense the Marxists represent a continuation of the Russian revolutionary tradition. But whereas the earlier revolutionists had looked primarily, and in vain, toward the peasants as a lever by which to overthrow the Tsarist autocracy, the Marxists turned toward the workers of the city. As early as 1899, at the founding Congress of the Socialist International, Plekhanov, the theoretical founder of Russian Marxism, declared to the assembled delegates: "In Russia political freedom will be gained by the working class or it will not exist at all. The Russian Revolution can only conquer as a working-man's revolution—there is no other possibility, nor can there be." [22] This conception, taken from Western Europe, constituted the Russian Marxists' most distinctive contribution to the variety of political movements struggling with one another and the Tsarist authorities.

The announced goals of the Russian Marxists for many years, beginning with their first Manifesto of 1898, involved a complete transformation in the system of status and authority prevailing in Russia. Broadly speaking, they anticipated and desired first a "bourgeois" parliamentary republic, to be followed at a later stage of history by a socialist society. The Marxist interpretation of the past emphasized the conception of distinct stages, while its predictions for the future stressed the role of the industrial working class. The Russian Marxists, viewing the conditions of Tsarist Russia through the Marxist prism, arranged their goals accordingly. Other non-Marxist opponents of Tsarism, perceiving the situation through other prisms, arrived at diametrically opposite goals. As F. I. Dan points out, believing in the necessity of a prior capitalist transformation of Russia, Plekhanov and Lenin faced a dilemma: how could a socialist party of the working class become the leader in the struggle for the political liberation of a capitalist form of social organization? [23]

In turn this dilemma was part of a larger one. Given the conditions of the Tsarist autocracy, resting upon a peasant mass apparently incapable of more than sporadic writhings under the knout, how could one go about the task of setting up a society that would give full scope to strivings for individual human dignity? It is hardly necessary to point out that the existence of these humanitarian goals, and the consequent dilemma of how to achieve them, was in itself the product of social change brought about by contact with Western institutions and ideas.

The Russian Marxist answer, to which all factions more or less agreed, was to permit and encourage the forces of Western industrialism to undermine and transform the old social structure. Beyond this immediate starting point overt and covert doubts and disagreements arose. Many Marxists asked themselves: Will not the capitalists be as bad as the masters they displace? And will the capitalists necessarily displace these barbaric and semi-feudal masters? May they not simply ally themselves with the old regime to keep the workers in their place? And finally, will the masses be intelligent enough to perceive that we have the correct answer to these problems and not be led astray by false promises?

The temporary solution of this dilemma was to separate the ultimate socialist goal from the immediate one of a democratic republic. The Party declaration of 1903 argued that although capitalism had become the ruling form of production in Russia, the survival of precapitalist institutions made it necessary to restrict the current program to the destruction of the Tsarist regime and its replacement by a democratic republic. The immediate democratic program was set out in quite specific form under the following headings:

1. Rule by the people, that is, the concentration of the supreme governing power in the hands of a lawgiving assembly made up of representatives of the people and in the form of a single chamber.

2. Direct elections by secret ballot, with equal electoral rights for all sections of the population, including women.

3. Widespread local government.

4. The inviolability of the person and of the home.

5. Unrestricted freedom of conscience, of speech, of the press, of association, and the right to strike.

To these were added several other demands, such as the separation of church and state, and a progressive income tax.[24]

These specifically democratic goals were in one sense an end in themselves. Yet in another sense they were but a means to the ultimate end of socialism. The first Manifesto issued by the Russian Marxists as a party declared: "And what does the Russian working class not need? It is completely deprived of that which its comrades abroad may freely and peacefully use: participation in the operations of government, freedom of speech and of the press, freedom of assembly and of union organization, in a word all the weapons and means by which the Western-European and American proletariat improves its position and at the same time battles against private property and capitalism for its ultimate liberation —and for socialism. Political freedom is necessary for the Russian proletariat in the same way that fresh air is necessary for healthy breathing." [25] Again in 1905 a Party declaration asserted that one of the desired results of the revolution against Tsarism would be the attainment of "more favorable conditions for the struggle for socialism against the possessing classes of bourgeois democratic Russia." [26]

It is often argued that because the ultimate aim was socialism, the Russian Marxists made use of democratic ideology as a screen to fool the masses and achieve their final goal. While there are some grounds for this assertion, particularly in regard to the Bolshevik wing of the Russian Social Democratic Labor Party, it neglects the fact that Lenin himself remained, overtly at least, an ardent believer in some variety of democratic transformation until the Party came to power. This argument also underestimates the vitality of the individualist version of the democratic tradition in Russian Marxist circles.

An incident at one of the Party Congresses reveals the strength of this tradition. At the time of the Second Congress in 1903, Plekhanov foreshadowed in his speeches the authoritarian tradition that had begun to play an important, though by no means exclusive, role in certain Russian Marxist circles. At one point Plekhanov asserted that the good of the revolution ought to be the supreme law of revolutionary activity, even if it meant temporary restrictions on one or the other of the democratic principles. In a prophetic sentence he said he could conceive of the eventuality that the Party might under some circumstances be in favor of restrictions even on the right of universal suffrage.[27] Only one minor delegate supported Plekhanov on this issue, at which point there were shocked exclamations from the audience and cries, "How about the inviolability of the person?"[28]

As will become clear in the course of this book, these individualist and democratic goals entered into the body of Communist doctrine. They remain an important part of this doctrine today, finding their reflection in the Stalinist Constitution of 1936, and in numerous pronouncements and actions by the Soviet regime.

Between the time of the Party's first adoption of an official program in 1898 and the seizure of power by the Bolsheviks in 1917 the conceptions of democracy, dictatorship, and revolution underwent significant modifications, particularly at the hands of Lenin and his immediate associates. To some extent these modifications can be traced to the political weakness of the Bolshevik position, and the Party's attempts to get around this weakness.

One of the major difficulties faced by Russian Marxists of all factions was the small size of the Russian industrial working class. The percentage of industrial workers in Russia in 1860 was 0.76. By 1913 it had risen only to 1.41.[29] Although the Marxists had hoped to make this group the core of their activities, it rapidly became obvious that they would have to turn to other groups for allies. Many twists and turns in prerevolutionary ideology can be traced to the efforts to attract other sections of Russian society to the revolutionary banner, and at the same time to retain both doctrinal purity and a free hand for the self-styled leaders of the proletariat.

From the point of view of size and potential opposition to the status quo, the most important section of Russian society was the peasantry, even though it was lacking in organization and distinct political objectives. However, Marxist doctrine taught, in part correctly, that the sources of change and upheaval in Russian society were to be sought in the ferment produced by the penetration of industrialism. Perhaps blinded by this emphasis, the Bolsheviks paid little attention to the peasants until the 1905 revolution. Then Lenin turned temporarily to the Socialist Revolutionaries, a non-Marxist socialist group, the intellectual descendant of earlier movements that had sought social reforms through the peasantry.

This search for allies led Lenin during the 1905 revolution to a new formulation of Bolshevik objectives. From the point of view of Western democracy, the new objectives, in which intermediate and ultimate goals were intermingled, represent a mixture of incompatible authoritarian and democratic elements. The mixture is well shown in Lenin's slogan of a "Revolutionary-democratic dictatorship of the proletariat and the peasantry," formulated in the middle of 1905.

At that time Lenin perceived two possible varieties of a strictly bourgeois revolution in Russia: a partial or "abortive" revolution in which the big bourgeoisie retained its predominance, and a "really great revolution" in which the peasant and proletarian elements predominated.[30] Despite the predominance of these elements, he still conceived of this as a bourgeois revolution, though one "in the highest degree advantageous to the proletariat." [31] Such a revolution must be carried to its democratic completion, that is, the destruction of the Tsarist regime and all remnants of feudalism. To attain this end a dictatorship was necessary, since the "introduction of reforms which are urgently and absolutely necessary for the proletariat and the peasantry will call forth the desperate resistance of the landlords, the big bourgeoisie

and Tsarism." Without a dictatorship, Lenin continued, the resistance of the counterrevolution would be too strong. "But of
course it will be a democratic and not a socialist dictatorship. It
will not be able (without a series of intermediary stages of revolutionary development) to affect the foundations of capitalism." [32]

In other words, under the specific conditions of early twentieth-century Russia, Lenin did not believe that democracy could
be achieved except by totalitarian means. The Marxist concept of
the dictatorship of the proletariat was shifted by Lenin from its
application to the transition between democracy and socialism to
the transition between Tsarism and democracy.

Lenin's views did not meet with a warm reception, even among
his own followers in the Party. The Bolsheviks adopted that portion of them which implied that the democratic revolution must
be carried to its completion in the destruction of reactionary
forces among the big bourgeoisie, as well as among the remnants
of feudal society. But instead of advocating a "democratic dictatorship," they demanded the calling of a constituent assembly. [33]
Trotsky decided that the revolutionary-democratic dictatorship
was politically unworkable, because the revolution could not stop
at the democratic stage. It would have to continue to the stage of
socialism. [34] Like Lenin, Trotsky feared both the intransigence and
the powers of recovery of antiproletarian interest groups. The
Mensheviks, who were the first to perceive the ebb of the 1905
revolution, clung to the conception of the Social Democratic
Party as a left-wing pressure group that should push the bourgeoisie as far as possible along the road to parliamentary democracy. [35]

It was also at the time of the 1905 revolution that Lenin set
down in the clearest and most overt form the principles that, he
thought, ought to govern the making of tactical alliances with
other groups and parties. In this respect he emphasized the conception, implicit in the first Manifesto, that alliances with nonproletarian elements were temporary expedients. They were to be
concluded only for the purpose of strengthening the position of
the proletariat. When this purpose had been served, the proletariat should turn upon its former enemies and destroy them.

This viewpoint differs sharply from the ideals, if not always the practices, of the Western democratic tradition. The latter recognizes the conflict of interest groups, but treats it as a guarantee that no single interest group will win out and destroy the others. In Bolshevik intransigence there is very little of the philosophy of live and let live.

While asserting in 1905 that the leaders of the proletariat must make the best possible use of their allies, Lenin was equally specific in pointing out fundamental differences and the occasions that would, he thought, bring about an eventual break. He said: "A Social Democrat must never, even for an instant, forget that the proletarian class struggle for socialism against the most democratic and republican bourgeoisie and petty bourgeoisie is inevitable . . . From this logically follows the provisional character of our tactics to 'strike together' with the bourgeoisie and the duty to carefully watch 'our ally as if he were an enemy,' etc." [36] The same line of thought applied equally to the peasantry. "The time will come when the struggle against Russian autocracy will be over, when the period of democratic revolution will also be over, and then it will be ridiculous to talk about 'unity of will' of the proletariat and the peasantry, about a democratic dictatorship, etc. When that time comes, we shall take up the question of the socialist dictatorship of the proletariat." [37]

It is hardly likely that such statements served to calm the fears of the bourgeois and peasant leaders whom the Bolsheviks sought for the purpose of a limited tactical alliance. Were it not for Lenin's great tactical flexibility, together with his capacity for concentrating on a single goal, one might suspect that the remarks just quoted, a tiny sample of their type, reflected an effort to achieve doctrinal purity rather than power.

Fears for doctrinal purity clearly existed then as they do now. Throughout Bolshevik history these forces have been partly countered by the requirements of doctrinal concessions in the interest of winning political power. In the course of continual polemics in and outside the Party, Lenin did not regard doctrinal purity as an end in itself, but as a means toward the achievement of other goals. He demanded, but did not always obtain, complete adherence to the tactical line of the moment; yet he was the source of more dramatic reversals of Bolshevik tactics than any other of their leaders.

When in 1917 a second revolutionary upheaval in Russia suggested to Lenin the possibilities of success, he left behind him in Switzerland the ideological baggage of parliamentary democracy, without taking with him a definitely socialist program. The projected Republic of Soviets was a compromise between the two. From Lenin's copious notes and writings of this period, it is apparent that he abandoned the idea of a "bourgeois democratic" republic some time in March 1917. This abandonment took place only when he became convinced that the Provisional Government was, because of its bourgeois nature, too closely connected with the Romanovs and with "imperialist" social forces abroad to carry through the program Lenin thought necessary. This revealing development may now be traced in some detail.

As late as 1915 Lenin continued to propound his ideas of 1905 and wrote that the task of the proletariat in Russia was to carry to the end the bourgeois democratic revolution in Russia, and to set on fire the socialist revolution in Europe.[38] This statement serves, however, as an indication of Lenin's primary interest in the ultimate goal of socialism, which he then apparently thought would first develop outside of Russia.

His reaction to the news of the March Revolution and the downfall of the Romanov dynasty, together with the formation of the Provisional Government under Prince Lvov, still carries out some of the 1905 ideas, though evidently modified under the impact of events. Lenin complained of the paucity of news, though it was apparent that he had already seen some of the programmatic statements of the new regime. He asserted that the new regime could not give the people of Russia peace or bread, because it was representative of the capitalists and large landowners and was tied by treaties and financial obligations to England and France. Continuing with a number of other criticisms, he concluded that the proletariat could only maintain its struggle for a democratic republic and for socialism.[39] In other words, when the time for action came, Lenin showed little or no disposition to trust the bourgeois parties or coöperate with them. However, it should be pointed out that highly conservative elements—in Marxist terminology, prebourgeois reactionary feudal ones—such as the Procurator of the Holy Synod, had a place in the Lvov Cabinet.[40]

Yet, it was not to the reactionary elements that Lenin voiced his strongest objections, but to the leftist elements. A further comment by Lenin on the new regime was as follows: "Not only the government in question but a democratic bourgeois republican government, if it was made up only of Kerensky and other Narodniki and 'Marxist' social patriots [a reference to socialists who supported the war], would not be in a position to save the people from the imperialist war and guarantee peace."[41] So far as I am aware, this statement is the first indication of Lenin's disenchantment with a bourgeois republic. A few days later he called for the creation of a network of soviets as a proletarian organization to counteract the organization of the bourgeoisie, and spoke of the possibility of a second revolution.[42]

In April, on his return to Russia in the famous sealed train, he announced the definite conclusion that the demand for a parliamentary regime should be scrapped, and that the soviets were the "only possible form of revolutionary government." "Not a parliamentary republic—to return to a parliamentary republic from the Soviets of Workers' Deputies would be a retrograde step —but a republic of Soviets of Workers', Agricultural Laborers' and Peasants' Deputies throughout the country from top to bottom."[43]

This rapid evolution of Lenin's thought caught the Party by surprise. However, such was his prestige and power within the Party that the confusion ended rapidly, and the Party was able to proceed with the task of winning over the soviets and eventually taking power in the country as a whole.

2

Lenin's Plans for the New Society

Tactical flexibility in meeting new situations has long been re-garded as Lenin's political forte. Toward the end of his life, as he looked over a history of the Russian Revolution written by a Menshevik journalist, he remarked that these "petty bourgeois democrats" were slaves to the past with only a pedantic compre-hension of Marx. They fail, he continued, to see the key point in Marx, that revolutionary moments demand the greatest flexibility. In this, Lenin's last article in *Pravda,* he reminded his followers of Napoleon's maxim: *On s'engage et puis . . . on voit.*[1]

Occasional remarks of this type by Lenin, and his ability to adapt his position to the power requirements of the moment, have led many persons to regard him as a pure careerist, interested only in power and lacking in political principles. Granting the tremendous importance of Lenin's desire for power, one may still conclude that it does not constitute the whole story. Lenin's thirst for power was closely connected with his conviction that he (and sometimes only he) had the right answer to the basic ques-tion of what caused human misery and what ought to be done about it. Although he changed his mind on these questions many times during his political career and many times admitted pre-vious errors of tactics and interpretation, there does not seem to be a single word of Lenin's that indicates any internal doubts about the course he was following at a given moment. In Marx-ism he felt that he had found the tool for coming to grips with social and economic realities. There he could find the questions to be asked about the political environment, though he and his followers would always deny that the answers themselves could be read mechanically out of Marxist writings. The general method of questioning constitutes one of the more stable aspects of Marxist-Leninist theory.

Reacting to situations as they arose, Lenin continued to add new conceptions and to abandon or modify old ones. The same process of growth and attrition has been maintained since his death. Superimposed upon this simpler process, a cyclical tendency may be observed in the development of Bolshevik theory and also in Bolshevik practice. Each new addition to Marxist theory and each modification established a bench mark to which Lenin or his followers could, and often did, return at a later date and under still different circumstances. Quarrels, which to an outsider resemble arid theological disputations, often arose among his followers concerning which was the correct point of return. The continuity in general method of questioning, combined with the flexibility and variety in the answers produced, is among the major factors that give to Russian Marxist theory the superficially paradoxical appearance of dogmatic permanence and opportunistic change.

Therefore, if one speaks of Leninist theory, it is usually necessary to speak of it as it existed at a given point in time and at a given stage of its development. In order to clarify the point of departure, the period just prior to revolutionary success may be selected for a general survey of those aspects of Leninist doctrine that are relevant to the remainder of this study. Taunted by his opponents who accused him and his followers of being mere demagogues incapable of assuming political responsibility, Lenin at this time was forced to make a number of statements about the type of society that would be established if the Bolsheviks came to power.

The affirmation and denial of authority

In line with the general Marxist tradition, Lenin emphasized the oppressive features of the state in his famous pamphlet *State and Revolution,* completed in August 1917, during the midst of the struggle against the Provisional Government. Standing armies, the bureaucracy, the police forces, and similar features were described by Lenin as the paraphernalia through which the ruling class maintained its power. Democratic institutions did not alter the fact, according to Lenin, that the state was an organ of class rule. He dismissed them in the famous remark: "To decide once every few years which member of the ruling class is to misrepresent the people in parliament is the real essence of bourgeois parliamentarism, not only in parliamentary-constitutional monarchies, but also in the most democratic republics." [2]

On the basis of this interpretation, Lenin and other Marxists drew two important conclusions. The first was that the victorious proletariat could not take over the existing repressive apparatus of the state, but would have to destroy it. The second conclusion, which distinguished the Bolsheviks from other, more idealistic, revolutionists, was that the working class would have to exercise oppression in order to maintain and consolidate its power. In Lenin's words, "The 'special repressive force' for the suppression of the proletariat by the bourgeoisie, for the suppression of the millions of toilers by a handful of the rich, must be superseded by a 'special repressive force' for the suppression of the bourgeoisie by the proletariat (the dictatorship of the proletariat)." [3] In other passages he argues that the proletariat and the peasantry must "take political power in their own hands, organize themselves freely in communes, and *unite* the action of all the communes in striking at capital, in crushing the resistance of the capitalists, in transferring the ownership of the railways, factories, land and so forth to the *entire* nation, to the whole of society." [4] In still another pamphlet, written less than three weeks before the November Revolution, Lenin asserted that the Bolsheviks were in favor of centralism and of a plan, "but it must be the centralism and plan of a proletarian state—it must be a proletarian regulation of production and distribution in the interests of the poor, the toilers, the exploited *against* the interests of the exploiters." [5]

In the foregoing statements there is at least an implicit recognition of the need for some system of status and authority in the workers' state, or, more accurately, in the beginning stages of this state. These ideas were, however, mingled with a set of anti-authoritarian goals that explicitly denied the need for a system of authority and organized inequality in the new society. These equalitarian ideas appear to be the product of hostility to the system of organized inequality prevailing in capitalist society. Among social groups opposed to the existing order of inequality in society, there frequently recurs the argument that all social inequalities are unnecessary. Although the Bolsheviks did not go as far in this direction as other nineteenth- and early twentieth-century groups opposed to the contemporary status quo, there are strong traces of this viewpoint in Bolshevik theory.

While the economic institutions of capitalism represented a step forward in Bolshevik eyes, they were not ready to grant that the apparatus of government in a capitalist state represented progress. The Russian Marxists of 1917 and earlier belonged for the most part to the tradition that regarded all nonmanual labor as unproductive, though they did not apply this doctrine with complete logical rigidity. In accord with this viewpoint, bureaucracy and a standing army were described by Lenin as a parasite on the body of bourgeois society, "a parasite created by the inherent antagonisms which rend that society, but a parasite which 'chokes all its pores' of life." [6]

Since the Bolsheviks could see no useful purpose to be served by the apparatus of control of the bourgeois state, and also recognized that this apparatus would be the strongest center of opposition to the revolution, they argued that the whole machinery should be smashed. A few weeks before the November coup, Lenin declared that the proletariat could not take hold of the state apparatus and could not wield it, but that they could "smash all that is oppressive, all that is routine and incurably bourgeois in the old state apparatus." [7]

The equalitarian aspects of Bolshevik doctrine are prominent in Lenin's proposals concerning what should replace the smashed machinery of the bourgeois state. As successor to the former bourgeois institutions, Lenin wanted to place the soviets. (As is generally known, the soviets were councils of workers, peasants, and soldiers that sprang up during the 1905 and 1917 revolutions.) Under the soviets, Lenin asserted, both legislative and executive functions could be combined and united in the person of the elected representatives of the people.[8] These new institutions would be not only elective but also "subject to recall at the will of the people without any bureaucratic formalities," and hence, from the Bolshevik viewpoint, "far more democratic" than any preceding form of state.[9] The army and the police were to be replaced by the "universal arming of the people."[10]

Shortly before the November Revolution Lenin apparently believed in the possibility of widespread mass participation in the processes of political control and decision-making. He argued that the Bolsheviks had a "magic means of increasing our state apparatus *tenfold* at one stroke" by getting the "toilers, the poor, to share in the day-to-day work of governing the state." Then he added, as if to show that he was aware of the limitations of this approach, the famous remarks, "We are not utopians. We know that not every labourer or cook could at present undertake the administration of the state. In this we agree with the Cadets . . . But we differ from these citizens in that we demand the immediate abandonment of the prejudice that assumes that only the rich . . . are capable of *governing* the state."[11]

On the basis of this tradition, the Communists in the USSR continued until as late as 1932 to give lip service to the ideal of the destruction of the bureaucracy and the creation of a state in which eventually every cook could govern.

The problem of status in economic affairs

In August 1917 Lenin also advocated the suppression of all outward signs of status distinction in the administration of the new workers' state. He also favored eliminating the possibility that such distinctions would grow up on the basis of income differentials. Under the new conditions of the workers' state the functions of rule should be stripped, he argued, of "every shadow of privilege, of every semblance of official grandeur." Then he continued, "All officials, without exception, elected and subject to recall *at any time,* their salaries reduced to the level of 'workmen's wages'—these simple and 'self-evident' democratic measures, while completely uniting the interests of the workers and the majority of the peasants, at the same time serve as the bridge between capitalism and socialism." [12]

Bolshevik goals for the future economic organization of the post-revolutionary society reflected the same partial recognition of the social function of inequality, woven in with a strong strand of emotional equalitarianism, that has been pointed out in connection with their goals for the future political organization. There was, however, this important difference. In the sphere of industrial institutions the Bolsheviks expected to take over a going concern, the factories, railways, mines, and so forth, that had been developed by the capitalist system, together with a limited portion of the administrative apparatus necessary to operate these organizations. This legacy of the bourgeoisie they had no intention of smashing.

Lenin and his associates were by no means unaware of the nature or the importance of the economic problems they would have to solve, even if in retrospect their solutions sometimes appear simple to the point of utopianism. The Bolshevik leaders definitely recognized that if they intended to eliminate or alter the market mechanisms controlling the production and distribution of commodities in capitalist society, they would have to find something else to take their place. "The main difficulty of a proletarian revolution," Lenin remarked, "is to establish on a nation-wide scale a precise and scrupulous system of accounting and control, *control by the workers,* over the production and distribution of commodities." [13]

Lenin and other Party officers were clearly aware likewise that the new economic order would require, at least in the beginning, some form of status distinctions and a ladder of authority in order to function. "We are not utopians, we do not indulge in 'dreams' of dispensing *at once* with all administration, with all subordination," said Lenin in 1917. [14] To the Bolshevik way of thinking, such "utopian" and "anarchist" views served reactionary purposes, since they implied the postponement of the socialist revolution until human nature had changed. The Bolsheviks wanted their revolution with "human nature as it is now, with human nature that cannot dispense with subordination, control, and 'managers.' " [15]

The general Bolshevik plan by 1917 with regard to economic organization was to take over the industrial organization of Russia, together with its administrative apparatus, but at the same time to make use of the soviets to ensure that the workers enjoyed real power and control over industry. Lenin pointed out that besides the preëminently coercive machinery of the modern state (the army, the police, and the bureaucracy) there had grown up through the banks and syndicates an apparatus that performed a vast amount of work of an accounting and statistical nature. It is characteristic of Lenin's thinking at this juncture that he saw in the managerial functions of industry and banking merely the "simple operations of registration, filing and checking that . . . can be easily performed by every literate person." [16]

This managerial apparatus, or, as Lenin saw it, this accounting apparatus, was not to be destroyed, but merely wrested from the control of the capitalists and subordinated to the proletarian soviets. In Lenin's own words, "*Without big banks socialism would be impossible of realization.*" He continued with the argument that the big banks were the state apparatus which the proletariat would take from capitalism ready-made.[17] In addition, the Bolsheviks planned to take over the wartime measures of the grain monopoly, bread cards, and universal labor service, putting them under the control of the proletariat.[18] As in the political sphere, the problem of economic control would be solved through the soviets.[19] This could be done, Lenin argued, because the problem was merely a question of smashing the resistance of a handful of people. "We know them all by name," said Lenin, "we have only to take the lists of directors, members of boards, big shareholders, and so forth. There are a few hundred of them in the *whole* of Russia, at most a few thousand, each of whom the proletarian state, with its Soviet apparatus, its employees' unions, and so forth, can surround with tens or hundreds of controllers." [20] There are no indications at this time that the Bolsheviks foresaw any of the difficulties that might arise from such a diffusion of responsibility and authority. How Lenin himself modified his views when these problems arose will be indicated in the course of this study.

In 1917 Lenin evidently anticipated that inequalities of income and consumption would continue after the Revolution, as a temporary measure, in order to induce those with scarce skills to coöperate with the new regime. He is equally specific in pointing to equality as an eventual Bolshevik goal. "We shall probably only gradually introduce equality of pay for all work in its full extent, leaving a higher rate of pay for such experts during the transition period." [21] On other occasions, perhaps carried away by enthusiasm for the equalitarian goal, Lenin asserted that the "immediate object" was to organize the whole of the national economy "so that the technicians, managers, bookkeepers, as well as *all* officials, shall receive salaries no higher than 'workmen's wages.'" [22] The latter type of statement is, however, relatively rare even in Lenin's writings of 1917. For the most part, he expressed clearly and pungently Bolshevik willingness to pay the "experts" for their services, provided they were kept under the control of the proletariat. This issue became the source of important splits in the top Party leadership shortly after the November Revolution.

The equalitarian and anti-authoritarian aspects of Bolshevik doctrine appear most clearly in the conception of the "withering away of the state." In the course of an unspecified period of time, the Bolshevik argument runs, both the coercive and the incentive features that have characterized past societies, as well as the early stages of socialist society, will disappear. This early Bolshevik belief reflects a certain idealistic and perhaps naïve faith in the plasticity of human nature. "When people have become so accustomed to observing the fundamental rules of social life and when their labour is so productive that they will voluntarily work *according to their ability*," the state will be able to wither away completely, according to Lenin. Perhaps he did not have a very firm belief in the possibility of attaining this eventual goal, because he went on to say that no socialist would promise that this higher phase of communism would arrive. Instead, he pointed out that the earlier great socialists, in foreseeing its arrival, assumed both a greater productivity of labor than existed and a new human nature: "a person *unlike the present* man in the street, who . . . is capable of damaging the stores of social wealth 'just for fun' and of demanding the impossible." [23]

Plans for the peasants

Lenin and other Marxists devoted more attention than is generally realized to the role of the peasantry in both the existing society of the day and the society they hoped to create. Points of departure for the Marxist analysis are found in the writings of Marx and Engels, and especially in Karl Kautsky's *Die Agrarfrage*. Early in 1899 Lenin took copious notes on the Kautsky study,[24] the influence of which is evident and acknowledged in many subsequent writings.

The belief in the inevitability of capitalist development in agriculture [25] was central to the Bolshevik analysis of the peasant problem and provided the stick with which they beat their opponents among non-Marxist parties opposed to the status quo. For Lenin and his followers in the years before the Revolution, the chief question was merely what type of agrarian capitalism would develop in Russia.

According to the Leninist analysis, two lines of development were possible. One was according to the Prussian model, through the gradual transformation of the large estates into "Junker-bourgeois" estates, by turning the mass of peasantry into landless peasants and keeping them down to a pauper standard of living. Parallel with this development there would be, in his opinion, the growth of a class of well-to-do peasants (*kulaks*), who would participate in the exploitation of the masses. This process would break up the village commune (*mir*) and other "antiquated" and semifeudal institutions in the interest of the landlords. The second line of development Lenin regarded as the American model. This too required the destruction of the old feudal forms, but in the interest of the peasant masses and not the landlords. The result would be a mass of free farmers. Both these possibilities he regarded as strictly capitalist develop-

ments, though he stressed that the latter would be far more beneficial to the masses.[26] On the basis of this interpretation of the
economic and political situation in Russia prior to the Revolution,
Lenin stated very clearly that the Party ought to promote the
latter type of development, namely, the "bourgeois" growth of
a mass of free farmers. This bourgeois goal was not to be confused, however, Lenin cautioned his followers, with the ultimate one of socialism.[27]

The capitalist means proposed by Lenin to destroy the remnants of feudalism and the institution of the *mir* was the nationalization of the land. Although this term is now associated with
socialist measures and, at the time it was proposed, included
the "total abolition of private property in land," Lenin regarded
it as a purely bourgeois device for the purpose of destroying
precapitalist arrangements and clearing the way for capitalist
(and eventually socialist) institutions. This argument, which
may strike the modern reader as paradoxical, was based on certain conclusions arrived at by Marx, to the effect that private
property in land was unnecessary and even economically harmful under strictly capitalist conditions. Such a line of reasoning
may also reflect a certain subconscious desire to strike a blow at
capitalism. Still another factor in the apparent paradox may
have been Lenin's desire at this time to attract the peasantry
to the banner of Social Democracy.

In criticizing not only the Narodniki, who thought that "the
repudiation of private property in land was repudiation of capitalism," but also that section of the Russian Marxists who followed a similar train of thought, Lenin drew upon the following argument by Marx. Marx asserted that under a system of
private property in land, the expenditure of money-capital in
the purchase of land diminished by that amount the capital
available for agricultural investment. In other words, he did not
regard the purchase of land as investment of capital in land.
Instead, he regarded it as just the opposite: a diminution of the
amount of capital available for investment in land.[28] Though the
actual validity of Marx's analysis is not of concern here, it is
difficult to see why this argument should apply any more to the

purchase of land than it should to the purchase of a factory. At
all events, it provided the grounds for the Marxist-Leninist doctrine that the landowner was "absolutely superfluous in capitalist
production." [29]

Lenin continues with a quotation from Marx, drawing certain
conclusions about the consequences for the bourgeois attitude
toward private property in land: "That is why in theory the
radical bourgeois arrives at the repudiation of private property
in land . . . In practice, however, he lacks courage, for an attack on one form of private property in the conditions of labour
would be very dangerous for another form (Theorien über den
Mehrwerth, II. Band, I. Teil, S. 208)." [30] For these reasons the
abolition of private property in land was the "maximum of what
can be done in bourgeois society for the removal of all obstacles
to the free investment of capital in land and to the free flow of
capital from one branch of production to another." This situation
in turn would lead to the rapid development of capitalism and
the unleashing of the class struggle, in which Lenin was, perhaps, primarily interested.[31]

The Bolsheviks were aware that the peasants were not interested in such elaborate discussions, and that they were mainly
anxious to divide up the large holdings of the landlords, the church,
and the Tsar among themselves. Lenin himself remarked that all
the peasant wanted was the expansion of small-scale private
plots.[32] Probably for these reasons the official Party program
of 1903 adopted a highly equivocal position toward the peasant
question in an effort to harness the peasants to the revolutionary chariot. "While supporting all revolutionary action on the
part of the peasantry," the Party declared, "including the confiscation of the large estates of the landlords, the Russian Social
Democratic Labor Party is absolutely opposed to all attempts
to hinder the course of economic development. While striving for
the transfer of confiscated lands to the democratic local government bodies in the event of a victorious development of the
revolution, the Russian Social Democratic Labor Party will, if
circumstances prove unfavorable for such a transfer, declare
itself in favor of dividing among the peasants landed estates on

which small husbandry had previously been conducted or which are required in order to round out the peasants' holdings." [33]

The Marxists were opposed to the development of small-scale peasant agriculture on the overt grounds that it was less efficient than large-scale agriculture, which permitted a wider use of mechanization. It is highly likely that a more important reason for their opposition was the fear that the growth of a class of established small property owners would block the road to socialism. Lenin's 1907 proposal to nationalize the land instead of turning it over to "democratic local government bodies," as advocated in the 1903 program, was probably designed to strengthen the hand of the central authorities in coping with such a situation. However, he recognized that even nationalization might achieve no more than to clear the way for the transformation of Russia into a country of small independent farmers. After a successful agrarian revolution and the nationalization of the land, he observed, the peasants might demand that the plots of land they rented from the state become their personal property.[34]

In 1907 Lenin was able to supply only a very general solution to this dilemma, which was to plague the Bolshevik rulers during the first decade and a half of their power. According to this solution, the proletariat should support the "militant bourgeoisie [which in this connection included the peasants] when it is waging a genuinely revolutionary struggle against feudalism. But it is not the business of the proletariat to support the bourgeoisie when it is calming down." Anticipating that the peasants might become a conservative force as soon as their land hunger had been satisfied, Lenin at this juncture offered no more than the formula that the proletariat must "defend revolutionary traditions." [35]

Nevertheless, there was latent in the prerevolutionary Marxist tradition the solution that was eventually adopted by the Party in the great campaigns for the collectivization of agriculture. Although this solution underwent significant alterations in the intervening period, there is no difficulty in recognizing the essential similar elements. Hints of the solution are found in the occasional glimpses of the ultimate goal of socialism and the peasants' way of life thereunder. In the late nineteenth century Karl Kautsky devoted a few lines to a sketch of the "socialist latifundia" of the future, peopled by prosperous coöperatives of free and happy men. He expected that in the future the flight from the peasant dwarf holdings to the city slums would be reversed by a stream of young men and women pouring into the coöperative estates. In this way the small peasant would disappear of his own volition, and "barbarism would be driven from the last fortress . . . of modern civilization." [36] Perhaps this picture was somewhat too rosy for Lenin's cast of mind, since he does not appear to have paid special attention to it in his notes on Kautsky. But he did note the general thesis that capitalism was preparing the ground for socialism in agriculture, as in industry, by the increasing cultivation of large areas of land and the increasing use of wage labor on the land. [37]

Where Kautsky in a less rosy analysis asserted that the peasant in contemporary society would not go over to socialized production of his own accord and that the initiative could come only from the victorious proletariat, Lenin used vigorous italics in approval. [38] Those already familiar with the actual history of the collectivization of agriculture in Russia will recognize that this forceful aspect of the Marxist tradition played a more important role than did the optimistic picture of the attractions of the socialist latifundia.

Lenin was quite cautious in his open advocacy of large-scale socialist farms and evidently conceived of them merely as the best way to make use of the big estates. By turning the big estates into coöperative farms he hoped, perhaps, to check the peasants' drive toward a mere division of the land. In 1903 he presented in brief form his ideas on this topic, which are worth quoting in full, since they foreshadow clearly later plans for collective farming:

When the working class is victorious over the whole of the bourgeoisie, it will take the land away from the big proprietors and introduce *coöperative farming* on the big estates, so that the workers will farm the land together, in common, and freely elect trusted men to manage the farms. They will use machinery to save labour; they will work in shifts for not more than eight (or even six) hours daily. Then the small peasant who prefers to carry on his farm in the old way on individual lines will not produce for the market, to sell to anyone who comes along, but will produce for the workers' associations; the small peasant will supply the workers' associations with corn, meat, vegetables, and the workers in return will provide him with machinery, livestock, fertilizers, clothes, and whatever else he may require, without his having to pay for it. Then there will be no struggle for money between the big and small farmer, then there will be no wage labour for others; all workers will work for themselves, all labour-saving devices and all machinery will benefit the workers and help to make their work easier, to improve their standard of living.[39]

As late as May of 1917 Lenin limited his proposals for co-operative farms to the confiscated estates. In his proposed revisions of the Party program he urged that the original (1903) proposal to permit the division of such estates be replaced by advice to the rural proletarians to set up model farms to be conducted for the public account by local soviets of agricultural workers under the direction of agricultural experts.[40] The proposal in almost identical wording was included in the decisions promulgated at the crucial Conference of May 1917, which adopted Lenin's program of the "April theses," reversing the official Party viewpoint on a number of issues.[41]

Revolution and international affairs

Around the turn of the century the Russian Marxists began to raise among themselves more frequently the broader question of what would happen to the Russian state and to world politics as a whole if their revolutionary ideas triumphed. The answers that were given to this question were closely related to the views held by their authors concerning both the probable and the desirable situation in Russia following a successful revolution.

By the spring of 1905 Lenin had come to the conclusion that the "revolutionary-democratic dictatorship of the proletariat and the peasantry" might succeed in establishing itself for a brief period in Russia. Such a victory would in turn rouse Europe to "throw off the yoke of the bourgeoisie" and enable the Russians to carry out a socialist revolution.[42] At the same time Lenin anticipated that the establishment of the "revolutionary-democratic dictatorship of the proletariat and the peasantry" would rapidly encounter the resistance of the property-owning classes in Russia. The struggle to preserve the gains won in this "democratic" revolution and to proceed toward socialism would be "almost hopeless for the Russian proletariat alone," and its defeat would be practically inevitable "if the *European socialist proletariat* should not come to the assistance of the Russian proletariat." [43]

Lenin's views differed from those of more conservative Marxist theorists, especially the Mensheviks, who expected the proletariat to play a role no more significant than that of a left wing of the liberal bourgeoisie in a parliamentary revolution in Russia. The practical implication of this viewpoint was a postponement of the revolutionary goal.[44]

The conception developed by Lenin also differed from Trotsky's views at this time. Arguing from the experience of the abortive revolution of 1848, and from the internal conditions in Russia, Trotsky came to the conclusion that political power in Russia would and should pass into the hands of the proletariat before the bourgeoisie could check the onward rush of events.[45] Pressing the argument further, he declared that the industrial workers should participate in the revolutionary government only in the position of a dominant power group.[46] Lenin's key conception of a dictatorship of the proletariat and the peasantry simply could not be realized, Trotsky announced, because the peasants were incapable of forceful political activity. They could neither identify themselves with the existing bourgeois parties, nor form a party of their own. Therefore, the workers would have to seize political responsibility themselves.[47]

After the seizure of power, class antagonisms were bound to increase as soon as the representatives of the proletariat went beyond policies of a purely democratic character and began to put into effect the policies of their own class. In this respect the leaders of the proletariat would have no real choice, according to Trotsky's reasoning. If, for example, the government dominated by the proletariat passed the "democratic" legislation of an eight-hour day, the violent resistance of the capitalists would force the government to take control of the factories.[48] In this fashion the distinction between the democratic and socialist programs of social democracy would inevitably disappear.

The increasing class struggle in Russia would, in turn, make it impossible for the Russian working class to hold power without assistance from the European proletariat.[49] At the same time, conditions in the capitalist world would make possible a clean sweep of the established order by a series of socialist revolutions. Capitalism, Trotsky asserted, had "drawn all reactionary forces into one world-wide co-partnership." [50] For the maintenance of its power the bourgeoisie depended largely on the "pre-capitalist pillars of reaction," [51] that is, such groups and institutions as the large landowners, the Russian, German, and Austrian monarchies, the police, the standing army, and the bureaucracy. All these institutions and capitalism itself could and should be swept away, Trotsky declared, in a chain reaction of revolutionary explosions. At the time when this was written, during the ebb of the 1905 revolution, many Marxists regarded Trotsky's views as an expression of personal idiosyncrasy. Yet they formed a latent contribution to Marxist doctrine that was destined to revive and win considerable acceptance in powerful Bolshevik circles, when circumstances seemed more favorable to their application.

A further stimulus to the development of Russian Marxist theory on world politics was the outbreak of the First World War and the collapse of the socialist movement along the lines of national fissures. For these events the Bolsheviks sought to find a theoretical explanation. It was not in the tradition of the early Marxist intellectuals to explain and dismiss striking events with tabloid catch phrases. The exact opposite was the case and so remained for many years after the establishment of the new regime. Long discussions of political affairs were the rule, a tradition that continued among opposition elements in the jails of the secret police.

For enlightenment on the war Lenin turned in 1915 to the

writings of Clausewitz. As was his practice, Lenin took copious notes, which throw a great deal of light on his thought processes as a whole, as well as on the aspects of Clausewitz's theory that appealed to him. He left untouched the purely military and strategic portions of Clausewitz. Instead, he paid careful attention to the political sections. Apparently he was particularly impressed by Clausewitz's analysis of the role of the masses in wartime. Clausewitz's observation that a good military leader should not have too much faith in the people or believe the best about them attracted his favorable attention.[52] Likewise, he was struck with Clausewitz's explanation of Napoleon's victories in terms of the spread of political and social changes associated with the French Revolution.[53] Lenin also seemed to enjoy Clausewitz's way of making fun of the distinction between aggressive and defensive war. In Lenin's notes is found Clausewitz's remark: "The conqueror is always peace loving (as Bonaparte always claimed); he would just as soon march peacefully into our state; since he cannot do this we must want war, and also prepare for it." [54]

Elsewhere Lenin copied out verbatim, and in the original German, some of Clausewitz's observations on the role of empirical judgments in political and military matters.[55] Lenin's expressed interest in the importance of an unsystematic and more or less intuitive approach to politics is significant. Although he was by far the most prominent theorist among the Bolsheviks, he was also the leader least bound by his past theories. While his numerous changes in policy were always presented with elaborate theoretical justification, there appears to have been in these changes a strong element of sheer intuition.

From these notes on Clausewitz, as well as in his own writings on the organizational problems of a conspiratorial elite (to be discussed in the next chapter), Lenin reveals many characteristics of the modern propagandist and manipulator of the masses. There is in Lenin the typical combination of cynicism concerning the role of the masses, who are regarded as merely objects for skilled political manipulation, and fanatical devotion to a cause that is characteristic of twentieth-century totalitarian movements.

It is, however, Lenin's *Imperialism, the Highest Stage of Capitalism,* written in 1916, the year after his reading Clausewitz, that constitutes his chief contribution to a theory of world politics and the source of much subsequent Marxist writing and thinking on this topic. In this work Lenin claimed that the concentration of production and capital into larger and larger units had led to the creation of enormous monopolies. An outstanding characteristic of monopoly capitalism was that control had fallen into the hands of the banks. In turn, Lenin argued, this situation had created the necessity for the export of capital and the development of colonial empires.

Since the territorial division of the world among the great capitalist powers had already taken place, the consequence could only be a continual struggle by peaceful and warlike means for a redivision of the world. Relations established by alliances among capitalist states were based on the economic partition of the world. Because a forceful redivision of the world was unavoidable under capitalism, Lenin continued, these alliances could be nothing more than temporary truces leading to new wars.[56]

Another feature of capitalism, according to this interpretation, was the rise of chauvinism and opportunism among the leaders of the working class. The receipt of monopoly profits by the capitalists made it possible for them to corrupt a minority of the working class and win them over to the side of the capitalists of a given nation.[57] By this argument Lenin endeavored to explain to his own satisfaction, and that of his followers, the growth of nationalist and nonrevolutionary sentiment among the leaders of the European working class, and their defection from the banner of class warfare and working-class solidarity at the time of the outbreak of the war.

In *Imperialism* the full tactical conclusions for Russia were not openly asserted. However, the Leninist doctrine of imperialism has provided the theoretical justification for the conclusion that the proletariat should struggle for the defeat of its own government in wartime and should do its best to "turn the imperialist war into a civil war." As Lenin put it elsewhere, "A revolutionary class in a reactionary war cannot but desire the defeat of its own government." [58]

It should be pointed out that this tactical conclusion already possessed a theoretical basis in the general tradition of European Marxism. The *Communist Manifesto* had already asserted that the working class knew no fatherland. Numerous Congresses of the Second International had in their declarations foreshadowed the position taken by Lenin. But it was only in Russian Marxist, and particularly Bolshevik, circles that this tradition was taken sufficiently seriously to become the basis for action. In September of 1914 the Central Committee of the Russian Social Democratic Labor Party, at that time controlled by the Bolsheviks, issued a Manifesto against the war, declaring that the task of socialism was to turn the conflict into a civil war. Accusing the other parties of treachery to the cause of socialism, the Manifesto called upon socialists of each country to defeat their own bourgeoisie. On the occasion of the voting of war credits in the Duma, both the Menshevik and the Bolshevik deputies refused to vote in favor of the credits and left the meeting hall.[59] However, nationalist sentiments were sufficiently strong in Russian Marxist circles to bring about a complete regrouping within the Party. Among the most prominent to go over to the "patriotic" viewpoint was Plekhanov, the father of Marxism in Russia.

Scattered through Lenin's writings of 1915–1917 are a number of remarks concerning the policy the leaders of the proletariat should adopt if they were successful in turning the imperialist war into a civil war and in seizing power. For the most part they followed the same line of thought as that adopted more than a decade earlier: that the proletariat should seize power and by so doing set on fire the socialist revolution in Europe, which would in turn enable the workers to retain power in Russia. To this he added, in 1915, that "we would propose peace to *all* the belligerents on the basis of the liberation of the colonies and of *all* the dependent, oppressed and disfranchised peoples." [60]

This is the course of action the Bolsheviks followed after the seizure of power. However, Lenin was unable to foresee many of the consequences of this action. Though he prophesied correctly that neither Germany nor England nor France would accept the peace proposals, he was incorrect in stating that this refusal would make it necessary for Russia "to prepare for and wage a revolutionary war." [61] After the assumption of political responsibility, Lenin himself prevented the Bolshevik leaders from adopting such an adventurous course. Similarly, as late as October 1917, he failed to foresee the possibility of intervention against the Soviet state. He regarded as "utterly absurd" the assumption that the French and Italians might combine with the Germans in order to attack Russia. In this he was correct only to the extent that the Germans did not coöperate with the Allies in the intervention, although they invaded Russia on their own account after the peace of Brest-Litovsk. At one point, however, the Bolsheviks sought German assistance against Allied intervention.[62] Furthermore, Lenin regarded as very unlikely that England, America, and Japan would declare war upon Russia, because of the conflict of their interests in Asia.[63] Here he might be described as "wrong for the right reason," in that American intervention was motivated largely by a desire to prevent the extension of Japanese power. While these matters will be considered in more detail in a subsequent chapter, it is well to point out here that the Leninist doctrine of imperialism and incipient revolution did not provide an accurate tool for political analysis and prediction, and that Lenin himself was the first to abandon the attempt to carry out certain of its implications.

Main points of the Leninist program

What, then, was the Bolshevik program on the eve of the *coup d'état?* The immediate objective was to establish a republic of soviets based on the proletariat and the poor sections of the peasantry, and to abolish the police, the army, and the bureaucracy. In the economic field, Leninist doctrine demanded the replacement of the existing managerial groups with a centralized system of control by the industrial workers, together with a sharp reduction of inequalities in pay and the eventual introduction of full equality. In agriculture, Lenin proposed the introduction of coöperative farming only on the large landed estates, while the disposal of the rest of the land was left up to the local population. At the same time he wanted to avoid, if possible, the transformation of Russia into a land of small peasant proprietors. In the international field, he expected that a successful revolution in Russia would set afire the socialist revolution in Europe, with the result that the Western proletariat would come to the aid of the hard-pressed workers of Russia.

Nearly every one of these hopes and expectations was disappointed. Yet these beliefs constituted a point of departure to which the Bolsheviks were to return in times of trouble. Before the nature of these defeats and the subsequent reinterpretation and readaptation of Russian Marxist doctrine can be understood, it is necessary to examine briefly the instrument of revolutionary victory, the Party.

3

The Party Faces the Dilemma of Means and Ends

Why the route of conspiracy?

In the first chapter certain aspects of the structure of Russian society favoring the overthrow of the established order by a conspiratorial elite were pointed out. Closer examination may now be made of the theory and practice of conspiracy developed by Lenin as a means for destroying one social order and replacing it with another. In the subsequent development of the Bolshevik regime such doctrines concerning the means to power were to play a more significant role than the doctrines concerning the ends to which power should be put. Some explanation is necessary, therefore, of the way in which these traditions arose, and the extent to which they corresponded to actual political behavior in the prerevolutionary period.

The first problem to be considered is why the device of a conspiratorial elite was invented or chosen by any of the groups that were in opposition to the Tsarist order. In addition to the hindrances imposed on open political activity by the conditions of Tsarist autocracy, an important reason for selecting the conspiratorial road to power appears to be that the persons who felt the social tensions of Tsarist society most keenly, the intelligentsia, had little or no widespread or organized support among the masses. There is a touch of historical irony in this situation. If mass discontent with the status quo had been greater, and if the level of education had been higher, the Marxist movement in Russia might have achieved a broader base of mass support and greater influence upon the decisions of the government. In this case, it might conceivably have followed the Western European, instead of the Bolshevik, line of development and emerged eventually as a peaceful left opposition.

The gap in Russian society between the intelligentsia and the masses had two far-reaching consequences in the development of Russian Marxism and Russian society as a whole. In the first place, it led to the conception of a dictatorship of the Party over the working class, because the intellectual leaders of the Party feared that the revolution would never come of its own accord.[1] In the second place, this split favored the development of a centralized control by an intellectual elite within the Party itself.[2] While in modern times the intellectuals of the Party have been replaced by practical administrators, the feature of centralized control has remained and even been intensified.

When the issue of a conspiratorial versus a mass organization first arose, it was not nearly as clear-cut as later historical synthesis, together with the exigencies of later Party polemics, might make it appear. Although Lenin had already formulated and circulated in numerous pamphlets and speeches his ideas on how the Party should be organized, and although these organizational principles became the issue over which the Party split into the Menshevik and Bolshevik fractions at the Second Congress (held in Brussels and London in 1903), it entered no one's head at the time the discussions commenced that the split would take place. Indeed, Lenin himself remarked at the time to Axelrod, later the outstanding Menshevik leader, "I do not in any way consider our differences so important that the life and death of the Party depends on them."[3] Nevertheless, the organizational principles expounded by Lenin as a means to an end became the basis for the organization of the Party, the Communist International, and eventually the Soviet State itself. While the ideology of ends has been much modified or discarded, the ideology of means has had lasting importance.

The ambivalent attitude toward the masses

The relative absence of mass support for the goal of revolution, combined with the intellectual's fanatical belief in the desirability of this goal, produced in official and unofficial Leninist doctrine an attitude of distrust toward the masses. Coupled with this attitude was a firm belief in the possibility of persuading the masses to follow the "right" path. This attitude and its relationship to the modern propagandist has already been pointed out in connection with Lenin's reaction to Clausewitz. A third element in the Bolshevik doctrinal view of the masses, which stands in contradiction to the other two, was a highly favorable opinion of the creative ability of the masses. This talent had merely to be released from the shackles of capitalism and feudalism in order to build a freer and happier society than man had ever known.

When the problem of organizing a party first arose, Lenin expressed the attitude of distrust, tinged with contempt, in a sentence that eventually became a cliché of Communist doctrine. "The history of all countries shows that the working class, exclusively by its own effort, is able to develop only trade union consciousness." [4] He went on to point out, by way of contrast, that both in Germany and in Russia the ideas of socialism had developed among the intellectuals. Elaborating his ideas further, he asserted, "There is a lot of talk about spontaneity, but the *spontaneous* development of the labor movement leads to its becoming subordinated to bourgeois ideology." Trade unionism in turn "means the ideological enslavement of the workers to the bourgeoisie. Hence our task, the task of Social-Democracy, is to *combat spontaneity*, to *divert* the labor movement from its spontaneous, trade unionist striving to go under the wing of the bourgeoisie, and to bring it under the wing of revolutionary Social-Democracy." [5]

Lenin's explanation of the failure of the workers to develop of their own accord a revolutionary viewpoint is in the form of a tribute to bourgeois ideology. Since the latter was "more fully developed," according to Lenin, and since the opportunities for its dissemination were enormously greater, the workers were likely to follow it instead of the revolutionary doctrine of social-ism.[6] No third ideology could develop, according to Lenin's argu-ment, because it is in general impossible to develop an ideology that is above class lines in a society torn by class antagonisms.[7]

This somewhat hostile and suspicious attitude toward the everyday demands put forth by the rank-and-file industrial work-ers did not imply that the Bolsheviks underestimated the im-portance of mass support. Lacking this support, the Bolsheviks did all they could to obtain it, especially in the months preceding the November Revolution. Repeatedly Lenin asserted that the Revolution could not succeed without the support of the masses. "We are not Blanquists, we are not in favor of the seizure of power by a minority," he declared in 1917.[8] His arguments in favor of the final armed uprising that put the Bolsheviks in power, an undertaking several of his most important followers regarded as sheer adventurism, were based on the premise that the psycho-logical moment had arrived when the masses would support the Bolsheviks.[9] It is significant that in Leninist theory the gauging of this support was to be an act of intuition on the part of the conspiratorial leaders. "It would be naive to wait for a 'formal' majority for the Bolsheviks; no revolution waits for that." [10]

The necessary mass support was something that had to be earned through positive and active leadership. Lenin had nothing but scorn for the leader who proceeds by finding out what the masses want and then offers it to them. For such tactics Lenin coined the picturesque term "tail-endism" (*khvostism*), an offense he lashes out against time after time throughout his career. In-stead, the Bolsheviks, and particularly Lenin, argued that one must explain patiently to the masses what the "real" political situa-tion was, and what tactics were necessary in order to achieve goals that would "really" help the masses.[11] It is clear that such a viewpoint implies that the Bolsheviks had the correct answers to the problems facing the masses. On this point the Bolsheviks at any given time did not entertain any public doubts, though they did not hesitate to alter their interpretation of events and their tactics when the situation appeared to require it.

This ambivalent attitude toward the masses, a mixture of

suspicion and admiration, has remained an important element in Bolshevik thinking down to the present day. There will be occasion later to speak of Stalin's "revolution from above," in which the ordinary citizens of the USSR were called upon to make enormous sacrifices for the sake of distant goals and were driven by frequently cruel means to make these sacrifices. Likewise, note will be taken of Stalin's various efforts to curb public expression of contempt for the masses by members of the Communist Party and the new use to which the Marxist version of *vox populi, vox Dei* has been put in the new social order.

Lenin's theories concerning the organizational forms that the Russian Marxist Party ought to take were closely related to the ambivalent attitudes toward the masses that have just been described. They also represented in his opinion, and that of his followers, the only possible adaptation to the conditions of police repression in Tsarist Russia. Although this repression was mild and inefficient by the standards that have been set subsequently by the totalitarian and police states, it included far greater restrictions on the political and economic activities of the industrial workers than prevailed at the same time among the workers in Western Europe with their legal socialist parties and trade unions.

As is generally known, Lenin believed in a highly centralized organization of professional revolutionaries. They were to be "professional" in the sense that they should devote their whole time to revolutionary activity. The writing of revolutionary literature, its dissemination, the organization of strikes, demonstrations, and other activities directed toward the overthrow of the established order could no longer be left to persons for whom it was an avocation.[12] "Secrecy is such a necessary condition for such an organization," Lenin stated, "that all other conditions (number and selection of members, functions, etc.) must all be subordinated to it." [13] As a result of these conditions, he argued, power would have to be concentrated in the hands of a small number of leaders.[14]

It is significant that Leninist doctrine recognized clearly the need for a system of status, authority, and discipline within the Party as a means for achieving the goal of a new society, while at the same time it took very little account of these necessities in the organization of the new society itself. By means of a conspiratorial elite the Bolsheviks hoped to set up a regime that would eliminate the bureaucracy and other authoritarian features of bourgeois society and create the conditions for the widest possible participation of the masses in the processes of government.

The Bolsheviks were aware of the conflict between the needs of conspiracy and their professed objectives of freedom, whether of the "bourgeois-democratic" or socialist variety. In the course of their prerevolutionary history they gradually evolved the principles of democratic centralism as a device for reconciling the conflict.

Democratic centralism: the answer to the problem of authority?

The term "democratic centralism" seems to have grown up and become accepted as part of the current coin of discussion in Russian Marxist circles without finding its way into print for several years. Its first appearance in an official Party declaration was at the Tammerfors Conference of the Bolshevik wing of the Party in December 1905. On this occasion it was briefly referred to as the "indisputable" basis of Party organization.[15] It nevertheless remained undefined in official Party statements until after the November Revolution. Until 1906 the word does not occur in any of Lenin's voluminous writings on problems of Party organization.

Since the Bolsheviks have adopted the principle of democratic centralism as the theoretical basis not only of the Russian Communist Party but also of the Communist International and the Soviet State itself, it is worth while to point out the forces that shaped this ingenious conception. We shall begin with the centralist half of the idea, which emphasizes theories of discipline and authority.

Although the Russian Social Democratic Labor Party had held its first Congress in 1898, adopted a formal statute and rules of procedure, and issued a manifesto, this unity on paper was all the Russian Marxists were able to achieve for several years. Until after the 1903 Congress the Party existed in the form of a scattered group of discussion and agitational circles, tied together very loosely by adherence to a common viewpoint. Within these circles more energy was devoted to attempts to convince the other members of the correctness of a particular shading of the Marxist *Weltanschauung* than to the overthrow of the Tsarist regime, a feature that was destined to be carried over to much later times. Together with this high valuation on theoretical polemics, the circles were characterized by the absence of any strong spirit of compromise or give-and-take. Differences of opinion were resolved, as Lenin observed in 1902, not by votes according to the Party rules of procedure, but by struggles and the threat of resignation.[16] It is difficult to imagine more unpromising material out of which to weld a coherent, disciplined, and secretive organization of revolutionaries.

Yet this is the very task which Lenin undertook in earnest in 1902. It is readily understandable that at this time, in the light of the human material with which he had to work and the conditions of police repression, he was highly impatient with demands for strict adherence to democratic procedures. There are therefore in his early writings, which laid the foundations of the Party organization, few if any hints of democratic centralism. Indeed, the opposite is the rule. Lenin fought tooth and nail to give as much power as possible to the directing core of the Party, and to cut down as far as possible the power of the local units. In the organizational proposals of his opponents within the Party at that time he criticized sharply the "misplaced and immoderate use of the elective principle."[17] He poured vitriol upon the "high sounding phrases . . . of 'broad democracy' in the Party organization" which he considered "nothing more than a *useless and harmful toy.*" It is useless, he added, "because as a matter of fact no revolutionary organisation has ever practised *broad* democracy, nor could it, however much it desired to do so. It is a harmful toy, because any attempt to practise the 'broad democratic principles' will simply facilitate the work of the police in making big raids, it will perpetuate the prevailing primitiveness, divert the thoughts of practical workers from the serious and imperative task of training themselves to become professional revolutionaries to that of drawing up detailed 'paper' rules for election systems." [18] While he agreed that the lower units of the Party should have the right to bring various questions to the attention of the higher echelons of the Party, in 1902 he did not want any such provision included in the Party statutes, for fear of facilitating police infiltration.[19]

Although the conceptions of centralization and decentralization were current in Party circles at this time, Lenin favored decentralization only insofar as it implied that the Party center should have full information about the activities of each local unit. He drew the metaphor of an orchestra, whose conductor would have to know exactly which player struck a false note in order to correct him at once.[20] Again later conclusions may be anticipated by pointing out that in practice it was this aspect of the theory of Party organization that came to be realized after the establishment and consolidation of the Soviet regime.

The evidence available does not indicate that Lenin and his immediate associates regarded this form of highly centralized discipline as something desirable in itself. On the contrary, they appeared to regard it as a very necessary evil that should be done away with when the conditions of Tsarist repression were lightened. During the period of temporary freedom that marked the revolution of 1905, Lenin offered a resolution to the Third Party Congress, strongly urging that the elective principle receive greater application within the Party. Declaring that while the complete operation of this principle was possible and necessary only under the conditions of political freedom, he asserted that it could be applied much more widely than it was under the conditions then existing.[21] Although the resolution was not carried at the Congress, a closely similar one was adopted as the official Party position at a Party Conference in Tammerfors in December of the same year.[22]

History did not provide the Bolsheviks with a good test case to prove or disprove their intentions about the temporary nature of their somewhat autocratic internal discipline. For a moment it seemed as though the authoritarian trend might be averted.

Upon his return to Russia in April 1917, Lenin announced that "Russia is *now* the freest of all the belligerent countries of the world." [23] *Pravda,* the chief Bolshevik newspaper, was appearing openly. For the first time the Party was able to hold its Conferences and Congresses in Russia. However, on July 19, 1917, the Provisional Government ordered the arrest of Lenin, Zinoviev, and Kamenev, charging that the Bolsheviks were German spies. Lenin and Zinoviev decided to go into hiding, justifying their action on the grounds that "there are no guarantees of a fair trial in Russia at the present moment" and that "all the accusations against us are a simple episode of the civil war." [24]

During this interregnum period, the problems of Party organization were discussed at the Sixth Congress, held in August 1917, while nearly all the top Party leaders—Lenin, Trotsky, Zinoviev, Kamenev—were in hiding or under arrest. Very little interest appears to have been aroused by problems of inner Party democracy, since only a few moments were spent discussing this question. In the light of renewed police activity, it is understandable that there was no strong demand to put democratic centralism into practice. However, in some circles of the Party there was discontent with the prevailing state of inner Party affairs, as shown by the following interchange which took place during the voting on the new Party bylaws, section by section.

Zaks [who achieved the reputation of "conscience of the Party"] reads Section 5: "5. All organizations of the Party are constructed according to the principles of democratic centralism."

Skripnik [an important leader of the Party in the Ukraine]: "The organizational section should have deciphered what this point means. In this formulation it ought to be thrown out, for it is not a decision, it is not a section of the by-laws, but a wish."

Section 5 is put to a vote and is passed by 16 in favor and 5 opposed.

Soloviev [a minor delegate]: "I insist on a re-voting of this point, since not all the comrades took part in the voting."

On the second voting Section 5 is adopted by a majority of 23 votes.[25]

When the democratic aspects of democratic centralism are considered, it is clear that one of the major elements, the responsibility of executive groups to the body that has elected them, was recognized from the very beginning of the Party's history as an organized group. The first Congress of the Party in 1898 decided that the Central Committee, the major central and executive organ, should be guided in its decisions by the general directives laid down at the Party Congresses.[26]

Lenin's contributions to the democratic aspects of the doctrine were apparently motivated by quite specific circumstances, basically the fact that he was out of power in the Party. When Lenin was in power in the Party, he beat the drums for discipline and authority. When out of power, he beat the drums equally effectively for the right of free discussion and other democratic conceptions. In the beginning, Lenin's opponents within the Party were the strongest advocates of democratic procedures. On later occasions, when the Bolsheviks were a vociferous minority within the Party, the positions were reversed.

Although Lenin and his followers had won a majority and carried most of their proposals at the Second Congress of the Russian Social Democratic Labor Party in 1903 (whence the name Bolshevik from the Russian word *bol'she* meaning "larger"), soon afterwards they found themselves the weaker fraction. In February 1905, Lenin complained that the Mensheviks had "more money, more literature, more ways to distribute it, more agents, more big names, more contributors." [27]

The following year a brief reconciliation between the Bolshevik and Menshevik wings of the Party took place, formalized at the Stockholm Congress of 1906. At this Congress the Mensheviks predominated and were able to carry their views on certain important topics, particularly the peasant question. Under these conditions Lenin turned again to the democratic aspects of Russian Marxist theory, elaborating and defining them, in the hopes of winning converts to Bolshevik views.[28]

In connection with the discussion of the attitude that the Bolshevik losers should take, Lenin gave a fairly full account of their interpretation of the allegedly accepted principle of democratic centralism. While the principle may have won general acceptance on a high level of abstraction, there were sharp conflicts between the Bolsheviks and the Mensheviks concerning what it meant at the level of day-to-day behavior in Party controversies. It is one of the many ironies of Bolshevik history that the present-day interpretation of democratic centralism is much closer to the Menshevik version of 1906 than it is to Lenin's. This superficial paradox is readily explained by the fact that at that particular time the Mensheviks were in power and therefore advocated a restricted interpretation of democratic centralism.

Lenin summed up the essence of democratic centralism in the familiar phrase "freedom in discussion—unity in action." [29] At this general level there was widespread agreement. In the application differences at once became apparent. The Mensheviks wanted to avoid criticism of the decisions of the recent Congress in public gatherings, although they agreed that such criticism should be freely permitted in closed Party circles. Lenin on the contrary insisted on the free discussion of the decisions, both before the general public and before closed Party groups.[30] He was especially vehement in his assertions that those decisions with which he disagreed should be subjected to widespread analysis in the Party press and all sorts of local Party gatherings. He demanded that each and every workers' organization should, with full knowledge of the facts, declare its approval or disapproval of the Congress decisions. In particular they should have the opportunity to express their opinion of the Party's decisions on the peasant question "without fear of destroying the proletariat's unity in action." The argument he advanced was that the resolution on the peasant question concerned action to be taken some time in the unspecified future, and that therefore present-day debate would not interfere with unity of action.[31]

One may easily perceive that this interpretation of freedom of discussion is much broader than that which later became accepted Party doctrine. After the November Revolution it became a very severe violation of Party discipline to attack a policy upon which the Party had, through the decision of a Congress, adopted an official viewpoint. This more restricted definition of Party discipline and the operation of democratic centralism was promulgated in the first set of Party bylaws adopted after the November Revolution (1919).[32]

Concerning the other half of the slogan of democratic centralism, "unity of action," Lenin still advocated in 1906 a restricted definition. As an example he gave the problem of whether or not to participate in the coming elections of the Second Duma. Lenin favored participation in the Second Duma, although he had been in favor of boycotting the First Duma.[33] Thus he argued: "The Congress has decided—we will all vote where elections are held. At the time of the election, no criticism of participation in the elections. The *action* of the proletariat must be unified. The Social Democratic fraction in the Duma, when this fraction will exist, we will all of us always recognize as *our* Party fraction." [34] By way of further explanation he added: "The principle of democratic centralism and of autonomy of the local [Party] units means namely full and universal *freedom of criticism*, so long as *unity in a specific action* is not destroyed thereby —and the inadmissibility of any criticism *whatever* which undermines or makes difficult *unity* of any action decided upon by the Party." [35]

Under roughly parallel circumstances, Lenin added in 1907 the conception of a referendum as an essential part of the process of democratic centralism. The immediate situation was again a question of electoral tactics, upon which Lenin apparently believed he had the support of the powerful St. Petersburg Party organization against the Party leadership. On this occasion Lenin declared that the democratic organization of the Party required that on all important questions the point of view of each and every individual Party member should be ascertained.[36] To this doctrine of referendum may be traced the post-revolutionary practice of holding formal Party discussions, in which certain controversial questions were thrown open to general discussion from conflicting points of view.

In general, the concept of democratic centralism was an original contribution, at least at the theoretical level, to the problem of reconciling the need for a system of status, authority, and discipline with the requirements of a democratic system of values.

Before turning to the problem of the way in which the theory of democratic centralism coincides with practice, it is necessary to put the doctrine in its proper perspective with a few remarks on the Bolshevik theory concerning the role of force and violence in social organization.

Terror and violence in Leninist theory

Bolshevik doctrine on the use of terror and violence was formulated at an early stage. Of violence in general, it is sufficient to point out that the essence of Lenin's contribution to Marxism lies in his effort to restore violent revolution to its place as a major element in Marxist calculations. This was the central theme in Bolshevik attacks on the revisionist theories of Marxism that had grown up under the more peaceful conditions of German socialist development, even though Lenin never realized the degree to which the rank and file of the German Socialists supported such doctrines. Concerning individual acts of terror, the Bolsheviks sought to differentiate themselves from their non-Marxist predecessors. "We have never rejected terror on principle, nor can we do so," Lenin asserted in 1901.[37] From this point of view, terror was a device that the Bolsheviks should not hesitate to use, when the situation called for it. But individual acts of heroism and terror, unless they were carried out "in close connection and complete harmony with the whole system of fighting," might merely lead to the distraction of both Party leaders and rank-and-file members from more significant political goals.

In this doctrine there is a reflection of Marxist determinism. If political events are determined largely by the broad sweep of economic developments and the relationships between the productive classes of society, the assassination of single individuals is unlikely to have profound effects. There is still a further element in the negative Bolshevik attitude toward acts of individual terror. From the Bolshevik viewpoint, force was not enough by itself to enable any group to hold power, once power had been achieved by revolutionary means. Lenin put the matter succinctly shortly before he was to assume power: "The guillotine only intimidated, it only crushed *active* resistance. *For us that is not enough."* [38] In other words, the Bolsheviks regarded consensus as necessary for effective political action, while force was to be a mere auxiliary. It should be used without squeamishness in crisis situations against the enemies of the revolution, as the concept of the dictatorship of the proletariat suggests. Yet it was considered a temporary expedient that would eventually disappear altogether with the withering away of the state.

Contrast between theory and practice

An analysis may now be made of how far the theory of Party organization, as exemplified in Lenin's conception of a conspiratorial elite, the doctrine of democratic centralism, and the use of violence, corresponded to the actual behavior of the Party in prerevolutionary times. There is considerable evidence for the conclusion that, contrary to Bolshevik hopes, the organization of the Party was much looser in the period of the conspiratorial underground than it became following the seizure of power. To be sure, Party policy was determined almost entirely by the intellectuals at the apex of the Party organization. At the various Party Congresses the intellectuals heavily outnumbered the workers.[39] The executive organs of the Party, its nerve center, were composed exclusively of intellectuals. Among them Lenin played the outstanding role. In several crucial instances he was able to bring about a shift in Party policy almost singlehandedly through the force of his personal prestige alone. One such instance was the ideological shift on the question of the proletarian dictatorship, announced by Lenin on his return in April 1917 to Russia, which has already been mentioned in Chapter 1.

Another controversy, which reveals the mechanics of decision-making at the apex of the Party and Lenin's role therein, concerned the date and technique of the actual seizure of power. This crisis occurred in October and November 1917. For some time Lenin had been arguing in favor of armed insurrection, winning adherents to his views in the top circles of the Party. In the course of the controversy Lenin showed little regard for the formal requirements of Party discipline. On several occasions he went over the heads of the Central Committee, sending copies of his letters and messages to the more important local Party organizations, and seeing to it that extra copies of his appeals got into the hands of the more active local Party workers.[40] At one time he resigned from the Central Committee in order to agitate among the rank and file of the Party in favor of his views, though the resignation was apparently ignored or passed over. A few days later Kamenev resigned from the Central Committee on the ground that Lenin's policy was highly dangerous.[41] Kamenev's resignation was apparently not accepted either, since he was present at the meeting which adopted the resolution in favor of insurrection, though he voted against it.[42]

Shortly afterward it was Kamenev's turn to appeal to the rank and file, and eventually to the general public, in the course of which he again resigned from the Central Committee, accompanied by Zinoviev, Lenin's close collaborator during their exile in Switzerland.[43] Evidently Lenin's 1902 comment that disputes were not settled according to Party statutes but by threats of resignation still held good, though the Party had supposedly left this stage behind more than a decade before.

On October 31, Kamenev and Zinoviev published in a non-Party newspaper, controlled by Maxim Gorky, an attack on the Party's plans for insurrection, without, however, revealing the date. Their action placed Lenin in a predicament that is not without its humorous aspects. In a letter to the Central Committee discussing this dilemma he declared:

> Kamenev's and Zinoviev's outbreak in the non-Party press was despicable for the added reason that the Party was not in a position to refute their *slanderous lie* openly. . . .
> How can the Central Committee refute that?
> We cannot tell the capitalists the truth, namely that we have *decided* on a strike and have decided *to conceal the moment chosen for it.*
> We cannot refute the slanderous lie of Zinoviev and Kamenev *without doing still greater damage to the cause.*[44]

The significance of this revealing incident lies not only in the violations of formal Party discipline of which both sides were guilty. It lies also in the appeals and threats of appeal to the rank and file of the Party. Later schisms after the seizure of power were to be concealed from the rank and file, though their exclusion from the decision-making process and the concentration of even greater powers at the apex of the Party system was a gradual process that was not completed until after Stalin's accession to power. Another significant feature of these early quarrels was the relative absence of vindictiveness. Both Kamenev and Zinoviev soon obtained posts of marked responsibility under the Soviet regime. Later struggles were to end with the imprisonment and death of defeated factional leaders, including these two individuals.[45] The quarrels just described reveal the importance attached to the opinions of the rank and file. In practice, the chief role of the latter appears to have been that of choosing between alternative policies and points of view presented by the Party leaders.

According to Party bylaws, the mechanism through which the rank and file was to exert its influence was the Party Congress. In addition to the Congress there was the Party Conference, a similar gathering of delegates, held at more frequent intervals than the Congresses before the Revolution. Although the Congress was theoretically more important than the Conference, in practice there was no apparent distinction between the two. In this connection it is worth noting that the Party bylaws of 1903, 1905, 1906, 1907, and 1917 all included a provision that regular Congresses be held annually.[46] (The bylaws made no mention of the Conferences.) Since only six Congresses and thirteen Conferences (some of which had very limited representation) took place between the official founding of the Party in 1898 and the November Revolution, it is clear that the opportunities provided by such meetings for the expression of rank-and-file opinion were somewhat restricted even in prerevolutionary times.

Nevertheless, the Congresses and Conferences were characterized by open debates at which the conflicting views were often heatedly set forth by various Party leaders. For those who could attend the sessions and bring back reports to their local Party units, there was no lack of opportunity to hear the arguments presented on both sides. Because of the police the gatherings were held outside Russia until 1917. As much as possible, efforts were made to insure adequate representation and attendance at these meetings, although this was not always easy to achieve. In connection with one such gathering, held in Germany in the beginning of 1912, Lenin finally became convinced that the Moscow delegate must have been arrested. Without a delegate from Moscow Lenin was unwilling to begin the sessions. Therefore, he requested one of his associates to send someone to Moscow to arrange for the election of a new delegate.[47] Whether he would have gone to such lengths to secure a replacement from a less important section of the Party than Moscow is rather doubtful. As a rule, to avoid such situations, alternates were chosen for the more important Party positions, a procedure that still survives in the choice of alternates for the Party Central Committee.

The discussion of issues that were to be raised at the Congress was not confined to the Congress itself. Theses and summaries of divergent points of view were circulated among the membership for comment and discussion well in advance of the meeting. According to Piatnitsky's *Memoirs,* the agenda of the Party Congress of 1907 were circulated among all the local organizations of the Party. In addition, the Central Committee decided to send Bolshevik and Menshevik speakers to each meeting for comment on the main resolutions of each faction.[48] While the Congresses and Conferences represented somewhat more formal occasions for the discussion of policy, the ideological battles and wars of pamphlets and brochures continued unabated between these occasions. The rank and file of the Party had access to these materials, although their understanding of them was perhaps limited to what could be presented in simple and slogan-like form.

A high degree of factionalism formed a prominent feature of the Party's attempts to reach policy decisions both before and after 1917. Because of this a large proportion of the group's hostility toward the Tsarist system was turned inward against internal opponents. Lenin, in his firm belief that the Party must be purged of unreliable elements before it could be an effective political instrument, deliberately increased the degree of internal factional tension. The following incident is a characteristic one. At an important Party gathering Piatnitsky complained about the uncomradely personal attacks that were appearing anonymously in the Party press, and read several excerpts aloud. A somewhat obtuse chairman, who did not realize that Piatnitsky was reading from the Party press, reproved him for using such insulting language. At this point, Lenin announced that he was the author of the articles, whereupon all burst out laughing.[49]

Internal quarrels were encouraged with considerable success by the Tsarist police in order to weaken the Russian Marxists. The greatest fear of the police seems to have been that Mensheviks and Bolsheviks might succeed in settling their differences and form a unified opposition. Perhaps the most dramatic case of this type is to be found in the career of Roman Malinovsky, one of four police agents who succeeded at various times in gaining Lenin's close confidence. Malinovsky attended the Prague Conference of the Bolshevik wing of the Party in January 1912 as a police spy, and so captivated Lenin that he became a member of the Bolshevik Central Committee and Lenin's choice for the Duma. His election was facilitated by the arrest of a competing candidate. Since both the police and Lenin were anxious to split the Russian Social Democratic Labor Party, Malinovsky had little difficulty in following the instructions of both. In a short time his efforts were successful. The Party's unified fraction in the Duma was split. Malinovsky resigned from the Duma in May 1914, after creating an artificial uproar, in order to prevent the scandal of potential exposure. At this time the chairman of the Duma was informed by the police about Malinovsky's double role, and his usefulness as a spy came to an end. Meanwhile, suspicions that he might be a spy had arisen within the Party itself, particularly in Menshevik circles. Since Lenin continued to defend him, these suspicions served to deepen the Party split.[50]

In general, the Party's relationships with the police had the curious effect of both increasing and diminishing internal solidarity. The formal, and presumably most approved, type of relationship with the police was one of hostility toward an out group. Piatnitsky's account again provides useful testimony:

> Since those who were arrested used to be beaten at the police stations, there was danger that while under examination they might involuntarily and unconsciously disclose their comrades. Therefore, the active and class-conscious comrades carried on energetic propaganda on how to conduct oneself when arrested and questioned. (Later on a special booklet on that subject was even published; I think by the *Bund*.) Those who did not conduct themselves properly when questioned were expelled from the workers' midst, and were shunned like the plague. Those who deliberately gave away their comrades were dealt with unmercifully and summarily.[51]

From this account it is clear that the individual Party member under the stress of police interrogation would have strong motivation for remaining loyal to his organization. Nevertheless, the police were able to persuade a number of members to act as informers and *agents provocateurs*. There is good evidence for the conclusion that the top Party leaders, as distinct from the rank and file, did not always discourage a man from turning informer, since by his connections with the police he might be able to serve the Party in a useful fashion. In at least one such instance it appears that a "double agent" of this variety obtained material from the police on the identity of other *agents provocateurs* in the Party.[52]

Under the prevailing conditions of police surveillance it was extremely difficult, if not impossible, for the selection of leadership within the Party to take place along democratic lines. It is safe to conclude that in this respect democratic centralism was honored chiefly in the breach. Within Russia the Bolshevik organizations, as a rule, selected their leaders by coöptation, according to Piatnitsky, who had wide experience with these matters. In the various factories Bolsheviks who worked there coopted to membership other workers whom they considered to be devoted to the cause. The regional committees of the large towns divided among their members the tasks of uniting all Party cells of a given district or subdistrict. Organizers of the sub-districts coöpted persons of their choice from among the Party cells to serve on the subdistrict committee. If one member of the committee was arrested or moved away, he was replaced by co-option. This was the procedure up to the level of city commit-tees. When a city committee was arrested as a body, the Party Central Committee designated one or more Party members to form a new committee. Those appointed in turn coöpted suitable members from among the local workers to complete the new com-mittee.[53]

Outside Russia, among the organizations of exiles, which at many points in the Party's history constituted the heart and brain of the organization, coöption was applied with very great fre-quency. Many of the early Party quarrels revolved around in-trigues formed over the choice of editors for the Party publica-tions and similar positions of importance. At the Congresses and Conferences of the Party it appears that the elections to the Central Committee were secret, in order to safeguard the persons chosen, although everybody at the meeting knew the identity of the candidates.[54]

Prolonged acquaintance with the literature of early Bolshevism is likely to give rise to the impression that a disproportionate amount of this group's energy was turned inward on matters of internal organization, factional struggles, and the like. Never-theless, Bolshevik activities directed toward the outside world, which assumed rapidly increasing importance following Lenin's return to Russia in April 1917, deserve brief mention.

Systematic Bolshevik propaganda after 1900 included as its major targets industrial workers, students, and peasants, among whom a good deal was done by word of mouth (the peasants were largely illiterate), and members of the Russian armed forces. Some notion of the extent of the distribution of Russian Marxist propaganda in prerevolutionary times may be gleaned from the following partial figures given by *Iskra* (The Spark),[55] at one time Lenin's chief mouthpiece:

Name of committee	Date	No. of types of proclamations	No. of copies
Don Committee	1902	46	60,000
Siberian Union	March– April 1903	13	40,000
Odessa Committee	April– May 1903	12	50,000
	July 1– October 1	39	108,000
Gornozavodsky Union	March– September 1903	39	104,500

Although these figures must be taken with several spoonfuls of salt, they strongly suggest the existence of an organization that has developed beyond the stage of intellectual discussions to a genuine attempt to influence mass opinion.

Bolshevik propaganda found its greatest effect in military circles, probably since disaffection was already widespread, both in 1905 and again in the World War after the March revolution of 1917. In 1905 the Bolsheviks played a leading, though not exlusive, role in the dramatic mutiny of the cruiser *Potemkin*. For thirteen days this vessel cruised the Black Sea under the control of her rebellious sailors, led by members of the Odessa committee of the Party.[56] Further mutinies took place the next summer at Kronstadt, under the local leadership of the Finnish Party members.[57] In 1917, after the failure of the Kornilov attempt at counterrevolution, the disintegration of the Russian army proceeded rapidly. (It is significant that disaffection was much greater among troops in barracks than among those exposed to the danger and discomfort of the front.) While the Bolsheviks after the seizure of power tried to shift the blame for this disintegration onto other factors, a very careful and competent student concludes that Bolshevik influence among the masses of soldiers was a major source of this collapse.[58]

Terror and violence were used by the Bolsheviks in prerevolutionary times chiefly as a means for financing their activities, and only secondarily as a political weapon. A favorite project was the looting of the cash funds of banks in transit. One of Stalin's early claims to fame in Bolshevik circles derives from his alleged role as a behind-the-scenes organizer of such a robbery in Tiflis.[59] These terrorist activities were under the direction of a Bolshevik Center, composed of Lenin, Krassin, an engineer with wide connections in bourgeois circles, and Bogdanov, a writer, philosopher, and economist. This Bolshevik Center was accused of exercising a secret dictatorship within the Party behind the backs of the Central Committee.[60] The secret "technical office" of the Central Committee in St. Petersburg was able to turn out 150 bombs a day. Arms were also obtained from soldiers, especially those recently returned from the Far East.[61] On several occasions the Bolsheviks carried out their exploits in coöperation with other revolutionary groups, the Anarchists and Socialist Revolutionaries.

The fact that the Bolsheviks were known to be willing to use terror added considerable force to their disruptive activities in other connections, such as street demonstrations, strikes, and the like. Rumors of what the workers were about to do heightened the anxiety of the general Russian population and at times gave even the Party members themselves an exaggerated idea of their power.[62] Such rumors are frequently found in a situation tense with imminent group conflict; they are closely parallel to the rumors that circulate among the whites in the Southern states of the United States at a time of increased tension with the Negroes.

As might be anticipated, Bolshevik "expropriations" attracted numerous elements from the criminal fringe, who had no political objectives whatever. For a time there was evidently a tendency for local Bolshevik units to degenerate into nothing more than robber bands without political goals. These difficulties were aggravated by related ones at the higher echelons: accusations of embezzlement, extortion, and blackmail were bandied about in a series of internal scandals.[63]

By the spring of 1907 the fear that these expropriations were deranging the entire organization was widespread throughout the Party.[64] The Fifth Congress (April 1907), at which the Bolsheviks were in a majority, announced that "these anarchist methods of fighting bring about disorganization in the ranks of the proletariat, obscuring its class consciousness, and giving rise therein to the illusion of the possibility of replacing its organized struggle by means of the efforts of self-sacrificing, single individuals." [65] Although the dramatic Tiflis robbery took place the following June, expropriations and similar measures declined in significance. In the 1917 Revolution there is no indication of acts of individual terrorism or of robberies organized by the Bolsheviks. Then the problem of the correct use of force and violence for political ends involved the persuasion of whole regiments to abandon their allegiance to the Provisional Government.

In attempting to appraise the extent to which the Leninist theories of secrecy, discipline, and conspiracy corresponded to the general pattern of prerevolutionary behavior, one is likely to conclude that the Bolsheviks were a strange form of conspiratorial elite, if indeed that term may be accurately applied to them at all. If the Tsarist police were at crucial times in the dark concerning Bolshevik intentions, as has been stated by one of the highest police officers,[66] that situation must have been the result of truly extraordinary incapacity on the part of the authorities. With all their emphasis on secrecy, the Bolsheviks made no secret of either their general tactics or their aims. Instead, they discussed them in innumerable pamphlets, books, and newspaper articles, both in Russia and abroad. Their discipline was violated frequently, and on highly critical occasions, such as just before the seizure of power. Democratic centralism seems, on the basis of the available evidence, to have been more of a pious wish than a basis for political decision-making.

From the point of view of the present study the most significant feature of the ground covered so far is the contrast between the aims and the methods of Bolshevism. In this contrast there is a double paradox. Lenin and his followers set out to achieve for humanity the goals of freedom and equality by means of an organization that denied these same principles. It was anticipated that the denial would be temporary and that the fruits of victory would bring the goals desired. Instead, discipline, authority, and inequality had to be intensified after victory. To what extent the experiences of political responsibility have led to a revision of theory, and to what extent theory has been a guide to action in the difficult task of adjustment to new experiences—these are the questions we must attempt to answer in the succeeding chapters.

PART TWO

THE DILEMMA OF AUTHORITY FROM
LENIN TO STALIN

4

Victory Creates Dilemmas

The problems faced

By the successful coup d'état *of November 7, 1917, the Bolshe-*viks passed from opposition to political responsibility. For the next decade and a half they faced five closely interrelated problems of major significance. The answer chosen for any one of these problems very largely determined the answers given to all the rest. The details varied during the period under discussion, as did the answers presented by different factions within the Party. Nevertheless, one may readily discern the continuity of the major problems down to the time when Stalin was firmly established in power.

One of these problems was how to organize industry in the new toilers' state. In turn, this problem broke down into a series of questions that have to be faced by any economy. What should the factories of Russia produce—guns or butter, shoes or butter-fly nets? The answer was only partly given by the nature of existing plants and their capacity. Another question, and perhaps the most vexing one, was how to combine machinery, men, and raw materials in an effective manner in order to produce the goods. The managers and engineers who had performed this function under the old regime were by and large hostile to the new one. Furthermore, the Bolsheviks were by their doctrine committed to the elimination of private property in the means of production and the institutional mechanisms of capitalism that had in the past performed the functions of joining labor, plant, and raw materials. In the third place, there was the question of distributing the products of industry. Should this be done by means of money, by a universal system of rationing without the use of money, by the combination of the two, or by some other device? Finally, there was the question of replacing old machinery with new and of increasing the industrial capacity of a primarily peasant country. Except to bar most of the answers given by the past, the literature of Marxism provided few if any answers to this complex of pressing questions.

A second major problem, or series of questions, closely connected with the preceding ones, concerned the status and organization of the industrial workers in the toilers' state. Would labor unions continue to be necessary in the new society? What would their functions be? How was the necessary discipline of labor to be achieved?

Still a third crucial problem was how to get the peasant to produce enough to feed the workers of the towns. At the same time, a way had to be found to make this vast majority of the population support the regime or at least refrain from active and effective opposition. The peasant might refuse to feed the townsman if he did not receive at least a minimum of salt, kerosene, cloth, and other manufactured goods from the workers. And even if this absolute minimum were achieved, it would hardly suffice to support the industrialization of Russia, which both doctrine and political expediency seemed to require. As has been seen, the existing body of theory provided suggestive leads, but little more, for the answer to this set of questions.

Closely related to all three preceding problems was the question of what system of status, authority, and discipline should be set up within the ruling group, that is, the Communist Party (as it was called after March 1918),[1] and within the country as a whole. On this point, at least, Leninist doctrine provided some fairly definite answers. However, it was soon found that by no means all of them were workable.

There remains the fifth problem, which with some justification was widely regarded as the key to all the others: what should be the relationship between the new toilers' state and the rest of the world? If it perished in a brief struggle, as many of the top leaders thought likely, there would be no other questions to answer. Should this happen, the best the Bolsheviks could hope for would be the creation of a glorious tradition like the Paris Commune which would inspire future generations of workers to continue the struggle. If, on the other hand, the toilers' state survived, the problems were much more complex. How much energy should be devoted to spreading or producing a socialist conflagration in Europe? Or should the Communists retire into a socialist fortress? Might it not be necessary to find at least temporary allies in the capitalist camp? To what extent could the resources of the capitalist world be tapped in order to build up the world of socialism? Once again the body of Marxist-Leninist theory provided a tool of analysis and some tentative answers, whose adequacy might now be tested.

The five basic problems just sketched were real problems. That is to say, they were not created by the specific set of values and desires current among the holders of power. Any group that took over political responsibility in Russia would have had to find a way to organize industry, create labor discipline, arrange for the production of food, develop some system of internal authority, and conduct relations with other states. A reactionary supporter of Tsarism, a Manchester Liberal, and a convinced Marxist would of course develop quite different answers to these problems. The Bolshevik tradition ruled out some answers that would have been given by the reactionaries or the liberals, while it favored others. Within the Bolshevik tradition itself a number of varying interpretations of the problems and answers to these questions arose at different times.

Until the time of Stalin's consolidation of power, each "solution" put into effect by the dominant group in the Communist Party "solved" one set of problems, only to have them reappear in the form of a new type of unstable equilibrium in Russian society. At each stage the instability of the situation was reflected in a variety of new proposed solutions, presented by distinct factions within the Party.

Early controversies and solutions

The problem of the relations between the new revolutionary state and its capitalist neighbors, still in the midst of the First World War, was the first one to arise in acute form. Specifically, the question in December 1917 concerned peace with Germany. Since the answer to this question would determine the type of policy that could be followed in Russia itself, Party factions elaborated answers to the entire series of questions that has just been outlined.

Lenin, almost alone among the Party leaders, favored signing peace with the Germans on the latter's terms. A group, calling themselves the Left Wing Communists, led by the Party's outstanding theorist, Nikolai Bukharin, proposed instead the slogan of revolutionary war: that is, they demanded a propaganda and revolutionary offensive that would destroy the German Empire from within and bring the flames of revolution to Western Europe. Bukharin's proposal was derived from earlier doctrines that had been advocated by Lenin before the Revolution. The advantages of such a plan, if there had been any chance of success, were obvious to the hard-pressed Bolshevik leaders; the difficulties were not so immediately apparent. Thus it was possible for a time to promote this conception on both practical and idealistic grounds, at least until it became clear that no revolution was around the corner in Germany. It was on the latter practical basis that Lenin was able to carry through his policy and compel the signing of the Brest-Litovsk Treaty.

In domestic affairs the Left Wing Communists pushed for as rapid an approach to socialist goals as possible. They demanded a much more rapid and sweeping confiscation of private enterprises than was being carried out, in order to crush the resistance of the bourgeoisie and achieve a clean break with the forms of the past. In addition, they opposed the tightening of discipline over the workers and accused the Bolshevik leaders of supporting the petty bourgeoisie against the workers.

Although not averse to centralized economic control, at least in theory, they advocated a form of nationalization which should embody a considerable measure of "direct democracy" and "committee management," that is, control by the workers of the factories in which they were employed. Their alleged object was to free the "creative impulses" of the masses.[2]

At first the Left Communists were unsuccessful. But on June

28, 1918, they won at least a partial victory in the decree on general nationalization. This measure was rapidly applied to whole industries by a stroke of the pen, and included even quite small enterprises below the size mentioned in the decree. A centralized bureaucracy, which attempted to eliminate market dealings as much as possible by organizing a giant system of state barter, was quickly established. Under this arrangement the state financed the enterprises directly, and frequently in kind, while the enterprises delivered their products directly to the state for distribution to other enterprises, the countryside, and the army.

A mixture of ideological and practical considerations apparently produced this shift. Among the more important factors, and perhaps the immediate cause of the nationalization decree, was the possibility that the Germans might continue their advance into the industrial regions of Russia and gain control over important industrial concerns. There were indications in Berlin that the Germans planned to claim that major Russian enterprises were now owned by German citizens, and hence exempt from any nationalization decree. Lenin acted quickly to forestall such claims.[3] Thus, what appeared to be utopian idealism under one set of circumstances became defined as hardheaded practicability and accepted by those in political power under another set of circumstances.

War Communism: main road or detour?

The decree on nationalization of June 28, 1918, was the prelude to the system of War Communism. For the next two years the Bolshevik regime was fighting a war for survival against both domestic and foreign enemies. While there were numerous disagreements on matters of tactics and strategy, under the pressure of the struggle the Party remained overtly united.

The political and economic institutions of War Communism represented a mixture of apparently utopian and practical policies. In industry the system of state-organized barter without the use of money tended to take the place of free market exchanges. Factory discipline was put on a semimilitary basis. Within the

Party also discipline was strengthened. Appointments to office replaced election to a wider extent than ever before and became the rule in many sectors of political life outside the Party, such as the trade unions. The peasants were subjected to numerous and purely arbitrary requisitions.[4]

To what extent was this set of answers to the problems faced by the new workers' state influenced by Marxist doctrine? Were these practices regarded as the realization of long awaited goals, or as the product of unfortunate necessity? At a later date Lenin described the period of War Communism as a "temporary measure," and one thrust upon the Bolsheviks by war and ruin. This statement and other similar ones by Bolshevik leaders have given rise to the interpretation of War Communism as an improvisation which the top Party leaders recognized as temporary. Only a few academic individuals, according to this view, regarded the system of War Communism as a major step toward Marxist goals.[5]

On the whole, however, the evidence strongly suggests that the institutions of War Communism were the result of both ideological and nonideological pressures which for a time operated in the same direction. The force of circumstances may be observed from the fact that many of the features of War Communism are familiar devices in capitalist states at war. The partial replacement of monetary incentives to production by others of a different kind, the introduction of rationing as a restriction on the operation of a free market in the exchange of goods, and a high degree of centralized control over the apparatus of production have been economic features of capitalist states in both World Wars. In themselves they can hardly be regarded as distinctive products of Marxist ideas. In fact, the Russian Marxists based some of their earlier programmatic suggestions on the institutions of wartime Germany. All this may be granted, yet there is abundant evidence in the public statements of the most responsible Bolshevik leaders that at the time War Communism was in full swing they regarded it as a major step in the direction of Marxist goals.

In 1919 Lenin himself declared, "The organisation of the Com-

munist activities of the proletariat, as well as the whole policy of the Communists, has now assumed a final and stable
form, and I am convinced that we are on the right road, and that
progress along this road is fully ensured." [6]

The speeches, including Lenin's, made at the Eighth Party
Congress, held at the height of the period of War Communism
in March 1919, gave no hint that the measures adopted were
temporary expedients, to be abandoned as soon as the emergency passed. While recognizing the tremendous difficulties
of the day, they were full of revolutionary enthusiasm and
optimism. Bukharin declared that the Party program, which was
to be adopted at this gathering, was closer to reality and less of
a paper program than any previous one. Many of its demands,
he believed, might be outdated any day by their transformation into actual achievements. [7] He even anticipated the end of
the first stage, the dictatorship of the proletariat and Russia's
development into a classless society in the not too distant future.
"From the exclusive domination of the working class, the domination of the proletariat, we proceed by degrees, by way of a
whole series of steps, measures, and stages, to the destruction of
classes in general, to the transformation of the proletarian dictatorship and the governing power of the working class into the
stateless and classless communist society." [8]

The system of War Communism was a successful attempt in
the trial-and-error process of group adaptation in that it was one
of the factors that enabled the Bolsheviks to remain in power.
That is to say, they won the Civil War. But the system of War
Communism in solving, at least partially, the problem of how to
win the war also created new problems. The double fruits of
the Civil War and the methods of War Communism were political unrest and a catastrophic decline in production and consumption. The production of large-scale industry dropped in 1920 to
12.8 per cent of the prewar level. During the summer of 1921
the net output of coal in the Donets Basin fell to the zero point. [9]
It is conservatively estimated that during this same period the
output of agriculture diminished by at least 30 per cent in comparison with the prewar level, perhaps considerably more. [10] Even

more significant from the political point of view was the collapse of the top-heavy system of rationing and distribution, which reached a stage of operating almost without money.[11] As a result, not all of the reduced supplies of goods produced and available reached those who needed them.

While political opposition to the Bolsheviks showed itself most clearly in the form of peasant revolts, there were also numerous signs of discontent among the industrial workers. A revolt in a section of the Red Navy at Kronstadt, symbolic starting point of the Bolshevik Revolution, was perhaps the final straw that brought about an abrupt change of policy and the adoption of the New Economic Policy (NEP) in the spring of 1921.

There is considerable evidence showing that the top leaders of the Party were aware that the system of War Communism was leading them into an impasse. Even though they may have believed that they were on the high road to socialism, Marxist ideology did not completely blind them to the danger signs along the way. In fact, there were so many signs that some of them later declared that the highway must have been a detour. Various alternative routes were proposed as the signs increased, first in secret sessions among the leaders, and later in the daily press.

Trotsky claims that in February 1920 he advanced a program similar to the NEP on the basis of his experience in directing economic work in the Urals, but was voted down in the Party Central Committee.[12] Similarly, Simon Liberman, a non-Party specialist in charge of the timber organization, asserts that he brought the situation to Lenin's attention in 1920. Lenin is said to have replied that he was well aware of the need for changes, but that he could not "change the banner in the midst of . . . battle" for fear of destroying the enthusiasm of the soldiers in the Civil War.[13] Even the Left Opposition of 1918 had foreseen the possibility that a change might be necessary, and had specifically mentioned the partial restoration of capitalism as a move that might be forced upon the Party in order to conserve revolutionary strength in Russia alone.[14] Similar ideas probably circulated among the Party leaders in 1920 and 1921.

Open polemics began with a discussion of the position and

function of the trade unions in the new toilers' state, but spread rapidly to more general questions. Much of the discussions concerned the prevailing system of status and authority. Trotsky proposed the extension of military discipline to the labor front, with the selection of leaders from above as the chief way out of the dilemma. Other sections of the Party, which became known as the Workers' Opposition and the Group for Democratic Centralism, took a diametrically opposite point of view, claiming that the major source of difficulty lay in the growing power of the top Party leadership, which was supposedly leading toward a bureaucratic stiffening and paralysis of the new regime.[15]

Retreat to the NEP

The Party controversies that closed the period of War Communism scarcely touched upon the problem that to Lenin, at this particular moment, held the key to all the others. In 1917–1918 he had seen the crux of the matter in foreign affairs and peace with Germany. Now he found it in the relationship between the peasants and the town workers. Impatiently brushing aside the Party discussions about the trade unions and the system of authority in the Party and country at large, he forced through the famous New Economic Policy, officially promulgated in March 1921. As in the case of Brest-Litovsk he found it necessary to use all his power of persuasion and personal prestige in order to compel the adoption of policies that seemed to many a betrayal of ideals.

The central measure of the NEP was the granting to the peasantry of the right to trade in the open market in whatever produce they had left, after a certain specified amount had been turned over to the government. This decision meant the return of the profit motive and exchange relationships to an important sector of the economy. In the field of industry the government retreated to the "commanding heights" of control over banking, transportation, and certain large industries, permitting private enterprise to take over the rest. In one of his speeches Lenin candidly described the NEP as a partial return to capitalism. He declared that Communists would now have to become good traders and learn to beat the capitalist at his own game. No wonder a member of the Workers' Opposition referred to the NEP as the "New Exploitation of the Proletariat"!

The problem as Lenin saw it was basically one of obtaining a proper exchange of goods between the partly socialized industrial sector and the individually owned agricultural sector. Under War Communism the government had taken nearly everything it could get from the peasant and had returned to the peasant what industrial products could be spared from other needs, largely without the intervention of money. At the end of the Civil War the system broke down, since there were no adequate incentives for production and no adequate measurements of costs. It was hoped, and the hopes were eventually justified, that through new exchange relationships incentives would be provided which would bring greater production in both industry and agriculture.[16]

At the same time the Bolshevik leadership did not give up all hope of ultimately bringing the peasant to participate in a socialist society, even though the goal was postponed to a very indefinite future. The scattered attempts to set up socialist peasant communities, begun on certain large estates during the enthusiastic days of War Communism, were summarily abandoned. Instead, socialist hopes were placed in the coöperative movement. In one of his last writings Lenin declared: "If the whole of the peasantry were organized in cooperatives, we would be standing firmly with both feet on the soil of Socialism."[17] But at least one or two decades would be needed, he felt, before the way of life of the tradition-bound Russian peasant could be changed and this goal achieved.[18]

In the meantime events in the international arena had led to a pessimistic reappraisal of revolutionary possibilities, at least for the time being, especially after the defeat of the Red Army before Warsaw in the summer of 1920. Instead of carrying the revolutionary torch, the Russian leaders found themselves increasingly engaged in ordinary diplomatic negotiations and employing the traditional tactics of balance-of-power politics. Nevertheless, the revolutionary torch was not altogether extinguished. When it seemed, during the twenties, that revolutionary forces might be harnessed to strengthen the international position of the USSR, attempts were made again to light the flames.

The NEP represented a solution to the problems facing Russia in the second decade of the twentieth century, in that the major social and economic institutions could again function. By 1923 the decline in population was arrested. Between 1915 and 1923 the total population losses are estimated to have been about nine million, with the heaviest losses falling in 1919 and 1920, or during the period of War Communism.[19] By 1926–1927 gross industrial production had regained the level reached in 1913, though the production of iron ore was only 52 per cent of the earlier level.[20] Grain production had recovered more slowly and had not reached the prewar level, especially in regard to marketable surplus, by the end of the NEP period. Nevertheless, the recovery was very substantial, amounting, with a 10 per cent increase in population, to 4 centners per person in 1927–1928, in comparison with 4.9 centners per person in 1913.[21]

Despite this economic recovery, Russian society remained in a state of unstable equilibrium. The reasons for this situation were that the forces of recovery were largely anti-Bolshevik, or, at best, passively opposed to the new regime. A substantial portion of the industrial recovery resulted from the recovery of the retail trade and smaller consumption industries, which were not in government hands. Likewise, the peasantry was largely beyond Bolshevik control. The exact figures were a matter of hot dispute in the controversies of the time, but there is no doubt about the situation as a whole.

In this respect the dilemma facing the Communist Party at the end of the NEP was very largely one of ideology and political power. If a group of Manchester Liberals had been in control of Russia at this time, they would not have perceived any dilemma. They would have been content to let the social and economic forces of the day have their full play, with the probable consequences that Russia would have developed along more or less familiar capitalist lines. Presumably, they would have dismantled at an even earlier date the entire apparatus of government controls that were a product of the war years, instead of retreating to the commanding heights of industry as the Bolsheviks did in 1921. But Russia was not in the hands of Manchester Liberals, and the question of what steps ought to be taken produced open and bitter struggles within the Communist elite.

5

Alternative Solutions

The legacy of Lenin

In solving the problems posed by War Communism through the measures taken under the NEP, Lenin overcame one set of difficulties and created a host of new ones. Such in its essentials was the legacy he bequeathed to those who competed for his mantle.

In the course of the struggle over issues and personalities, which began with Lenin's illness and partial incapacitation in 1922 and became acute even before his death in January 1924, the Party remained overtly united upon two fundamental objectives. In the first place, there was complete unity on the goal of retaining power in Communist hands. Also, there was broad agreement on the desirability of achieving at some future date a socialist transformation of Russian society.

Given this unity on objectives, there was room for sharp disagreement about the way to achieve them. Industrialization might be accepted as a means to extend the social base of the regime as well as a method for strengthening the toilers' fatherland against aggression. But the question immediately arose regarding the problem of supplying sufficient food for the industrial workers. Secondly, where was the capital to come from? If both were provided by the peasants, might not peasant resistance smash any such program?

Further vexing questions presented themselves. How should the management of industry be organized? What should be the role of organized labor in the process of industrialization? The whole problem of relationships with the capitalist world had to be taken into account. Would it be politically safe to obtain the capital for industrialization from the capitalist states? Or would it be better to work for a socialist revolution in these states, after which they could come to the aid of backward Russia? Or would some totally different policy be necessary?

During the twenties the fundamental problems facing Russia, outlined at the beginning of the preceding chapter, presented themselves in roughly this fashion to the leaders of Russia. Three major solutions were offered. Reduced to its barest essentials, Trotsky's solution was to press forward on both the domestic and the international fronts toward a socialist revolution. Bukharin, on the other hand, was the advocate of caution and of a search for some kind of answer within the institutional framework left by Lenin and the NEP. Stalin, in a series of brilliant political maneuvers, made use first of Bukharin's general approach, and in the process was able to discredit and eliminate Trotsky as a political opponent. Then, since Bukharin's solution appeared to be leading into a blind alley, he took over many, but not all, of the essential features of Trotsky's program and eliminated Bukharin from power. Finally, in the course of adopting Trotsky's program, Stalin developed certain distinctive features of his own.

The Trotskyite solution

A year after Lenin's death Trotsky pointed out what many of the responsible Communist leaders must have realized already —that the Russians had been living upon the accumulated construction or real capital of previous times, and that the problem of creating new factories would soon be acute.[1] Furthermore, he pointed out, external pressures from the capitalist world prevented the Soviet Union from making its own choice concerning the tempo of industrialization.[2] Commenting on the backwardness of Soviet economy he observed, "A lion is stronger than a dog, but an old dog is stronger than a lion cub." Victory in history, he asserted, goes to those societies that give human society the highest economic level.[3]

Part of the answer to this problem Trotsky recognized as lying in widespread improvements in the internal organization of industry. He demanded a better managerial group that would pay more attention to details,[4] a demand that has been raised in nearly similar language down to the present day. In statements that foreshadowed Stalin's later slogan, "Cadres decide everything," Trotsky laid strong emphasis on the need for improved selection of managerial personnel by the Party.[5] Likewise he sensed, even if vaguely, some inadequacies in the system of incentives that were intended to spur the workers to produce for the toilers' state. It is a shame, he wrote in 1925, to hear Soviet managers and even engineers complain that the specialization of production crushes the spirit of the worker. The opinion that factory work was monotonous and boring he dismissed as reactionary and utopian. Instead, he declared, the task of turning industry into an automatic mechanism was in fact a grandiose and inspiring one.[6] Evidently Trotsky was feeling his way toward a program for the systematic overhauling of status relationships in industry in the interests of productivity. The task of carrying this out, however, was destined to fall into other hands.

Economic planning had long been part of the Marxist answer to the asserted disorganization of capitalism, and was also brought forth by Trotsky as a solution to the chaotic condition of Russian industry in the twenties. Two points are worth noting about Trotsky's conception of planning. One is that he did not envisage a single plan for the entire country. Rather, he appears to have had in mind the elimination of the confused situation whereby government-controlled industries were forced to sell at fixed prices, while the state made its purchases in an open and uncontrolled market.[7] In this respect he was much less bold than later Soviet planners. But in his attitude toward planning as a technique of deliberately controlled social change, he was in accord with later events. Socialist planners, he said, should not have the attitude toward their figures that an astronomer has toward the movement of the stars, which he can predict but cannot control. Socialist plans he professed to regard not as products of passive prediction, but as tools for action.[8]

It is typical of Trotsky's approach that he saw the answer to the peasant question in the field of industry. Industry, he argued, represented the key point in peasant-worker relations, and the area toward which energy should be directed. In 1925 he observed that the peasant put on the market less than one third of his total production. To improve the exchange of manufactured articles for food, industry would have to put on the market not only cheaper consumers' goods, but also better agricultural machines, "requiring collective forms of cultivation." [9] In this phrase by Trotsky there occurs one of the first hints of the eventual reorganization of agriculture on a collectivized basis.

A group of economists, associated with Trotsky, had begun the year before to ask the question of how the capital might be raised to increase the output of industry. They reasoned that there were only three possible sources for the accumulation of capital: loans from abroad; profits within the state-controlled industry itself (more accurately, the difference between the value of its production and what it paid out in wages and salaries); and finally, what could be obtained from "exploitation" of small-scale private undertakings—in effect, the peasants—by extracting from them a greater sum of values than was given to them in the form of industrial products. This doctrine found its clearest expression in the writings of E. Preobrazhensky, a former coauthor with Bukharin of the *ABC of Communism* and later one of the important figures in the Trotskyite opposition.[10] Such views became the basis of the accusation that Trotsky intended to exploit the peasantry. However, as shall be seen, Trotsky himself laid greater emphasis on other techniques for obtaining capital, which were, perhaps, even less practicable than those suggested by his associates.

If we distinguish Trotsky's own views on the peasantry from those of his associates during 1924 and 1925, there does not appear to be any large difference between his position and that which Lenin had reached in his 1923 paper, "On Cooperation," the guiding line of official policy in the early stages of the NEP. Like Lenin, Trotsky asserted that the socialist reconstruction of agriculture should be carried out through the coöperative movement. In turn, the coöperatives should be based upon a mechanized agriculture.[11]

At a later date Trotsky and other leaders of the Left Opposition criticized violently the official policy of going easy on the peasants, accusing Stalin and Bukharin of favoring the rich peasants at the expense of the poor and middle peasantry.[12] By 1927, when he had almost completely lost power, Trotsky arrived at the conclusion that the collectivization of agriculture was the only way out of the dilemma. In what purports to be a draft of a program for the Fifteenth Party Congress, Trotsky declared: "The growth of private proprietorship in the country must be offset by a more rapid development of collective farming. It is necessary systematically and from year to year to subsidize the efforts of the poor peasants to organize in collectives."[13] At the same time Trotsky repeated his arguments concerning the necessity for a technical revolution in agriculture, without which collectivization was impossible. But by this time Stalin had already stolen his fire. In his report to the Fifteenth Congress, Stalin too proclaimed that the only way out was the collectivization of agriculture on the basis of a higher level of technique.[14]

Trotsky's attitude toward the system of political authority in the Soviet Union changed sharply as his own position in that system deteriorated. Immediately after the Civil War, it will be recalled, he had been the advocate of authoritarian measures by the Party to "shake up" the trade unions and solve the problems posed by the system of War Communism. Two years later, when his influence had been sharply reduced, he became much more critical of the Party leadership. Then, in a series of articles published during December 1923 in *Pravda*, he spoke openly about the possibility of degeneration among the Bolshevik old guard and the loss of their revolutionary fire. In these articles he also defended the individual Party member's right to think matters out for himself and to battle for his own interpretations against those put forth by the Party leaders.[15] The next year he published a thinly disguised attack on the Party leaders, the so-called Triumvirate of Stalin, Kamenev, and Zinoviev, in the form of a historical study, the *Lessons of October*.[16] The immediate occasion of the attack was the defeat of the German revolution of 1923, about which more will be said later. The rather obvious implication of *Lessons of October* was that revolutionary uprisings would fail if they lacked revolutionary leadership. From then on Trotsky attacked with increasing savageness the "bureaucratic degeneration" of the Party and the concentration of authority in its upper echelons.

As his position continued to weaken in the internecine struggle with Stalin and Bukharin, it appeared more and more to Trotsky and his followers that the only hope for Russia's escape from this "bureaucratic degeneration" lay in successful revolutions abroad. By bringing the technical resources of the West into the socialist orbit, or even by weakening imperialist pressure through successful revolutions in the East, the need for a quasi-military atmosphere at home would diminish. The Soviets, he argued, could not build up their economy on the basis of their own resources alone.[17] Indeed, as he maintained in *Permanent Revolution,* it is impossible for a socialist revolution to succeed within the national boundaries of a single country.[18] Thus, the Left Opposition hammered away at the theme that the building of socialism in the Soviet Union could only succeed "in immediate connection with the revolution of the European proletariat, and in the struggle of the East against the imperialist yoke."[19] For Trotsky and his followers the choice became increasingly clear-cut: either international revolution or the abandonment of the socialist experiment in Russia. Following the failure of the first, and his own fall from power, he devoted most of his energy to proving the truth of the second.[20] The core of Stalin's approach was to refuse to accept the dilemma as posed in Trotsky's terms, or, for that matter, in those of Bukharin.

Bukharin's solution

Bukharin's position in the Party, even at the height of his power, was a somewhat curious one. Unlike Trotsky, Stalin, or Lenin, he never held a position of direct and first-rate administrative responsibility. His counsels in the Politburo were for a time highly influential, though they were not connected with specific organizational tasks. His positions, as editor of *Pravda* and as a high officer of the Communist International, involved the manipulation of symbols rather than of men. Even though

he was acknowledged in Lenin's testament as "the most valuable and biggest theoretician in the Party," [21] his theories over
time represent perhaps even less of a consistent whole than do
those of Lenin, Trotsky, and Stalin. Between 1918 and 1923 he
made a complete traverse from the extreme left to the extreme
right of the Communist political spectrum. However, after the
completion of this traverse, his opinions represented for many
years a fairly consistent view of the world.

In his writings from about 1925 onward, Bukharin attempted
to demonstrate that the NEP was not really a retreat, which
Lenin had freely admitted, but actually a new road on the way
to the original goal. In so doing he developed a series of interpretations and justifications that strongly resembled the gradualist views of Western Social Democracy, whose vehement critic
he had once been and in fact continued to be, at least in his
published statements, despite the rapprochement of views.

Under Bukharin's reinterpretation the Marxist doctrine of the
class struggle became softened into a peaceful contest among
opposing interest groups in the relatively tranquil arena of the
market place. Eventually under NEP conditions, he wrote, big
capital in industry would beat out little capital. Since big capital
was in the hands of the proletariat, his argument continued, socialism would be the ultimate victor.[22] In another passage of the
same reinterpretation he asserted: "The center of gravity shifts
more and more from the work of immediate and mechanical repression of the exploiters . . . to the economic reorganization
of society—to peaceful organizational work, economic competition with private firms, [and] the work of constructing socialist
economic forms (government, coöperatives, etc.)." [23]

His views and proposed solutions of the peasant question were
in line with this gradualist interpretation. In general, his opinion
was that the Communists ought to give the peasants what they
wanted, for the time being at least, in order to attract them to
the proletarian banner.[24] On one occasion, the cause of quite an
uproar in the Party, in a newspaper article he put forth for the
peasants the slogan, "Enrich yourselves." Six months later Bukharin was forced by the Politburo to retract this slogan.[25]

Bukharin's slip of the pen was in line with his negative atti-

tude toward the collective farms. Following Lenin, he argued
that the chief way to incorporate the peasant into a socialist
society was through the coöperative movement. "The peasant
will grow into the general socialist system through the coöperatives," he declared in the spring of 1925.[26] Collective farms were
"not the main road by which the peasant will come to socialism,"
but merely a subsidiary route.[27] In 1925 the basis of his argument
was that the Soviet government did not yet have at its disposal
sufficient material means to make the collective farms attractive
enough for the peasants to overcome their traditional hostility to
such new arrangements. At the same time the government could
point out concrete advantages for the individual peasant in the
coöperative movement.[28] In this way Bukharin returned to the
conception that the class struggle in the countryside was chiefly
an economic struggle. Against the shops of the village traders
the government should not use force, but instead rely on the
material advantages of the coöperatives. And against the village
usurers the government and the Party should bring up its bat-
tery of credit unions.[29]

In 1927 and 1928, when the problem of collectivization had
become really acute, the major discussions of the question were
carried on behind closed doors. It is therefore difficult to reconstruct Bukharin's opinions and those of the Right Opposition in
general. However, it is reasonably clear that Bukharin feared a
renewal of the Civil War if Stalin persisted in his newly adopted
policy of exploiting the peasantry. In the middle of 1928 he
finally went so far that he broke with Stalin over this issue (though
not in public) and made tentative maneuvers toward a political
bloc with former associates of Trotsky, as well as certain other
leaders, in the hopes of ousting Stalin from control.[30]

Bukharin's answer to the problem of industrialization was also
consistent with his generally conservative approach. Originally,
he believed that heavy industry in socialist hands could compete
successfully with the nonsocialist sector of industry and gradually drive the latter to the wall. Because of this viewpoint he was
a useful ally for Stalin against Trotsky.[31]

After Trotsky's defeat, Stalin began in 1927 and 1928 to adopt some of the policies advocated by his defeated opponent. Bukharin continued to oppose these policies and managed to get some of his views before the Soviet public, at least in a disguised form. In a *Pravda* article [32] that posed as a critical evaluation of the Left Opposition, but was actually directed against Stalin, he pointed out how agricultural shortages might endanger and even wreck the whole process of industrialization. For publishing this article he was later reprimanded by the Party Central Committee.[33] In another article some months later, ostensibly a critique of capitalism, but which could easily be taken as a criticism of the Five Year Plan, he pointed to the dangers of an expanded bureaucracy inherent in certain types of industrialization. Organizational techniques, which should be means to achieve economic ends, tend to become, as he pointed out, ends in themselves. The result, he contended, was paper pushing, material losses, and the general routinization of society.[34]

On still another occasion he used the not too subtle device of quoting extensively from one of his earlier speeches, a major programmatic announcement that was supposedly above suspicion, delivered some seven years before at the Fourth Congress of the Communist International, defending the Bolshevik adoption of the NEP. By this device he was able to repeat his opinion that the major problem of any country in which the proletariat held power was to distinguish between the forms of production that the proletariat could organize, and those which, in the beginning stages, it could not control. If the proletariat tried to take over too much, or injured the small producer and the small peasant, production declined. Furthermore, an enormous and economically unproductive bureaucratic apparatus was required to carry out the economic functions of the small producer and the small peasant if the latter groups were destroyed. Instead of increasing production by these measures, the exact opposite would take place.[35] It is fairly safe to assume that arguments along these lines were also advanced by Bukharin and his associates in the stormy and secret sessions of the Politburo.

In his opposition to the ambitious program of industrialization, Bukharin was joined by Rykov, a member of the Politburo from

1919 onward, and long prominent in the role of an economic administrator, and also by Tomsky, president from 1917 to 1929 of the All-Union Council of Trade Unions. Rykov's opposition appears to have been based largely on the ground that Stalin's industrialization program was simply not economically feasible.[36] The union leader Tomsky, however, joined on grounds that require further clarification.

During the NEP the unions gained a considerable degree of independence. They represented the interests of the workers in opposition to the claims of the government, as well as against other interest groups in Russian society of the early twenties. To Stalin it was clear that the program of industrialization would require heavy sacrifices from the workers, at least in the beginning stages. To ensure that the workers would make these sacrifices, he apparently believed that it was necessary to reduce the independence of the unions and subordinate them to the Communist Party. On April 23, 1929, the Party Central Committee issued a warning to this effect. It announced that the unions were called upon to play a decisive role in the construction of socialist industry, the increase of the productivity of labor, and the improvement of labor discipline, and that they must therefore get rid of all the remnants of a narrow trade-unionist mentality.[37]

One of Stalin's moves in extending control over the unions was to put his close follower, Lazar Kaganovich, on the presidium of the All-Union Council of Trade Unions. To this and other actions Tomsky, together with Bukharin and Rykov, reacted strongly in various statements to the Politburo. They were, however, rapidly defeated. On the same occasion the Central Committee declared: "On the question of the trade unions Comrades Bukharin, Rykov, and Tomsky proceed in a most dangerous fashion by setting the trade unions against the Party, and in fact take a course of weakening Party control over the trade union movement, cover up the weaknesses of trade union work, and conceal trade-unionist tendencies and manifestations of bureaucratic ossifications in part of the trade union apparatus, representing the Party's struggle with these weaknesses as a Trotskyite 'shaking up' of the unions." [38] For these and other reasons Bukharin and Tomsky were deprived of their posts in the Comintern, *Pravda* (of which Bukharin was the editor), and the unions, and were ejected from the Politburo as violators of Party discipline.[39] Rykov was spared for the time being.

In foreign affairs Bukharin was identified with the conservative wing of the Party, which sought to obtain the support of non-Communist groups abroad to serve Soviet aims. The strongest application of this policy took place in China in the years 1926 and 1927. Bukharin was the chief public spokesman for the policy of coöperation with Chiang Kai-shek. At that time the latter had worked closely for a considerable period of time with the Chinese Communists and the Russian advisers sent to China by the Soviet government. Severe conflicts between Bukharin and Trotsky took place over this policy. Trotsky wanted to speed up the revolutionary processes and bring about an open break with non-Communist elements while the Communists had some possibilities of success. Bukharin argued that coöperation was necessary because of the all-important role of the peasants in Chinese society, which consequently was not yet ready for a proletarian revolution.[40] For reasons that will be discussed more fully in another chapter, the Chinese adventure ended in disaster for the Communists and constituted a major debacle in Soviet foreign relations. Similar attempts to win the support of the British trade unions for Soviet ends and efforts to put into effect a united front with the German Social Democrats had turned out equally unsuccessfully.

On this account the policy of the Communist International was reversed at the Sixth World Congress of 1928. The Right deviation was proclaimed the chief danger of the day. Social Democrats and other sectors of the non-Communist Left were denounced as the "working class allies of the bourgeoisie" or branded as "social fascists" in what was essentially a return to Lenin's opinions of the non-Bolshevik left.[41] In the vivid language of Communist polemics it was asserted that "in order to grasp the bourgeoisie by the throat, it is necessary to step across the corpse of social democracy."[42]

Although Bukharin was most prominently identified with the earlier policy, he was chosen to be the major spokesman for the new at the meeting of the Comintern Congress. At one point he even went so far as to assert in a public address that the right-wing danger was the major one in the Comintern.[43] In his somewhat anomalous position he appears to have followed one point of view in his public statements and another while attacking Stalin in the relative privacy of the Politburo sessions; and at the same time he tried to outmaneuver Stalin at the Congress. The difficulties and disagreements did not become known to the Party rank and file until considerably later.[44] Their appearance was a clear indication that Stalin had decided to embark on a course diametrically opposed to all that Bukharin stood for in the twenties.

Stalin's solution

Trotsky had demanded an acceleration of the revolution as an answer to the problems posed by the NEP, but never faced the problem of full political responsibility after Lenin's departure from the helm. Bukharin had sought a retention of the status quo and its gradual modification through economic forces he asserted were inherent in the situation. His policies faced defeat abroad and appeared to be strengthening the enemies of the regime at home. Could Stalin resolve the tensions at home and abroad generated by Lenin's initial retreat?

Stalin's answer, developed piecemeal in intense factional struggles over the years, was composed of five elements: (1) rapid industrialization; (2) planning; (3) collectivization in agriculture; (4) socialism in one country; and (5) a more intransigent and leftist policy for the Communist International. A brief examination of the development of these policies may throw light on one important question: to what extent was ideology used as a mere screen by Stalin in order to achieve power? Or, to put the question in another fashion, did doctrinal considerations play any role in the decisions reached by Stalin during these crucial and formative years of the present regime, or were they mere camouflages to be changed at will in what was basically a struggle for personal power?

At the outset it is worth noting that Stalin did not belong, at least as an insider, to the circle of Westernized intellectuals that constituted the core of the Bolshevik movement before the Revolution. He was an organization man rather than a weaver of theories. Until 1924 Stalin made no claims to be considered an important Party theorist. While his role in Party councils up to this time has been systematically underrated by Trotsky and his followers, his own writings show that, with the exception of the problem of national minorities, he concentrated for the most part on practical administrative matters. Unlike Lenin, Trotsky, and Bukharin, he did not attempt before 1924 to develop a world view into which the events of the day would fit and from which tactics for future action would flow with apparently inexorable logic.

Stalin's first significant statements on the question of industrialization were made at the Fourteenth Party Congress in December 1925, a meeting that marked a crucial defeat for the Left Opposition. Declaring that it was impossible to build socialism "with white gloves," Stalin in a major report recommended that Russia should be transformed from an agrarian into an industrial country in a way that would guarantee the independence of the Soviet economy under the conditions of capitalist encirclement. After fierce and bitter debates over Stalin's general policy and his qualifications for leadership, the Congress adopted his program.[45]

Although Stalin had by this time developed a clear conception of his goal, he displayed very little grasp of what the goal implied concerning measures necessary to pursue it. He wanted a strong, independent, industrialized, and socialist Russia. Such an objective implied a heavy program of capital investment. But in the same speech in which he put forth this goal, he anticipated that the rate of industrial progress would decline in the near future. To "cross the threshold" from a policy of restoration to a policy of new construction would be extremely difficult because of the shortage of capital.[46] Just when Stalin reversed himself and became a proponent of heavy capital investment is not altogether clear, although it is well known that this question was a major issue with the Right Opposition in 1928. In a speech of

November 19, 1928, he sarcastically attacked the People's Commissariat of Finance for setting its sights too low in drawing up figures for the capital construction of industry.[47] After further public and secret discussions, the Party adopted for the First Five Year Plan a maximum variant among the proposals for capital investment in industry. The final figure agreed upon envisaged a capital investment in industry of 15.6 billion rubles. This amount is estimated to be nearly five times the prerevolutionary value of the basic capital in Russian industry.[48]

Although discussions about some form of collective enterprise for agriculture had taken place in Russian Marxist circles ever since Kautsky's observations on socialist latifundia, in Stalin's public statements references to collectivization appear suddenly and for the first time in his report to the Fifteenth Party Congress in December 1927. As late as October 1927 he gave no clue that he might adopt the policy of collectivization and forced repression of the *kulaks*. Instead, in polemics with the Left Opposition, he continued to defend the policy of concessions to the peasantry.[49] But by December of the same year he had begun to veer away from the status quo policies of Bukharin and to turn toward the policies of the defeated Left Opposition.

In his report to the Fifteenth Party Congress, Stalin pointed out that the increase in the productivity of agriculture lagged far behind the corresponding increase in industry. This lag threatened to upset the balance between industry and agriculture. It could therefore upset the whole program of economic self-sufficiency which had been decided upon at the Fourteenth Congress in 1925. The reasons for this lag, he said, lay in the fact that agriculture was conducted in an unplanned manner by scattered owners of small plots. Industry, on the other hand, was operated in large units, subject to planned socialist control.[50] On the same occasion, the well-known agricultural economist, Yakovlev, produced numerous figures purporting to show that large-scale farmers were much more productive than small ones.[51] Supporting the same argument, Molotov pointed out that the curbing of the capitalist elements in the countryside was merely a policy of palliatives, no matter how well it was done.[52] From this general interpretation of the situation, Stalin drew the following conclusion: "The way out is in the transition from small-scale peasant enterprises to large-scale, unified enterprises on the basis of a socialized working of the land, in the transition to collectivized working of the land on the basis of a new and higher technique." [53]

Soon afterward, steps were taken to promote the movement of the peasants into the *kolkhozy*, though reliance on voluntary methods continued for a while. A little more than two years were to elapse, during which the First Five Year Plan was announced, before the Party embarked on its policy of the "liquidation of the *kulaks* as a class" and widespread forced collectivization. [54]

The collectivization of agriculture served the purpose of ensuring a more reliable food supply for the town workers and a way of extracting capital for the industrialization program that resembles Preobrazhensky's proposals to exploit the peasantry. The late date and the suddenness with which Stalin reached this answer again points to his difficulties in deciding how to implement a policy once the goal had been set.

Although the idea of an independent socialist state, or socialism in one country, may be found occasionally in quite early Marxist writers, it is usually regarded as Stalin's most distinctive contribution to contemporary Marxism. [55] Combined with the conception that such a state should be the focal point for socialist, or better communist, movements elsewhere, which should derive strength from this state and contribute support to it, the idea of a single socialist state constitutes one of the more continuous and permanent features of Stalin's thinking. As early as 1920 he was willing to declare that the new Soviet Republic could stand on its own feet without the aid of revolutions in foreign countries. [56] However, he did not deny then or later that such revolutions might be of great service to the Soviet Republic.

Again in April 1924, in his first major theoretical speech, he pointed out that older Marxist opinions concerning the impossibility of a successful proletarian revolution in a single country did not correspond with the facts of history. [57] At that moment he was apparently unwilling to carry the break with tradition much further. He argued, as did Trotsky, that without assistance from proletarian revolutions abroad it was impossible to proceed from the revolution itself to the construction of a socialist society.[58]

In December 1924, for reasons that are not altogether clear but may have been derived from a desire to distinguish his position from Trotsky's, he modified this opinion and revised all subsequent editions of his April speech. In the new version he asserted that it was indeed possible for a single country to carry out a revolution and to proceed to the building of socialism unaided by revolutions abroad. But, he continued, this country could not consider itself secure, that is, free from the danger of destruction by hostile capitalist powers, until successful revolutions had taken place in other countries.[59]

In one very important sense Stalin's conception was still similar to Trotsky's. Both emphasized, overtly at least, that the November Revolution could not be secure until it was universal. In other words, as others have pointed out, Stalin's difference with Trotsky on this as well as other points concerned timing and immediate tactics, rather than long-range objectives. Yet the choice of tactics has important effects upon the verbal expression of political goals, and still greater consequences for the possibilities of achieving them.

Stalin's tactical conception of revolutionary strategy during the period of his struggle with Trotsky was a variety of the united front. The essence of this policy was the utilization of other leftist and non-Communist groups for the promotion of Soviet influence abroad. Expressions of this policy in England via the Anglo-Russian Trade Union Committee, an unsuccessful attempt to capitalize on the sympathy of the British trade unions for the Soviets, and in the abortive German and Chinese revolutions led to failure. In response to these failures Stalin moved toward the policies of his Left opponents.

The shift became apparent in 1928, when the Communist International took a turn to the left, at least on the verbal level. The thesis was put forth that the temporary stabilization of capitalism was indeed temporary and scarcely stable. Communist Parties abroad were ordered to close their ranks, get rid of wavering elements, including adherents of both Left and Right Oppositions, shun the reformist socialists, and defend the USSR against imperialist attack while awaiting an inevitable uprising. One consequence of the new policy was increased antagonism between the German Communists and Social Democrats, which in turn facilitated Hitler's rise to power.

However, the Soviet Union under Stalin's leadership did not by any means follow a consistently doctrinaire policy. The Comintern provided only one of several techniques available for dealing with other states. In 1927 the Soviet Union embarked on the so-called Litvinov period in foreign policy, conducted under the doctrinal flag of the "peaceful co-existence of two social systems at a given historical epoch." The details of this policy and the Soviet search for security through the channels of orthodox diplomacy will be considered in another chapter. Here it is sufficient to point out that the simultaneous use of orthodox diplomacy and the Comintern to promote the strength and security of the new socialist state reveals once more the duality and even inconsistency of Stalin's techniques in pursuit of goals that were stated with considerable clarity.

The role of ideology in factional struggles

Viewing the record of Stalin's tactics during the period of storm and stress in the Party, one is likely to be struck with his intuitive flair for finding a workable political formula. Like Lenin he showed himself willing to reverse himself or his predecessors on various doctrinal points for the purpose of gaining or consolidating power. It is a quality that Stalin's enemies within the Party have condemned in him, while praising it in Lenin.

Nevertheless, this intuitive adaptation to the political situation of the moment shows a specific form of its own. Stalin did not reveal any trace of the ideal, frequently expressed in Western society, that a political leader ought to find out what the people want and then proceed to give it to them. For both Lenin and Stalin such an approach would be the rankest form of opportunism. While deviations from earlier programmatic goals might result from popular pressures, the response to popular pressure was consistently regarded as a concession and not as a virtue in itself. Although Stalin's solutions to the problems he faced have a highly eclectic character, his borrowings were all drafts upon the treasury of Marxist intellectual tradition. The same might be said for the solutions offered by the competing opposition groups. They were variants upon a single theme, or deductions from the same body of unstated premises. It is indeed difficult to see how men immersed for years in a specific intellectual tradition could have freed themselves from it completely even if they wished, especially when competing intellectual traditions were largely excluded or explained away in terms of the dominant set of ideas. Even in the case of Stalin there is sufficient internal consistency and continuity in his objectives, if not in his techniques for reaching them, and enough agreement between his professed goals and his major policies from the early twenties onward, to reject the conclusion that he had no political principles.

At the same time one must reject with equal force the oversimplified interpretation which sees in Stalin's partial return to earlier Marxist principles on this and other occasions a simple case of strategy and tactics. According to this interpretation, various Communist deviations from earlier principles, such as the peace of Brest-Litovsk and the NEP, were merely tactical retreats, while the general strategy remained unaltered. By this line of reasoning Stalin's final program emerges merely as the "real" intentions of the Communist Party, which they had never really abandoned while waiting for the opportunity to put them into effect. Such an interpretation fails to take account of the complicated and varying interrelationship between men's ideas and the political forces in the world around them. It overlooks the trial-and-error process through which the Bolshevik leaders tried to find solutions to the insistent problems they faced. It ignores the marked differences between prerevolutionary intentions and the doctrines that developed under the impact of political responsibility. Finally, it exaggerates out of all proportion the role of ideology in determining political conduct.

Perhaps a more useful analysis would consider both doctrinal goals and the opportunistic adaptation to circumstance as a combination of factors, both sets of which were usually present, in varying degrees, when a decision on any crucial policy was reached. Ideological factors appear, inasmuch as all the contestants for power in the Party were at least verbally agreed (and, with the uncertain exception of the Right Opposition, more than verbally agreed) upon the objectives to be attained. These objectives included the transfer of the means of production to the community as a whole, the industrialization of Russia, and the utilization of non-Russian Communist parties for the defense and aggrandizement of the power of the toilers' homeland. Disagreements occurred on matters of timing and techniques, and also over some of the details of social organization in the future system of society.

In general, the role of the Marxist-Leninist tradition appears to have been to provide the major questions to be asked about the political environment, as well as a few of the answers. These questions included: (1) Who holds power? (2) How do economic and other developments affect the distribution of power? (3) How may these forces be controlled to favor the Communists? The victorious answers included rapid industrialization, the transfer of the means of production to the state, and the collectivization of agriculture. A similar analysis was applied to the situation in foreign countries, with the important distinction that the Russian leaders knew they exercised effective control over only one factor in the situation: the tactics of the Communist Parties together with the official attitude of the USSR.

A mixture of ideological and nonideological factors appears in what may be termed the necessity for an authoritarian solution of the tensions in Russian society generated by the NEP. The need for an authoritarian solution came from the hostility to the Bolshevik regime of a large portion of the population, that is, nearly all of the peasantry as well as those who made their living in the cities from the nonsocialist sectors of the economy. In addition, the alleged and real hostility of the capitalist world was an important factor in the adoption of an authoritarian solution. This internal and external hostility was in turn based to a considerable extent on the fact that the Bolsheviks were the carriers of a specific ideological tradition.

The Communist leaders had stated on a number of occasions that the respite offered their enemies in Russia and in the capitalist world at large was only a temporary one. Despite occasional flurries of hope that the Communists might be undergoing a change of heart, distrust and hostility remained strong, both within and without Russia.

If one concludes that there was a very limited possibility that some ideological acceptance of the NEP conditions could take root in the Communist elite, and that Stalin's solution presented approximately the only way out through which the Party could retain its power, the grounds for this conclusion are found largely in the domestic and foreign opposition to the Bolshevik leaders. These antagonisms were in turn based very largely upon matters of ideology.

If, on the other hand, one concludes that a genuine Thermidor situation existed, and that the Communists could have retained power by adopting and considerably extending the program of the Right Wing Opposition, it is then all the more necessary to fall back upon Marxist ideology as a significant factor in the adoption of Stalin's program. Thus the degree of significance attached to ideological considerations depends upon certain other interpretations and assumptions about the nature of Russian society at this crucial period in its history. However, it does not seem possible to discover any tenable interpretation that will eliminate this factor altogether, or even relegate it to secondary importance. Had the rulers of Russia been of another political persuasion, this hostility might not have developed, and there then would have been no compulsion, ideological or otherwise, to reshape Russian society.

6

Political Dynamics: Who Shall Command?

General factors

On the first anniversary of the Bolshevik Revolution Lenin proclaimed that the organized workers had created a Soviet government without bureaucrats, without a standing army, and without privileges.[1] To many members of his audience the claim must have had a strange ring. Already the march of events had compelled the Bolsheviks to make use of privileges, bureaucrats, and standing armies; to develop in practice, if not in theory, a system of status, authority, and organized social inequality. It will be the task in the next few chapters to trace the development of this system of authority and the associated system of ideas.

Among the more important factors that determined this development of ideas and institutions was the chronic crisis situation in which Russian society found itself from 1917 onward. Following the devastation of War Communism there came the abrupt about-face of the NEP. Despite the economic progress made during the NEP, these years were characterized by several severe crises of an economic nature, as well as by the internecine struggle in the Communist Party. In the thirties came the crises of forced-draft industrialization and the campaigns for the collectivization of agriculture. This state of chronic political and economic tension favored the development of a campaign psychology and the further elaboration of the authoritarian aspects of the Marxist-Leninist tradition.

The new system of authority and its accompanying system of ideas developed under a set of conditions where there was little or no common acceptance of a set of shared values. Political life became a fight to the death against internal enemies: first those of the days of War Communism, and later the *kulaks* and the *nepmen.* The Marxist-Leninist tradition, as it had developed under Tsarism, did not conceive of a social system composed of balanced and opposing social forces—capital versus labor, farmers versus townspeople—in which the guiding principle should be one of live and let-live.

Under somewhat different conditions the ideas of democratic centralism might have provided a substitute device for the reconciliation of opposing social forces. At various points in the history of the Communist Party between 1917 and 1930 this democratic tradition displayed no little vitality. One indication of this vitality was the series of attempts to revive democratic procedures, when popular enthusiasm flagged because of the concentration of power and responsibility in fewer and fewer hands. Even though the democratic aspects of the Marxist-Leninist tradition were retained in this period, they also underwent an adaptive transformation to fit them to the emerging authoritarian structure. It was discovered that democratic ideas and practices could, with but little manipulation, be utilized by those in power to deflect the hostility of large sections of the population away from themselves and against their opponents. The stream of self-criticism could be turned against minor officials who violated the general line of the Party. Finally, these democratic aspects of the earlier tradition were made to serve not only as a basis for the claims of mass support, but also as a stimulus for efforts to achieve this support.

The elimination of political competitors

One of the first steps in the development of a new system of authority was the elimination of organized political competition. During this stage, which lasted more than four years, the Communist leaders did not put into effect any long-range and detailed program of destroying their enemies in a Machiavellian fashion, one by one. In fact, the record of the events suggests that unforeseen incidents together with the mutual intransigence of the Bolsheviks and their competitors led to the collapse of a collaboration that was commenced in good faith. Nevertheless, in their doctrinal writings, especially in comments on the dictatorship of the proletariat, the Communists declared openly that they would not tolerate any real threat to their power, whether from their avowed enemies among the bourgeoisie, or from their competitors among the leftist parties.

On November 27, 1918, Lenin gave clear expression to the conception of the dictatorship of the proletariat. He said that the proletariat must rule over all other classes. Such classes would remain until the exploiters—big bourgeoisie and the landlords— had been destroyed. At the same time the proletariat must win the allegiance of the petty proprietors (chiefly the peasantry). Thus the proletariat should say to the petty bourgeoisie and the Mensheviks, "We will be glad to legalize you—but we will keep power." [2] We should act toward the petty bourgeois, he continued, as "towards a good neighbor who is under the strict control of the governing power." [3] The *kulak* or wealthy peasant, on the other hand, was to be repressed "physically, when he tries to creep into the soviet." [4]

One of the first and most important incidents which put Bolshevik political doctrines to a test was the dissolution of the Constituent Assembly in January 1918. In the dispersion of this body, which was to have decided the political forms of the post-revolutionary Russian state, the Communists were apparently motivated almost entirely by the desire to retain power—if necessary in the face of popular opposition. During these critical weeks one may perceive in Bolshevik statements and actions the influence of latent hostility to bourgeois "formal democracy," together with strong traces of the deliberate manipulation of ideology for power purposes, and, finally, equally strong traces of self-deception.

Before the seizure of power, the Bolsheviks had been among the loudest in insisting that the Constituent Assembly be called, probably to embarrass their political opponents, who were temporizing on this question as well as on others. Following the November coup, Lenin was strongly in favor of postponing the elections to the Assembly, but he did not succeed in carrying his views. It was decided to carry through the election and permit the Assembly to meet, but to dissolve it if it showed signs of refractoriness. Evidently some of the Bolsheviks entertained hopes that the Assembly might provide some sort of legitimizing authority for the new regime.

Others shared Lenin's suspicion. Volodarsky, leader of the Petrograd Party organization, declared as early as November 21, 1917, "We may have to dissolve the Constituent Assembly with bayonets." [5] On November 27, in reply to someone who said that the work of the Constituent Assembly would depend on the mood of the country, Lenin snapped, "Trust in the mood, but don't forget your rifles." [6]

The results of the election to the Constituent Assembly, as Lenin himself later acknowledged, were not favorable to the Bolsheviks. They received only 25 per cent of the votes; the "petty-bourgeois democratic parties" (Socialist Revolutionaries, the leading peasant party; Mensheviks; and so forth), 62 per cent; and the Cadets and other groups (labeled by Lenin the landlord and bourgeois parties), 13 per cent.[7]

Trotsky gives a vivid account of the sequel. The Bolshevik delegates to the Assembly were carefully distributed so that they might be an important element in the organizational machine for the "supplementary revolution" of January fifth. As for the peasant delegates, "Essentially these provincial burghers had not the slightest idea what to do with themselves . . . But to make up for that, they worked out the ritual of the first session most meticulously. They brought along candles, in case the Bolsheviks were to turn out the electric lights, and a large quantity of sandwiches, in the event they were deprived of food. Thus, Democracy came to do battle against Dictatorship—fully armed with sandwiches and candles. It did not even occur to the people to defend those who considered themselves the elect of the people." [8]

In the absence of effective popular support for the Constituent Assembly, its dissolution took place without bloodshed and and almost without incident. Lenin's reaction, as reported by Trotsky, was that this action represented a "frank and complete liquidation of formal democracy in the name of the revolutionary dictatorship." [9] The revolutionary dictatorship was, however, not officially considered as something imposed upon the people. In fact, *vox populi* was invoked by Lenin to justify the dissolution: "And now we have carried out the will of the people—the will that says all power to the Soviets." [10] A further reason for the dissolution, advanced on several occasions before and after it took place, was that it was not genuinely representative of the people, since the major peasant party, the Socialist Revolutionaries, had split into two wings, and therefore the people had voted for a party that no longer existed. [11] In this general fashion the democratic aspects of Marxist-Leninist doctrine, and particularly that limited portion which placed a high evaluation on the approval of the masses, was used by the Bolshevik leaders as a public justification for the concentration of power in their own hands.

In the elimination of competing political parties, which commenced at the same time as the dissolution of the Constituent Assembly, the Bolsheviks showed no hesitation about declaring the Cadets enemies and agents of the counterrevolution, which had already flared up in southern Russia. [12] But there are no indications at the time that Lenin or his associates intended to carry this process to its eventual and logical conclusion. For tactical reasons it was necessary for the Bolsheviks to coöperate with other groups, largely in order to obtain at least the passive support of the peasantry. From the Left Socialist Revolutionaries and their peasant supporters Lenin, by his own acknowledgment, borrowed the first Bolshevik measures concerning land reform, issued in the form of a decree on the day following the November coup. [13]

Shortly afterward a formal agreement was reached between the Bolsheviks and the Left Socialist Revolutionaries. On December 22, 1917, the latter entered the government, receiving the posts of People's Commissars for Agriculture, Justice, and

Post and Telegraph. They quit the government soon after, however, in protest against Lenin's capitulation policy at Brest-Litovsk, but maintained a loose alliance with the Bolsheviks until the summer of 1918.[14]

Trotsky declares that far from spurning the coöperation of other socialist revolutionaries, the Bolsheviks in the early days following the November coup sought it eagerly on every occasion. He claims that he and Lenin once seriously considered allotting certain territories to the Anarchists to let them carry on their experiment of a stateless social order.[15] It is possible that such a proposal was actually made in the flush of revolutionary victory, though, as Trotsky points out, nothing ever came of it. In general, however, it seems out of character for Lenin to consider granting concessions to a competing political movement for other than tactical reasons.

Mutual intransigence, the lack of common goals, and inexperience in the compromises of democratic politics rendered the attempts at collaboration brief and ineffective. In July 1918 certain Left Socialist Revolutionaries working in the Commissariat of Justice assassinated the German ambassador, Count Mirbach, and attempted an uprising against the Bolsheviks. These acts were a protest against Lenin's conciliatory policy toward the Germans, which found expression in the Treaty of Brest-Litovsk and subsequent diplomatic relationships. The Central Committee of the Left Socialist Revolutionaries immediately announced its responsibility for the assassination. The announcement may be taken as a major indication of the political attitude of this group,[16] which was, if anything, less favorable for the development of an ethics and pattern of political compromise than Bolshevik political philosophy and practice. This incident in effect brought to a close the attempts at political collaboration with other leftist groups, although minor steps toward mutual tolerance took place later in the year.[17]

The last openly organized political opposition of any consequence faced by the Bolsheviks was in connection with the Kronstadt rebellion of 1921. This rebellion was the culmination of a series of revolts against Bolshevik measures of forced grain collection from the peasantry, as well as other grievances, and undoubtedly influenced Lenin to adopt the New Economic Policy. The program of the mutineers is significant, since it reflects the grievances not only of the peasantry but also of the workers who supported the Bolsheviks throughout the Civil War. Some of the points are the following:

1. Reëlection of soviets by "secret voting" with "free preliminary agitation."

2. Freedom of speech for workers, peasants, Anarchists, and Left Socialist Parties. (Evidently the tradition of free speech for everyone was not current even among Lenin's leftist opponents. But note the preceding point.)

3. Freedom of meetings, trade unions and peasant associations.

5. Liberation of the political prisoners of the Socialist Parties.

11. The granting to the peasant of the right to do what he saw fit with the land, without employing hired labor.

15. Free artisan production with individual labor.[18]

In subsequent years there were some slight indications that the old political parties maintained an underground organization and managed to work upon the various continuing cleavages in Russian society. Thus, in 1922, the Communist Party declared that the coöperatives and other organizations were used as a basis of counterrevolution, and that the Constitutional Monarchical Party (probably the Cadets) and the Socialist Revolutionary Party had obtained the leadership of the coöperatives.[19] Again, in 1926, the Party referred to the political use made of economic, cultural, and religious organizations against the dictatorship of the proletariat, and to the "counterrevolutionary agitation" in favor of special peasant parties and organizations,[20] an indication that Party control had by no means become as complete as was the case after about 1932. Despite such relatively minor signs, it is safe to conclude that, after the Kronstadt rebellion of 1921, the process of presenting alternative solutions to the problems facing the country was confined to the ranks of the Communist Party itself. In another chapter it will be pointed out how this process was gradually restricted to the upper ranks of the Party.

The doctrine and organization of terror

By the elimination of competing political parties and the consequent concentration of authority in their own hands, the Communists had approached their goal of the dictatorship of the proletariat.

A major device, though by no means the only one, through which the Communist Party consolidated its ruling position in Russia was the systematic application of terror. There were apparently two points of view within the Party concerning the use of terror. By far the strongest and most important attitude was that terror and force must be used ruthlessly on occasion for the ultimate benefit of the masses, even though terror could not in the long run be a substitute for persuasion. Mass support could eventually be obtained only when the masses saw the economic and other benefits of a new form of society. Thus terror was regarded as a temporary measure, necessary to sweep aside the exploiting minority and the remnants of their followers after the workers had seized power in the interests of the masses.

The opposite view was never clearly or openly formulated into a complete system. Its existence must be inferred from occasional actions and statements of Party officials, as well as from the vigor with which Lenin attacked it. This opposing tradition might be described as having a tinge of Western liberal humanitarianism, which regarded force, violence, and compulsion as a necessary evil, but distinctly as an evil to be avoided whenever possible.

In the days immediately following the November Revolution there was little or no need for terror. According to W. H. Chamberlin, Moscow was the sole place in central and northern Russia where the Bolshevik seizure of power encountered serious, sustained, and sanguinary resistance.[21] At the same time, important leaders of the Party both before and after the seizure of power felt that Lenin was embarking on a dangerous course, dangerous both in the sense that the coup might fail and in the sense that, even if it succeeded, it could do so only by means of force and violence.

The negotiations with other left-wing parties following the Bolshevik coup brought to light these fears of what might perhaps be termed the antiterrorist wing of the Party. On November 17, 1917, Kamenev, Zinoviev, and a few other Party leaders resigned from the Central Committee on the grounds that the new government was instituting police terrorism. It will be recalled that Kamenev and Zinoviev had shortly before opposed the seizure of power. One declaration (not signed by these two but by the other leaders) went so far that it accused the Party Central Committee of having entered on the path of "maintaining a pure Bolshevik government by means of police terror." [22] Zinoviev was the first of these individuals to withdraw his resignation, and later all of them became active in posts of high responsibility within the Party, perhaps an indication that their convictions on these matters were not overly strong.

Although the Bolshevik secret police (Cheka) was founded on December 20, 1917, only a few weeks after the seizure of power, the use of terror on a mass scale did not begin until the end of August 1918. The immediate occasion was the murder of the head of the Petrograd office of the Cheka, and the attempted assassination of Lenin by a former Anarchist turned Socialist Revolutionary. In reprisal for the murder of the head of the Petrograd Cheka, five hundred persons were shot.[23] During the Civil War terror was widely used by both the Reds and the Whites. Yet in 1919 opposition to the indiscriminate use of terror and repression was again expressed at the Congress of the Communist Party. In the program adopted at this Congress the Party declared that the deprivation of political rights or any other limitation on freedom should be regarded as "exclusively temporary measures" necessary in the struggle with the exploiters.[24] This statement was directly in line with earlier views concerning the temporary nature of terror. In his report to the Seventh Congress of Soviets during the same year, Lenin similarly blamed the terror on the Entente, saying in effect that the Red terror was a necessary reply to the White terror, and that success over the

Whites would mean that this method of persuasion could be abandoned.[25]

Events turned out otherwise. The pressure of both internal and external opposition to the regime provided the grounds for the continuing expansion of the terrorist bureaucracy. Chamberlin estimates, on the basis of a moderate amount of data, that the Cheka put to death about fifty thousand persons during the course of the Civil War.[26] Beginning only with Dzerzhinsky and a handful of assistants, the Cheka expanded rapidly to a total of 31,000 employees before 1921.[27]

Simon Liberman, one of the non-Party specialists who had close contacts with Lenin in the post-revolutionary period, reports that the Cheka in the search for sabotage expanded its activities rather rapidly into economic matters. This expansion was resented by other sectors of the bureaucracy. On some occasions important officials, learning of the arrest of certain of their subordinates, telephoned Dzerzhinsky, the head of the Cheka, demanding their immediate release.[28]

In 1921 Lenin attempted to use his own prestige to check the expansion of the secret police. At the Ninth Congress of Soviets he described the Cheka as an instance in which "our weaknesses are a continuation of our virtues." Conceding that without the Cheka the power of the workers could not exist so long as there were capitalists and exploiters, he asserted that the Cheka ought to be reformed. Specifically, its functions and competence ought to be defined and limited to political matters. Greater revolutionary legality should be the slogan of the day.[29] From the available evidence this seems to be the last time in which a high official of the Party criticized the secret police in a public statement. While the secret police has undergone a number of administrative overhaulings and changes of name, it has continued as an important feature of the Soviet regime down to the present day.

For Lenin and other Bolsheviks of his day terror was, of course, not an aim in itself but a means to an end. Lenin evidently tried to check the expansion of the secret police because he did not want the tail to wag the dog. His post-revolutionary theoretical position was elaborated in the famous pamphlet, *The Pro-*

letarian Revolution and the Renegade Kautsky, first published in 1918, in which he replied to the criticism by Western or liberal socialists of the Communist dictatorship.[30] The core of the argument was that the Bolshevik terror was exercised in the interest of the masses against the exploiting minority of the population and was essential in order for the masses to benefit. The same general viewpoint was also set out in Trotsky's reply to Kautsky,[31] as well as in other Bolshevik writings of the day. They are in essence an elaboration of the prerevolutionary position without essential change.

The political end toward which terror was directed was crystal clear to the top leaders of the Party, if not to others. A little more than a year after the November Revolution Lenin spoke with sarcastic derision about the request of the Austrian Socialist, Friedrich Adler, for the release from jail on humanitarian grounds of certain Mensheviks. The request gave Lenin one of his many opportunities for comments on the weakness of Western European democracy, which, he asserted, failed to perceive the class position of the petty bourgeois parties and the threat to the Russian Revolution brought about by their "wobbling." [32] In part this speech was addressed to members of his own Party, among whom there was considerable reluctance to apply physical repression against former fellow revolutionaries. Until about 1922 Mensheviks, Socialist Revolutionaries, Anarchists, and other leftists received a privileged position and comparatively mild treatment in Soviet jails, even though they were accused of aiding the bourgeoisie and counterrevolutionary forces.[33] It was in the same year, however, that Lenin wrote, in one of his many administrative notes, that the courts must not do away with terror, but must give it a legal basis "without false adornments." There follows a suggested law to the effect that "membership or participation in an organization supporting that section of the international bourgeoisie that tries to overthrow the Communists should be punished by death." Lenin's suggestion was adopted into the Soviet criminal code.[34]

In this fashion, and through such concepts as the dictatorship of the proletariat, the Bolsheviks gave a certain legitimate quality and overt recognition to the social necessity for the forcible repression of groups and individuals opposed to the existing institutions of society. They applied the Marxist theory of class relationships as a blanket explanation for all hostility to their new status quo. Likewise, the Marxist viewpoint gave rise to a strongly environmentalist explanation of crime and, in the early period at least, to a denial of the existence of any universal code of morals, and consequently of any objective conception of guilt. It is only since about 1935, and with the stabilization of Soviet society in general, that a new conception of crime, closer to orthodox Western conceptions of personal guilt and individual responsibility, has arisen. Even now strong traces of the older view remain.[35]

Problems of mass support: the soviets

In their prerevolutionary and post-revolutionary writings the Bolsheviks expressed no intention of establishing a regime based upon force alone. Instead, Lenin hoped for the creation of a regime that would be far more responsive to the needs of the masses and more readily subject to their will than any political organization previously known to man. The institutions that were intended to bring about this close connection with the masses were the soviets.

In the days immediately following the November Revolution some of these ideas found their way into the Constitution of the Russian Socialist Federated Soviet Republic, adopted by the Fifth Congress of Soviets on July 5, 1918. The first paragraph of the Constitution proclaims that "Russia is a Republic of Soviets of Workers, Soldiers, and Peasant Deputies. All power in the center and locally belongs to these Soviets." [36] Another paragraph described the Russian Republic as a "free socialist society of all the toilers of Russia." Within this territory "all power belongs to the entire working population of the country, united in city and village Soviets." The commentator adds in explanation, "We wish to rule ourselves through the soviets of toilers in the cities and the villages." Provision, of course, was made for some centralization of authority and responsibility. Section 12 stated that the "supreme authority" belonged to the All-Russian Congress of

Soviets (made up of delegates from lower soviet organizations by a system of indirect elections), and, between Congresses, to the All-Russian Central Executive Committee.[37] According to the Constitution, local soviets were supposed to carry out the decrees of higher soviet organs, to take care of economic relationships within their own areas of control, and to decide all questions of purely local significance on their own initiative.

At this early date any constitution or attempt to define the role of the soviets was largely a statement of intentions, insofar as local authority was concerned. The local situation was chaotic. The commentator on the Constitution notes that in one place power belonged in fact to the Military Revolutionary Committees, quasi-military groups set up by the Bolsheviks and nominally subject to the Party and the soviets, while in other places power was in the hands of non-Party soviets.[38] The situation was probably even more complicated than that, since in many places the city Dumas and *zemstvos,* relics of Tsarist days, existed for weeks side by side with the soviets.[39]

While statements of intentions granting widespread autonomy to the local soviets were being issued by responsible Party officials,[40] the Party was at the same time engaged in consolidating its authority. As early as April 1918 the Left Wing Communists began to complain about the loss of independence of the local soviets and restrictions on their activities brought about by officials sent out from the center.[41]

The concentration of authority in the hands of the Party proceeded rapidly during the period of War Communism, by which time other competing political groups had lost their right to exist. At this time all ideas about the soviets as a new social invention sensitive to the will of the masses were pushed rudely into the background. As a Soviet author wrote, local soviet democracy was "compressed," subordinated to the interests of the government as a whole. Because of the necessity for prompt action, decision-making through "broad collectives" was replaced by policy formulation through "narrow ones and by individuals." All authority and all administrative work were in fact concentrated in the governing centers, in the executive committees, their presidiums, and their chairmen. The subordination of the lower to the higher units increased.[42] Under the stress of emergency conditions the need for a system of discipline and authority was promptly recognized in practice, and Lenin's earlier anti-authoritarian views were disregarded.

In 1919, at the Eighth Congress, the Party proclaimed the goal of obtaining decisive influence and complete control of all organizations of the workers, and ordered that in all soviet organizations there must be set up Party fractions strictly subordinated to Party discipline.[43] Considerable energy was required to unite all the soviets and subordinate them to a single will. In the course of the campaign the slogan, "All power to the Soviets," upon which Lenin had come to power, was turned against the Communists.[44] In addition to methods of persuasion, the Bolsheviks evidently resorted to force to a wide extent. The details of the suppression of the soviets, both higher and lower echelons of the system, and alleged terroristic methods of administration are given in a resolution of the Socialist Revolutionaries to the Eighth Congress of Soviets, December 23, 1920.[45] The fact that such complaints could be made openly indicates that Party control was not nearly as successful as it became later. Owing to the system of indirect elections as well as other causes, Party control by the beginning of the NEP was strongest at the top levels of the Soviet system, in the Congress of Soviets and its Executive Committee, quite strong in many of the city soviets, and weak and precarious in the village soviets.

In the course of this struggle the idea came increasingly to the forefront that the Communist Party, as the representative of the vanguard of the proletariat, had a moral right to sole power in the soviet organization. This idea was both a form of justification for actions that were taken to meet the power requirements of the moment and a continuation of Lenin's ideas concerning the elite role of the Party. From a conspiratorial elite and vanguard of the oppressed, the Party had advanced to the position of a ruling elite. An early Soviet legal authority raised and answered the question of the Party's new role in this manner: "I will not mention here that the possibility exists of the Communist candidates' failing to be elected to the soviets and of the government's being overthrown in this fashion by the soviets . . . Thus the one and only truly soviet party was and remains the Communist Party." [46] In a similar vein the Soviet *Encyclopedia of Government and Law,* published by the Communist Academy in 1925, declared: "Not a single political or organizational question is decided by a single government establishment in our republic without leading directives from the Central Committee of the Party." [47]

The peasant revolts of 1920 and the Kronstadt rebellion of 1921 with its slogan of "soviets without Communists" served warning that some of the controls would have to be relaxed. By this time it was clear that the Party faced a serious problem. If it retained an iron hand over the soviets, the workers, and more especially the peasants, would develop at best a lack of enthusiasm and at worst downright hostility. On the other hand, if the Party relaxed its controls, there was a considerable danger that hostile elements might take over the local soviets.

The solution adopted in 1924 was an attempt at the restoration of soviet democracy under the slogan of "enlivening the soviets." The discussions of the time reveal a clear awareness of the problems involved. The Congress of Soviets in a resolution of 1925 declared that the major weaknesses of the soviets consisted in a lack of contact with the masses, their failure to act as collective organs, the replacement of the soviet by its chairman, the inadequate discussion of economic and political matters at plenary sessions, and similar matters.[48]

The problem of mass support was considered in detail at the Fourteenth Party Conference, held at the end of April 1925. L. M. Kaganovich, subsequently one of Stalin's top administrators, observed: "If a deputy of a soviet goes to a meeting and knows beforehand that all questions and decisions have been already decided by a narrow committee of the Party, he won't show much liveliness." [49] Although Kaganovich was not altogether clear about how the two objectives of winning greater popular support and maintaining Party control were to be simultaneously attained, he appears to have believed that they might be achieved by diminishing the appearance of command without reducing its substance. His immediate practical solution was to suggest that, since the Party leaders were often the same individuals as the local soviet leaders, they should talk matters over more frequently with their non-Party colleagues.

In these and other "top level" discussions of the problem, it is quite clear that the Party had no intention of giving up its preeminent position and permitting the growth of a "loyal opposition." Instead, it wanted to widen the basis of mass support and and in so doing drive out of strategic positions any groups or individuals who opposed its policies. A declaration of the Party Central Committee in July 1926 proclaimed that the policy of enlivening the soviets was directed toward "the final destruction of the remnants of the influence of bourgeois elements (*nepmen, kulaks,* and bourgeois intelligentsia) upon the toiling masses."[50] On the positive side it was directed toward attracting the broad masses of the peasantry and the proletariat into participating in the task of soviet construction. In this task, according to the declaration, the proletariat should preserve its directing role.[51]

The objective was one of voluntary and enthusiastic support. Such support, however, could not be obtained and might even be destroyed by a dictatorial approach on the part of local Party officials, as had been the case under War Communism. Therefore, at this time the petty tyranny of the less effective local Communist leaders received severe criticism. Apparently some of them were rather upset when, in Communist terminology, "they lost their ideological monopoly in the village"—that is, when the props of Party support were pulled out from under them.[52] For the same reasons the practice of appointing persons to the soviet instead of holding elections, as well as the practice of mere formal ratification of a list of candidates, received severe criticism from the highest quarters in the Party.[53] Understandably enough, this policy of relaxation of restrictions was viewed with considerable misgivings in various Party circles. Molotov in 1925 had considerable difficulty in juggling the electoral statistics to show that the drop in the number of Communists in the local soviets did not imply any reason for the Party to fear the realization of the "white guard slogan 'soviets without Communists.' " [54]

The results of this attempt to revive soviet democracy were only partly satisfactory from the Bolshevik point of view. They were particularly disappointing at first. In January of 1925 a decree was issued annulling elections in which the participation of the voters fell below 35 per cent of the electorate.[55] In cases in which the elections were repeated, the results were even more disappointing, until finally the authorities had to intervene to annul the results of the repeated elections.[56] In the course of subsequent discussions the Party admitted that it had made a mistake in widening the franchise at these elections, since the increased growth of *nepmen* in both the city and the country revealed the error of diminishing the number of persons deprived of electoral rights.[57] In time better results were achieved, at least insofar as actual participation in the elections was concerned. Although in 1922 only 22.3 per cent of the electorate participated in the elections of village soviets, 69.1 per cent participated in 1931. The corresponding figures for the city soviets are 36.5 per cent and 78.4 per cent.[58]

As an indication of increasing mass participation in the work of government, Soviet writers point to the very high percentage of renewal or turnover in the city soviets. In the Russian Socialist Federated Soviet Republic in 1927 the average turnover in the city soviets was 64.5 per cent, while in the other republics it was only a little lower.[59] However, the authors concede that the goal of having every worker participate to some extent in the work of government was far from achieved. In the USSR as a whole, less than 1 per cent of the electorate in the cities took on the burden of continual work in connection with the soviets.[60] Presumably this work was concerned with the various more or less voluntary sections of the local soviets which dealt with local matters such as playgrounds, housing, and the like.

The reports of an investigation made by the Party revealed in 1928 that the ordinary soviet deputy did not do any continuous work in the operation of local government. According to this report, the organ that made the decisions in the city and village soviets was the presidium. Open meetings merely ratified decisions that had already been reached.[61] In the village soviets, the same source reports, all the work was done by the chairman and the secretary, and secretly at that.[62]

There are several further indications that the Party by no means achieved its goal of popular support by the device of enlivening the soviets. Party statements of the time are full of references to a variety of forms of opposition to its policy. Since criticism of the work of the soviets (justifiable from the Communist viewpoint) was at times identified with counterrevolutionary activity, according to the admission of Bolshevik writers themselves,[63] the extent of opposition cannot be estimated with much hope of accuracy. Some notion of the type of opposition can be gleaned from the comments on the results of the 1926 elections. In writing of this campaign Party historians speak of the existence of "counterrevolutionary agitation" on behalf of a special peasants' party, and mention special peasant organizations in opposition to the "hegemony of the proletariat and its vanguard, the Communist Party." They also complain of "false leftist and purely proletarian" slogans. Allegedly as a result of inadequate preparation on the part of the Party, "hostile class elements" managed to penetrate into the soviets.[64] On other occasions the theme of the opposition was, according to the same report, "Why is there no secret voting? It is unpleasant to vote openly against the administration." At some election meetings opposition speeches were made, reputedly counterrevolutionary pamphlets distributed, and a struggle conducted against the candidates nominated by the Party. In other cases the opposition went so far as to nominate its own candidates, an action described in tones of horror by the Party writers.[65] In still another instance a purge of the election committees reportedly uncovered a number of cases in which the *kulaks* had succeeded in getting elected even to the committees themselves. In Siberia two thousand persons were removed from the election committees.[66] Still more cases are mentioned in which the soviets passed anti-Communist resolutions, such as the instance of one soviet in the Nizhnii-Novgorod Guberniya which declared that the "Soviet power ought not to divide the peasants into poor, middle, and *kulak*." [67]

Taken together, these instances of opposition to the Party's policy, and the way in which the Communists reacted, indicate a clear effort by the Party to maintain strict control over the soviets, even if this effort was not always successful, and even if it was carried out under the slogan of the restoration of democracy. It is well that this point should be underscored, because several writers have spoken of the absence of interference by the Party in these early soviet elections.[68]

In rural areas the Party's difficulties were increased by the fact that in many places the soviet failed to take root as a form of political organization. Village affairs were still very largely governed by the periodic meeting (*skhod*) of the village community.[69] According to official Soviet historians, almost all questions concerning the local peasant population were considered at the *skhod*, over which the village soviet exercised almost no control. Indeed, the soviet frequently fell under the leadership of the *skhod*.[70] The latter was even guaranteed important rights, especially in the field of taxation, by Soviet law.[71] The description of the *skhod* in a manual for local soviet officials gives further details about the meetings of the village community and its relation with the soviet. The manual states: "Among the soviet organs in the countryside the *skhod* has a special place. The *skhod* is not the executive organ of the village soviet. The *skhod* is the general assembly of citizens of a given village or villages who elect the village soviet." The assembly is called to decide or discuss questions "requiring the expression of the general opinion of the toilers" and can be summoned by the village soviet.[72]

Still further difficulties were derived from the fact that in the rural areas the thin red line of Party workers was stretched to the utmost. In 1926, out of a rural population of about 120 million,[73] there were only 154,000 Party members working in the villages. Of these, 100,000 were in office jobs of one sort or another.[74]

From the Communist point of view, the attempts to win enthusiastic mass support in the soviets by means of a relaxation of Party controls had been far from an outstanding success. In the crises at the end of the twenties and early thirties that derived from the collectivization of agriculture and the initiation of rapid industrialization, the soviets were found incapable of serving as an adequate contact between the Party and the masses. Therefore, the top Party leadership decided once again to tighten its control over the soviets. This time the pattern of strict control crystallized into a form that has remained more or less stable for the past two decades. Parallel developments took place in the trade unions and in the Party itself.

In December 1930 the Party Central Committee announced new elections for the soviets and plans for a complete reorganization of their work in connection with the new role that they were called upon to play in collectivization and industrialization.[75] According to this proclamation, "In the period of an expanded socialist offensive the Party especially cannot tolerate right-wing opportunist practices in the direction of soviet organs, which practices not only do not secure the adopted Bolshevik tempos of construction and a consistent battle with bureaucracy on the basis of an expanded proletarian self-criticism, but also in effect mean the sabotage and on occasion outright disruption of the most important Party directives."[76] Molotov remarked at the time that, under the new conditions, "It is impossible to permit . . . the slightest difference between the line of the Party and the line of the soviets."[77]

In 1930, Kaganovich admitted frankly that the soviets, especially the rural and to some extent the city ones, had failed to concentrate on the basic tasks of the day, that is, the socialist reconstruction of agriculture and industrialization. "It is impossible," he stated, "to be satisfied with the situation when the gigantic wave of collectivization passes over the heads of the soviets; when the soviets, organs of the proletarian dictatorship, which ought to be in the center and the leadership of every revolutionary undertaking, drag at the tail of this vast movement of social change."[78] The majority of the soviets, it is reported, failed even to discuss the major problems of the Five Year Plan.[79]

One of the measures adopted to correct this situation was the strengthening of the control of the local soviets by the "higher organs of power," that is, the higher soviets, where Party in-

luence was much stronger.[80] It is also at this time that local Party
officers tended increasingly to issue orders themselves instead of
through the soviets, and to carry out policy directives over the
heads of the soviets. For so doing they were, paradoxically, still
subject to reprimand and criticism.[81]

The paradox may be explained by the fact that the official
ideology concerning the necessity for voluntary mass support,
well expressed in the Webbs' phrase concerning the Party's "vocation of leadership," was still retained and even elaborated
during this crisis. Kaganovich, in the course of his criticism of
Party and soviet activities, expressed clearly the ideology of the
vocation of leadership:

Leadership of the masses [requires] not only a correct policy,
not only good explanations of this policy, but also the force of example
on the job . . . In mobilizing the workers around productive tasks
it is necessary to pay especially close attention to their enquiries, to
their needs in regard to living conditions, their material and cultural
requirements. One should not command, but lead; instead of flattery
there should be mutual criticism of one another's errors, correcting
them along the way, arming one's self with new strength, new examples and new energy for the successful execution of the hardest
tasks of socialist construction.[82]

The vocation of leadership was, of course, to remain in strictly
Party hands. As early as 1923 Zinoviev asserted that the Party
should have the courage to declare that the dictatorship of the
proletariat meant the dictatorship of the Party. This was nothing
to be ashamed of or to conceal, he added. The motto should be,
he concluded, the "division of labor—yes; the division of power—
no." [83]

The Party's degree of success or failure in achieving its goal
of mass support may perhaps be measured by the expansion of
the secret police during this period. Between 1929 and 1934, the
main years of the so-called Stalinist revolution, the scope of
terrorism had reportedly expanded greatly.[84] Even the Webbs,
who have produced the most laudatory of the reports that deserve serious consideration, declared that in 1935 the OGPU was
an organization of great magnitude, extending to every corner

of the USSR." [85] The fact that the development of secret police activities was apparently encouraged rather than viewed with alarm, as had been the case in Lenin's day, indicates that its function by this time coincided with high policy under the Stalinist regime.

As has been seen, the Party's problem of reconciling its goal of mass support with the necessity for safeguarding its own power position was resolved largely in its own favor. Lenin's objective of mass participation in the political process had encountered severe obstacles. For fear of losing power the Communists were unable or unwilling to relax their authority to any great extent. The second obstacle was of a more general nature, often referred to as the "iron law of oligarchy." While it is rather extreme to consider such phenomena as an iron law, it is an observable fact that, as a rule, power and responsibility tend to become concentrated in the hands of the few rather than in the hands of the many. In part this is a result of the general conditions of decision-making, which demand that responsibility be granted to one or a limited number of persons in order to have any decisions made at all. In part it appears to be the result of a general lack of interest in political affairs among the masses, so long as daily life proceeds in a familiar fashion.

In spite of the consequent abandonment in practice of Lenin's ideas concerning the function of the soviets, both the structure and the official ideology have been preserved to a great extent. The structure has been retained, since the soviets now serve, among other things, as an administrative extension of the Party. The ideology has survived because, through such devices as carefully controlled elections, the Party is able to give at least the appearance, and even to some extent the substance, of popular support for its policies.

7

The Transformation of the Rulers

The theory of decision-making: democratic centralism

In the preceding chapter it was pointed out how the crisis-strewn history of the Bolshevik regime contributed to the concentration of political authority in the hands of the Communist Party. Within the Party itself similar forces were at work. In time they led to the elimination of open disagreements in the Party ranks and the concentration of authority at the apex of the Party pyramid. Though the official ideology recognized these changes in part, the recognition was not complete. Strong anti-authoritarian remnants of the older view remained. To a very great extent they were transformed, as in the case of the soviets, to an ideology alleging the existence of mass support for the new social order. To a somewhat lesser extent they remained an ideal that from time to time produced tensions and consequent efforts to restore "true" inner Party democracy.

In the post-revolutionary years the doctrine of democratic centralism as the theoretical principle which reconciled the need for authority with the desire for democracy received further elaboration and definition. Democratic centralism, according to an authoritative Soviet source published toward the end of the period of social readjustment in 1931, consisted of three major elements: (1) "the election of higher and lower Party organs at general gatherings of Party members, Conferences, and Congresses." Thus the principle of election was an indirect one. (2) "The periodic accounting of Party organs before their electors." (3) The "obligatory nature of the decisions of higher Party organs for the lower ones; strict discipline; and rapid execution of the decisions . . . of controlling Party centers." Moreover, centralism must be democratic and not bureaucratic. It included the possibility of changing the personnel of all Party organs. Furthermore, it included the "right and obligation of each member of the Party to speak out independently and on his own concerning a question disputed within the Party."[1]

These principles theoretically governed the Party in all of its deliberations and activities, according to the Party statutes, first adopted in 1919 and subjected to very little change thereafter. Thus, in theory, the broad lines of Party policy were laid down at Party Congresses which set the tactical line of the Party on current questions. The Central Committee, while given considerable discretionary power, was conceived of as responsible to the Congress and as the executor of policy formulated by the latter. Discussion of all controversial questions was to be completely free until a decision had been reached. The enumeration of the Central Committee's executive functions included the power of determining relations with other parties (a task which soon ceased to exist) and the management of other Party organizations, such as the press. The statutes merely mentioned the Politburo, describing its functions only as "political work."[2] Although new statutes were adopted at the Eleventh Party Conference in 1922, at the Fourteenth Congress in 1925, and again at the Seventeenth Congress in 1934,[3] only one change reflected an alteration in the distribution of power: in 1934 the new statutes provided that a Party Congress should be called at least once every three years, instead of annually.[4] The preceding Congress had been held three and a half years before, and the next one was not called for five years.

Actual patterns of decision-making

As might be anticipated, Party folkways governing the making of policy bore only a distant resemblance to the formal statements that claimed to describe these behavior patterns. In the first place, the number of crucial decisions was so great, and in many cases required such secrecy, that it would have been physically impossible to convene a Party Congress to consider all of them.

Because of this, just before the November Revolution on October 23, 1917, a small nucleus was created within the Party Central Committee at the suggestion of Dzerzhinsky, later chief of the secret police. The original members were Lenin, Zinoviev, Kamenev, Trotsky, Stalin, Sokol'nikov and Bubnov.[5] The main task envisaged at this time appears to have been little more than the management of the details of the November uprising. Nevertheless, the idea of concentrating decision-making powers in the hands of a very few leaders persisted, owing to the continuing need for immediate and far-reaching decisions in the crises directly following the Revolution. By March 1919 the Eighth Party Congress set up, as a permanently acting body, a Political Bureau consisting of five members, who were "to decide on questions which do not permit delay" and to report bimonthly on all its work to a regular plenary session of the Central Committee.[6] At that time the Politburo consisted of Lenin, Trotsky, Stalin, Kamenev, and Bukharin.[7] At no time during the period from 1919 to 1946 did the membership of the Politburo, including candidates, exceed seventeen individuals.[8]

Although originally this elite within an elite was theoretically established to decide upon political questions of an urgent nature, after its first year of existence its range of authority had increased enormously. Lenin, in a report of the Central Committee to the Ninth Party Congress in 1920, stated that not only had the Politburo "decided all questions of international and domestic politics" but that "any question at all could be considered a political question, upon the request of a single member of the Central Committee" to the Politburo.[9] By 1928, according to the published work plans of the Politburo, its functions (together with those allocated to the Plenum of the Central Committee, a larger body to which the Politburo was theoretically responsible) covered almost the entire scope of political, economic, social, and cultural problems in Soviet life.[10]

In spite of its actual position as the center of authority, and although its members undoubtedly realize their high role in the state, there has never been an open admission that power is thus concentrated. At the Fourteenth Party Congress in 1925, Stalin declared: "The Politburo is sovereign as it is, it is higher than all organs of the Central Committee except the Plenum. The Plenum decides everything among us and it calls its leaders to order when they begin to lose their balance." [11] This distinction may perhaps be regarded as a deliberate effort to preserve a fiction which not only accords with official ideology but might tend to satisfy popular belief that high decision-making is conducted through legally recognized channels and in an orderly representative fashion. Although the allegedly superior body of the Central Committee, the Plenum, has met at decreasingly frequent intervals since 1917, while the Politburo has increased its number of sessions manyfold,[12] the myth of the Central Committee's superior role is steadfastly maintained in published materials. In more recent years and at the present time when Party decrees of major significance have been published, they are always issued in the name of the Central Committee as a whole, without mention of any role played by the Politburo.

The urgent flavor of the atmosphere in which early decisions by the Politburo were reached was well captured by Lenin in his report of the Central Committee to the Ninth Party Congress in 1920: "There were so many questions that we had to decide them one after another under conditions of extraordinary haste. It was only possible to carry out the work, thanks to the members' complete knowledge of each other, their awareness of each other's shades of opinion, and their complete trust [in one another]. We often resorted to deciding complicated questions by telephone conversations instead of holding meetings." [13]

This simple method of reaching decisions, as well as the dominant role of the Politburo, are sharply illustrated in an informal report by Lenin himself. On December 22, 1921, he telephoned the Politburo, saying, "I ask a discussion of the question, shouldn't the Congress of Soviets adopt a special resolution against the adventurist policies of Poland, Finland and Rumania? (About Japan we'd better keep quiet for a number of reasons.) The resolution should say in detail how we have shown by actions that we value . . . peaceful relations with the countries that formerly belonged in the Russian empire . . . The resolution should end with a sharp threat that if . . . these adventurist pranks do not stop . . . we will rise up in . . . war . . . A resolution of the Congress along these lines would be useful if we could spread it around among the masses in all languages." [14] The Ninth Congress of Soviets, which opened on the following day, adopted a resolution closely following Lenin's suggestions.[15]

Trotsky in his autobiography corroborates the impression of great haste and the mood of emergency among the decision-makers when he reports: "On the decisions made and the orders given in those days depended the fate of the nation for an entire historical era. And yet those decisions were made with very little discussion. I can hardly say that they were even properly weighed and considered; they were almost improvised on the moment. But they were none the worse for that. The pressure of events was so terrific, and the work to be done so clear before us, that the most important decisions came naturally, as a matter of course, and were received in the same spirit." [16] From other information available it is clear that Lenin's and Trotsky's descriptions applied only to situations in which the ruling ideology of the Party provided a ready answer to the problem at hand. Whenever there existed a consensus among the Party leaders concerning objectives and the proper techniques to achieve them, the decisions probably did come "as a matter of course."

When this consensus was lacking, alternative interpretations of the existing situation and alternative courses of action were presented with much heat. As a rule, though by no means always, Lenin's prestige was sufficient, when added to the force of his arguments, to win adoption for his views. The case of the discussions concerning war or peace with Germany, the issue of Brest-Litovsk, illustrates this situation. In the beginning of the negotiations Lenin was almost alone in his opinion that war against Germany was physically impossible and that Russia would have to take what terms she could get. Trotsky, who was in charge of the actual negotiations but returned for consultation, developed the formula of "No war—no peace," in essence a delaying tactic in the hopes that revolutionary disintegration might set in behind the German lines. Bukharin wanted to wage a revolutionary crusade against Germany. On several occasions Lenin was outvoted in meetings of the Central Committee as the negotiations teetered back and forth. Eventually his formula triumphed in the face of the stark realities of a German offensive.[17]

In accord with the theory of democratic centralism, members of the Politburo and other high decision-making units were supposed to adhere to the decision of the majority in public statements at least, no matter what their personal convictions. Of course, this was not intended to prevent them, in the early days at least, from giving vigorous expression to their convictions behind the closed doors of secret committee meetings. As the Brest-Litovsk case shows, the system tended to break down as soon as disagreements became severe.[18]

The Brest-Litovsk controversy is also significant in bringing to light from the very beginning the role of a single leader. Lenin got his way through the threat of resignation as well as through the force of argument, a continuation of the early prerevolutionary situation before the Party had passed beyond the stage of discussion circles. However, the position of the single leader was not as strong then as it became subsequently. On other issues Lenin was overruled. The case of the Constituent Assembly was described in the preceding chapter. Lenin was again overruled or persuaded, perhaps a combination of the two, on the question of abandoning Petrograd to the Whites,[19] as also in the question of whether or not to end the war with Poland.[20] In the interregnum preceding and following Lenin's death, the Party was ruled for about a year by a self-appointed triumvirate (Stalin, Kamenev, and Zinoviev). Though factional struggles continued, no one proved successful in challenging Stalin's leadership after the Fourteenth Congress in 1925.

The issues of Party discipline in connection with "fractional behavior" and freedom of discussion came shortly to the fore in 1921, just preceding the marked reversal of Communist policy that took place with the adoption of the New Economic Policy. The immediate issue, it may be recalled, concerned the role of the trade unions in the toilers' state. According to Lenin, the disagreements on this problem within the Central Committee made necessary an appeal to the Party as a whole.[21] During January of 1921 a series of polemical articles by various top Party leaders in *Pravda*, the Party daily, presented a wide variety of views. In sharp contrast with later practice, the "official" draft platform of the Party did not appear until January 18. Discussion did not cease then; on the twenty-fifth Bukharin criticized Lenin's views in polite language, and the theses of the Workers' Opposition, a left-wing group within the Party, also appeared. On the whole, the discussion resembled one which might be found on any major issue in American newspapers of large-scale circulation. That is, the major premises concerning the desirable forms of social organization were largely accepted by all participants, whereas the discussion revolved chiefly around interpretations of the best way to achieve generally accepted goals.

But the discussion was not fated to be a step in the direction of Western democratic practices. Lenin rapidly grew annoyed with what he felt were empty theoretical discussions while Russia and the Party were still in a crisis of survival. His ideas, to which Stalin turned in his efforts to crush the later opposition, deserve full quotation:

Probably there are not many among you who do not regard this discussion as having been an excessive luxury. Speaking for myself, I cannot but add that in my opinion this luxury was really absolutely impermissible; by permitting such a discussion we undoubtedly made a mistake and failed to see that in this discussion a question came to the forefront which, because of the objective conditions, should not have been in the forefront; we wallowed in luxury and failed to see to what an extent we were distracting attention from the urgent and menacing question of this very crisis that confronted us so closely.[22]

As a result, Lenin obtained at the Tenth Party Congress the passage of measures to eliminate such discussions in the future. Calling attention to the danger of factional groups with special platforms and their own group discipline, the Congress empowered the Central Committee "to carry out the complete destruction" of these groups in the future. This was a long step in the direction of the monolithic conception of the Party, which eventually became the official one. A secret clause, later revealed by Stalin, provided for the expulsion from the Central Committee of a member who had violated the new rules against fractional behavior.[23] In this manner a bench mark was established, to which the Party was to return in the struggle with the various subsequent oppositions and, still later, in the purge trials following the consolidation of Stalin's power.

In 1921, however, the Party was by no means ready to shut off all public discussion within its own ranks. Lenin himself asserted that the mere prohibition of discussion would not solve the problem. Therefore, he sought to drain off the antagonisms arising from divergent views by creating outlets for the presentation of different theoretical viewpoints in special publications, symposia, and the like. With a trace of sarcasm he observed, "If anyone is interested in studying the quotations from Engels down to the last word, here is his opportunity!" [24] Though the results of these symposia were to be published, Lenin evidently regarded them mainly as a way to prevent argument among the masses of the Party. In this manner he sought to create an outlet for the Party intellectuals that would not diminish Party unity. Roughly parallel devices, the appointment of committees of inquiry, and so forth, are a familiar phenomenon in contemporary democratic states.

The taming of the rank and file

Parallel to the concentration of the decision-making power in the hands of the top Party leaders, there took place a corresponding diminution in the influence of the rank and file on matters of major import. Debates at the early Party Congresses were lively affairs in which there was a genuine interchange of opinion on the important issues of the day. Speakers were by no means limited to the elite of the Party, and on occasion one may find in the stenographic reports sharp attacks on general Party policy by relatively unknown delegates. While there is no reason to spare the salt in evaluating Lenin's frequent comments on the way he "picked up" solutions to important problems from his conversations with ordinary delegates at the Congresses, there is also abundant evidence of the way in which he kept his ear to the ground. One incident at a meeting of the Central Committee shows the attitude of this body toward the Congress quite clearly. In reply to Lenin's attack, Riazanov, later the editor of Marx's works in Russian, asserted that he could not refrain from criticism when he considered the policy of the Bolsheviks deeply mistaken. In such cases, he explained, in which the decisions of the Central Committee are "dictated by political combinations and are not based upon the decisions of the supreme organ of the Party Congress, I consider it my duty to struggle against them." [25]

There are also indications during the early years of widespread discussions. These were formal occasions, when the matters upon which the Central Committee could not agree were thrown open to the Party for general discussion. Between 1917 and 1925 four of these took place, concerning the Brest peace, the trade unions, the Party bureaucracy including problems of economic planning and the peasant question, and finally the discussions on permanent revolution and world revolution. After debate in the Party cells and other groups, a vote expressing the opinion of the group would be taken and the results forwarded to higher Party units. *Pravda*, for instance, reported that in the trade-union discussion of 1921 a large number of meetings were held, four fifths of which in the Moscow area voted for the official theses put out by Lenin and his associates.[26] Even though the "official" theses enjoyed enormous prestige and were adopted in every important case, until 1921 competing theses were presented fully and with supporting arguments for the rank and file to choose among. According to official Party doctrine, the masses made the actual decisions on these and other crucial occasions. In the case of the trade-union discussion, Lenin described the situation in these terms: "In this discussion, the Party proved itself to be so mature that, seeing a certain wavering among the 'upper ranks,' hearing the 'upper ranks' saying as it were, 'We cannot agree, sort us out,' it quickly mobilised itself for this task, and the overwhelming majority of the larger Party organisations quickly answered us, 'We have an opinion and we shall tell you what it is.' " [27] Thus, for a time at least, the official mythology concerning the role of the rank and file approached the conception of *vox populi, vox dei*. It is important to remember, however, that this conception never extended to the whole of the population, but only to the rank and file of the Party. It did not even extend to the whole of the industrial working class, a large portion of which was considered culturally "backward."

Nevertheless, the limitations on the powers of the Party rank and file had already begun in Lenin's time. As early as the Eighth Congress in 1919 there were numerous complaints about the lack of opportunities for the rank and file to participate in discussions, about the bureaucratization of the Party, the presence of too many "decorative figures" in the Central Committee, the procedure of voting for Central Committee members by list instead of by individual candidates, and similar matters.[28] The next year the complaints were even stronger. One outspoken delegate in a sharply worded attack on Lenin went so far as to call the dictatorship of the proletariat the dictatorship of the Party bureaucrats.[29]

During Lenin's lifetime the major influence, if not the sole one, brought to bear upon the rank and file was perhaps the prestige of the leaders and the force of their arguments. After Lenin's death there is increasing evidence that more concrete measures were brought to bear and that Stalin displayed considerable skill in the manufacture of rank-and-file opinion.

Stalin rapidly took advantage of the devices created by Lenin to prevent the outbreak of factional disputes. One of these was the series of Party Control Commissions, created at the Tenth Congress in 1921. Stalin gained control of them the following year when four of his supporters were elected to the seven-man board of the Central Control Commission.[30] These Commissions were a bureaucratic device established to combat bureaucracy. Their tasks were described at the time as conducting the struggle against bureaucracy, careerism, misuse by Party members of their official positions, and particularly against the "spreading of rumors and insinuations . . . destructive of the Party's unity and authority." [31] Their functions were so broadly defined that they made any member of the Party with independent views subject to investigation by the Commissions.

In the spring of 1923 the Party declared that the Control Commissions should not limit their work to the collection and verification of facts concerning the violation of Party decrees, "but must become initiating organs in learning about, and removing the causes themselves, of anti-Party acts and diseased manifestations in the Party." [32] Some years earlier the Party had approved the creation of investigative staffs for the Control Commissions, which were regarded by opposition sources as a new variety of secret police within the Party itself. This impression was no doubt strengthened by another Party declaration of 1923 which demanded that individuals of the "Chekist type" ought to be elected to the Central Control Commission. [33] A Soviet source states specifically that the services of the Control Commissions were shown especially clearly in connection with their struggle against the Trotskyite opposition, and attributes the exclusion of "hundreds of thousands" of persons (no doubt an enormous exaggeration) to their tireless activities. [34] Again after the defeat of the Right Opposition the Sixteenth Party Congress congratulated the Central Control Commission upon its success in eliminating from the Party "ideologically foreign elements." [35]

Another important step in Stalin's manipulation of rank-and-file opinion took place immediately after Lenin's death and after the struggle between Stalin and Trotsky had broken out into the open. Early in 1924 the Party proclaimed a mass enrollment of new members, the so-called Leninist levy. The official Party history, first published in 1938, in its account of the levy reveals clearly its motives: "In those days of mourning every class-conscious worker defined his attitude to the Communist Party, the executor of Lenin's behest. The Central Committee of the Party received thousands upon thousands of applications from workers for admission to the Party. The Central Committee responded to this movement and proclaimed a mass admission of politically advanced workers into the Party ranks." [36] It is perhaps not too much to infer that the new members were screened to exclude those opposed to Stalin and his followers, who were already the dominant group in the Central Committee. The importance of this flooding of the Party with new members may be noted from the fact that in 1923, at the Twelfth Congress, 386,000 members were represented; in 1924, at the Thirteenth Congress, the membership had risen to 735,881.[37] In subsequent years the flooding continued. By 1929 the membership figure had reached 1,551,238. Of these, 73.4 per cent had entered the Party after 1923.[38]

In his voluminous writings of the opposition period and afterward, Trotsky accused Stalin time and again of highhanded methods in packing Party Congresses with his own supporters, using the secret police to intimidate his opponents, and similar techniques. As early as 1923 Preobrazhensky revealed that 30 per cent of the secretaries of the *guberniya* Party committees were "recommended" for their positions by the Party Central Committee, and expressed fears concerning the abuse of the Party's power to transfer its members from one type of job to another.[39] Several others complained that no one who had ever been in an opposition group could get a responsible post.[40] Even if one makes considerable allowance for political spite, it is unlikely that these complaints were without foundation. Stalin rapidly developed his position as Party Secretary General, to which he was elected in 1922, into one that enabled him to maintain close contact with local Party organizations. In this way he was able to reward his friends and punish his enemies.

In addition to the above devices, Stalin and his followers exerted increasing pressure to prevent the opposition from presenting its views before the Party rank and file. One incident from the year 1927 reveals the mechanics as well as the psychology of this repression. In October Stalin declared that the Central Committee had not printed the opposition platform "not because we fear the truth"; stenographic reports of the Plenums of the Central Committee and the Central Control Commission containing opposition speeches were distributed, he said, by the thousand to members of the Party. The platform was not printed, he asserted, because it was a sign of "fractional behavior." Then he cited Lenin's resolutions and actions at the 1921 Party Congress forbidding fractional behavior in support of the refusal to print the opposition document.[41] These reports had, of course, a much more limited circulation than the general Party press, which had previously been available from time to time for the presentation of opposition views. By the time the Right Wing Opposition had begun to develop, in about 1928, Stalin's suppression of opposition policies had become so successful that it is now extremely difficult to reconstruct the objectives of the Right Opposition from published sources.

In subsequent years Stalin attempted to minimize the extent and importance of the opposition groupings within the Party. So far as I am aware, no figures were ever published to indicate the degree of mass support obtained by the Right Opposition. In the case of the Left Opposition, the official Stalinist Party history of 1938 reports that, in the October 1927 discussion, 724,000 members voted for the policy of the Central Committee, while only 4,000 members, or less than 1 per cent, voted for Trotsky's platform.[42] Ten years before Stalin gave a quite different evaluation of Trotsky's strength. Referring to the same discussion, Stalin then reported that 10,000 persons voted against the Central Committee's platform, while there were in addition about 20,000 persons who sympathized with Trotsky but refrained from attending the meetings or voting.[43]

The taming of the rank and file was very largely completed by the end of 1925. After the Fourteenth Congress, held in December of that year, public attacks on the persons and policies of the leaders ceased almost completely. It is impossible to determine to what extent this shutting off of mass criticism resulted from the difference between Lenin's personality and Stalin's, and to what extent it was due to differences in external circumstances. In the light of Lenin's action in temporarily repressing discussion and fractional behavior in 1921, it seems reasonable to attribute greater significance to the circumstances than to the personalities. From 1925 onward public criticism by the rank and file was directed toward the way in which policy was executed and practically never toward the policy itself or those who formulated it. In this way the Bolshevik version of the tradition of free speech was transformed into a weapon that the central authorities were able to use to keep their subordinates in place and to break up any incipient clusters of power that formed around local leaders.

Conflicting conceptions of rule

The concentration of power in the hands of the Central Committee, and actually within the Politburo, together with the elimination of opportunities for the presentation of alternative interpretations and solutions to the problems facing Russian society, was accompanied by a severe ideological struggle. In this struggle the authoritarian conception of the Party emerged greatly strengthened. In its more or less final form the authoritarian conception was exemplified in Stalin's doctrine of a "monolithic" Party.

In the prerevolutionary period there was a strong undercurrent of opposition to the authoritarian conception of the Party promulgated by Lenin. In the post-revolutionary period this antagonism formed a common element in the platforms and complaints of the various opposition groups, who differed widely from one another on other matters. In 1917 it was the theme of Bukharin's Left Opposition, as well as of the hesitancies and objections raised on individual issues by Kamenev, Zinoviev, Lunacharsky, and others.

As early as 1919 a faction within the Party organized itself under the specific banner of opposition to dictatorial methods in the Party and the country as a whole, calling itself the Democratic Centralism Group. In that year the members proposed that the petty-bourgeois parties which were not opposed to the Soviet regime should be permitted freedom of the press and freedom of assembly. By 1920 this group had obtained considerable local support in the Ukraine. In the fall of that year they demanded the legalization of oppositional groups in the Party in statements that approach the Western doctrine of a "loyal opposition." One of their members wrote in *Pravda*, "Without the conflict of opinions, without the struggle of movements and groups, without an opposition, proletarian democracy cannot exist." [44] They were later accused of trying to turn the Party into an educational society that would be no more than an appendage of the soviets.[45] It is difficult to determine to what extent the members of this loose grouping were motivated by a genuine interest in the extension of proletarian democracy, and to what extent they were disturbed by their failure to receive adequate consideration and rewarding posts in the Party hierarchy.

In general, and throughout the Party's history, it was the groups excluded from power that propounded an anti-authoritarian version of Bolshevism. Trotsky underwent a conversion from an extreme authoritarian position to one that resembled closely modern Western liberalism. For his authoritarian views on the necessity for discipline and the introduction of the death penalty in the Red Army, he clashed with other Party leaders, but was supported by Lenin. His proposals for the militarization of labor, which set off the discussions preceding the adoption of the NEP, were a part of the same pattern. In 1917, when Lunacharsky was greeted with applause for an attack on Lenin that ended with the prediction that some day only one man would remain—a dictator, Trotsky jumped to Lenin's defense and poured contempt on those who adopted a "bookish attitude" toward the class struggle. "The moment they got a whiff of the revolutionary reality, they began to talk a different language." [46]

In 1923 and 1924, when Trotsky had already lost much of his power in the internal struggle in the Central Committee, but was still regarded as a loyal supporter of the regime by the rank and file who knew little or nothing about this struggle, he published a famous series of articles that immediately aroused a storm of controversy. In these he presented a criticism of the Party bureaucracy and an analysis of the decision-making process that resembled the views of the Democratic Centralist opposition. At this time he evidently hoped that his differences with other Party leaders could be reconciled after public discussion. In his articles he showed a keen awareness of the dilemma of authority: the need for both discipline and flexibility. He also made several suggestions on how to meet it.

According to Trotsky's interpretation of 1924, Party policy emerged from the conflict of views within the Party. To localize this process in the Party bureaucracy and present the final results in the form of slogans would, he argued, emasculate the Party. On the other hand, to make the entire Party participate in the decision-making process meant running the danger of fractions. Fractions in turn derived from the fact that the Party was the only political group possible under present-day conditions, and hence contained some representatives of different interest groupings.[47] Citing the instance of strong disagreement within the Party over the peace of Brest-Litovsk and over the organization of the Red Army, Trotsky argued that events handled with success led to the reconciliation of factions instead of to the danger of splits and disunity. In effect, he claimed that since the Party had overcome previous emergencies without stifling criticism, it would continue to do so in the future.[48] In another passage he remarked, "The collective Party view gradually extracts from the discussion that which it needs, becomes more ripe and self-confident." Again, he declared that the dust would settle from present controversies, and the truth emerge.[49] The similarity is striking between Trotsky's conceptions at this time and the assumption that truth will prevail in the competition of ideas in a free market, perhaps the basic assumption behind the modern Western ideal of civil liberties.

Trotsky's conception of the right and duties of a Party member likewise resembled closely certain tenets of modern Western individualism. A Bolshevik, he said, is not only a disciplined person; he is also a person "who works out for himself on each and every occasion a firm viewpoint and in a manly and independent way defends it not only in the fight against the enemy, but also within the organization itself." [50] If he is in the minority, Trotsky continued, he subordinates himself because it is his Party. But that does not always mean that such an individual is wrong. It may simply mean that he has seen the need for a change in policy before others have seen it. Such a person persistently brings up the same question, once, twice, ten times. In this way he performs a service for the Party and helps it find the right way "without fractional convulsions." [51] In these passages Trotsky comes very close to the conception of a responsible and loyal Party opposition. The idea was not altogether new. In 1918 the Left Wing Communists regarded themselves as a group maintaining complete unity with the Party, even going so far as to suggest that they might become a "responsible proletarian opposition." [52]

The debates produced by this series of articles by Trotsky were hot and heavy within the Politburo. Bukharin, it was revealed later, wanted to have Trotsky arrested for publishing them.[53] Instead, he was given the task of producing an official reply. Therein he expressed the viewpoint that was destined later to be victorious, and which was in time to be turned against him. The Communist Party, he declared, never was, and never could be a mere federation of groups, as implied by Trotsky. So long as the Party was at its fighting post, unity could not be abandoned.[54] Finally, in April 1924, the Party issued a resolution, declaring that the Trotskyite opposition was endeavoring to replace the "Bolshevik conception of a monolithic Party with the conception of the Party as the sum of all possible tendencies and fractions." In so doing, said the resolution, the opposition was abusing the principles of Party democracy.[55]

This is one of the earliest occasions on which the term "monolithic Party" was used, and as such marks an important turning point in the history of Communist doctrine. The seeds of the monolithic conception in Stalin's mind may be found in a remarkable speech delivered to local Party workers on December 2, 1923. The speech was reprinted in *Pravda,* along with several others by important top leaders, and later gathered into a pamphlet marked "for Party members only." [56]

In contrast to several of the other leftist contributors who referred to the demoralization of the Party and the rise of self-seeking elements in it, resulting from contact between the Communists and the profiteers of the NEP, or the growing division within the Party between those who made decisions and those who carried them out, Stalin's tone was for the most part optimistic. In general, he said, the Party line as expressed in the Congresses and major actions of the Party was correct. At the same time he warned against two extremist tendencies within the Party. One was the demand for complete democracy and the abolition of the requirements concerning length of Party membership for election to offices of Party responsibility. This demand could not be met, he asserted, under present-day NEP conditions, when bourgeois elements attempted to creep into the Party. This comment was in reply to Trotsky's criticism of the Party old guard, which he had already accused of bureaucratic degeneration. The second extremist danger, said Stalin, was the demand for complete freedom of discussion. In this he opposed as inadequate the conception of the Party as a "voluntary union of those who think alike." It is also, he averred, a military union of those who act alike on the basis of a common program. The first conception, Stalin argued, can have only two possible outcomes. On the one hand, the Party might become a narrow sect or philosophical school where all think alike. On the other hand, it might become a discussion club, eternally debating and never acting. In either case it would lose its capability of effective political action. Discussion is necessary, he agreed, but there must be definite limits set.[57]

Like Lenin before him, Stalin appeared tired of endless theoretical discussion and impatient to get down to immediate practical matters. Acknowledging the widespread incompetence of the Communist cells in the rural areas, he asked why they should not set to work spreading a little elementary knowledge of good farming practices among the peasants. Do you know, he said in effect, that if every peasant did a little work cleaning seeds we'd get a ten *pood* increase in the yield per *desyatina?* This means a milliard *poods* per year in gross production with no new machinery. "Is this really less important than conversations about Curzon's politics?" he concluded, with a heavy touch of sarcasm.[58]

In the course of further clashes during the twenties, the conception of a monolithic Party became hardened and elaborated. The development, however, did not proceed in a straight line. As late as 1926 Stalin quoted Marx and Engels to prove that the Communists, like other parties, developed and grew by means of an internal struggle.[59] At the same time, the mixture of rational and mystical elements characteristic of Russian Marxism, which sometimes seem ridiculous to a Westerner, cropped out periodically. Sir John Maynard mentions the time when for several days Party circles discussed the question of whether or not the Party was infallible.[60] On another occasion, when Stalin in 1928 was explaining the monolithic conception, someone from the floor asked quite seriously if a split was possible under these conditions. Stalin replied that the question was not the possibility of a split, but whether a split could be justified on Leninist grounds. Because of the class purity of the Party, he went on to show, such a split was not justifiable.[61]

By 1931, after the Right Wing had been completely defeated, a new tone may be detected in Stalin's pronouncements. The occasion for his major statement was a magazine article on prewar Party history, which might seem an academic subject until one recalls Trotsky's similar use of Party history to cast doubts on the competence of Stalin's leadership. Stalin wrote to the editors of the offending magazine: "This [publication of the article] means that you intend once again to draw people into a discussion on questions which are axioms of Bolshevism. It means that you are again thinking of turning the question of Lenin's Bolshevism from an axiom into a problem needing 'further elaboration.' . . . Why? On what grounds? . . . Perhaps for the sake of a rotten liberalism, so that the Slutskys and other disciples of Trotsky may not be able to say that they are being gagged? A rather strange sort of liberalism, this, exercised at the expense of the vital interests of Bolshevism." [62] The evolution of Stalin's views is clearer if the above statement is contrasted with his observation in 1924 that the Party would have been "a caste and not a revolutionary party had it not allowed certain shades of opinion in its midst." [63]

Stalin's attack on rotten liberalism was widely distributed throughout the USSR and repeated and elaborated by Party pamphleteers. It is perhaps in this statement that one finds for the first time the overt recognition of a monolithic dictatorship over intellectual and political life. In essence, Stalin was saying that certain theories of Bolshevism were above and beyond criticism, because such criticism endangered the foundations of the regime.

While it is not possible to put a finger on any specific date for the adoption of this viewpoint in official circles, by its adoption the Communist Party crossed a great divide. Despite his dogmatism and intransigence, Lenin had permitted direct criticism of his major assumptions by his Party colleagues. Both Lenin and Stalin, as well as other Party leaders, had admitted their mistakes on several public occasions. But now Party doctrine, formulated by a very small elite, was to be regarded as above and beyond criticism. Likewise, the leaders were above and beyond criticism by ordinary mortals. In time the conception of Stalin as an infallible leader emerged.

The question is often raised whether the authoritarian elements of Bolshevism were inherent in the original tradition of Leninism. Quite frequently the question is answered in the affirmative. Those who do not answer with an unqualified affirmative sometimes draw attention to Stalin's personality as the key factor in the growth of the authoritarian system. Granted that the tradition of Leninism provided a significant starting point, the preceding chapters have missed their mark if they have not drawn attention to the existence and role of an anti-authoritarian tradition in Communist circles, as well as the significance of political and economic conditions in the transformation of this tradition in the service of authoritarian ends.

8

The Mythology of Status and the New Bureaucracy

Early fumblings

Just before the assumption of political responsibility by the Bolsheviks, Lenin expressed the opinion that modern capitalism had so greatly simplified the functions of management and control in modern society that they could be performed at workmen's wages by any literate file clerk. All that was necessary was some variety of political control by the workers over this relatively simple machinery. Armed with these ideas the Bolsheviks took over the sprawling colossus of prostrate Russia.

Before the November *coup d'état* Lenin had been in favor of planning and centralized political control over the economic processes, though he did not consider in detail how this political control would be achieved beyond references to the effect that the soviets would take care of all such matters. When the time came to put these ideas into practice, political circumstances were such that for the moment centralized control or planning was out of the question.

Instead, the factories were turned over to the workers to manage as best they could under the famous decree on Workers' Control. In effect, the decree meant little more than an official blessing for the workers' attempts to take power in various cities, a movement the Bolsheviks could hardly afford to discourage at the time. According to its provisions, drafted by Lenin himself, general elections should be held in each plant over a certain size to determine who was to represent the workers and manage the plant. These representatives were to be given access to all the books and documents of the plant. Their decisions, subject to rather vague control from the higher Soviet authorities and the trade unions, were to be obligatory upon the owners of the enterprises.[1]

About 40 per cent of the factories in the area of Russia controlled by the Bolsheviks were affected by the system of workers' control.[2] Where the factory representatives did assume control and continue production, the workers proceeded to promote the interests of their own factory with little or no regard to the interests of the community or the state. The role of the state was reduced practically to that of paying subsidies. One careful student of the movement has concluded that these first months after the November Revolution constituted a time—and the only time —when a real dictatorship of the real workers existed. In this case, however, the power of the workers, as this writer points out, rested basically upon the temporary impotence of the state.[3] By the beginning of 1918 the experiment was at an end and the plant committees reduced to organs of the trade unions within the factory, with functions that had little, if anything, to do with the control of production.[4]

The experiment in workers' control resembles other applications of the more naïve versions of equalitarianism in the first months following the Revolution. When Trotsky took over the Tsarist Ministry of Foreign Affairs to transform it into the Bolshevik People's Commissariat, he is reported to have called together those willing to work with the new organization and announced, "Comrades, don't forget, everybody from commissar to watchman is equal now! 'Your worship' [the old term for addressing superiors] doesn't exist any more." [5] Ivan Maisky, who later became ambassador to England, reports that the Commissariat was organized on a democratic basis, and that the employees tried to form a collective to govern the foreign policy of the new workers' state. Machine guns were placed in strategic corners of the corridors of the former Ministry Building, while the vice-commissar always wore a large pistol in his belt, much to the discomfort of visiting diplomats. Occasionally, diplomatic conversations were carried on above the sound of machine-gun fire from the guards who practiced their weapons to while away the tedium of their jobs.[6] Nevertheless, concern with status and protocol asserted itself almost at once. The French mission consistently refused to use the word "People's" Commissariat in papers addressed to this office. In turn, the Soviet officers refused to accept the incorrectly addressed French communications and always returned them to their sender.[7]

Not all the early thinking and acting of the Bolsheviks displayed this somewhat utopian equalitarianism even at this date. Bukharin, for one, faced the problem of status differential squarely and recognized the need for a division of labor in society between those who make decisions and those who carry them out. In the course of a general analysis of the economic problems involved in the transition to a workers' state, he observed:

Here before all the entire sum of the newly arising production relationships must receive theoretical consideration. For there arises here a question of basic significance: *how is an entirely different combination of persons and elements of production possible, if the logic of the production process itself brings forth relationships of a specific type?* An engineer or a technician must of course give orders to the workers, and must therefore stand *over* them. In exactly the same way must the former officer in the Red Army stand *over* the common soldier. Here as there an inner, purely technical, objective logic is involved, which must remain in any given social order. How should this dilemma be solved? [8]

Bukharin's attempted solution to this dilemma followed Lenin's general line of reasoning, which provided the rationale for numerous subsequent attempts to "solve" the problem of bureaucracy in the Soviet state. Bukharin argued that the technical intelligentsia and others who performed the social function of administration and control in capitalist society would continue to hold the same relative position in the new society. On the other hand, they would no longer be engaged in extracting surplus value from the workers. Instead, they would be engaged in extracting a "surplus product," that is, in aiding the new society to accumulate capital, replace worn-out equipment, and build new equipment. Bukharin did not go into the question of whether

the rank-and-file workers would gain any material and psychological satisfactions from such a finespun distinction.

At the same time, his solution was not limited to the transition from surplus value to surplus product. While the administrator and technician would still retain a "middle position" in socialist
society, as he had in capitalist society, he would now be subordinate to the proletariat instead of to the capitalists. The proletariat,
organized in the Communist Party, the soviets, trade unions, and
other economic and political forms, would under the new situation give orders to the administrators.[9] Furthermore, in the course
of time the psychological viewpoint of the technician engineer
and administrator would change because of the change from a
capitalist to a socialist milieu in which these individuals func-
tioned. Finally, the technical intelligentsia would lose its caste-
like character insofar as new individuals rose into this group
from the ranks of the proletariat.[10] At a later date all of these
arguments formed part of the stock-in-trade of the Communist
leadership and were used to justify inequalities in power and
prestige that emerged with the development of the Soviet system.

Lenin himself was quick to realize the problem created by
the absence of skills and immediately ceased to talk about the
operation of the state as something any literate file clerk could
perform. Instead, in his report to the Eighth Congress of the
Party (1919), he spoke of how the "incredible burden of admin-
istering the country" had fallen on such an insignificant number
of individuals. The number was so small, he added, because
there were so few educated, and capable, political leaders in
Russia.[11] The more plausible portions of the old idea were retained. Russia's administrative difficulties were blamed by Lenin
and the Party on her general cultural backwardness, with the
implication that these difficulties would disappear when the international revolution came to Russia's aid from the civilized
countries of Western Europe, or when Russia overcame them
through her own efforts. Without doubt Lenin and his followers
were at least partly correct in their emphasis on the low level
of education in a peasant country as a major source of their difficulties.

Though the Communist Party could not at first provide administrative skills, it could provide what was more important—men of proven political reliability. Thus the Bolsheviks soon came to fill the key posts in political and economic affairs. By the time of the New Economic Policy, however, the top Party leadership had realized that good revolutionaries do not necessarily make good administrators. In his report to the Eleventh Party Congress in 1922, the last one he attended, Lenin concluded with his usual candor, "We must not be afraid to admit, that in ninety-nine cases out of a hundred the responsible Communists are not in the jobs they are now fit for, that they are unable to perform their duties, and that they must sit down to learn them." [12] The reason was, according to Lenin, that responsible Communists who had acquitted themselves splendidly during the Revolution had been put to commercial and industrial work about which they knew nothing, while "rogues and swindlers hide behind their backs." [13]

In the absence of an adequate skill group, the old Tsarist bureaucracy managed to hang on to a surprising extent. A valuable Soviet account published in 1932 reveals that in some sections of the bureaucracy as high as 50 per cent of the personnel were former Tsarist officials.[14] Instances were likewise uncovered about this time of the patterning of Soviet administrative decrees on Tsarist models.[15] This situation prevailed in spite of fairly intensive efforts to replace the old Tsarist bureaucracy with workers and peasants and to build up a new Soviet intelligentsia, efforts that before the Stalinist regime evidently enjoyed only limited success in limited fields, despite earlier claims to the contrary.[16] In addition, the Bolsheviks in the beginning drew fairly heavily for scientific and technical skills on the prerevolutionary intelligentsia, though important elements in the Party were strongly opposed to pampering the specialists or *spets,* as they were usually called. Lenin was frequently forced to intervene on their behalf. Probaby one reason that made it possible to use these individuals was that a considerable section of the intelligentsia had been opposed to the old regime and was aware of its inefficiencies.

Figures on the total size of the Soviet bureaucracy prior to the Stalinist regime are not easy to find. In 1925 Molotov revealed in his report to the Fourteenth Party Congress that there had been a 10 per cent increase in the government personnel, which then numbered 1,850,000 persons.[17] In 1926, according to the *Large Soviet Encyclopedia,* the bureaucracy of the entire soviet apparatus included 2,500,000 people.[18] For a regime which had come to power on the program of destroying bureaucracy, and which continued to give lip service to this idea into the early 1930's, this was a sizable figure.

Decision-making: inequalities of power

Under the conditions of the Civil War various conceptions of democratic management of industry, of which workers' control had been merely an extreme manifestation, had to give way in practice to a bureaucratic management, exercised through special officials. Returning the factories to their owners was, of course, out of the question for political and military reasons; [19] nevertheless, about one fifth of them, particularly those concerned with war industries, continued during the first months of the new regime to work under their old ownership and management.[20]

By about 1919 the prevailing practice in management consisted of collegiums or boards composed of two-thirds workers and one-third engineers or technicians approved by the trade union.[21] Even this diffusion of responsibility led to enormous difficulties. According to Soviet authors, during the period of War Communism the transition from a system of broad representative collegiums to a system of small workers' collectives or even individual responsibility and one-man management made considerable headway.[22] By 1920, 85 per cent of the enterprises in the new regime were controlled by individual managers,[23] though the powers of these managers were still weak and subject to marked interference by other organs representing the interests of the workers or the state.

During 1920 there was considerable discussion in high Party circles concerning the problems of democratic management. The trade-union leader, M. Tomsky, and members of the Workers' Opposition defended collegial management as the only method capable of achieving broad mass participation in the management of industry. They asserted that one-man management was not up to handling the complex problems of the day.[24] Other arguments adduced in support of collegial management asserted that it provided the only way through which the proletariat could learn to take over real control of the country.

Lenin repudiated these views in blunt language. He told the Ninth Party Congress in the spring of 1920, "You cannot escape . . . by declaring that corporate management is a school of government . . . You cannot stay forever in the preparatory class of a school. That will not do. We are now grown up, and we shall be beaten and beaten again in every field, if we behave like school children." [25]

The sharpness of this repudiation is striking. Quite frequently Communist ideals that could not be achieved at the time were put into cold storage to be realized at some distant and undefined future. An example of this type is the "withering away of the state." But in the case of the specific institutional form of collegial management, Lenin refused to regard it even as a goal. Instead, he spoke of it as something embryonic, essential only in the first stage of construction when it was necessary to build anew. But in the transition to practical work, one-man management, he asserted, made the best use of human skills.[26]

The Congress did not go as far as Lenin in the repudiation of the collegial principle. It adopted instead a compromise resolution, declaring that although the collegial principle had a place in the process of reaching decisions, it should without question give place to individual responsibility in the execution of decisions.[27]

The conflict between collectivist and individual conceptions continued for many years afterward. The official line swung back and forth between two extremes. In general, the collegial principle was more widely retained in the upper branches of the government, where matters of policy were considered, while the principle of individual responsibility was increasingly applied at the level of factory management, where the situation involved more the execution than the formulation of policy.[28]

Both the conceptions and the practice of democratic administration were further modified through the gradual elimination of the influence of the trade unions in matters directly associated with the management of the economy. The initiative in this movement came from the top ranks of the trade-union bureaucracy, which was closely connected with the Party. In the spring of 1920 Tomsky declared that the trade unions should not interfere directly in the problems of management. It was sufficient, he stated, that the unions were represented in the economic organs of the state and participated in the problems of management through these organs.[29] This move may well have been an effort on the part of the trade-union leaders to strengthen their position vis-à-vis their followers. The Ninth Congress of the Party in the same year gave the *coup de grâce* to the doctrines and institutions of workers' control by declaring that the factory committees should not interfere in management.[30] The blow was partly softened by the Party declaration that the unions should concentrate on the task of preparing officer cadres for industry from among the workers by means of professional and technical education.[31]

Two years later the Eleventh Party Congress repeated this formula in even stronger terms, declaring that any immediate interference of the unions in the management of the factory must be considered without qualification harmful and impermissible.[32] Early in the same year (1922), the Trade Unions Congress declared that the unions must give up the principle of equal rights in the naming of industrial managers and other officials concerned with economic administration. In this fashion most of the power over the selection of industrial leadership, as well as over the latter's day-to-day decisions, was taken away from the unions and turned over to the organs of economic administration. For the remainder of the NEP period the Communists kept to this arrangement.[33]

One aspect of the pattern of collective decision-making, which gave the unions a certain limited power in the administration of

he factory, remained in force until well into the thirties. This
vas the so-called "triangle," composed of the plant manager, the
rade-union organization or workers' plant committee, and the
'arty cell within the plant. A struggle for power among these
hree elements took place all during the twenties. According to
ioviet sources, the plant management frequently censored the
vall newspaper of the workers, the Party cell tried to decide
[uestions of a purely business nature, and the trade-union group
vould do the same thing, forgetting all about its tasks as a union
rganization.[34]

In September of 1929 a Party decree attempted to set up a
ystem of one-man management in the factory, which, though
ieither the first nor the last decision of its kind, may be regarded
s official recognition that the triangle arrangement was unsatis-
actory. Subsequently complaints continued to the effect that au-
hority and responsibility were still divided. It was not until 1937
hat a top Party officer, Zhdanov, could declare that the triangle
iad no more justification for existing.[35]

During the NEP there was a definite conflict between the
equirements of efficiency, or what Bukharin had called the logic
if the production process, and the goals of the Communist Party.
'reobrazhensky put his finger on the difficulty, pointing out that
mder the NEP, in which government and private industry com-
ieted to a considerable extent, the socialist managers who were
ble to operate their plants with the greatest possible profit might
iot be the ones who were doing the Party and the working class
he most good on a long-run basis.[36] Since labor conditions were
requently better in the privately owned and managed plants than
n those operated by the regime, the situation contained a threat
o the Party's leadership of the industrial workers.

In addition, certain circles in business administration began
o express ideas similar to the conservative American view of
more business in government and less government in business."
These groups gathered around Krassin, an old Bolshevik with
onsiderable business experience from prerevolutionary times.
Though Krassin denied some of the ideas attributed to him, he
tressed the need for good Party administrators, organizers, and

managers in the course of sharp debates on this question at the Twelfth Party Congress.[37] About this time he is said to have complained that the top Party leaders were the same as they had been two decades previously, "newspaper dilettantes and litterateurs," who interfered in the choice of business personnel without knowing anything about the subject.[38]

Not all the directors sought power, of course. Some found it more advantageous to avoid responsibility, taking advantage of the triangle or other similar institutions, in the hope of escaping direct accountability for decisions that might involve disastrous personal consequences.[39] Nevertheless, the problem continued to cause difficulties down to the beginning of the Five Year Plans. As late as 1929 one of the Party leaders brought up at a Party Conference the case of a prominent trust director with a good reputation for efficiency who complained of "too much control— the Workers' and Peasants' Inspection and the unions get in the way." [40]

Until the complete change of policy involved in the rapid industrialization and extension of Party control under the Five Year Plans, there was very little the Party could do about this situation. On the whole, it endeavored to solve the dilemma during the NEP by strengthening the power of the managers and backing them up with the weapon of high-policy declarations. In defining the duties and functions of the director, the Party declared that his main job was to increase the productivity of labor, lower the cost of production, and increase the quantity of material goods available for the workers' government.[41] In 1924 the Party declared that the local Party leaders must give the managers full support and must not permit them to be disturbed by minor distractions.[42] Furthermore, the Party during this time gradually managed to create its own managerial group. Some interesting figures on this point were presented by Kaganovich at the Sixteenth Party Congress in 1930.[43] He reported, on the basis of sample of about 1300 factory directors, that 29 per cent of the directors were Party members in 1923, 48 per cent in 1924, and 9 per cent in 1929. In this way the factory directors obtained status not only as administrators, but also as Party members. From 192

nward the state extended its control over all sectors of the econ-
my, eliminating the problem of competition with private indus-
ry. By these devices many of the difficulties produced by the
bjective necessity for status differentials and the goals of Communist policy were solved.

Role of the equalitarian myth in the execution of decisions

It is a commonplace observation that making policy is much
asier than executing it. Most organized human groupings, and
articularly such large ones as the modern state, have had to
volve methods for coping with this problem. They have devel-
ped a wide variety of formal and informal techniques for seeing
) it that the decisions made by those in authority are at least
artly carried out by those subject to authority.

In a socialist society these difficulties tend to be more severe
han they do in a free-enterprise system. Under a capitalist regime
he decisions about what goods should be produced, and how
abor, plant, and raw materials should be efficiently combined
) produce them, are largely left to the individual producer, who
uides himself by the indexes of cost and selling price. On the
ther hand, a socialist economy must control deliberately and
onsciously this range of decisions, instead of leaving them to the
ree play of market forces. In the latter situation the checks of
onsumer resistance and the spurs of consumer demand play a
much less significant role.

As an excellent English economic historian of the Soviet re-
ime has pointed out, the Soviet administrative problem was
normously magnified from the very beginning by the disap-
earance of market price as an indicator of what to produce,
nd in what quantities. For a time military needs took the place
f market price. Certain war industries were selected for shock
reatment while other subordinate plants were neglected. When
he Civil War ended, and military needs no longer were the major
riterion for production and consumption, the system broke down.
t had to be replaced by the semi-market economy of the NEP.[44]

Furthermore, a state dominated by a single political party
acks many of the devices for checking up on the execution of

decisions that are found in states with competing political par
ties. In a state with the latter type of political organization, the
party that is temporarily in power can be sure that its opponent
will be on the lookout for any signs of incompetence in the exe
cution of policy.

The preceding observations do not imply that a socialist or a
one-party state is necessarily less efficient in the utilization o
human and material resources than a multi-party and capitalis
state. Too, the proposition is yet to be proved that a socialis
state is necessarily a totalitarian state, even though definite pres
sures in this direction must be recognized. The point to be made
is that for a number of reasons the Soviet regime faced an extraor
dinarily difficult problem in developing adequate techniques fo
verifying the execution of policy decisions. As one illustration
among many of the scope of the problem, an administrative
house cleaning in the Gosplan in March 1931 uncovered 190
unfulfilled orders issued by the government, some of which were
almost three years old.[45] These problems were not only the prod
uct of the new social system the Soviets were endeavoring to
establish. They were also the product of history and the cultura
traditions of Russia, which did not include the precise and punc
tual execution of bureaucratic orders.

On the whole, the problem of execution has been met by set
ting one part of the bureaucracy to watch another part. Quite a
number of different organizations have been established at vari
ous times for this specific purpose. For a while this was the chie
purported function of the Workers' and Peasants' Inspection. The
Party Control Commissions, and particularly the Central Con
trol Commission, described in Chapter 6, fulfilled a number o
functions of checking up on the execution of decisions. Afte
1930 these mechanisms were overhauled and extended with re
sults that will be considered later.[46]

Perhaps the most important role in the task of verifying th
execution of major policy decisions has fallen to the secret police
Despite the lack of quantitative data, Simon Liberman's mem
oirs [47] and other sources show that the secret police expande
rapidly into the economic field in the search for sabotage. Th

distinctions among deliberate sabotage, administrative incompetence, and reaction to hostile local pressures are difficult enough to draw in any case, and it was not to be expected that the secret police would be overly meticulous in drawing them.

Under such pressures administrative errors tended to become not only criminal offenses but also, under the watchful eye of the Party, to partake of the nature of counterrevolutionary sin. The resulting stifling of initiative and high degree of insecurity on the part of administrative officials have been dramatized in a number of accounts by individuals who have turned against the regime and fled. The extent to which this factor has affected efficiency cannot be measured, though it is unquestionably important.

Partly because the major way of verifying administrative performance lay in the creation of competing bureaucratic elements, the Soviet bureaucracy prior to the Stalinist regime did not develop into a homogeneous unit. There were a number of intense struggles between various sections of the bureaucracy, some of which were conducted mainly behind the scenes. At various times the Red Army showed signs of restiveness and tended to become an independent sector of the bureaucracy, despite the efforts of the Party to keep it under control. Likewise, many of the internecine Party struggles were reflected in the Army.[48] Between 1928 and 1930 the trade-union leadership opposed Stalin's policies associated with rapid industrialization. Stalin was compelled to turn nearly all the top leaders out of office and replace them with his own supporters. The Party itself during this period was not a homogeneous group and was rent by serious divergencies over matters of major policy prior to Stalin's accession to power.

Soon after the establishment of the Bolshevik regime, various sections of the bureaucracy had begun to create defenses against the attacks on it that derived from competition among elements in the administrative structure and from the specifically Soviet situation under which administrative errors became counterrevolutionary sins. In Trotsky's complaints of 1922 one learns about the growth of bureaucracy in the Party and state institutions, the combination of the two apparatus, and the practice of mutual shielding among the influential groups around the Party secretaries.[49] Widespread bribery, of which Lenin complained in 1921,[50] was also a device by which the clash between unpopular policies and popular opposition was softened and mitigated. In other cultures bribery and political corruption frequently arise to soften the conflicts between two or more irreconcilable groups or sets of social demands—witness the prohibition era in the United States. The continuity of all these problems is revealed by the complaints of a high Party official in 1929 concerning the lack of individual responsibility and the practice of mutual shielding of all administrative workers, with the result that every paper was countersigned by so many people it was impossible to trace who was responsible for any decision. Furthermore, the strong opposition of the villages to the socialist offensive of collectivization resulted in numerous instances, he stated, of agreements between Party and state officials with "representatives of the class enemy." In many cases under this pressure, the same source reports, important local leaders had joined forces with the class enemy.[51]

To increase the participation of the masses in the work of administration was almost the only way that occurred to the Bolsheviks in their attempts to cure these and other "distortions" of the bureaucratic apparatus. It is worth noting at this point the divergence between what the leaders thought they were doing in their efforts to increase mass participation and the actual results. As has been seen, the "real" way in which the problem of bureaucracy was met was in large part the setting of one section of the bureaucracy to watch another section, a divide-and-rule policy. There does not seem to be any overt recognition by the Bolshevik leaders prior to 1932 that this was their actual policy.

The emphasis on mass participation is well illustrated by the article on bureaucracy in the *Large Soviet Encyclopedia*. The author asserts that the Soviet system of government, based on attracting the toilers into the work of the government, eliminates the possibility of the development of bureaucracy in the form created by every bourgeois government. But, the writer continues, the danger of bureaucratic distortion was remarked at the very beginning of the organization of the Soviet government. There follows, in a quarter column of fine print, a list of the various

Party decrees and other official actions related to the attempt to increase mass participation in government and to eliminate bureaucracy.[52]

Lenin strongly advocated in 1920 that all workers—men, and particularly women—should participate in the Workers' and Peasants' Inspection in rotation, and that even illiterate peasants should do what they could.[53] A few years later Trotsky began in earnest his diatribes against the bureaucratic degeneration of the workers' state, a theme that he emphasized from that time onward. But even Trotsky's cure repeated the same formula of increased participation of the workers, of the youth, and so forth.[54] Again in 1928 the Party declared that the working class runs into the "worst bureaucratization of its government apparatus," referring to its size, indirectness, and red tape. These difficulties were attributed to the heritage of the past, "the absence of culture among the masses, their inadequate ability to rule, and the inadequately rapid bringing of the masses into the task of managing the government and the government economy." [55] Similarly, at the Sixteenth Party Conference in 1929, one of the Party officers, in a long speech devoted to the problems of Soviet bureaucracy, declared that the struggle against bureaucracy could only succeed if the masses were "raised up against it." [56]

In their efforts to increase mass participation, the Bolsheviks hit upon several devices. For instance, the visits of a collegium of a commissariat to a factory to listen to the complaints and criticisms of the workers is described in a Soviet study as one of the most deep-rooted ways of attracting the masses into the act of governing.[57] Another method, which evidently sprang up in the early thirties and then was permitted to die a natural death, was called "patronage" (*sheftsvo*), usually the patronage of a specific factory or of a specific group of workers over some section of the administration. Similar forms of patronage were occasionally applied to rural areas. The workers were charged with overseeing the operations of a portion of the bureaucracy and pledged themselves to increase efficiency and eliminate red tape.[58] This form of control, however, evidently showed a tendency to develop into mere festive occasions at which formal patronage agreements or contracts were signed but which did not bring real results. In addition, the bureaucracy tended to protect itself by turning the arrangement into one of mutual verification and control, a development strongly condemned by the Party.[59]

In all of these efforts to increase the importance of the masses and to bring about some form of control from below, certain practical results of the Leninist ideal may be observed. By creating an atmosphere aptly termed an "open season on bureaucrats," the Party managed to deflect against the bureaucrats a great deal of mass hostility that might otherwise have been directed against the policies of the Party. At the same time, this procedure helped to prevent the consolidation of any section of the bureaucracy into a self-contained group that might form the basis of organized opposition to the top Party leadership. In this way the equalitarian traditions of revolutionary Marxism were of use in consolidating the hegemony of the Party leaders. A similar phenomenon has already been pointed out in connection with the soviets, where the conceptions of democratic control from below were used to eliminate from the soviets the various groups that sympathized at one time or another with opposition elements in the Communist Party.

Together with the force of tradition, the political advantages of the conception of mass participation in the work of the bureaucracy may help to explain why these views were so rarely challenged. In a wide though by no means complete survey of Soviet writings on bureaucracy, I have found only very few occasions on which this view was questioned. In 1920 Lenin, in one of his fits of impatience with the Party intellectuals, remarked acridly that there was too much theorizing on the idea of insuring "the participation of the masses by a collegium of seven or three people." [60] Again in 1928, in the course of one of the campaigns to simplify the bureaucracy, one writer, a local judge, challenged the entire Communist conception of bureaucracy. He pointed out that cheap administration is not always the same as good. In industry the work of a well-trained specialist is paid at a higher rate than that of a rank-and-file beginner. Therefore, the writer continued, it is not desirable for the state to replace qualified specialists with any worker that comes along. Bureaucracy, he observed, must be adapted in the best possible way to the function it is expected to perform. The simplest way may not necessarily be the best. The best cream separator, he remarked sarcastically, is not necessarily the simplest one—after all, one can separate cream from milk with a fork—but the best is one that gives the largest amount of cream in the cleanest and most efficient fashion.[61]

In addition to stressing the importance of mass participation as a cure for the evils of bureaucracy, the official ideology continued to emphasize the elimination of status differentials as a goal of Soviet bureaucracy. Kalinin in 1928 repeated the slogan attributed to Lenin that every cook should be able to run the government. For this purpose the process of governing must be greatly simplified, and the cultural level of the masses raised.[62] In 1930 a Party resolution on the patronage of factories over the soviet apparatus described this movement as a step in the direction of Lenin's goal of the execution of government functions by the workers without pay.[63] Again, in 1932, the fulfillment of Lenin's will concerning the unpaid performance of government duties was described by prominent Soviet writers as having been raised to a "new and higher level." They also declared that the struggle for this goal remained an important task in the Second Five Year Plan.[64]

On a few occasions the need for status differentials broke through the official ideology and received overt recognition from the Party leaders. Although these differentials emerged rapidly in practice, the official view was rarely challenged. Lenin's defense of the bourgeois specialists was regarded as a purely temporary measure until the workers could take care of matters themselves. In 1923, however, Lenin did suggest that the core of the Workers' and Peasants' Inspection should be a group of "highly skilled, specially tested, specially reliable, and highly paid" employees.[65] In the same year Stalin confessed that pre-revolutionary notions about the creation of a commune or association of workers without a bureaucracy was an ideal that would have to be postponed until a high level of culture in Russia and absolute peace in the world at large prevailed. In the meantime, he concluded, "Our government apparatus is bureaucratic, and will be bureaucratic for a long time." [66] Occasional comments of the type just quoted reflect the pressure of political realities and the objective need for a system of status and authority. At first glance it is surprising that these comments are so few, and that the equalitarian views of Leninism in regard to bureaucracy and the administrative process maintained themselves into the thirties with relatively little change. The continuation of these doctrines can, however, be explained by the services they performed in strengthening the position of the top leaders of the regime.

The doctrine of no class struggle

The absence in prerevolutionary Marxist-Leninist tradition of any conception that there could be a conflict of interest between management and the labor force in a workers' state played an important role in the development of both the theory and practice of post-revolutionary status relationships.

While even the most theoretically inclined Bolsheviks were quick to realize the need for "proletarian labor discipline" after the November Revolution, [67] they did not draw the implication that discipline reflects some form of conflict of interests between the discipliners and the disciplined.

In the beginning Lenin attributed the inescapably visible conflicts of interest to the chaotic conditions of the day, regarding them as remnants of a psychological attitude that had been built up in the workers under capitalism. In this analysis he was no doubt at least partly correct. Within a few weeks of the seizure of power, he pointed out that the Party would have to fight the old notions of the workers, "the habit of shirking burdens, of trying to get as much as possible out of the *bourgeoisie*" that were being carried over into the new situation. The newcomers who entered into factory life during the war, he complained, were especially bad in this respect: they "want to treat the *people's* factory, the factory that has come into the possession of the people, in the old way, with the sole end in view of 'making' as much as possible and clearing out." [68] Again, in 1919, he was suspicious of the proposal that the functions of the government and the trade unions should be merged, on the same grounds as those just mentioned. If the unions took over the functions of government, he observed, a mess would result. Too much of the old "petty-bourgeois" tradition, "every man for himself and God alone for everybody," remained in the psychology of the workers. The trade unions, he added sharply, would think that God alone takes care of the management.[69] A year later, at the Ninth Party Congress, he complained that not everybody realized the change that had taken place since the trade unions had passed from the old stage, when they were organs of resistance to the oppressors of labor, to the new stage, when the working class had become the governing class.[70]

At an early date signs accumulated that the conflict of interests between the industrial workers and the management, or the Soviet government—the two were synonymous at the higher administrative levels even then—was a very real one. At the Second Congress of Trade Unions, held between January 16 and January 25, 1919, the Mensheviks introduced the following resolution: "The Trade Unions cannot regard the Soviet power as representing the interests of the working class, as the embodiment of its dictatorship, as the Soviet power bases itself on the repression of the independence of the workers, on the use of force against the expression of their will." Since the Congress was dominated by the Bolsheviks (449 Bolsheviks out of 648 delegates), it is not surprising that the Menshevik resolution received only thirty votes.[71] Since the Mensheviks, at least before the Revolution, had a much wider base than the Bolsheviks among the Russian working class, it is probable that this resolution reflects a fairly widespread discontent in the Russian working class with the new conditions. Within the Bolshevik ranks themselves this discontent appeared in the Left Wing Opposition of 1918 and the Trade Union and Workers' Opposition of 1920 and 1921, both of which groups were easily defeated by the Party majority.

For the time being, the Bolsheviks' majority was content merely to deny the existence of the problem, which according to Marxist-Leninist ideology ought not to exist. In other words, their

traditions tended to screen out of their consciousness any awareness of the problem. At the Ninth Congress of the Party in March
and April of 1920, the Party declared: "As it is the dictatorship
of the proletariat, the Soviet government is the lever for the transformation of the economy. Therefore there cannot be any question of a conflict of interests between the organs of the trade
unions and the organs of Soviet power." [72]

During the period of War Communism a similar line of
thought was elaborated by Trotsky to justify the military discipline applied to the industrial workers. To the Third Congress of
Trade Unions he announced, on April 9, 1920, that the unions did
not have the task of fighting against the government in the interests of labor. Instead, they ought to coöperate with the government in the task of constructing a socialist economy.[73] He attacked
the Mensheviks for circulating the idea that compulsory labor was
inefficient. "If that is true, then the entire socialist economy is
destined to crash, for there can be no other road to socialism except the compulsory distribution of the entire labor force of the
country by the central economic authority, which will distribute
this force according to the needs of an over-all government
economic plan." [74] This and other statements by Trotsky at this
point foreshadow clearly what took place in 1929 and 1930 when
industrialization and planning were begun in earnest. In 1920 he
argued that a military approach to the problem was essential. The
free movement of workers from job to job could not be permitted.
Instead, the militarization of labor was necessary, in which the
unions should help in allocating workers to their posts.[75] To the
Menshevik accusation that this was Egyptian slavery, Trotsky
replied that the Egyptian peasants did not decide through their
soviets to build the pyramids.[76]

Following the same line of thought in October 1920, he refused to admit that the trade unions and the government could
have conflicting interests. He declared that it was meaningless
to talk about protecting the worker against the government in a
proletarian state. On the basis of his experiences with the army
and in the reorganization of the transport system, he demanded a
"shaking up of the unions" to wrench them away from their tradi-

tion of antagonism to the management, and the introduction of quasi-military discipline, by merging the top levels of the unions and the government.[77] Trotsky's declaration set off a general discussion that was the prelude to the NEP.

For the time being Trotsky's views formed a high-water mark in the development of the theory that there could be no conflict of interests between the workers and those in authority. At a later date Stalin and his followers were to return to this doctrine for guidance and support in the reorganization of labor relations that accompanied the Five Year Plans. These earlier views, including Trotsky's, are now the official doctrine of the Soviet State and are incorporated in legal texts on Soviet labor law.

At the time, however, Lenin came out with a sharp attack against Trotsky's assertions. In an exchange of polemics with both Trotsky and Bukharin, he denied that Russia had as yet achieved a workers' state. He emphasized the transitional nature of the regime and the overwhelming importance of the peasantry, to whom he shortly afterward granted far-reaching concessions. The present Soviet state, he remarked, was a workers' and peasants' state, with bureaucratic distortions. Under such conditions, he said, "we must utilise these workers' organisations for the purpose of protecting the workers from their own state and in order that the workers may protect our state."[78] In this same speech he developed the famous theory of the trade unions as "transmission belts" for passing along to the backward Russian masses, including the more backward (from the Bolshevik point of view) sections of the working class, the ideology of its more advanced sections, particularly the Communist Party. In this fashion he hoped to overcome gradually the older exploitative attitudes of the workers and to teach them that their welfare depended upon increased production. In addition, he expected to show them that it was in their own interest to protect the Soviet state. While Lenin did not go so far as to advocate a plural state composed of competing interest groups—in fact, he hinted at the eventual disappearance of the trade unions in the distant future—he recognized directly both the conflict and identity of interests between the workers and those in authority.[79]

Although the Tenth Party Congress of 1921, immediately following the discussion on trade-union matters, adopted a long resolution on the trade-union question which followed out the lines of thinking adopted by Lenin, the Party was apparently not yet quite ready for a programmatic recognition of the conflict of interests so clearly perceived by Lenin. Such a recognition was achieved only a year later at the Eleventh Party Congress in March 1922. On this occasion the Party announced that under the new conditions of freedom of trade, inaugurated by the NEP, together with the increased requirements for a higher productivity of labor, there had arisen a "definite conflict of interests on questions concerning the conditions of labor in the factory between the toiling masses and the directors in charge of government establishments." [80]

The recognition of a conflict of interests between workers and management implies an equal recognition of the right of the workers to defend their interests by appropriate means, such as the strike. During the NEP this was a very difficult point for the Communists, who were unwilling either to prohibit strikes or to recognize them. To prohibit them probably would have been a severe psychological blow to the Party's chief supporters, who had, in NEP days, enough other reasons to ask, "Is this what we made a revolution for?" The possibility of an outright prohibition received some consideration at the highest level in the Party. In the course of the trade-union discussion preceding the Eleventh Party Congress of 1922, Miliutin, a member of the Party Central Committee, asked for and suggested to Lenin a categorical prohibition on strikes in government industries. His proposal was not upheld either by the preparatory commission of the Congress or by the Congress itself. [81]

Lenin tried to tread a thin line between opposing pressures on this question. Under capitalism, he said in 1922, the object of a strike is the overthrow of the government in power. Under the workers' government, on the other hand, the task of the trade union must be the reconciliation of conflicts with a maximum of advantages for the workers. [82]

The Eleventh Party Congress adopted an equally evasive

formula. According to its pronouncement, the resort to a strike in a state with a proletarian government in power could be justified only on the grounds of the "bureaucratic distortions" of the proletarian government on the one side and lack of political development and cultural backwardness of the toiling masses on the other.[83]

With the onset of large-scale industrialization in 1929 and 1930, the limited beginnings in the direction of a pluralistic society were brought to an abrupt halt. The workers were called upon to make tremendous sacrifices in this campaign, and were compelled by the Party to give up nearly all the independent representation of their interests that they had achieved to date through the trade unions. In return, the Party promised an improvement in their living conditions. Before the Sixteenth Congress of the Party (June 1930), almost the entire leadership of the All-Union Council of Trade Unions was removed and replaced by men willing to support Stalin's program of greatly increased labor productivity. There was practically no pretense that such an action by the Party Central Committee was in accord with Soviet conceptions of democracy. Kaganovich dismissed such objections bluntly, declaring, "One might say that this [action] is a violation of proletarian democracy, but, comrades, it has long been known that for us Bolsheviks democracy is not a fetish; for us, proletarian democracy is a means for arming the working class for the better execution of its socialist tasks."[84] This "shaking up" changed not only the leadership of the All-Union Council of Trade Unions, but also the central committees of the various constituent unions. In some cases, still lower officers were removed from their posts.[85]

The old trade-union leadership, which had been acting more or less in accord with Lenin's precepts of protecting the workers against their own state, was now accused of following the "Menshevik" line of setting the interests of the workers against the interests of the dictatorship of the proletariat.[86] Lenin's recognition of the conflict of interests could no longer be permitted under the conditions of a campaign for the construction of socialism. Instead, the Party returned to the older formula, elaborated in the twenties by Trotsky, that a conflict of interests was out of the question because of the logic of the situation. "Since the workers do not work for the capitalists, but for their own government, their own class," the Sixteenth Party Congress declared, it is therefore to their own advantage to promote the most rapid development of Soviet industry. The Party defined the task of the unions as one of indoctrinating the "broad masses" of the workers with this viewpoint.[87] In 1919 Bukharin had used almost the same words: "The workers do not work now for the capitalist, nor for the money-lender, nor for the banker, but for their own selves. They are doing their *own* work; they are building the building that belongs to the toilers." [88]

In the attempt to resolve the conflict of interests between the workers and the bureaucracy, Soviet official ideology underwent two major changes. One was the return in the late twenties and early thirties to the doctrines that were promulgated during the period of War Communism. While this return was a widespread, though not universal, feature of the times, it is most striking in respect to the doctrine of no class struggle. When faced with a crisis situation, the regime went back to a familiar symbolism. Freudian notions of "regression" need not be called upon to explain this phenomenon, since the political and economic problems faced during War Communism and the years of the Stalinist Revolution were similar in a number of essential respects. In the second place, one may take note of the utilization of the more "idealistic" aspects of the Marxist-Leninist tradition, that is, the doctrine that the workers were the masters of their own fate, to support a highly authoritarian regime.

The repudiation of equality

The prerevolutionary Bolshevik attitude toward inequalities of wealth was an ambivalent and uncertain one. Like Marx before him, Lenin felt that certain inequalities might remain in the early stages as socialism emerged with violent birth pangs from the womb of capitalism. But he had not hesitated to affirm the eventual goal of equality. In general, the feeling was strong among the early Bolsheviks in both prerevolutionary and post-revolutionary days that inequality was somehow wrong and immoral, a temporary evil that would only have to be endured for a time. There was no realization that inequalities might be a permanent social necessity as part of a system of incentives to labor.

The idealistic equalitarian point of view remained strong during the period of War Communism. The first program of the Bolsheviks following the November Revolution, adopted at the Eighth Party Congress in March 1919, proclaimed that among the outstanding tasks of the moment was the ideological and educational work required "to destroy completely all traces of previous inequality or prejudices, especially among the backward strata of the proletariat and the peasantry." [89] In accordance with Lenin's and Marx's earlier writings, the authors of the program acknowledged that equality could not be brought about at once, but chose this propitious moment to reaffirm the goal: "While aspiring to equality of remuneration for all kinds of labor and to total Communism, the Soviet government cannot consider as its immediate task the realization of this equality at the present moment, when only the first steps are being made towards the transition from capitalism to Communism." [90]

During the period of War Communism both doctrinal considerations and the necessities of wartime siege favored equality in the distribution of goods and incomes, even though it was an equality perilously close to the zero point. Inequalities remained in the payment of the *spets* or vital technical personnel, inequalities that many Party leaders regarded as purely temporary concessions. In addition, there was a rough system of priorities in the distribution of consumers' goods to the workers in different industries, as well as to different plants within an industry. But by 1920 rationed goods and services distributed free of charge, which constituted almost the sole income of the wage earner, were distributed equally among the workers of any one enterprise. The use of apartments was free, as were theater and tramway tickets. [91]

Not until the spring of 1920 did it apparently occur to the Communist leaders that equality might result in a loss of production, when production was vital to the survival of the regime. At this time Tomsky, the trade-union leader, declared that the payment of labor ought to depend immediately upon the results of labor.[92] At this time also the Ninth Party Congress went far enough to declare that an incentive system of payments ought to be one of the most powerful means for awakening competition, and even announced that a good worker should be better supplied with the necessities of life than a negligent worker.[93] This line of thinking received a marked impetus with the transition to the NEP and the general overhauling of economic incentives in March 1921. Lenin himself declared in October of the same year that "every important branch of national economy must be built up on the principle of personal incentive." [94]

By the end of the NEP underlying economic factors, together with the Communist retreat from their equalitarian position, had produced a situation in which variations in wage payments did not differ very markedly from corresponding differentials in capitalist countries at a similar stage of economic development. On the basis of careful and detailed study of variations in wage rates, Abram Bergson has concluded that the "capitalist" principles of supply and demand were the fundamental factors determining wage differentials in the Soviet Union during this period. In others words, these differentials depended primarily upon the productivity of different workers.[95] In the month of March 1928 the earnings of workers varied from less than 30 rubles to more than 250 rubles. Six per cent of the wage earners earned less than 30.01 rubles; only 0.2 per cent earned more than 250 rubles. However, the wages of 47.9 per cent of the earners varied between the rather narrow range of 40 to 80 rubles.[96] Though the variation or inequality of wages in the Soviet Union in 1928 was less than had been the case in Russia in 1914, the differences were slight.[97]

Wages are by themselves not a completely accurate index of variations in real income, owing to the number of services provided for the workers by government and civic organizations for the improvement of material and cultural living standards. In the Soviet Union these extra factors are important at all income levels, because of the practice of giving responsible officials houses, the use of automobiles for official purposes, and the like. Furthermore, figures on wages do not cover more than a fraction of the population. Therefore, figures on the distribution of savings, available for 1930, provide a welcome addition to those on wages. Total savings in the hands of the banks in that year amounted to 722 million rubles. They were allegedly distributed in the following proportions:[98]

Workers	91 million
Clerical workers and members of the bureaucracy	205 million
Others (professional men, craftsmen, etc.)	134 million
Individual peasants	46 million
Collective farms and other "juristic persons"	246 million

Even though this information may arouse rather than satisfy curiosity at many points, it is plain that the Soviet system had by this time developed a system of organized social inequality with marked similarities to that in capitalist societies.

In response to forces beyond their control, the equalitarian idealists in the Party were compelled to compromise and rationalize at several points. For example, in 1929 the rule limiting members of the Party to a maximum income was modified to exclude from its limitations several of the major occupations in which it was possible to earn more than the legally defined maximum. It may also be significant that the maximum itself was not indicated in this decree.[99]

Nevertheless, the period of the twenties was not one of complete retreat from the equalitarian position. Latent pressures among the industrial workers helped to keep the tradition alive. It showed some vitality in high Party circles down to the time of Stalin's caustic repudiation in 1931.

Factory workers, particularly those at the lowest paid level, were suffering in 1925 and afterward under the impact of monetary inflation,[100] which gave rise to demands for an upward leveling of wage rates. Likewise, there were objections among the workers to the use of incentive differentials as a whip to increase production. This was particularly strong among small groups of workers in continual face-to-face contact, who objected to what they felt were injustices in differing rates of payment for fairly similar tasks. The situation was exacerbated by the attempts of the Left Opposition to capitalize on this discontent.[101] On this account the Party approved, in November 1926, a rise in wage rates as the "first and an important step in the direction of eliminating the plainly abnormal differences in pay among various categories of workers." [102] Similarly, at the Seventh Congress of Trade Unions in December 1926, Tomsky spoke of the gap between the wages of skilled and unskilled labor, which supposedly violated prevailing conceptions of "elementary class justice," a tribute to the continuing equalitarian tradition. "In the future we must reduce the gap in wages between qualified and ordinary labor," he concluded. Actually, a widespread revision of wage scales, which resulted in some diminution of inequalities, was undertaken at that time under the supervision of the All-Union Central Council of Trade Unions.[103]

These events may be regarded as the last flicker of the equalitarian tradition, at least in official circles—a final effort to achieve equality of rewards for all. Not long after the drive for industrialization, embodied in the First Five Year Plan, had gotten under way, Stalin removed Tomsky from the leadership of the trade unions and specifically repudiated his conception of "elementary class justice."

Speaking in 1931, Stalin pointed out that while the Plan called for an over-all increase of industrial production of 31 to 32 per cent in 1930, the actual increase amounted to only 25 per cent.[104] In the key industries of coal mining, iron, and steel, the increase was only from 6 to 10 per cent.[105] Obviously, the objectives of the Communist leadership were in serious danger.

A major line of attack lay in the overhauling of the wage system, one of the central features of Stalin's policy. Commenting on the heavy turnover in the labor force, Stalin said:

The cause is the wrong structure of wages, the wrong wage scales, the "Leftist" practice of wage equalization. In a number of our factories wage scales are drawn up in such a way as to practically wipe out the difference between skilled labour and unskilled labour, between heavy work and light work. The consequence of wage equalization is that the unskilled worker lacks the incentive to become a skilled worker and is thus deprived of the prospect of advancement; as a result he feels himself a "sojourner" in the factory, working only temporarily so as to earn a little and then go off to "seek his fortune" elsewhere.[106]

These remarks were dinned into the consciousness of Soviet citizens by every means of communication at the Party's disposal. Stalin emphasized what Lenin had merely suggested—that inequality served a necessary social function in a socialist as well as in a capitalist society. It is this point which constitutes a new element in Russian Marxist ideology, and which serves as the basis for the contemporary justification of organized social inequality.

The Stalinist slogan for the system of distribution under socialism is: "From each according to his abilities, to each according to his labor." Equality is stigmatized as "petty bourgeois." The goal remains that proclaimed by Marx: a higher (Communist) form of society in which the slogan "From each according to his abilities, to each according to his *needs*" will supposedly prevail. Older Bolshevik theorists, perhaps not in accord with the strictest logic, interpreted the latter to mean equality of rewards for all.[107] Such interpretations are now conspicuous by their absence.

There is a significant contrast between the fate of early doctrines concerning equality of power and similar doctrines concerning equality of rewards. In practice, inequalities developed rapidly in both areas. On the basis of various prerevolutionary features of Bolshevik ideology and behavior, that is, the theory and practice of a conspiratorial elite, the stage was set to an important extent for the development of inequalities of power. At the same time, the concurrent stream of ideas to the effect that the new regime would be sensitive to the needs of the masses, that it would represent the highest expression of the will of the toilers, and that the masses would soon be the masters of their fate, was retained and in some respects even amplified to give a further atmosphere of legitimacy, consensus, and mass support to the new regime. On the other hand, the conception of equality of rewards was repudiated as incompatible with the major goal of industrialization, or at best allowed to slip into forgetfulness as a possible feature of an indefinite future. The difference between the fate of the two sets of ideas may perhaps be explained as a consequence of the differing social function each set could play under the new social conditions.

9

Revolution and World Politics

The pattern of world politics

Before the Revolution of 1917 the Tsarist rulers of Russian so-
ciety had shown considerable skill in adapting themselves to the
prevailing pattern of world politics that had grown up with the
modern system of independent and competing sovereign states.
This pattern, which has undergone a number of significant structural changes but remains in many essentials the same today, has
been widely described in terms of the balance of power. Without
assuming that the balance of power explains every facet of international relations, this conception can nevertheless be used as
a simple theoretical framework to account for a very significant
portion of the behavior of modern states.

The chief principle of the balance-of-power system is the following: if any state attempts to expand its power and influence,
other states will singly or in combination attempt to prevent this expansion. (The Allied coalition against Hitler provides a familiar
recent example.) In this way the existing distribution of power
may be regarded at any one time as a system of equilibrium that
has a tendency to return to its original state as soon as it is
disturbed. An important corollary of the balance-of-power principle is that any state that wishes to preserve its power and territorial integrity must ally itself with the opponents of an expanding state. If the existing distribution of power is static or
nearly so, a relatively weak state that wishes to preserve some
freedom of action will, as a rule, ally itself with the opponents
of the strongest power. Thus the victors in a war frequently find
themselves faced by a coalition of the discontented. In addition,

the most powerful victor is frequently deserted by certain of its allies, who fear an undue expansion of the victor's power and therefore join the coalition of the discontented.

The balance of power leads in this fashion to a system of coalitions and countercoalitions. Although it may legitimately be regarded as a system with a tendency toward equilibrium, the equilibrium is precarious and unstable. The numerous factors which constitute the power of any state—military preparations, technology, population, morale, diplomatic skill, and a host of others—are in a continual state of flux, which means that the distribution of power among states is likewise continually changing. Furthermore, no state can obtain real security by being just as strong as its potential opponents. This security can be won only by becoming a great deal stronger than the potential or prospective opponents. But the very effort to gain this strength upsets the delicate equilibrium and sets in operation the development of a still stronger countercoalition.

Among the major skills required for success and survival under balance-of-power conditions is the ability to evaluate correctly the strength and weaknesses of potential allies and enemies in order to shift one's position in the distribution of power as rapidly and effectively as possible. Failure to do so may lead to conquest and defeat. By the same token, it is often necessary for the statesman to be on guard lest an ally become too strong, in which case it may be necessary to shift allegiance to the opposite camp. In a similar way, successful statesmen have to be skilled in detecting signs of dissension in the enemy's camp and in playing upon such conflicts to further the survival of their own state.

At times the shiftings from one coalition to another are rapid and frequent. A sharp observer has commented that one of the charms of power politics is that no one has time to become tired of his friends. The epigram draws attention to the amoral aspects of any struggle for power. Allies have to be sought where they may be found, and in the international arena it often occurs that the choice dictated by power considerations does not correspond with ideological ones or those of cultural affinity.[1]

The Bolsheviks, before they came to power, did not interpret world politics along these lines. There is, to be sure, some overlapping in the conclusions reached by Lenin and those presented in the preceding analysis. Both agree concerning the amoral nature of politics and the tendency toward conflict in the modern state system. The Leninist theory of imperialism explained such conflicts as the result of certain special features of modern capitalism, which led to a struggle for the redivision of the world among the industrial giants. Lenin hoped that a successful revolution in Russia would set on fire a world revolution that would bring the entire system to an abrupt end. It does not appear that he or his followers had any very clear idea about what they would do if the conflagration failed to materialize. All that Lenin had to offer in this case, by way of prerevolutionary advice, was a series of scattered remarks to the effect that if the proletariat were victorious at first in only a single country, they would then confront the rest of the capitalist world and attempt to raise up revolts against the capitalist masters. Apparently Lenin thought that the capitalist states would drop their struggles with one another and face the infant socialist state in a single hostile phalanx. In his prerevolutionary writings, Lenin was so preoccupied with the class struggle inside the various states that he seems to have left out of account the possibility that conflicts between states might continue even after the advent of socialism and provide the socialist state with its chief opportunity for survival. In other words, prerevolutionary doctrine emphasized horizontal or class cleavages, to the neglect of vertical or national cleavages.[2] This chapter will examine to what extent Lenin's ideas became the basis of Soviet foreign policy, and to what extent the failures of Leninist policy forced the Soviets to adopt balance-of-power methods.

The impact of political responsibility

From the very beginning Bolshevik actions in foreign affairs were influenced by the simple consideration of self-preservation, as well as by more recondite considerations of doctrine. Perhaps the most accurate appraisal of their behavior during the first few weeks is that they sought self-preservation through means suggested or implicit in their doctrine.

Almost the very first step the Bolsheviks took was to issue a propaganda appeal designed to rouse the masses to force an end to the war upon their political leaders.[3] Since the Russian military forces were in a weakened state, at least partly due to the defeatist activities of the Bolsheviks themselves, an all-round armistice would of course have served Bolshevik interests. However, attempts to bring about an armistice through propaganda and regular diplomatic channels were failures, leaving the Bolsheviks alone to face the still formidable military machine of Imperial Germany.

In this situation the Bolshevik leaders at first acted on the hope that a proletarian revolution might break out behind the German lines and solve their problems in a dramatic and simple fashion. The Russians secured a truce, whose terms provided for an "exchange of views and newspapers" and the consequent entry of Bolshevik antiwar propaganda into Germany.[4] Then the Bolshevik negotiators under Trotsky's leadership attempted to protract the conversations in the hope that the revolutionary situation would ripen. Over the heads of the diplomats Trotsky issued revolutionary proclamations claiming that peace could be guaranteed only by the victorious proletarian revolution in all countries. German trenches were flooded with appeals to throw out the Kaiser and declare a revolutionary peace. For a moment it appeared that revolutionary tactics might succeed, for a great strike movement broke out spontaneously in Austria and spread to Germany, even though the Russians exercised no direct control over this expression of sympathy for the Russian Revolution. But the strike was soon brought under control.[5]

In the course of the negotiations Lenin rapidly came to the conclusion that for the moment there was no hope of a revolution in Germany, and that the Russian army was too weak to offer effective resistance to anything the Germans demanded. Revolutionary hopes would have to be put aside, he insisted, at least for the time being, and the German terms accepted. Against strong opposition within and without the Party, he forced through the Russian signature of the Treaty of Brest-Litovsk. Defending his policy before the Party, he declared, "Yes, we will see the international world revolution, but for the time being it is a very good fairy tale, a very beautiful fairy tale—I quite understand children liking beautiful fairy tales." [6]

Faced with the choice between a revolutionary crusade whose outcome seemed dubious and the preservation of the Soviet regime, Lenin had no hesitation in choosing the second course. It was a problem that would occur many subsequent times in the history of the Soviet regime. To date it has always been answered in the same way. Indeed, it was only on this early occasion that the forces within the Party hostile to Lenin's choice stood any real chance of imposing their version of "correct" revolutionary strategy.

Bukharin and others, opposed to the "capitulation" at Brest-Litovsk, accused Lenin and other members of the Central Committee of having betrayed the interests of the revolution, both in Russia and in the world at large. "The conduct of the Central Committee strikes a blow at the international proletariat," declared the Left Communists, led by Bukharin. [7] The decision to conclude peace at any price, asserted the Bukharin group, inevitably meant that the proletariat would lose its role as leader in Russia, as well as in the world. Instead of abject surrender, the proletariat should try to bring about a civil war on an international scale. "We turn aside with contempt," Bukharin said, "those appeaser elements who . . . instead of a civil war against the international bourgeoisie wish to wage a national war against Germany on the basis of class unity and a union with the Anglo-French coalition. The renunciation of the dictatorship of the proletariat in the name of war is just as inacceptable for us as its renunciation in the name of peace." [8] This statement is a complete denial of the principles of international power politics in favor of a pure revolutionary tactic.

With the wisdom of hindsight, one may readily assert that the Left Communists, in their refusal to accept assistance against Germany and their insistence on a revolutionary civil war, were impractical utopians who pushed Marxist doctrine to its logical

and absurd conclusions. Perhaps in the light of the objective
situation at that time such comments are an accurate evaluation
of their position. Nevertheless, they and their followers in subsequent decades, who have accused the Central Committee of
selling the international revolution down the river, have un-
ceasingly based their arguments on the allegedly practical
grounds that the promotion of world revolution was the only
way to preserve the new socialist state.

Lenin denied Bukharin's accusations and tried to show that
the peace of Brest-Litovsk had helped rather than hindered the
world revolution. Overtly at least he professed to regard the interests of the Soviet state and the world revolution as identical.
Like his opponents, he seemed to think that one could not survive without the other. "If we take the position on a world historical scale, there can be no doubt that if our revolution remains
alone, if there are no revolutionary movements in other countries, our position will be hopeless," he declared to the Party
Congress in 1918.[9] Therefore, he continued, "every . . . revolutionary . . . will admit that we were right in signing any
disgraceful peace, because it is in the interests of the proletarian
revolution and the regeneration of Russia." [10] "If we manoeuvred
in the Bukharin way," he stated in the course of a bitter debate,
"we would ruin a good revolution." [11]

In addition to this first postponement of revolutionary hopes,
another ideological consequence of the assumption of political
responsibility was an increased awareness that the capitalist
world did not represent a solid hostile phalanx. Two incidents
in 1918 indicate the general pattern. In February of that year
the Germans were still on the march, although the Russians had
already announced their willingness to sign a dictated peace.
On the twenty-second, at a meeting of the Party Central Committee, Trotsky proposed that the Bolsheviks should ask the
Allies for aid against the Germans. Lenin could not attend the
session, but sent a note saying, "Please add my vote in favour of
the receipt of support and arms from the Anglo-French imperialist brigands." [12] In August, when the situation was reversed and
the Whites and the Allies were pressing upon the Bolsheviks,
Chicherin asked the Germans for aid against Allied intervention.[13]

The effect of these and other similar experiences may be traced in various doctrinal statements of the time. By May 1918 Lenin's prerevolutionary view of the workers' state confronted by a united imperialist world was considerably modified. He declared to the Moscow Soviet at this time that the struggles of the imperialists among themselves made it impossible for these powers to form a union against the Soviet Republic. The waves of imperialist war, Lenin observed, might drown the little island of the Socialist Soviet Republic, but might also break up against each other.[14] At the same time, he continued to deny that his diplomatic maneuvering was directed solely toward the preservation of Russian national interests. Instead, he maintained that the defense of the Soviet Republic was the defense of worldwide socialism. Lenin declared that the Bolsheviks had become "defencists" after the November Revolution. ("Defencists" was a term of abuse used by the Bolsheviks before the November Revolution to describe those who wanted to continue the war.) "We do not defend . . . national interests; we declare that the interests of socialism, the interests of world socialism are higher than national interests . . . We are defenders of the socialist fatherland."[15]

The impact of political responsibility in the first months of the regime led to a temporary renunciation of revolutionary goals in favor of the preservation of the infant socialist state. This renunciation was not overtly recognized as such and was concealed through the rationalization that the strengthening of Russia inevitably implied the strengthening of the revolutionary forces. In addition, political responsibility very rapidly led to an awareness of splits in the enemy camp and to techniques for taking advantage of them, which received doctrinal sanction and recognition. The analysis of world politics hammered out in prewar years had been tried out in practice and found at least partly deficient, which Lenin himself was the first to admit.

Revolutionary hopes and disappointments

Despite their first disappointments, the new leaders of Russia continued to express the opinion that they could not survive without revolutionary outbreaks in some more industrially advanced country. Shortly after the first anniversary of the November Revolution, Lenin told the Congress of Soviets that the complete victory of a socialist revolution was "unthinkable in a single country" and that it required "the most active co-operation of at least a few progressive countries in which we cannot include Russia." [16]

As an advanced industrial country whose technology and highly skilled population would provide a tremendous asset in the Communist camp, Germany was widely regarded among the Russian leaders as the key to the international situation. Trotsky in a public speech on October 3, 1918, declared: "The German proletariat with all of its technical skill on the one hand and, on the other hand, our Russia—disorganized but extremely rich in natural resources and with 200 million inhabitants—present a most powerful bloc against which all the waves of imperialism will break. For us there can be no allies from the imperialist camp. The revolutionary camp of the proletarians, advancing in an open battle with imperialism—these are our allies." [17] Such responsible leaders as Trotsky and others predicted that the processes which brought the Bolsheviks to power in Russia would repeat themselves because of parallel and irresistible social forces, aided by only a minimum of Russian assistance. [18] Their reliance on the logic of history may in this case have been an indirect confession of their inability to render more concrete assistance to their sympathizers in Germany, who became increasingly active with the collapse of German arms.

Nevertheless, the Russians did what they could. Adolph Joffe, the Soviet diplomatic representative in Berlin after the Treaty of Brest-Litovsk, behaved as a revolutionary agent rather than as an ordinary diplomat. More than ten Left Social Democratic newspapers were directed and supported by the Soviet Embassy in Berlin. In December 1918, Joffe admitted having paid 100,000 marks for the purchase of arms for German revolutionists, and claimed that he had established in Germany a 10 million ruble fund for the support of the German revolution. [19]

Soviet financial assistance and conspiratorial advice failed to turn the upheavals in Germany into a copy of the November

Revolution. In January 1919, the Spartacist Union, a group that had split off from the majority socialists and favored the seizure of power by violent means, was decapitated in an unsuccessful uprising by the killing of its two leaders, Rosa Luxemburg and Karl Liebknecht. The majority socialists turned to conservative forces in the army to suppress the uprising, and thereby saved their own position for the time being.

Similar outbreaks in Munich (April 7, 1919) and in Hungary (March 21, 1919) likewise ended in failure. These rebellions were led during their communist phases by flamboyant and doctrinaire revolutionaries who soon alienated local support by attempts to organize economic and political life on what they believed were Soviet models. This policy made it relatively easy for their internal and foreign enemies to crush them.

The communist phase of the Munich uprising lasted only two weeks, scarcely time for the Communist International to extend greetings.[20] In the Hungarian revolt Lenin gave its leader, Béla Kun, tactical and general advice. But Lenin was in no position to enforce the acceptance of this advice. He lacked both the disciplinary power and the information upon which to make an informed judgment. Béla Kun sent flattering letters to Lenin, enclosing copies of his decrees and telling Lenin how his writings were serving as a model for the Hungarian proletarian revolution. From them it is clear that he was making most of the decisions on his own, decisions that we need not record, but which ended disastrously for him and his followers.[21]

The present-day concept of a tightly disciplined Communist Party blindly following detailed instructions from Moscow, a conception that distorts even the contemporary relationships between Moscow and its satellite parties, certainly does not apply to these early attempts to extend the Soviet system to other lands. At this time the leaders of the Russian Revolution served as inspirers, and as contributors of occasional advice and assistance, but not as directors. Although they often claimed they were riding the wave of the future, they were scarcely able to direct it into the channels they chose.

The only attempt to extend Soviet influence over which the

Russian Communist leaders exercised considerable control took place in Poland, more or less by accident, during the spring and summer of 1920. What had begun as a defensive war against Pilsudski became transformed for a brief time by the military successes of the Red Army into a revolutionary crusade. The Russians established a Polish "Provisional Government" behind the lines of the Red Army and attempted to set up soviets as they went along. Local Polish support was not forthcoming, and the invasion of the Red Army unified Polish national sentiment behind Pilsudski, whose forces defeated the Red Army.[22] A few months later Lenin confessed that he had made a political miscalculation.[23]

A significant sidelight on Soviet foreign policy appears from the fact that, when the Red Army was at the height of its campaign against Poland, the Russians continued their negotiations with the British in an effort to bring to a close hostilities between the two countries and to establish normal diplomatic relations. These actions indicate that the Communist leaders were anxious to keep a second string to their bow. They also suggest that the Bolsheviks had already begun to entertain serious doubts about the imminence of a world-wide revolutionary conflagration.[24]

The revolutionary failures of 1918, 1919, and 1920 were attributed very largely by the Russian Communist leaders to a poor choice of tactics on the part of local leaders, over whom they felt they had inadequate control, and to a lack of disciplined organization in general.[25] The Communist International had been founded formally at its opening Congress in March 1919. But as Zinoviev, the chairman of its Executive Committee, observed, the Comintern was merely a "propaganda society" during the entire first year of its existence.[26] Now the time had come, the Russian leaders argued, for it to become something concrete. The Russian Party had succeeded in overthrowing the Tsarist autocracy by creating a strictly disciplined conspiratorial elite. Might not a similar organization be able to succeed on an international scale? In the spring of 1920 Lenin wrote that "the Russian model reveals to *all* countries something that is very essential in their near and inevitable future." [27] "The experience of the victorious dictatorship of the proletariat in Russia," he added, "has clearly shown even to those who are unable to think . . . that absolute centralisation and the strictest discipline of the proletariat are one of the fundamental conditions for victory over the bourgeoisie." Similar arguments were hammered home by Zinoviev at the Second Congress of the Communist International, in July 1920.[28] Waverers on both the Right and the Left, particularly those who wished to have dealings with the alleged traitors to the proletarian revolution among the moderate socialist parties, must be eliminated from Communist ranks.

Such was the background of thinking and circumstances that preceded the adoption of the famous "Twenty-One Conditions" for admission into the Communist International at its Second Congress. On paper at least these conditions established a centralized organization very similar in structure to the Russian Communist Party.[29] Henceforth the failures of the Comintern were to be rationalized by the explanation that they were due either to treachery or to the failure of various Communist leaders to understand Marxist-Leninist (later Marxist-Leninist-Stalinist) doctrine correctly and to apply it properly. The same argument was used against the leaders of the Comintern by those who lost power within its ranks.[30] At no time was the suggestion made openly that the Russian experience might be irrelevant or that Lenin's conception of the dynamics of modern capitalist society could be seriously mistaken.

Despite the adoption of the Twenty-One Conditions in 1920, the Comintern remained for some time a loose gathering rather than a tightly centralized organization. As late as 1922, at the Fourth Congress, Zinoviev complained that the twenty-one points had not been "brought to life." He spoke bitterly about the misbehavior of the French and Italian Parties, and observed sadly that internal discipline was so weak it had not proved possible to carry out even such a minor festival as "Comintern Week" on an international scale.[31] However, some improvement was noted by this time in Comintern connections with Germany. There, according to Zinoviev's claim, almost no political event took place without an exchange of opinions between the German Party and the Comintern Executive Committee.[32]

In general, the Comintern was torn throughout its history by factional disputes frequently ending in wholesale expulsions. These disputes were the reflection of oppositional movements within the Communist Party of the Soviet Union, personal rivalries, and genuine differences of opinion over the correct policies to be adopted. Often these differences arose from the fact that the interests of the local Parties in adapting themselves to local conditions did not agree with the interests of the dominant Russian Party, or at least were interpreted in widely divergent fashions.

In the beginning, debates were often hot, long, and heavy at Comintern Congresses, where disagreements were brought out into the open. Such continued to be the case as late as the Fifth Congress in 1924. At the Sixth Congress in 1928 disagreements were largely prevented from coming out openly. However, the delegates were obviously concerned about rumors of differences within the Russia Politburo as Stalin prepared to liquidate the Right Opposition. The Seventh and last Congress in 1935, at which Comintern policy underwent one of its many sharp reversals, was a well-rehearsed affair in which policy was adopted without serious objection from the floor. These and many other facts show that the same process of transferring power to a narrower and narrower circle took place within the Comintern as well as in the Communist Party of the Soviet Union.

According to the Twenty-One Conditions, the formal procedure for reaching decisions within the Comintern was supposedly that of democratic centralism, as in the Russian Party. Actually, decisions were reached for the most part by prominent factional leaders taking their troubles to the top Russian authorities. Factional groups attempted to persuade the Russians that their policy was the correct one. If they succeeded, their policy was adopted as the formal line of the International.[33] If they failed yet insisted on their point of view, they would, in time, be cast out as traitors to the working class. Naturally this situation put a great premium on personal contacts and accurate nformation on currents of opinion among the Russian leaders. A career and even survival often depended on guessing correctly which way the Soviet cat would jump. Those who out of principle disdained to make such guesses increasingly failed to survive. This situation has had important effects upon the present-day leaders of the Communist Parties outside the USSR. Most of them are skilled bureaucratic intriguers rather than flaming revolutionaries.

Thus the Russian Communists did not have at their command a revolutionary instrument until after the spontaneous postwar upheavals had died down. The earliest date at which the Russians may have attempted to direct a proletarian uprising was in March 1921, the time of an abortive outbreak in Germany. Even in this case the Russian role was at the very most no more than that of spurring on the German Communists to seize an apparently favorable moment for general strike throughout Germany.[34] The attempt was a failure. By this time the pressure of domestic events, combined with the failure of world revolution to materialize, had forced Lenin to sound the signal for a general retreat. On March 8, 1921, he gave to the Tenth Party Congress the famous speech outlining the New Economic Policy.

Once again the revolution was postponed. Lenin conceded this frankly, both in public and in private.[35] Other leaders adopted, officially at least, a more equivocal attitude. Trotsky's report to the Third Congress of the Communist International, held in the summer of 1921, and the Theses drafted by him which were adopted by that body, might be regarded as a model of political double talk. He argued that the conclusion of the peace treaties did not mean that the international bourgeoisie had renounced the goal of destroying the Soviet Republic.[36] Future perspectives remained revolutionary.[37] Capitalism was definitely not restored, and had instead entered a period of profound depression, according to Trotsky's interpretation.[38] On the other hand, he conceded that capitalist equilibrium displayed great powers of resistance, that the bourgeoisie felt it had grown stronger, and that in the future the advance would not be so feverish, that there would be a slowing down of the revolutionary tempo.[39] Therefore, he advised the Communist Parties to be ready for revolutionary upheavals or for a period of gathering their forces and winning the support of the majority of the working class.[40]

The equivocal nature of these statements and others of the same kind may be attributed to the conflicting pressures of the necessity for a new definition of political realities and the desire to cling to older definitions in the face of contradictory and refractory experiences. Even natural scientists have occasionally found themselves in this awkward predicament at the time of the breakup of one world view and the emergence of a new one.

On the whole, revolutionary hopes displayed a surprising tenacity in the face of repeated failures. Two more major attempts in Germany and China were undertaken before a long lull, lasting from 1927 until the Second World War, took place in Soviet endeavors to alter the social structure of the non-Soviet world. Before examining these attempts it is necessary to analyze the Soviet effort to adjust to a world of competing great powers by the more familiar methods of balance-of-power diplomacy, and its relationship to official Soviet doctrines.

Marx or Machiavelli?

Accepting in 1921 the supposedly temporary setback to the goal of self-preservation by revolution, the Communist leaders of Russia proceeded to display considerable skill in the techniques of balance-of-power diplomacy. As in the case of other contemporary states, the Soviets applied such techniques with but little open recognition that they were following an easily recognizable pattern of behavior. For the most part, their overt awareness of this fact was limited to statements about the necessity of splitting the imperialist camp, or to proclamations about their generally pacific intentions and willingness to coöperate with capitalist states "during a given historical period."

The Leninist conception of international relations, though it did not prevent the practice of balance-of-power politics on the part of the Communist elite, militated against any conception of international politics as a continuing system of political relationships, in which the participants themselves might change or change their positions, while the system itself remained relatively unchanged. Instead, the Russian leaders continued, though with decreasing frequency and emphasis, to predict the disappearance of the entire system and its replacement by an international proletarian community.

The first large-scale triumph won by the Soviets through the techniques of balance-of-power diplomacy was the detachment of Germany from a position of dependence on England and France by the Rapallo Treaty of April 16, 1922. The success of Rapallo appears to have been a hoped for, but unexpected, windfall. In the discussions that preceded Russia's participation in the Genoa Conference, Lenin continually emphasized Soviet economic rather than political goals. In fact, his published speeches contain no reference to the possibility of a Soviet-German rapprochement. The purpose of the Genoa Conference, as stated by its moving spirit, Lloyd George, was the restoration of European economy shattered by the war. From just such a conference Lenin apparently believed that Russia had much to gain. "From the very beginning we declared that *we welcomed Genoa and would attend it;* we understood perfectly well, and did not conceal it, that we were going there as merchants, because trade with capitalist countries is absolutely essential for us (until they have entirely collapsed), and that we were going to Genoa to discuss in the most correct and favorable manner the politically suitable terms of this trade, and nothing more." [41] There was, according to Lenin, no disagreement or controversy on this question in the Party Central Committee or among the rank and file,[42] an indication of the extent to which the hopes and desires for a revolutionary crusade had died down.

Even though the restoration of trade relations appears to have been the primary Soviet objective, it is evident that political matters were also under consideration. On the way to Genoa the Soviet delegation stopped off in Berlin and engaged in conversations concerning the possibility of a Soviet-German agreement.[43] Both sides had been feeling their way toward an agreement for some time in order to escape pressure from the victorious Allies.

According to Louis Fischer, the conversations that ultimately led to Rapallo began as early as 1920 in a prison cell occupied by Karl Radek.[44] They did not succeed until the Allies had been split by a combination of circumstances and Soviet-German diplomatic tactics.

In addition to England, the major participants in the Genoa Conference were Russia, France, Germany, and Italy. Certain economic interests temporarily united these countries against the Soviets before the conference. Various groups in England, France, and Germany joined together prior to the conference in a plan for dealing with the Russian problem that would in effect have resulted in the exploitation of Russian resources on what amounted to a basis of extraterritorial privileges. The hopes of these circles were perhaps unduly raised by the partial restoration of private property and private trade in Russia under the NEP, and by various official Soviet announcements concerning the opportunities for foreign capitalists to operate enterprises in the Soviet Republic in order to hasten the restoration of Russia's shattered economy.[45] However, the powers were able to reach an agreement only on this extreme basis, which would have virtually ended Russian sovereignty. Other political factors divided them.

Chief among these factors were conflicting Anglo-French views on the German problem. The British were suspicious of French desires to achieve European hegemony. The French in turn were suspicious of British balance-of-power policies, and of the German desire to play off their former enemies against each other to increase their own freedom of action. The entire situation was further complicated by a division of opinion within each country, which was at least partly reflected in the delegations of each power, including the Soviet one.

At the opening of the conference Chicherin was careful not to create a common antagonistic front by revolutionary phrase-making. Lenin had already advised him to "avoid big words" in discussing the text of his opening speech.[46] Instead, and presumably taking his cue from Lenin, Chicherin opened his speech by declaring that the Russian delegation, while remaining true to the general principles of Communism, recognized the need for economic coöperation between the old and the new system of the world during the present historical epoch.[47] This conception of the "peaceful co-existence of two social systems during a given historical epoch" was put forth on a number of subsequent occasions when the Soviet leaders were anxious to obtain the support of a specific capitalist country against other capitalist states. On this occasion, as on others, the search for support required the postponement or abjuring of revolutionary goals.

It is not possible to follow here in any further detail Soviet techniques at this conference, though they constitute a fascinating chapter in diplomatic history. Chicherin cleverly succeeded in splitting the Allies, so that they could not present a united opposition to Russian tactics. Then he managed to split the German delegation itself, which was divided between those favoring an Eastern and a Western orientation for German foreign policy. Finally, he telephoned a member of the German delegation at one-thirty Easter morning, saying the moment to sign was then or never. The same afternoon the Rapallo pact stunned other delegates to the conference.[48]

The three-cornered diplomatic struggle among England, France, and Germany continued for several years, and again provided an opportunity for the Soviets to prevent capitalist unification directed against them. Among other incidents, the Bolshevik leaders feared that the Locarno pact of 1925, guaranteeing the Franco-German frontier, might be a move inimical to them. Before the treaty was signed, Chicherin stated to the German press that the "entire guarantee pact policy of England is an integral part of her basic anti-Soviet activity." [49] At the same time both the French leaders, Poincaré and Briand, feared that Locarno would make England the arbiter between France and Germany and hamper French freedom of action. They therefore made an unsuccessful attempt to effect a rapprochement with the Russians.[50] Meanwhile the Germans, who were under pressure from the Russians to refuse Locarno, could not forfeit friendly relations with the Soviets, since this would weaken their bargaining position with the Western powers. Furthermore, there are indications that an arrangement was in effect at that time between Germany and the Soviet Union for an exchange of military experience, army experts, and munitions, though this fact has been denied by the Russians.[51] For these reasons Stresemann and Chicherin reached an agreement, repeating the essentials of the Treaty of Rapallo, by October of 1925. The Locarno Treaty was signed on October 16, 1925, but the Russo-German treaty was kept secret in order to avoid spoiling Germany's chances in the West. It was not published until the League Council refused to allow Germany to enter the League of Nations in March of 1926.[52]

This technique of pitting one power against another, the essence of balance-of-power diplomacy, was not confined to European affairs. It was also applied in the Near East, where the major antagonist again was England, and where the application of the policy also conflicted at times with revolutionary aspirations. Here, however, the conflict between doctrine and expediency was not so marked, since according to Leninist doctrine the forces opposed to colonial rule included local nationalist movements. After experimenting with propaganda appeals to throw off the imperialist yoke, and even in one case with the establishment of a Soviet regime in Northern Persia—the Gilan Republic which lasted until the autumn of 1921—the Russians contented themselves with the toleration or active support of local nationalist leaders such as Riza Shah Pahlavi in Persia or Kemal Atatürk in Turkey, who endeavored to westernize and modernize their countries. The anti-British policies of such leaders made them useful to the Soviets. Thus at the Lausanne Conference in 1923, called to discuss the status of the Dardanelles, Chicherin clashed with the British leader, Lord Curzon, and won the reputation of being "more Turkish than the Turks." Although Kemal used strong-arm measures to put down Russian Communist influence within his country, his actions had no appreciable effect upon the friendly relations between the two countries.[53]

During the twenties the Soviets continued to waver between attempts to maximize their power and security by prolonging the truce, as they saw it, with the capitalist world, and attempts to find a more radical solution by revolutionary means. Among the devices used to prolong the truce was the series of disarmament proposals that won for the Soviets much sympathy in non-Communist circles opposed to war.[54] The Soviet proposal, made on a number of occasions, amounted to complete and total disarmament. As a weak state in the military sense, the Soviets had much to gain from radical disarmament. They may also have anticipated gains from weakening what they regarded as the military props under capitalism, and have found some value in showing up the alleged hypocrisy of their capitalist opponents. Nevertheless, Soviet disarmament proposals were not merely propaganda statements, issued without any intention that they should be acted upon. As their actions show, the Russians regarded any step that might reduce the danger of armed attack on the USSR as desirable. They suggested partial steps, such as a mutual reduction of the Red Army and the armies of Russia's western border states to one quarter of their existing dimensions.[55] After sharp initial criticisms, the Soviets participated in the Kellogg Pact (1929), sponsored by the United States in an effort to outlaw war as an instrument of national policy, and at a later date in the League of Nations. At the same time the Russians continued to make it clear that even though they welcomed partial, or indeed any, disarmament, they still regarded such measures as palliatives. Capitalism, they repeated, was bound to produce war.

Another aspect of the Soviet policy of prolonging the truce and seeking allies where they could be found was exemplified in their search for *de facto* and *de jure* recognition by the other powers. By 1924 recognition had been granted by the major powers except for the United States. In that year the Commissariat for Foreign Affairs could make the somewhat unrevolutionary claim in its annual report to the Congress of Soviets that "the USSR has taken its due place in the system of great world powers." [56] In addition to the search for credits and other concrete advantages, the search for prestige—the desire to make the capitalist world and capitalist diplomats accept them as social equals— appears to have played no small role in this aspect of Soviet foreign policy. Italy, where Mussolini was one of the first dictators to succeed in suppressing the local Communist Party, managed to be the first country to grant *de jure* recognition, and thereby won a favorable trade agreement. Others followed rapidly.

As the Italian incident suggests, the search for allies and for recognition, conducted largely through the Commissariat for Foreign Affairs, conflicted on various occasions with the policy promoted through the Comintern. A frequently reproduced cartoon from *Pravda* shows Foreign Affairs Commissar Chicherin scratching his head in perspiring anxiety as Zinoviev, Comintern leader, thundered revolutionary phrases over the international air waves. Nor was the anxiety confined to Chicherin's organization. Bukharin found it necessary to reassure the delegates to the Fourth Congress of the Comintern that it was perfectly proper for proletarian states to accept loans and form alliances or blocs with bourgeois states, if the tactical situation of the moment demanded it. In such cases, he added, "it is the duty of foreign comrades to work for the victory of such a bloc. If in the future the bourgeoisie of such a country is itself defeated, then other tasks arise. (*Laughter.*)" [57] In other words, agreements with capitalist states were defended as one means among many for strengthening the socialist bulwark against the inevitable day of reckoning. Such statements were of course a repetition of Lenin's essential argument at Brest-Litovsk: that there could be no conflict between the national interests of the Soviet state and the ultimate interests of the world revolution.

This argument might satisfy doubts among those whose thinking took place at a high level of abstraction, but it gave few clues regarding what tactics or combination of tactics would be effective in a specific situation. The abortive revolution in Germany during 1923 reveals clearly the dilemma thrust upon the Russian leaders by the necessity of choosing between revolutionary and nonrevolutionary techniques in pursuit of their goals.

During the winter of that year Germany underwent a series of disturbances, set off by the French occupation of the Ruhr, that had many of the appearances of revolutionary turmoil. In contrast to the situation during 1918–1920 the Russians now had, in Germany at least, a Communist Party that could be counted upon to follow closely the Politburo's suggestions.[58] However, differing appraisals of the revolutionary potentialities of the situation in Germany led, along with other factors, to numerous delays and hesitations, which contributed to the adventure's failure.

These varying appraisals were related to hopes and fears concerning the fate of the revolution in Russia itself. As has already been seen, one current of opinion among the Bolshevik leaders pinned Communist hopes on a revolution that would incorporate German skills and technology into the Soviet system. According to this argument, such a turn of events would counteract the industrial backwardness of Russia and produce a strong proletarian bloc against the capitalist world. Zinoviev pointed out that a proletarian victory in Germany would put an end to those features of the NEP that were dangerous from the Communist viewpoint, increasing enormously the role of state industry and nipping in the bud the recovery of the bourgeoisie.[59] The other current of opinion was embodied in the policy of Rapallo and the search for economic and even military arrangements with the existing German government, as a counterweight to the power of England and France.[60] On this account, the proponents of this view advocated caution and held back from revolutionary adventures, evidently fearing to promote a renewed attack on the Soviet Union.

Various individuals among the major Soviet leaders shifted back and forth between the two positions. Stalin apparently opposed the revolution, at least in its beginning stages.[61] In the course of subsequent factional struggles, Stalin denied the accusation that he had opposed the German revolution, but revealed a number of other differences of opinion within the Politburo. "I and the whole Politburo," said Stalin, shared the view that the Communists should not make a premature demonstration (a reference by Stalin to a Communist demonstration attacked by "armed fascists"). When the situation changed after August 1923, Stalin continued, "I and other members of the Commission of the Comintern stood without reservation for the immediate seizure of power by the Communists." [62]

Trotsky, on the other hand, who had initially favored the revolution and worked out the details with the German Communist leader Brandler,[63] threw cold water on the attempt at a crucial moment, when the Reichswehr intervened to suppress the disturbance. To an American senator, who questioned him on Russian intentions, he made a statement which illustrates clearly the conflict between the Soviet need for a continuation of the truce with capitalism and the desire for a radical solution of Russian problems. His reply indicated strongly that the German revolutionaries could not count on effective Soviet assistance, but would have to fend for themselves. In his statement Trotsky said, "Before all and above all we desire peace. We shall not despatch a single Red Army soldier across the boundaries of Soviet Russia unless we are absolutely compelled to do so." Trotsky then went on to say that Russia would defend herself if the conflict in Germany ended in victory for the German monarchists and an agreement with France and England for combined action against Russia. But, he pointed out, the Russians could help the Germans only by first making war on Poland, which would provoke a general conflict. He then declared: "We do not conceal our sympathies with the German working class and with its heroic struggle for freedom, and to be perfectly frank, I can say that if we could assure victory to the German revolution without risking war we should do everything we could." [64]

Shortly afterward, and at the very last moment, the leaders of the Germany Party called off the plans for the uprising. One courier, however, departed by mistake for Hamburg with the signal to begin the battle. After a brief but bloody struggle the Hamburg revolt was put down, an event which extinguished for several years Soviet prospects of a Communist Germany. This failure was a crucial blow to those elements in Russia who still counted on revolutions outside the Soviet Union for assistance in solving its domestic and foreign problems. Recriminations over this failure helped to bring out into the open the split between Trotsky and Stalin. With the failure of revolution to materialize in the West, the Russians turned their revolutionary attentions to the Far East.

Anti-imperialism: the convergence of doctrine and expediency

In Europe, Russian revolutionary interests sometimes conflicted with her balance-of-power interests, with the result that the Bolsheviks had difficulty in choosing between the two. In the Near East, the conflict was less, though the Russians on the whole found it more expedient to support nationalists anxious to westernize their countries, and hence opposed to a position of colonial dependence, than to attempt outright revolution. In China, for a time, revolutionary and balance-of-power interests tended to coincide.

At first, however, such was not the case. In the beginning Russian national interests, inherited from the Tsarist regime, prevented the Russians from taking an active hand in Chinese domestic affairs. Despite high expectations on both the Chinese and the Russian sides, aroused by numerous Soviet expressions of sympathy for the "semi-colonial" status of China and Russian promises to abandon Tsarist privileges, relations between the two countries were cool and intermittent until 1923. Various Soviet attempts to achieve agreement with and recognition by the Peking government ended in failure, largely owing to Soviet reluctance to give up the territorial acquisitions in Outer Mongolia and Northern Manchuria that had been won by the Tsarist regime and over which the Bolsheviks managed to reëstablish varying degrees of control by methods that foreshadowed their policy in Europe after World War II, nearly a quarter of a century later.[65]

However, after the failure of protracted attempts to reach an agreement with the Peking government, in 1923 the Soviet emissary, Joffe, whose earlier activities in Berlin have already been described, sought out the Kuomintang leader, Sun Yat-sen. Following a number of discussions between these two, a statement was issued that set the tone of subsequent Russian policy for a number of years. According to this declaration, both Sun and

Joffe agreed that "neither Communist organization nor the system of soviets can be introduced into China at present because the necessary conditions do not exist there . . . [and] the most pressing problem of China is to achieve her national unification and to realize her complete national independence." [66]

The policy, suggested in the Joffe statement and followed by Stalin and Bukharin from this point until the end of 1927, had two main features. One was the giving of military advice and assistance to the Kuomintang, which included the services of Michael Borodin and General Galen, as well as the furnishing of a considerable quantity of military supplies. The other feature was the attempt to make the peasants the background of the antimilitarist and anti-imperialist movement and to draw them into the Kuomintang. In general, the Russian leaders debated and approved the major policies outlined above, in addition to many tactical details. When the adventure was drawing to a close in 1927, Bukharin revealed that the general tactics of the Chinese revolution were determined by the Politburo.[67]

Even the moderately leftist policy promoted by the Moscow leaders produced a split within the ranks of the Kuomintang. The cleavage appeared at the Second Kuomintang Congress held early in 1926. In March 1926, Chiang Kai-shek, who succeeded Sun as the leader of the Kuomintang, decided to ally himself with right-wing elements in the organization and executed a minor coup against the leftist group during Borodin's absence. Though this rift was temporarily patched up, Chiang managed to carry out a more successful coup in the spring of 1927.

As the Chinese coalition disintegrated, Trotsky demanded more and more insistently an outright revolutionary policy. The only way out after Chiang's second coup, Trotsky declared in heated sessions of the Executive Committee of the Communist International, lay in arousing the Chinese workers and peasants against imperialism by connecting their basic economic interests with the cause of China's liberation. He demanded a definite break with the bourgeoisie, the forming of soviets on the Russian model, and an intensification of the class struggle.[68] Fears that a truly revolutionary policy might provoke a dangerous reaction in Britain, whose government broke off relations with the USSR during these vitriolic arguments, Trotsky answered with the boast that a really revolutionary leadership could "make the waters of the Yangtse too hot for the ships of Lloyd George, Chamberlain and MacDonald." [69]

Stalin at first attempted to maintain the coalition in China. Then, since this policy failed, and since Chiang Kai-shek outmaneuvered the local Comintern forces, Stalin and the Comintern moved further and further toward an open revolutionary break.[70]

By such a policy neither the advantages of revolution nor those of compromise could be obtained. The relationship of political forces in Moscow was such that each side was strong enough to paralyze the other insofar as Chinese affairs were concerned, with the result that the weaknesses of both prevailed. The record of the debates shows clearly that both Stalin and Trotsky attempted to fit the facts into the rigid pattern of Russian experience, while interpreting that experience according to variant shadings of Marxist-Leninist theory.

There is no need to follow further the details of the disintegration of Kuomintang-Communist coöperation. In July 1927 Borodin was expelled. Although the Chinese Communists attempted to utilize a split between the right and left wings of the Kuomintang, they were unsuccessful and found themselves in open warfare against both wings during the summer of 1927. Finally, on December 11, 1927, there was a brief and bloody uprising in Canton which lasted for three days, when it was put down by Chiang's troops.[71] Thus ended the abortive Chinese revolution. The Chinese Communists took to the outer reaches of China, living as a state within a state for nearly twenty years, returning to the scene as a major factor in international politics after the Second World War.

The consequences of this defeat were far-reaching in terms of both ideology and behavior. The Soviet Union did not again attempt to engineer any mass upheavals. For nearly twenty years no Communist Party made a serious attempt to gain power.

Although the Leninist framework was retained as the official explanation of foreign affairs, the Soviet Union proceeded to follow the typical balance-of-power pattern of coöperating with one power or group of powers against an opposing group, and shifting its alliances in accord with obvious national interests. In addition, after the defeat of the Chinese revolution, Stalin pursued in earnest the slogan of "socialism in one country" and devoted a large proportion of the Soviet Union's energies to the task of transforming its internal social order.

Conclusions

The impact of Marxist ideology upon Soviet foreign policy is highly visible during the period just discussed. The interpretation of world politics developed by Lenin and others prior to the November Revolution became the basis for action on a number of occasions following the seizure of power. The very first actions of the new regime in its relationships with the non-Soviet world represented an attempt to put Leninist ideas into practice, an attempt that was repeated in varying ways for many subsequent years. Efforts to bring about the proletarian revolution occupied a large part of the energies and talents of the new regime.

In addition, Marxist ideology acted as a screen between the Communist rulers of Russia and political events in foreign lands, as well as in Russia itself. Their previous training in the Marxist pattern of analysis and interpretation of world events sensitized the new Russian leaders to certain facts and made them obtuse to others. Revolutionary optimism, which events showed to be unwarranted, played an important part in their decisions, although there were significant differences in the extent to which such optimism affected various individuals in Bolshevik ruling circles.

Each revolutionary attempt failed. In the years 1918–1920 circumstances were such that the Communist leaders of Russia were prevented from making attempts that extended beyond propaganda. The Communist uprisings of that period in Berlin, Munich, Hungary, and elsewhere cannot be considered manifestations of Russian policy to the same extent as the German revolution of 1923 or the Chinese revolution. But even in the latter instances, in which the Politburo could direct the tactics of local Communists in their mutual efforts to ignite apparently revolutionary tinder, the attempts failed.

This series of failures had important consequences in both behavior and doctrine. When the proletarian revolution did not materialize, the leaders of Russia were forced to fall back on the techniques of traditional balance-of-power diplomacy. In the employment of these methods they enjoyed no little success, which contrasted with their failures in the sphere of revolution. The structure of international relationships in the early twentieth century was stronger than the attempts of the Bolsheviks to overthrow it and replace it with a new system. Indeed, it was strong enough to force the Bolsheviks to abide by its rules and to adopt its time-hallowed techniques in order to survive as a state.

The failure of revolution placed the Russian Communists in a dilemma. They were compelled to split the capitalist front, or to take advantage of splits in this front, in order to preserve and enhance their own power and security. At the same time, the existence of the revolutionary tradition tended to encourage a unified opposition to the Soviet regime and to hamper it in its efforts to seek allies in the capitalist camp. In this fashion the goal of ultimate and complete security, to be gained after the victory of the proletarian revolution in the more important capitalistic countries, came into conflict with the goal of immediate security, to be obtained only with the acceptance of questionable allies.

A number of reactions to this difficult situation can be distinguished. It is clear that Lenin very rapidly realized the significance of divisions among the Soviets' enemies and that he displayed considerable skill in utilizing these splits for strengthening the Russian position in the existing distribution of power.

When the Communist leadership, however, was deprived of Lenin's intuitive grasp of political realities, fumblings and disasters followed for a time. The debates and actions concerning the German and Chinese revolutions reflect a doctrinaire blindness and lack of adaptability between opposing groups in the

Communist elite. Thus the actualities of the political situation in both instances escaped under the pressure of fitting them into the Marxist framework.

Additional factors prevented the emergence and overt acceptance of alternative, non-Marxist interpretations of world problems. The tendency in the latter twenties to revive Lenin's older view of Russia alone against the united onslaught of world capitalism probably helped to inhibit the development of competing non-Marxist formulas. Furthermore, the increasing limitations on free discussion of political matters aided in discouraging such interpretations.

However, during the first decade and a half of the Soviet regime, by far the most common reaction to the dilemma of Soviet foreign policy was to deny that one existed. From Lenin onward the Russian leaders maintained that the interests of the socialist fatherland were identical with the interests of the world revolution. If this argument was accepted, it became perfectly logical to sacrifice the interests of any given Communist Party, perhaps even to permit its total destruction, for the purpose of strengthening the Soviet Union's position in world politics. Such arguments cannot be dismissed as pure rationalizations. Under the conditions of world politics there was very often some portion of the world in which Soviet power interests coincided more or less with revolutionary interests. At the same time and for the same reasons, these interests conflicted in some other part of the world.

Still another frequent response was the device of postponing the goal of world revolution to an increasingly indefinite future. This device is a familiar one among social movements that possess a goal difficult or impossible to realize, and it was applied to other Bolshevik goals, such as the withering away of the state or the achievement of a communist, as distinct from a socialist, society. The doctrine of socialism in one country represents in part a postponement of the world revolutionary goal, as Trotsky insistently pointed out. Stalin himself did not deny this conclusion, but contented himself with the reply that socialism in one country meant the creation of a socialist bulwark in a hostile capitalist world, and hence the strengthening of the revolutionary forces.

Another and somewhat less frequently stated reaction to this dilemma was the assertion that coöperation between socialism and capitalism was possible during a given historical epoch. Such a statement was the complement of the doctrine that the interests of world revolution and the Soviet state were synonymous. That is, they were an approximately correct appraisal of the interests of the Soviet Republic in a certain portion of the world. However, no attempt was made in any Soviet writings that have come to my attention to relate these views to one another in the manner just described.

This chapter may be concluded with a brief consideration of the widespread hypothesis that the rulers of Russia were at all times following a "master plan" of world conquest, laid down by Lenin. According to this interpretation, the toning down of revolutionary propaganda and the abandonment of revolutionary activities represented mere "tactical" retreats to a stronger position and did not imply the abandonment of the original revolutionary goals.

The hypothesis of a master plan in Soviet foreign policy draws attention to one portion of the truth: that the Soviets exhibited a preference for revolutionary methods and professed to regard agreements with capitalist states as temporary maneuvers. Nevertheless, the hypothesis of a master plan errs by taking at face value the rationalization that there can be no conflict between the interests of the international proletariat and the interests of the Soviet Union in world affairs. Likewise, it very seriously under-emphasizes the role of pure empiricism, of simple trial and error, in the formation of Soviet foreign policy. There was a continuing interaction between ideology and events, in which the goals were modified as they began to appear unattainable. Even the revolutionary actions themselves were to a great extent efforts to adapt to existing circumstances and to seize opportunity by the forelock, even if the opportunity may not have been as great as the Bolsheviks hoped. If such a great proportion of Russian Communist behavior has been mere tactics, the hypothesis of an over-all guiding strategy fails to provide a useful explanation. It confuses Bolshevik hopes with Bolshevik policies. While their hopes were one of the many important factors that determined their policies, it is a mistake to elevate this one factor into some sort of primal cause and to regard all other factors as mere perturbations and temporary disturbances.

TODAY'S DILEMMA

PART THREE

TODAY'S DILEMMA

10

New Wine in Old Bottles: The Stalinist Theory of Equality

Stalin's political victory over the opposition was secure by about 1930, despite the existence of scattered groups of opposition members still at large, some of whom, among the Trotskyites at least, managed to maintain contact with their leader in exile.[1] Four years later Stalin was able to claim to the Party delegates assembled at the Seventeenth Congress that capitalism had been eliminated in the USSR and that the dilemma of the NEP had been solved. By that time the peasant had been forced into the collective farms, and a large-scale industrial base, firmly in the hands of the Party, was well on the way to completion. From about 1934 onward a very definite stabilization of political and economic relations in the Soviet Union may be perceived. Nothing like the upheavals that took place during the shift from War Communism to the New Economic Policy, or from the NEP to the Stalinist program of industrialization and collectivization, has occurred since the completion of the First Five Year Plan. Even the Second World War failed to bring about any fundamental changes in the structure and function of Soviet society. Though Soviet society has not been static from the thirties down to the present day, we are justified in treating this period as a more or less consistent segment in the development of Soviet ideology and social institutions.

One outstanding characteristic of this era has been the endeavor to reconcile the older Leninist doctrine that the masses are the masters of the country and of their fate with the fact of the concentration of power at the top levels of the Party. Lenin's theory of a conspiratorial and disciplined elite provided a basic starting point in this process. Under Stalin there is a recognizable tendency for the reigning ideology to approach more closely the actual facts of the distribution of power in the Russian state. At the same time, this trend is checked by the fact that it has proved possible to use the democratic and populist aspects of Communist ideology as a means for supporting and strengthening the power position of the top Party leaders.

The justification of coercion

In Leninist ideology the chief justification of social coercion was put in terms of class relationships. The dictatorship of the proletariat was represented as a temporary measure necessary to crush the resistance of the bourgeoisie that would—and did—continue after the workers' revolution. In the far more distant future, wrote both Engels and Lenin, when mankind had become thoroughly used to the new classless society, the state would wither away, and coercive powers would no longer be necessary.

The Stalinist justification of social coercion represents a modification of the position taken by Engels and Lenin. Stalin's doctrine was formulated in a series of *ad hoc* statements to meet specific situations and does not by any means represent a logically consistent whole. It has been left to the intellectuals to reconcile these statements as best they could, and even to prove that Stalin is the greatest of contemporary social philosophers.[2]

With the victory of industrialization and collectivization, voices were raised within the Party suggesting that the time had come to begin the liquidation of the coercive machinery of the state. In 1933, in a speech announcing the successful results of the First Five Year Plan, Stalin fired a rhetorical salvo at such suggestions. He called once more for a strong and powerful dictatorship of the proletariat in order to "scatter the last remnants of the dying classes to the winds." "The state will die out," he continued, "not as a result of a relaxation of the state power, but as a result of its utmost consolidation, which is necessary for the purpose of finally crushing the remnants of the dying classes and of organizing defence against the capitalist encirclement, which is far from having been done away with as yet, and will not soon be done away with." [3] At the Party Congress the following year, he spoke sarcastically of those who "dropped into a state of mooncalf ecstasy, in the expectation that soon there will be no classes, and therefore no class struggle, and therefore no cares and worries, and therefore we can lay down our arms and retire —to sleep and to wait for the advent of classless society." [4]

Only two years later, on the occasion of the promulgation of the Stalinist Constitution of 1936, Stalin announced the "fact" that "there are no longer any antagonistic classes in [Soviet] society." [5] Socialism, or the preliminary and lower stage of communism, had by now been achieved in the USSR, according to Stalin's declaration.[6] This achievement, which supposedly included the abolition of the exploitation of man by man and the elimination of class antagonisms, was to be reflected in the new Constitution. According to older Marxist theory, a relaxation of the dictatorship of the proletariat might have been anticipated. Instead, Stalin announced that the Constitution preserved the "regime of the dictatorship of the working class." In almost the same breath he pronounced the new Constitution the only thoroughly democratic one in the world.[7]

The alleged abolition of class antagonisms was used chiefly as a justification for the absence of political competitors for the Communist Party, whose dominant position was formally recognized in the 1936 Constitution. Competing political parties, said Stalin, were merely a reflection of class antagonisms. Since there were no such antagonisms in the Soviet Union, there was no reason, said Stalin, for the existence of competing political parties. At this point Stalin restated the argument, made familiar by Lenin, that democracy in capitalist countries was only "democracy for the strong, democracy for the propertied minority," whereas in the USSR the regime guaranteed democracy for all.[8] Stalin's arguments are widely repeated in the Soviet press today and have found their way into textbooks on the political structure of the Soviet regime.[9]

Finally, in 1939, Stalin postponed the withering away of the state to an even more indefinite future. Even after the achievement of Communism the state would remain, he declared, unless the danger of capitalist encirclement and foreign attack had, by that time, been eliminated.[10] Stalin's statement represented a definite break with Leninist doctrine, which, following Engels, had anticipated the disappearance of the state when society passed from the socialist stage to that of communism.

The reformulation of the Communist theory of the state is the product of at least three factors. One is the impact of political facts, such as the continuation of a world of warring states, which do not fit into the original doctrine. A second factor is the attempt to use the doctrine to provide a moral justification for existing internal political relationships, such as the dominance of the Communist Party. A third factor may be called the "revolutionary conscience" of the leaders, that is, their desire to convince themselves and others that the regime had achieved the promised benefits of a liberty greater than the liberty of capitalist society. That the product of these forces is not a symmetrical and logical system of political philosophy is scarcely surprising. Equal contradictions of logic and fact may be found in the case of any functioning political formula, including that of Western democracy. Nor is it surprising that the Soviet political formula is immune to logical attacks upon it by intellectuals nourished in another tradition. It has long been recognized that the power of ideas does not depend upon their logical coherence alone, but also upon the social functions that they perform.

Freedom and the individual's role in society

In contrast with Western ideas, which begin with the individual and extend to the group or to society as an instrument serving the needs of the individual, the Soviet concept of freedom stresses the role of society and the group. The Russians are fond of asserting that the full development of the individual's capabilities and personality is possible only under the socialist organization of society.

This stress on the role of society appears in the familiar Soviet emphasis on the economic prerequisites of freedom. Contemporary official Soviet ideology emphasizes the economic conditions that are to be met before men have any free choices that they can make. Stalin put the matter bluntly in a speech of 1935 that has frequently been quoted:

> If there is a shortage of bread, a shortage of butter and fats, a shortage of textiles, and if housing conditions are bad, freedom will not carry you very far. It is very difficult, comrades, to live on freedom alone. (*Shouts of approval*) In order to live well and joyously, the benefits of political freedom must be supplemented by material benefits. It is a distinctive feature of our revolution that it brought the people not only freedom, but also material benefits and the possibility of a prosperous and cultured life. That is why life has become joyous in our country.[11]

The year before Stalin had enumerated the material benefits supposedly brought by the regime: the end of the exploitation of man by man, the end of poverty in the countryside, the end of unemployment, and the end of urban slums.[12] The Soviet press today carries almost daily some variation on these themes.

Anti-Soviet writers frequently argue that the Soviets have neither political freedom nor the material benefits claimed by the regime, and draw the conclusion that the population is cowed and unhappy. The more scholarly among them buttress this conclusion with comparative statistics, endeavoring to show that the standard of living in the USSR is lower than that in capitalist societies, or even that it has not markedly improved since Tsarist times. Such analyses leave out of account the strong probability that the level of expectation of the Russian masses is not the same as that of the United States or Western Europe. Given a monopoly of means of communication, and the absence of opportunities for direct contact with the outside world, there does not seem to be any insuperable difficulty in convincing the Russian masses that they are better off than their predecessors in Tsarist days and their allegedly unfortunate brethren in the rest of the world. However, where contact with other cultures becomes more or less unavoidable, as in the case of occupation armies or officials sent on duty to foreign countries, disillusionment often sets in rapidly, as shown by the high desertion rates and the renunciation of the regime by several of its diplomatic officers.

The same conception of the importance of the group appears in the official doctrine concerning the liberties of the individual. At first glance this doctrine resembles Western ideas of liberty. Article 125 of the Soviet Constitution of 1936 guarantees to the individual the rights of free speech, freedom of assembly, including the right to organize street demonstrations, and a free press. But the concluding paragraph adds that these rights are secured by turning over to the workers and their organizations the printing establishments, stocks of paper, public buildings, streets, means of communication, and other material conditions necessary for making these rights real. As matters work out on this basis, the populace is free to organize demonstrations praising Stalin, and that is the end of the matter.

The Soviet conception of freedom and the role of the individual in society stands at the opposite pole from the Western glorification of the individual who is willing to follow his own conscience as a guide over and above the will of the group's constituted authorities. At times minority opposition groups among the Communists, including Trotsky, put forth such views. But they have never become incorporated into the official doctrine. In this connection it is well to point out that the Soviet doctrine is in some ways closer to the realities of social behavior than Western individualist doctrines. One very rarely finds an individual who really stands alone in opposition to the group. Nearly always the heretic or deviant receives comfort and support from his membership in a subgroup of other heretics and deviants, which enables him to withstand the pressures brought to bear by the larger society.

The contrast between Western individualism and Soviet collectivism appears clearly in differing conceptions of the role of the artist in society. The Soviet artist is not permitted to set up his own viewpoint in contradiction to that of the Party. Zhdanov, one of Stalin's close associates, stated clearly the official Soviet view on the position of the artist in the autumn of 1946: "Our literature is not a private enterprise . . . We are not obliged to give a place in our literature to tastes and manners that have nothing in common with the morale and qualities of Soviet people." Further, he adds, "If junk is produced in a factory," the producer is punished, and a stronger penalty must apply to one who "produces junk in connection with the education of human souls," since this is a far greater sin.[13]

The significance of the group and the insignificance of the individual who is not a member of the group appear in several fashions. One is in the semimystical worship of the Party line. Stalin expresses this viewpoint in typical language: "Our Party alone knows where to direct the cause; and it is leading it forward successfully." [14] Another instance is the attitude that the regime tries to encourage in the individual workers. Once again Stalin puts the matter in simple yet vivid language: "Here the working man is held in esteem. Here he works not for the exploiters, but for himself, for his class, for society. Here the working man cannot feel neglected and alone. On the contrary, the man who works feels himself a free citizen of his country, a public figure in a way. And if he works well and gives society his best —he is a hero of labour and covered with glory." [15] It is hardly necessary to repeat at this point that there is little or no reliable information concerning the extent to which this statement actually describes the feelings of the rank-and-file Soviet worker.

Soviet ideology regarding the place and value of the individual in society is also revealed in Soviet legal conceptions concerning guilt. In earlier days, certain Soviet theorists argued that "bourgeois legality" ought to be replaced by the application of repressive measures according to considerations of political or revolutionary expediency, conceived in class terms, without any claim that these repressive measures should correspond to individual guilt. These views were included in a draft of a new criminal code in 1930.[16] Since that time there has been some movement in the direction of formulating a conception of individual guilt along lines prevalent in Western democratic countries. Thus, in 1937, in a speech that was the prelude to an attack on alleged saboteurs, Stalin demanded an individual approach to each case instead of a mass witch-hunt.[17]

But in the same speech Stalin made several statements whose effect was to sow suspicion and bring about the mass hysteria he supposedly wished to avoid. He warned that one could not trust a person merely because he was an efficient worker or administrator who raised production; a spy or saboteur had to assume such a disguise, and the saboteur with a Party card, said Stalin, was the one to be most feared of all. One of the consequences of this suspicion was a wave of mass purges, of which the famous Moscow trials were only the froth on the surface. In January of 1938 the Party Central Committee attempted to call a halt, alleging that the mass exclusions that had been going on for several months were unknown to the top leadership of the Party and violated its directives.[18] This plea of ignorance can hardly be taken seriously.

In 1938 another move took place toward an individual conception of guilt and the protection of individual rights. A new statute on the constitution of the courts included in the latter's functions the safeguarding of the "political, labour, housing, and other personal and property rights and interests of the citizens of the USSR as granted by the Constitution."[19] If the numerous accounts of those who have fled from the regime are to be trusted on this point, this protection does not apply to those who are in any way suspected of being enemies of the regime. These accounts likewise give rise to considerable skepticism concerning the application of the rights mentioned in articles 127 and 128 of the 1936 Constitution: freedom from arrest (except by decision of a court or with the sanction of the procurator); the inviolability of the home (that is, freedom from search); and the privacy of correspondence. These alleged rights represent a polite bow to prerevolutionary Russian Marxist doctrines, which gave considerable prominence to the liberal conceptions of the West. They may also be a gesture to the sentiments of the democratic powers, whom the Soviet regime was endeavoring to propitiate in 1936 in order to protect itself against attack by the Axis.

Relations of leaders and masses

Political ideologies usually formulate an idealized conception of the relationship between the political leaders of the state and the masses of the population.[20] The current political ideology of the USSR contains a number of the authoritarian and populist elements of prerevolutionary Leninist doctrine, with some significant additions.

Beginning with the authoritarian elements, the most striking innovation since Lenin's day is the glorification of a single leader. This glorification first became apparent about 1929 and developed rapidly in subsequent years. In the thirties the term *vozhd'*, or leader, similar in connotation to the German term *der Führer*, was applied to Stalin with increasing frequency. Curiously enough, the equalitarian term of address, "Comrade," was also retained. Postwar Soviet newspapers carry on their front page nearly every day letters addressed to "Comrade Joseph Stalin, leader and teacher of the peoples of the Soviet country, and all of toiling humanity," or variations upon this theme. They contain personal promises to fulfill or overfulfill some portion of the Five Year Plan, or to carry out some other aspect of a highly publicized policy of the regime. In a similar vein, all good things for the past decade and a half, from victory in war to the achievements of the arts and sciences, are attributed to Stalin's personal qualities.[21] In contrast to Lenin, who publicly admitted errors of tactics on a number of occasions, since 1929 Stalin has cultivated the aura of infallibility. When matters do go wrong, the blame is put upon scapegoats at various levels in the administrative hierarchy. No public suggestion is ever made by lesser lights that Stalin himself could be or has been mistaken at any time. The break with the previous tradition is clear, since as late as 1924 one may find in Stalin's speeches admissions of doctrinal error and even of disagreements with Lenin, which were of course generally known facts in the Party at that time.[22]

The development of the conception of a "monolithic" Party, free of internal disagreements, has been described in an earlier chapter. With the victory of this conception there was no longer any room for honest differences of opinion within the Party. Karl Radek, on trial for his life on January 24, 1937, unwittingly expressed this situation, saying, "People begin to argue about democracy only when they disagree on questions of principle. When they agree, they do not feel the need for broad democracy, that goes without saying." [23] It is at this point that Soviet ideals diverge most sharply from those of Western democracy, which gives lip service, and often more than lip service, to the ideal of tolerating a complete range of political opinions within its midst. Speaking in 1937 of the struggle with the remnants of Trotskyism, Stalin demanded that the Party should make clear that the "old methods of discussion" could no longer be used. Instead, "new methods, methods of uprooting and smashing" were called for.[24] The consequence was a wave of purges that spread deep into the fabric of Soviet life. Stalin likewise coined the term "rotten liberalism" to describe any public expression of tolerance for former enemies of the regime.

The demand for "uprooting and smashing" opposite opinions may be contrasted with Stalin's remarks in December 1925 at the Fourteenth Party Congress, when he chided Zinoviev and Kamenev for demanding the expulsion of Trotsky from the Party. On this occasion Stalin declared, "We do not agree with Comrades Zinoviev and Kamenev, because we know that the policy of cutting off [deviant members] is fraught with danger to the Party, that the method of cutting off, the method of bleeding— and they do demand blood—is dangerous and contagious; today we cut off one, tomorrow—another, the day after tomorrow—a third. But by then, what will be left of the Party?" [25]

The third aspect of the authoritarian portion of contemporary Soviet political ideology is the increased recognition of the leading role played by the Communist Party. The Stalin Constitution of 1936 recognized this situation formally in article 126 in the familiar clause which states that "the most active and politically-conscious citizens in the ranks of the working class and other sections of the working people unite in the Communist Party of the Soviet Union (Bolsheviks) which is the vanguard of the working people in their struggle to strengthen and develop the socialist system and is the leading core of all organizations of the working people, both public and state." While statements of this sort had been made on numberless previous occasions, their incorporation into the Constitution implies a somewhat more open recognition of the locus of authority. In an even more direct

fashion the 1938 *History of the Communist Party,* a highly publicized document still in widespread use today, gives open recognition to the fact that the Stalinist revolution of forced industrialization and collectivization was a revolution "from above."
The *History* calls this upheaval a "profound revolution . . .
equivalent in its consequences to the revolution of October 1917."
It continues: "The distinguishing feature of this revolution is
that it was accomplished *from above,* on the initiative of the
state, and directly supported *from below* by the millions of
peasants, who were fighting to throw off kulak bondage and to
live in freedom in the collective farms." [26] This statement is one
of the rare occasions on which the role of the leaders in initiating
policy is openly and directly stated. Again, the way to an open
recognition of elite leadership may be found in Lenin's continuous lashings of the sin of following the masses. Nevertheless, one
may observe that in the statement above the recognition of an
elite leadership is very carefully coupled with specific claims of
mass support. The Soviet leaders are a long way from stating
openly any philosophy of "the public be damned." It is highly
unlikely that this phrase would apply to the actual sentiments
of the top Soviet leaders, who are probably convinced that they
are acting in the best interests of their country.

Much more common than the open recognition of the elite
role played by the leaders of the state are statements emphasizing the close connection between the leaders and the led. Political propagandists in the USSR are fond of quoting Stalin's use of
the Antaeus story from Greek mythology: the legend of the giant
who drew his strength from contact with the earth. The Bolsheviks, like Antaeus, says Stalin, draw their strength from contact
"with their mother, the masses, who gave birth to them, suckled
them, and brought them up." [27] The mixture of paternalist authoritarian notions with populist ones may also be observed in
the close of Stalin's famous speech, "Dizzy with Success," in
which he called a temporary halt to the collectivization drive:

> The art of leadership is a serious matter. One must not lag behind
> the movement, because to do so is to become isolated from the masses.
> He who wants to lead a movement and at the same time keep in

touch with the vast masses must wage a fight on two fronts—against those who lag behind and against those who rush on ahead. Our Party is strong and invincible because, while leading the movement, it knows how to maintain and multiply its contacts with the vast masses of the workers and peasants.[28]

In general, with the consolidation of the regime, the suspicious attitude toward the masses expressed so frequently by Lenin has disappeared from official statements. It has been replaced by an increased emphasis on the role of the "vocation of leadership" and by increased claims about the enthusiastic nature of mass support.

In the official ideology concerning the role of the masses, much of the original democratic and populist mythology has been retained. Democratic centralism remains the theoretical basis of the Communist Party, and is now extended to the soviet apparatus that exists alongside the Party.[29] Official manuals still repeat statements to the effect that socialist democracy means putting into effect "the most democratic political forms and institutions, securing the genuine and decisive participation of all the toilers in the control of the government through universally elected and genuinely universal and sovereign organs—the soviets, which constitute the political basis of the socialist state." [30] Self-criticism, too, remains one of the alleged pillars of Soviet democracy. According to official descriptions, self-criticism is the device whereby the weaknesses and mistakes of official agencies and individual officers are uncovered on the basis of a "free and businesslike discussion of the economic and political problems of the country." [31]

Whereas Westerners are accustomed to regard democracy and dictatorship as opposite ends of the political spectrum, the Soviets refer to their regime by the phrase, "the dictatorship of the working class—the highest form of democracy." Lenin, it will be recalled, developed a similar idea at the time of the 1905 revolution, when he put forth the slogan of a "revolutionary-democratic dictatorship." According to contemporary Soviet arguments based on Lenin, the dictatorship of the working class is the highest form of democracy because it brings into the direct control of the state the bottom levels of the masses, which under capitalism or any form of bourgeois democracy remain economically and politically repressed.[32] Since such arguments serve an important political purpose in the Soviet Union, that of convincing the masses that they are better off there than elsewhere, and since they have at least a slight basis in fact, they are impervious to any logical and factual demonstration of their inadequacy.

The democratic aspects of the Soviet "myth" are not without repercussions on Soviet behavior. As in the days before Stalin's accession to power, there have been several attempts by the top leadership to reintroduce the elective principle into practice in a wide sector of Soviet life. The rejuvenation of Party democracy was one of the main points in Zhdanov's recommendations concerning the reorganization of the Party made at the Eighteenth Congress in 1939.[33] Since the end of the war there have been similar efforts to reorganize the collective farms and the trade unions. New elections have been held for the soviets. While quantitative comparisons on this point are very difficult, it is a fairly safe conclusion that this "democratization from above" is even less effective than were parallel movements in the twenties. For example, nearly ten years have elapsed since the last Party Congress, despite the provision adopted in 1939 that such a meeting should be held at least once every three years. Furthermore, although these local elections are by no means the meaningless ceremonies they are sometimes said to be, there are very strong limitations on the degree to which they reflect popular sentiment.

In general, the power of the population to influence the policy of the Communist Party leadership is about equal to the power of a balky mule to influence its driver. The contemporary Soviet press can be searched in vain for any evidence of open popular criticism of the major aspects of the Party line. A derogatory reference to the top Party leadership or any of its policies evidently cannot appear in print and is likely to be reported to the secret police if it occurs in private conversation. Thus the Soviet population has no more choice concerning the road it will travel than the balky mule. At the same time, the masses are encouraged to criticize the way in which policy is executed. The Soviet press is full of complaints of inefficiency in the management of particular factories, particular collective farms, and similar matters. While a number of these complaints are made by roving correspondents of the major metropolitan newspapers or by regional Party secretaries, and hence must be regarded as coming from above, there are also a fair scattering of letters to the editors and plaints of individual citizens concerning bureaucratic mismanagement. This stream of complaint appears to be carefully channeled and directed by the Party for its own purposes.

The ways in which the democratic and populist aspects of the present ideology may be used to perform the paradoxical function of supporting the authoritarian regime are numerous. Elections, in which the candidates are carefully picked by the Party, have been utilized to clear the soviets of suspected opposition elements or persons otherwise undesirable from the point of view of the central authorities. Self-criticism is often used to break up bureaucratic cliques and knots of power with connections in the local community that would otherwise weaken control from the center. By channeling criticism against the execution of policy ways are provided for letting off steam and dissipating discontent that might otherwise be directed against the policy itself. A corresponding technique in the United States would be the encouragement of attacks on OPA officials, their inefficiencies, paper work, and bureaucratic obstructionism, in order to reduce discontent over rationing itself. For many people, and particularly the uneducated masses, it is much more satisfying to blame an immediate and visible local official than to attack a complex and intangible social system.

There are some indications that the Party leaders, including Stalin, are aware of this manipulation of democratic symbolism for authoritarian purposes. The cultivation of the myth of the "little man" who overcomes foils of the bureaucracy to solve some major problem facing the state is such a pat device for putting the bureaucrat in his place that it is difficult to believe it is not done in a deliberate and Machiavellian fashion. The language of one example suggests the motivation. In 1937 Stalin praised warmly the efforts of a woman from the rank and file, calling her the typical "little man," who had supposedly overcome the bureaucratic machinations and Trotskyite intrigues of the Kiev Party organization. "As you see," Stalin concluded with an obvious warning to the bureaucracy, "simple people sometimes are closer to the truth than certain high offices. It would be possible to bring forth tens and hundreds of similar examples." [34] It may safely be assumed that in the Soviet regime, as in any hierarchical organization, there are a large number of "little men" with grudges against their superiors who can be utilized by those at the top to control the latters' subordinates.

The Stakhanovite movement was used in a similar way as an attack upon engineers and business managers who were skeptical of plans for a rapid increase in industrial output. Speaking to the Stakhanovites in 1935, Stalin remarked:

What first of all strikes the eye is the fact that this movement began somehow of itself, almost spontaneously, from below, without any pressure whatsoever from the administrators of our enterprises, even in opposition to them. Comrade Molotov has already told you what troubles Comrade Mussinsky, the Archangelsk sawmill worker, had to go through when he worked out new and higher technical standards in secret from the administration, in secret from the inspectors. The lot of Stakhanov himself was no better, for in his progress he had to defend himself not only against certain officials of the administration, but also against certain workers, who jeered and hounded him because of his "new-fangled ideas." [35]

As the latter oblique reference to workers' objections to Stakhanovite methods indicates, the mythology of the "little man" can also be used to break up incipient clusters of opposition among the masses.

It would be rash to assume that the democratic aspects of current Soviet ideology are retained for purely Machiavellian motives alone. A sincere desire to bring theory and practice closer together may be one of the many factors behind the various shake-ups that endeavor to introduce democracy from above. Yet it should be stressed once more that it is not a democracy which emphasizes the rights of the individual over those of the group. The emphasis on the group and the elitist aspects of Communist theory combine with the populist and democratic ones to produce a system whose major consequence is that the solution of national problems is a task limited to those at the top of the pyramid of authority. The entire system of beliefs is officially considered as one within whose confines all truth, including that of the natural sciences, may be found. The elasticity that is permitted by the denial that Marxism-Leninism-Stalinism is a dogma is an elasticity that is permitted only to those at the apex of the system. Since about 1930 anyone who has attempted to reformulate any of the cardinal points of doctrine in opposition to those at the top of the power pyramid has been branded as a deviationist. The consequences are those pointed out by Mosca toward the close of the last century: "When power rests on a system of ideas and beliefs outside of which it is felt that there can be neither truth nor justice, it is almost impossible that its acts should be debated and moderated in practice." [36]

The ideology of inequality

Under the Stalinist regime the tendency toward organized inequality, which became evident soon after the November Revolution, has continued. The class nature of contemporary Russian society is a highly controversial question, to which there are almost as many answers as there are investigators. The paucity of recent statistical information that might throw light on this question adds to the variety of answers.[37] It appears that Soviet society is characterized by a distinct status hierarchy, with wide variations in income, authority, and prestige. As is generally recognized, however, such differences are not necessarily the indicators of a class system. There is a clear distinction in any society between high and low rank in the political or economic or military hierarchy, and membership in a high or low social class. Not all generals are aristocrats, and not all aristocrats are the holders of high political, military, or economic offices. Unless one can demonstrate that the differences in authority, income, prestige, and culture, which distinguish various sections of the population in Soviet society, are by and large transmitted from

ne generation to the next, it would appear wiser to refrain from
abeling it a class society. Since the present regime has been in
xistence for only a little more than three decades, it is unlikely
hat clear evidence could be found on this point, even if more
lata were available than the Soviets choose to publish.

Some indirect evidence on the transmission of inequalities
rom one generation to the next may be obtained from data con-
erning the Soviet educational system. It is reported that nineteen
ut of every twenty children in the USSR leave school before the
enth grade. The major reason appears to be about the same as in
apitalist societies: poor people need to have children earning
s soon as possible. Another, and less important, reason is the
lrafting of children for the state labor reserves. In September
946 the labor reserves took 434,000 boys and girls between the
ges of 14 and 16, whose educational opportunities were thereby
onsiderably reduced.[38]

These facts suggest that there are substantial obstacles in the
vay of economic and social advancement through the educa-
ional ladder, and that most children will probably remain at
bout the same level as that of their parents. The Party has fought
. slow rear-guard action against the trend in this direction. In
he late twenties it required that a major proportion of the uni-
ersity students should be of proletarian origin. Then, in 1931,
s part of the attempt to increase the number of specialists, the
estrictions against the entry of the children of engineers and
echnical workers into the universities were removed. Finally,
n the autumn of 1940, the system of labor reserves was created
nd tuition fees introduced into higher educational institutions
nd the last three grades of secondary schools, except for students
ligible for stipends on the basis of scholarship.[39]

The significance of these measures in limiting access to higher
ducation is, however, open to debate. Scholars with different
oints of view employ the same figures either as evidence that
pportunity has declined markedly, or that there is no significant
lecline. Evidence on the importance of the 1940 measures intro-
lucing tuition fees is inconclusive. Concerning the consequences
f the earlier measures, it may be noted that between 1935 and

1938 the proportion of workers and their children in the institutes of higher education fell from 45 per cent to 33.9 per cent, while the proportion of employees and intelligentsia rose from 36.2 per cent to 42.3 per cent. Likewise, the proportion of peasants rose from 16.2 per cent to 21.6 per cent.[40] Thus the diminished access of workers to higher education has been partly offset by the increase among the peasantry. In my opinion the most sig nificant conclusion that emerges from this information is that there is no longer any attempt to achieve equality by holding back those children who get superior educational opportunities through the social position attained by their families. Thus, in the Soviet system there are some of the same opportunities for the accumulation of advantages through the family as under capi talism. Equality of opportunity in the strict sense of an identical starting line for everybody in the race for achievement does not exist.

The development of a system of organized inequality in the USSR has been reflected in several ways in Communist ideology. One of the most important was the repudiation of the goal of equality of incomes, which had been put forth by Lenin before the November Revolution and repeated by Bukharin afterward.[4] For this repudiation there is, however, authority in Marx. Stalin in 1934 bluntly told his followers, "It is time that it was under stood that Marxism is an enemy of equalization." Simple equali tarian ideas Stalin attributed to "the remnants of the ideology of the defeated anti-Party groups," which were now to be regarded as a form of petty-bourgeois heresy. He poured out his sarcasm on the "infatuation" of certain Party members with equalitarian tendencies, calling them "Leftist blockheads, who at one time idealized the agricultural commune to such an extent that they even tried to set up communes in factories, where skilled and unskilled workers, each working at his trade, had to pool their wages in a common fund, which was then shared out equally." "You know," he concluded, "what harm these infantile equali tarian exercises of our 'Left' blockheads caused our industry." [4]

The trend toward the recognition of status differences was continued in Stalin's famous slogan, launched the next year in an address to the graduates of the Red Army academies, "Cadres decide everything," a slogan that is common in the Soviet press today.[43] Accompanying this slogan Stalin put forth an indirect justification for the differential treatment of the leadership group, saying that it was necessary to "learn to value people, to value cadres, to value every worker capable of benefiting our common cause." [44]

Since then the regime has taken pains to accentuate the external indications of status differentials. The resplendent uniforms of Soviet diplomats come to mind as one example, together with the sharp differentiation of ranks in the Red Army, which were often a surprise to American soldiers during the recent war. In 1947 the engineering and technical staffs of various industries were equipped with a series of uniforms that, in the case of the coal industry, for example, distinguished nineteen grades of authority and prestige.[45] A similar system of orders and medals was established for farmers on the collective and state farms.[46]

The official ideology concerning the class structure of the USSR reflects the conflicting pressures that derive from the officially encouraged system of organized inequality and the desire to remain loyal to some of the equalitarian ideals of Marxism. These conflicting pressures also help to account for a number of inconsistencies and contradictions in the official doctrine.

In 1934, on the occasion of the repudiation of "petty-bourgeois equalitarianism," Stalin declared that socialism implied and required the abolition of social classes.[47] Two years later, with the promulgation of the Stalinist Constitution, which was widely hailed as the constitution of a socialist society, Stalin altered this view. According to his 1936 statements, which are repeated today at frequent intervals in the Soviet press, Soviet society consists of two classes, the workers and the peasants, who live with one another in friendly and coöperative relationships, instead of hierarchical and antagonistic relationships, such as those between bourgeois and proletariat in capitalist society. Classes continue under socialism, so the argument runs, but class antagonisms have been abolished. The disappearance of class antagonisms is claimed to be the result of the abolition of "the exploitation of man by man." [48] It is hardly necessary to point out in this connection that the existence of the secret police and the concentration camps, which are occasionally referred to in the Soviet press though the number of their inmates remains a carefully guarded secret, is a sufficient indication of the continuation of social antagonisms, whatever their source may be.

To the above-mentioned groups of workers and peasants the Soviets usually add a third group, the intelligentsia. But, perhaps as a reflection of the strength of the equalitarian tradition, class status is denied to the intelligentsia in the official ideology. According to Stalin, the intelligentsia has never been a class and never can be a class. Instead, it was and remains a "stratum" (the saving power of words!) that recruits its members from all classes of society. In Tsarist times, the argument continues, the intelligentsia recruited its members from the ranks of the nobility, the bourgeoisie, and to a much less extent from the ranks of the peasantry and the workers. However, in Soviet society, according to Stalin, the intelligentsia is recruited mainly from the workers and peasants.[49]

As early as 1936 between 80 and 90 per cent of the Soviet intelligentsia were derived from the working class, the peasantry, and "other strata of workers." [50] The phrase "other strata of workers" is suspicious, for it suggests the possibility that a considerable portion of the intelligentsia may be derived from sources other than manual workers. The most likely group is that of office workers, which, together with their families, in 1939 constituted 17.5 per cent of the total population of the USSR, or 29,700,000 persons.[51] According to Molotov's speech at the Eighteenth Party Congress in 1939, the Soviet intelligentsia was composed of factory directors, engineers and technical personnel, scientists, teachers, artists, lawyers, military intelligentsia (presumably officers), and others, to a total of 9,591,000 persons. This was, with the inclusion of families, between 13 and 14 per cent of the population.[52]

From Molotov's statement it is clear that the intelligentsia is simply another word for those of high status in Soviet society. Hence the assertion that it is not a class. And in justice to the

Soviet claim, it should be pointed out again that there is as yet not much evidence to indicate that this group is a hereditary one.

The continuing vitality of the equalitarian portions of Marxist doctrine appears most strongly in Soviet ideology concerning equality of opportunity. In this respect Soviet ideals resemble those that command widespread, if not universal, allegiance in the United States. Speaking of the 1936 Constitution, Stalin declared: "It does not recognize any difference in rights as between men and women, 'residents' and 'non-residents,' propertied and propertyless [in itself a significant comment], educated and uneducated. For it, all citizens have equal rights. It is not property status, not national origin, not sex, nor office but personal ability and personal labour that determines the position of every citizen in society." [53]

Most literate societies have developed some rationale to explain and justify the position of the individual in society. Many of the arguments are based upon blood, or upon a religiously sanctioned order of nature. The idea that the individual's place in society is determined by his own efforts is largely limited to contemporary Western civilization. The Soviets have carried this doctrine to its ultimate extreme, in that even the position of women is made theoretically to depend upon their own achievements.

This conception of a universal equality of opportunity is a new element in Marxist doctrine. Previously, the industrial workers were regarded, in theory at least, as the elite, though this doctrine was never put into practice on any wide scale. Now the doors of achievement are supposedly thrown open to all. The abandonment in 1936 of the election system which had given a large advantage to the urban communities is another gesture with the same meaning. Remnants of the older preferences, however, may be found in the contemporary ideology, which still refers to the regime as the dictatorship of the working class.

Another facet of the Soviet doctrine of equality of opportunity may be examined in connection with the Communist viewpoint concerning the distinctions between mental and manual labor. In a culture with a written language the distinction between physical and mental labor is nearly always associated with status distinctions. In actual practice this is also the case in the Soviet Union. No amount of propaganda about the dignity of labor has been able to reduce mass desire to get into "desk work" and out of manual-labor occupations. American engineers and other technical personnel in the Soviet Union have reported that Soviet engineers prefer to stay in their offices and write out orders rather than go out and demonstrate directly to the workers. The disappearing American tradition that the boss should be able to walk into the shop, roll up his sleeves, and show the "green hands" how the job really ought to be done, has never developed very far in the USSR.[54] Probably the absence of this tradition may be traced to the generally sharper status distinctions of European society.

The official Soviet ideology attempts to combat in a rather halfhearted way the status distinctions between mental and manual labor. The orthodox doctrine, less frequently repeated of late, is that in the USSR "all the conditions are present for the elimination of the distinction between manual and mental labor."[55] This assertion may be explained by reference to specific circumstances in Soviet society. As part of the drive against the older equalitarian tradition, Stalin castigated the idea of leveling downward, of reducing the cultural and technical level of engineers, technicians, and mental workers to that of average skilled workers. "Only petty bourgeois windbags can conceive Communism in this way," he said. He added: "In reality the elimination of the distinction between mental labour and manual labour can be brought about only by raising the cultural and technical level of the working class to the level of engineers and technical workers. It would be absurd to think that this is unfeasible. It is entirely feasible under the Soviet system . . . where the working class is in power, and where the younger generation of the working class has every opportunity of obtaining a technical education."[56]

The assertion that the elimination of distinctions between physical and manual labor is just around the corner may be regarded as a continuation of the equalitarian tradition in a new form. By stressing the opportunities for social mobility, the claim can be made to have some color of reality. In this respect Soviet and American official beliefs are very similar. In America, too, the saying that the "sky's the limit" to personal achievement serves to explain and to justify marked inequalities. Both the United States and the Soviet Union have approached the point where the saying has begun to diverge more and more from the facts, although the USSR may not have traveled as far along this road as we have. In both cases one may anticipate tensions and difficulties in the efforts to match the official mythology with the existing social structure.

The Stakhanovite movement has provided the background for a similar elaboration of the doctrine of equality of opportunity. Alexei Stakhanov was, according to Soviet sources, an ordinary coal miner, who in 1935 suddenly discovered that by organizing his work and that of his assistants in a more efficient manner he was able to produce fourteen times as much coal as that indicated in the official norms. The entire apparatus of the Soviet propaganda machine immediately supported Stakhanov, who was received by Stalin and other dignitaries, until the movement spread throughout the USSR. Stakhanovite workers now constitute a new elite among Soviet workers. They may receive, in addition to their high piece-rate earnings, great prizes ranging from 50,000 to 100,000 rubles.[57] Stalin, and following him the Soviet press, have pointed to this situation as proof of the possibility of getting ahead in the Soviet system, "where the productive forces of the country have been freed from the fetters of capitalism." [58]

At whatever time the opportunities for social advancement decline in the USSR—and there are many observers who declare that the decline has already set in—the Stakhanovite legend will probably play a still more important role. If adjustments to this situation take place within the framework of the present ideology, they are likely to take the form of a denial that the ladder of achievement has become more difficult to climb, or that it has become broken at any point. The Stakhanovite legend can easily be used to support such denials, just as the legend of the self made man in the United States, supported by occasional factual instances, now performs this function in America.

The available data are not adequate to support more than the most tentative conclusions concerning changes in the oppor tunities for economic, political, and social advancement in the USSR.[59] It is clear, however, that a very large proportion of the past opportunities for advancement resulted from nonrepeating causes, such as the elimination of the former ruling classes and decimation of the professional and scientific personnel of Tsaris times. Likewise, the rapid industrialization of the country sud denly opened up many opportunities for getting ahead by cre ating a demand for persons with business and technical skill and by lifting them from the ranks of the peasantry and manual workers.

On the other hand, the latter factor may well be considered a continuing cause in the opening up of new avenues of achieve ment. As the industrialization of the USSR proceeds, the demand for these skills will continue to grow. Plans have been made to meet this situation. In 1939 the number of students in technical schools was 945,000. It is planned that by 1950 the graduates of these institutions will total 1,326,000. In addition, the number of university students is supposed to increase from a 1939 figure of 619,900 to 674,000 in 1950.[60] If the same rate of increase is maintained in the future, which is feasible in the sense that Soviet industrialization is unlikely to reach any saturation point for many years, and if these new positions are not monopolized by those who have access to them through the superior advantages of birth and position, the continuing industrialization of the USSR may offset to some extent the elimination of the nonrepeat ing causes for social mobility.

Certain potential and probable lines of development in the Soviet status system may also be inferred on the basis of the cultural characteristics of the new intelligentsia. The abundant complaints in the Soviet press concerning the weaknesses of Com munist indoctrination among this group, especially among engi neers, technicians, and scientists, indicate that the intelligentsia is largely apolitical. Since they owe their position to the new regime, it is unwise to infer that these complaints reflect actual hostility. It is more likely that a considerable portion of the new elite are patriotically interested in a strong state for its own sake, and are attached to Stalin as one who has achieved this. At the same time, they are repelled or perhaps bored by the mysteries of dialectical materialism. They are not Hamlets. One thing at least is certain: they are men of ruthless energy who have found both a source of energy and an opportunity for its release in the creative task of "socialist construction." In itself this is perhaps the most important reward of status in the Soviet Union. Ciliga, an anti-Stalinist to the core, tells the story of a man sent to organize the health services of a little village in the province of Leningrad. This person was deeply moved by the gratitude of the collective farmers, who were stupefied by the thought that the city had considered their plight and that the Leningrad city hospital had furnished, free of charge, medical equipment and beds for the village *crèche*. Commenting on the crowd of peasants gathered around the newly organized medical center, Ciliga's friend remarked, "This is the first time in my life that I have felt myself useful to the people." [61] In other cases, this sense of belonging and achievement may have little to do with the direct and immediate satisfaction of the needs of the people. Yet, in contrast to the tired cynicism of other days and other cultures, it undoubtedly has provided a tremendous creative stimulus that is psychologically its own reward. [62]

There is also, however, evidence of a cultural separation of the new holders of high status from the masses of the population. In their leisure time the intelligentsia mingle more with one another than with the uneducated. It requires no great insight to perceive that a Soviet executive or scientist would find the company of other executives and scientists more congenial than that of a peasant or manual laborer. In this way different habits of speech, manners, and dress are built up and transmitted from one generation to the next. In addition, the tendency for families of similar social station to live near each other in the same community leads to the choice of marriage partners from families with approximately the same background.[63] All of these forces are at work in the Soviet Union, and it is a safe prediction that they will eventually result in the emergence of a class system resembling in many ways that in the United States excluding the South.

11

The Organization of Authority

On paper the contemporary political structure of the USSR is composed of two hierarchical structures, the soviets and the Party, both governed by the principles of democratic centralism that supposedly reconcile the need for authority and discipline with strong popular control over the leaders. However, on examining how the leaders are actually chosen and how policy is formulated and decisions reached, it becomes apparent that, as in most political structures, there is a great discrepancy between the formalized rules of behavior and the actual patterns of behavior.

Selection of leaders: the elective principle

Within the Party the selection of leaders, according to the formal Party statutes, is supposed to be by election. Paragraph 18 of the latest set of statutes, adopted in 1939, repeats the statement that the guiding principle of the Party's organization is democratic centralism, which is defined as meaning the electiveness of all leading Party organs from the bottom to the top. This document declares (¶ 31) that the Party Congress elects the Central Committee. In turn, the Central Committee chooses from among its members the personnel of the Politburo (¶ 34).

There is no information concerning the actual operation of the elective principle at the top level of the Party. But the importance of other than elective principles in the selection of the top Party leadership is disclosed by certain events that took place between the Seventeenth Congress in 1934 and the Eighteenth Congress in 1939. It has been computed that out of the seventy-one individuals elected to the Central Committee at the Seventeenth Congress, nine were executed, twelve declared "enemies of the people" (and probably executed), and twenty-four had disappeared, accounting for forty-five out of the seventy-one. By 1939, of the sixty-eight candidates (or alternates for membership) in the 1934 Central Committee, fourteen had been executed, two had committed suicide, nine had been declared enemies of the people, and thirty-four had disappeared.[1]

At the lower levels of the Party hierarchy the elective principle plays a considerable role in both theory and practice. First, the formal provisions that are supposed to prevail may be briefly indicated. The basic unit of the Party is the primary organization, formerly called the cell. It may have from three to three thousand members. In the case of the larger units, these primary organizations are required by the Party statutes to elect officers for a one-year period (¶ 62). The election is supposed to take place at a general gathering of the membership. The same applies to the next higher unit of the Party hierarchy, the city, *rayon* (similar to a county), or village organization. The gathering of the membership of this unit is called a conference (¶ 21). These conferences, which are also supposed to be annual events, are the occasion for the election of the administrative officers who exercise power between conferences (¶¶ 52, 53). The same general principles apply to the next higher units in the Party hierarchy, organs of the *oblast'*, *krai*, and republics (both Union Republics and Autonomous Republics), with slightly longer time intervals between meetings and elections.[2]

There is scattered evidence in the Soviet press that these provisions for inner Party democracy are actually carried out. In cases where Party democracy is working in the manner approved and encouraged by the top authorities, the general procedure appears to be for the local Party official to give a report of his work, followed by a debate from the floor. (The Soviets attach great significance to the amount of participation from the floor, and usually report the number of persons who spoke in this fashion.) In groups where the work is not satisfactory, the officer or administrative committee is not reëlected.[3] *Pravda* for April 2,

1943, reported: "The Plenum of the Samarkand *oblast'* Committee of the Communist Party of Uzbekistan debated the questions of the committee's work during the spring sowing. Declaring itself dissatisfied with the committee's management of the spring sowing, the plenum removed from his work the first secretary of the committee, Comrade Ibragimov, as unsuited for his work. Comrade Makhmudov was elected as first secretary." Or, again, it is revealed that in the Gorky *oblast'* in 1940, 92 per cent of the Party primary organizations in recent elections approved the work of their bureaus and officers as satisfactory, in comparison with 68 per cent at the previous election.[4] On the other hand, to cite another random example, in the Donets *oblast'* in 1937, 65 per cent of the Party gatherings gave negative opinions concerning the work of their committees and Party officers.[5] This instance may reflect the purge, in which the top echelon of the Party encouraged the rank and file to attack the middle ranks. As will be pointed out shortly, this apparent autonomy of the grass-roots organs of the Party to determine their own affairs has very strictly circumscribed limits.

During the war the number of electoral meetings and the responsibility of the lower Party officials to their electors diminished sharply. However, the Party is making an effort to encourage the return to democratic methods. *Pravda,* in a prominent front-page editorial (October 25, 1946), proclaimed: "One cannot be reconciled with a situation where Party organizations permit violations of the Statutes of the CPSU concerning the time intervals and method of elections of Party organizations." In a way this is rather ironical, since the basic provision of Party democracy, the requirement that a Party Congress be held once every three years, has been consistently violated. Of special interest was the announcement, in the same editorial, that the wartime system of appointing Party officials in the Party organizations in the armed services was being replaced by elections, which were then going on.

It is extremely difficult, if not impossible, to estimate the extent of this form of grass-roots democracy in the USSR. In general, Soviet press accounts of electoral meetings along the lines quoted above have been much fewer since the war. Further-more, the apparent and perhaps genuine anxiety of *Pravda's* editors concerning the immediate restoration of inner Party de-mocracy must not be taken too seriously. In their official state-ments at least, the Party leaders display a certain form of naïveté, which takes the form of urging "one more last push and our troubles will be over." For instance, similar statements are made about the elimination of bureaucracy and "bureaucratic distor-tions" of Party policy, which sound as though these problems would be eliminated the day after tomorrow. Some of these difficulties, however, have existed since the beginning of the Soviet regime and appear to be an inherent feature of its basic social organization.

Strong forces are clearly at work preventing the extension of inner Party democracy and the free selection of Party leaders even at the lower levels. The program of collectivization and industrialization required enormous sacrifices and a sustained effort from the population, sacrifices and efforts that continue today. The lower levels of the Party, which are in continuous close contact with the population, could not avoid sharing some of the people's weariness and doubt, and could not help being moved and "softened" by some of the tremendous personal sacri-fices involved. It has often been observed that democratic organ-izations have great difficulty in carrying out a long-term policy, particularly one that requires unremitting sacrifices. Therefore, it is not surprising that the power of the lower Party organizations to choose their own leaders shows a repeated tendency toward conversion into an autocratic system of appointment from above.

According to article 95 of the Stalinist Constitution, elections to the local soviets are supposed to be held every two years. However, perhaps owing to the interruption of the war, no such elections were held between 1939 and 1947.[6] The first elections to the Supreme Soviet were held in 1937, and the second in 1946, although the Constitution provides (article 36) for only a four-year term for this body.

It is common knowledge that in Soviet elections there is only one candidate for each post. This arrangement has prevailed since the elimination of other political parties shortly after the establishment of the Bolshevik regime. Since there is only one candidate, it is especially important to understand the nominating process. Article 141 of the 1936 Constitution states: "The right to nominate candidates is secured by public organizations and societies of the working people: Communist Party organizations, trade unions, coöperatives, youth organizations and cultural societies." All of these organizations are carefully controlled and their policies directed by the Communist Party. Except at the lowest local level, the leaders are Party members. Therefore, the mention of the additional organizations serves largely to obscure the role of the Party.

There are, in addition, important limitations on the right of these "public organizations and societies of the working people" to nominate their own candidates. According to Soviet sources, the "primary cells of social organizations (local committees of the trade unions, cells of the *Osoaviakhim* [Society for the Defense of the Soviet Union and for the Development of Its Aviation and Chemical Industries], the MOPR [International Labor Defense], etc.) do not have the right to nominate candidates. The members of these primary cells take part in nominating candidates through their *rayon, oblast'*, and republic organs, and also at general meetings of workers and employees in factories, establishments, and other . . . meetings." [7] In other words, at the lowest level of these organizations, where Party representation and control is thinnest, there is no possibility of putting up a candidate for the local soviet. Candidates who are nominated in violation of these rules must not, according to the same sources, be registered by the local electoral commission.[8]

According to the official theory, the voters should have an opportunity to pick and choose among the potential candidates before the latter are put on the ballot. On March 1, 1936, Stalin told the American newspaperman, Roy Howard, that although there would be only one political party, there would be a lively struggle among the candidates before the election. The voters would question the candidates on their records, asking: "Did you or did you not build a good school? Did you improve living conditions? Aren't you a bureaucrat? Did you help to make our work more effective, our life more civilized?" [9] On the basis of these criteria, Stalin added, the voters would choose the good candidates and cross the bad ones off lists.

If this were the actual practice, it is almost certain that the press would give wide publicity to these meetings, not only as proof of the democratic nature of the regime, but also in order to draw attention to the weaknesses it wished corrected by the device of self-criticism. However, there are very few and very meager accounts of such meetings. To be sure, occasional reports in the Soviet press mention preëlectoral gatherings of factory workers in a given factory or meetings of other bodies for the purpose of choosing a candidate. Thus, *Izvestiya* of January 14, 1947, tells how everyone's heart swelled with pride when one Alexei Nikolaevich Kurakov was chosen to be a candidate for the Supreme Soviet by the "collective" of a factory in Tula and the representatives of 115,000 voters in the area. But it seems highly unlikely that as large a group as a set of factory workers could agree among themselves on a single candidate; and the account becomes more suspect in view of the failure to report any discussion of alternative candidates.

Further evidence of the Party's control over the elections to the soviets may be seen in the disappearance of thirty-seven candidates for the Supreme Soviet and their replacement by others in the course of the 1937 elections. While this was a relatively small proportion of the total number of candidates (over 1,100), as an excellent English authority on the soviets points out, it remains an indication of how the candidates were chosen and demonstrates clearly the Party's real authority in this sphere.[10]

In sharp contrast with the practices of Western democracy, the electoral campaigns in the USSR are the outstanding demonstrations of national unity. The candidates, the press, and the professional agitators vie with one another in proclaiming the loyalty of the Soviet population to the Party and to Stalin. The spirit and purpose of the elections from the Party point of view was well expressed by Kalinin, Chairman of the Presidium of the Supreme Soviet: "The Communist Party approaches the elections in order to throw before the masses its ideals, strivings, and tasks, which stand before the builders of communism, to organize the masses around these ideals, to infect the masses, and nourish them on the striving to achieve communism; the Party calls upon them, pushes them, and organizes them for socialist construction." [11] During the course of an electoral campaign, the Party propaganda machine operates at a feverish pitch, if not without occasional hitches that receive criticism in the press. Thus, during the 1947 elections to the local soviets, at one of the major speechmaking and propaganda stations, a local theater in one of the Kirghiz cities, none of the speakers knew the local Uzbek tongue.[12]

As is generally known, these campaigns usually result in at least 99 per cent victories for the slate of candidates chosen. Also, an extraordinarily high percentage of the electorate goes to the polls: in the 1947 elections for the local soviets held in the Russian Socialist Federated Soviet Republic, the lowest figure was 99.81 per cent. Of those who did vote, between 0.40 per cent and 1.31 per cent (depending on the different types of soviets) had the temerity to vote against the official bloc.[13] In the elections to the Supreme Soviet of the USSR on February 10, 1946, 819,699 persons, or 0.81 per cent of those who came to the polls, opposed the official nominees.[14]

It has been pointed out in this connection that these figures do not represent a sudden jump, but the culmination of a trend. The percentage of the electorate voting has risen as follows: [15]

1927	50.2%
1929	63.5%
1931	70.9%
1934	85.0%
1937	96.8%

The writer cited sees in these figures proof of the democratic nature of the Soviet regime and the increasing popular support that it enjoys. These data may also, however, be interpreted as evidence of the increasingly tight and effective control exercised by the Party.

Selection of leaders: the appointive principle

As the preceding section demonstrates, strong pressures exist within the Soviet system which tend repeatedly to break down the operation of the elective system in the selection of leaders, to which the regime is committed by its ideology. Within the Party there is a widespread tendency for appointment by coöption to replace election.

In 1937 Zhdanov reported that 11.6 per cent of the members of the *oblast'*, *krai*, and central committees of the Parties of the various national republics had been coöpted to membership. This was an average; in several cases, more than a quarter of the members had been coöpted. Lower in the hierarchy, the percentage of members coöpted was much higher, varying between 14 and 59 per cent for the city and *rayon* bureaus. While Zhdanov is not clear whether this set of figures applies to the USSR as a whole or only to a portion of it, he adds that in very widespread areas more than half the members of the local Party organs had been coöpted. Special cases are of course even more striking. In the city committee of Kharkov, only one third of the members had been legally elected.[16] In view of the fact that Party democracy was held in abeyance during the war, it is probable that the amount of coöption has increased rather than decreased since then.

Even when regular elections take place, there are wide deviations from the avowed ideal of examining and questioning each candidate on his merits. In the same speech, Zhdanov gives a revealing description of how, as he asserts, the choice of candidates is usually made. Some days before an election is due, a Party secretary writes down in a notebook what looks like a good slate of candidates. Afterward there is a gathering behind closed doors of the other Party secretaries, who go over the slate until agreement is reached. When this happens, Zhdanov observes, it is nearly impossible to propose a candidate from the floor of the general meeting.[17] The whole process is cut and dried and chokes off criticism by the Party rank and file.

In addition to the illegal device of coöption, there has grown up an elaborate legal machinery of appointment. Stalin reported to the Seventeenth Party Congress in 1934 that the Central Committee had handled the selection of personnel for the government administrative and economic organizations.[18] In 1939, at Stalin's suggestion, the Party established a Cadres Administration in the Party Central Committee, with corresponding units in each of the republic, *krai,* and *oblast'* Party organizations.[19]

Perhaps the most clear-cut indication of the extent of the operation of the appointive principle is the decree of the Party Central Committee, dated August 22, 1938, which required that the *oblast'* and *krai* committees, as well as the central committees of the national Communist Parties, should submit for confirmation by the Central Committee in Moscow the candidacies of the first, second, and third secretaries of all *rayon,* city, and *okrug* committees throughout the USSR.[20] To conceive of a parallel instance, it would be necessary to imagine that every candidate for election to a county office in the entire United States would have to be cleared by the Cabinet in Washington. The Cadres Administration was established no doubt in order to introduce somewhat greater system into this work.

It is highly likely that the Party Cadres Administration is the agency responsible in many areas for the selection of proper candidates for election to the soviets, although the Russian sources examined are not specific on this point. But it is perfectly obvious that the Party does not scruple too much about the formal privileges of those elected. In 1946 a member of the Politburo, Khrushchev, then Party boss of the Ukraine, revealed that the local (*rayon*) Party secretaries had changed 64 per cent of the chairmen of the executive committees of the *rayon* soviets during the preceding year and a half.[21] Even though these facts were reported in a manner indicating sharp disapproval, the situations are typical of many similar ones reported.

A high rate of turnover in the local leadership is a characteristic of the Soviet regime. The daily press is full of complaints that the local cadres sections of the Party move people around indiscriminately from one job to another, without attempting to match individual capabilities with the requirements of the job.

Only too often, the Party press complains, when a man makes a mess of one job, he is simply transferred to an equally unsuitable post, and an equally unsuitable man is put in his place. This fluidity may diminish as the regime succeeds in educating a greater number of people with the requisite skills.

It is characteristic of the tensions and contradictions in Soviet society that with the one hand the regime tries to restore inner-Party and soviet democracy and to eliminate the practice of coöption, while with the other hand it builds up an elaborate administrative apparatus for the appointment of individuals to all kinds of posts, including many that are in theory open to democratic election. This contradiction is a continuation of the long-standing conflict between the authoritarian and anti-authoritarian elements of Leninist doctrine. If the Russian masses are incapable of achieving the socialist salvation by their own efforts, as Lenin argued on numerous occasions, the obvious consequence is the necessity for administrative control from above through a self-chosen and self-perpetuating elite. Lenin recognized the force of this argument and did not hesitate to apply it. But he failed to recognize that this elite might have to continue its functions after the achievement of the preliminary goal of socialism, and that its operations would run counter to the objective of a society in which the masses were the masters of their own fate.

Changes in the composition and recruitment of the elite

Ordinarily, a self-perpetuating elite leads to a situation in which the composition of the elite remains stable for considerable periods of time. But in the case of the Soviet Union, the changes brought about by the assumption of political responsibility, together with the series of internal and external crises through which the regime has passed, have brought about a marked change in the composition of the elite during the past twenty years.

In fact, there has been a nearly complete turnover in the composition of the Communist Party since the elimination of the opposition elements. Figures published at the 1939 Party Congress showed that 70 per cent of the members had entered the Party after 1928.[22] Since 1939 the number of Party members has more than doubled. It is safe to assert, therefore, that, among the rank and file, those with memories of the old conflicts and old doctrines have been heavily outnumbered by new recruits.

So far as can be ascertained, the Communist Party at no time consisted primarily of factory workers, although strenuous efforts were exerted for a time to make it a real party of proletarians. Instead, in the early days, it was weighted heavily in the direction of intellectuals, the "scribblers" of Krassin's contemptuous phrase. Krassin, it will be recalled, was a former businessman himself, who during the early twenties wanted to see more efficient, businesslike men and methods introduced into the Party. Since his day, his wishes have been fulfilled. As early as 1934, Kaganovich, one of Stalin's top administrators, recognized the change that had taken place. Whereas in the early days, Kaganovich said, the Party worker was primarily an agitator or propagandist, now he knows production well. He has been through a rich school of economic activity and "his viewpoint has become wider, he has become a worker for the government." [23] In other words, a large proportion of Party members had by 1934 become government administrators, responsible for a small or large section of the economic and political life of the country.

The figures on page 258, taken from protocols of Party Congresses, reflect the sharp decline in proletarian membership between 1926 and 1934. No figures for 1939 were published probably because they would have indicated a further drop in the number of workers in the Party.

Insofar as the authorities concern themselves publicly with the decline in proletarian membership, they attribute it to the alleged circumstance that the disappearance of class distinctions in the Soviet Union has made it unnecessary to maintain the rule favoring ordinary factory workers in the recruitment of Party members. This regulation, adopted in 1922 when there was considerable perturbation about the corruption of the Party by alien elements, was abandoned in 1939.[24]

It is much more likely, however, that this decline in proletarian membership is the result of an effort to recruit and absorb

PROLETARIAN MEMBERSHIP OF PARTY [a]
(Per cent)

Year	Working-class kernel [b]	Workers from production
1926	58.4	35.7
1927	57.8	40.8
1930	68.2	48.6
1934 [c]	60.0	9.3

[a] See speech by Kaganovich in *XVI S'ezd VKP(b)*, p. 83; and speech by Ezhov in *XVII S'ezd VKP(b)*, p. 303.

[b] This category apparently refers to men with working-class backgrounds but not necessarily engaged at the time in manual labor. It presumably includes "workers from production."

[c] The 1934 figures refer only to the delegates at the Party Congress and would probably be weighted somewhat against workers from production.

into the Party the leadership group in all fields: political, military, economic, and scientific. The Party has skimmed the cream and taken the top leaders in every walk of life. At the same time, those who came to the top in any field gravitated toward the Party as the source of power and influence. Thus there has been a steady increase in the proportion of factory directors who are members of the Party. In 1923 only 29 per cent were Party members; by 1936 between 97.5 and 99.1 per cent belonged to it.[25] A similar process took place in connection with the Red Army, though it has not been possible to obtain strictly comparable figures for purposes of illustration.[26]

The change in the recruitment of the Party and the consequent shifts in the composition of the elite of the USSR have had their reflection in the ideas concerning how the Party ought to be recruited. The principal change, as has already been pointed out, is in a deëmphasis of the industrial working class, reflected most clearly in the dropping of the rules that gave preference to persons of working-class origin who wished to enter the Party. As Zhdanov pointed out in his 1939 speech introducing this change, the old rules made it increasingly difficult for a worker to enter the Party the more he increased his education or advanced to more responsible positions.[27] In a party that had already become the ruling nucleus and wished to remain a monolithic ruling group, the old viewpoint concerning the virtues of the industrial workers was obviously out of place. It is probable that there was considerable pressure within the Party itself to make this change. Zhdanov quotes a former factory worker, who had become a Vice-Commissar of Light Industry for the USSR after several intermediate steps and promotions, as saying, "How did I become worse as I was promoted from an ordinary worker to the head of a shop? How did I become worse when they made me the director of a factory? Why must I hunt up a larger number of 'recommendations' . . . than before, when I was an ordinary worker?"[28]

In other respects the requirements of Party membership and the paper regulations for the selection of the Soviet elite have remained unchanged. Recent discussions of these regulations still quote the paragraph, which was a bone of contention between Mensheviks and Bolsheviks in prerevolutionary days, defining a Party member as any person who recognizes the Party program, works in one of the Party organizations, subordinates himself to Party orders, and pays dues.

Perhaps because the prewar Party was overloaded with persons holding high administrative positions, the Party has since then tried to alter its social composition by broadening its membership base. Already by 1941 the membership had risen from the 1939 figure of 2,477,666 (including candidates) to 3,876,885 (including candidates).[29] According to *Pravda*, December 9, 1947, the current membership is 6,300,000, of which about one half joined during the war and postwar years. Many joined on the field of battle. Apparently, no figures have yet been published concerning the changes in the social composition of the Party brought about by this mass recruitment. However, it is safe to assume that the Party has been interested in becoming more representative of the population as a whole. In this connection, it is significant that the Party is no longer frequently described as the "vanguard of the working class." Instead, it is referred to as containing "the best representatives of the working class, the peasantry, and the intelligentsia." [30]

From about 1936 onward, the regime has shown a certain limited willingness to permit non-Party elements to share elite positions. The slogan of a bloc of "Party and non-Party Bolsheviks" was put forth in connection with the 1937 elections to the Supreme Soviet. By the term "non-Party Bolshevik" is meant an individual who is a loyal and enthusiastic supporter of the regime without holding a Party card. In the 1946 elections to the Supreme Soviet, there were 106 non-Party delegates out of a total of 682 in the Soviet of the Union, and 148 out of a total of 657 in the Soviet of Nationalities. [31] As has been pointed out, these delegates had already been hand-picked by the Party. There do not appear to be any grounds for concluding therefore, as some have done, that these actions represent a slackening of the authoritarian controls. It would be more accurate to interpret them as evidence that the Party has achieved sufficient consensus in the population to be able to find a number of enthusiastic supporters.

Formulation of national policy

Both the hierarchy of soviets and the Party hierarchy culminate, on paper at least, in representative bodies that allegedly formulate the guiding lines of national policy. The Party statutes define the Party Congress as the supreme policy-making organ of this body (¶¶ 29, 31). Article 30 of the Soviet Constitution declares, "The highest organ of state power in the USSR is the Supreme Soviet of the USSR," to which article 32 adds, "The legislative power of the USSR is exercised exclusively by the Supreme Soviet of the USSR."

Only two Party Congresses have been held in the last sixteen years, one in 1934 and one in 1939, despite the regulation that sets three years as the minimum interval between Congresses. Each of them has been a parade affair, in which policy has been announced in long set speeches. There were no open debates or discussions.

According to the bylaws, the Party Congress "listens to and confirms"—a curiously accurate rendition of the actual situation—

the reports of the Central Committee and other major reports of the central Party organization. It also has the task of reviewing and changing the Party program (not altered since 1919) and the Party statutes. Finally, the Congress supposedly determines the tactical line of the Party on basic matters of current politics (¶ 31). According to the general principles of Party organization (¶ 18), which include the "periodic responsibility of Party organs before their Party organizations," the Central Committee is responsible to the Party Congress and executes the policy laid down by the Congress. However, unlike its predecessors which gave detailed outlines of tactics and strategy to be followed, the last Party Congress of 1939 confined its policy resolutions to an outline of the Third Five Year Plan (interrupted by the war) and did not tie the Central Committee's hands in any other way.

Despite the very limited role of the Party Congress in policy formulation, certain of the older forms of democratic participation were maintained at the last Congress and may also be retained when and if another Congress is called. The Party ordered the publication of the "theses" or main points that would be made by some of the major speakers some months before the Congress. In addition, the main Party daily, *Pravda*, carried a discussion section on these theses.[32] In some instances, writers questioned the major points of the theses. Thus, in *Pravda*, February 4, 1939, two writers questioned the elimination from the new Party statutes of the regulation that gave preference to accepting persons of proletarian origin as new members of the Party. Asserting that the boundaries between workers and peasants were not completely erased, a viewpoint that was contrary to some of Stalin's official statements, these writers asked if this new provision were not premature. Such questionings, however, were rare. They were ignored in the official summary of the discussions, which claimed that the Party unanimously approved the theses although it made many suggestions about details.[33]

Since the end of World War II the sessions of the Supreme Soviet have been used as a forum for the announcement of major national policies in a manner that is reminiscent of the Party Congresses. The resemblance cannot be pushed too far, however, since Stalin has not addressed the Supreme Soviet. (In fact, he has made no long and detailed speeches since 1939.) It is worth noting that there has been no comprehensive review of Soviet policy as a whole, before the Supreme Soviet or any other body, since before the recent war.

The sessions of the Supreme Soviet have given observers the impression of a well-rehearsed play. A study of the stenographic reports of the sessions confirms this impression. It seems that each person who speaks has a set part to play. There are "bit" parts for making procedural motions, and longer parts with formal speeches. Everything proceeds smoothly without objections or interruptions from the floor or the chair until unanimous decisions are adopted.

The elections that take place have obviously been arranged beforehand. For instance, at the 1946 meeting, the first stage in the "choice" of the People's Commissars was a note of formal resignation signed by the chairman, J. Stalin. Immediately afterward a minor delegate made a brief but flowery speech, ending with the motion that J. Stalin be asked to present to the Supreme Soviet a list of People's Commissars. Four days later at a subsequent session, there was read to the assembled delegates a second note from Stalin, in which he asked for the confirmation of a list of Ministers. (The title Commissar had been changed to Minister in the meantime by the Supreme Soviet.) At the head of the list and as chairman of the Council of Ministers was the familiar name of Joseph Vissarionovich Stalin. Following this were eight more members of the Politburo as vice-chairmen of the Council of Ministers. In several cases these members were chosen for additional portfolios. After two brief speeches by delegates from the floor in favor of the list, it was adopted unanimously.[34] In the case of other elections the process was practically identical.

This procedure, with its insistence on open uniformity and unanimous decisions, is an inherent part of the present political ethos. If one may judge from their actions, nothing could be further from the intentions of the present leaders than the creation of a political system in which free play is given to opposing political forces. Unlike the Congress of the United States or the

British Parliament, the Supreme Soviet is by no means an arena in which these forces are intended to clash, with some consensus and compromise emerging from the conflict. No doubt a limited form of clash does occur among men who hold to a common set of fundamental principles (as happens for the most part in Congress and in Parliament); but in the Soviet Union it occurs behind the closed doors of the Politburo.

The preceding remarks should not be taken to imply that there is absolutely no discussion at the sessions of the Supreme Soviet. Such discussion does take place, in which various sections of the government may be made the objects of sharp criticism. Internal evidence indicates, however, that the outcome of such discussion is never for a moment in doubt once the session has opened, and that here too the actors are playing parts that have been well learned beforehand.

By way of illustration, the discussions concerning the 1947 budget of the USSR may be examined. On October 15, 1946, a detailed budget was presented in a long speech by the Minister of Finances to the Supreme Soviet. The following day equally detailed comments on the budget were presented by the chairmen of the budget commissions of the Soviet of the Union and the Soviet of Nationalities (the two chambers of the Supreme Soviet). In the two latter speeches certain changes were suggested, which resulted in identical totals. While the figures are difficult for a nonstatistician to compare, a number of the specific changes suggested were identical in both speeches. If the speakers had learned the contents of the address by the Minister of Finances only at the time it was given or only shortly beforehand, it would have been impossible to present these two detailed and harmonious sets of comments. All the speeches were obviously prepared and synchronized well in advance.

In addition to the comments on the budget presented by the Minister of Finances, the leaders of the budget commissions in the two houses made a number of sharp criticisms concerning the work of several government ministries. The heads of these ministries were also called upon to speak in the course of the debate on the budget. Those subject to censure conceded their faults in tones of *mea culpa,* although in a few cases explanations of objective conditions that had made efficient operation difficult or impossible were added. It is worth noting that no ministry headed by a member of the Politburo came in for criticism. Such criticisms serve several purposes: first, the obvious one of calling attention to inefficient work; secondly, to permit the masses to blow off vicarious steam by attacking an unpopular bureaucrat; and finally, to call public attention to real difficulties that stand in the way of improvement.

When the debates were finally concluded, the budget was voted with the suggested changes made by the budget commissions of the two houses of the Supreme Soviet. The cumbersome procedure of voting the budget section by section was used, although the vote was unanimous in each case. Some requests for additional appropriations, made by individual delegates, were referred to the Council of Ministers for further consideration.[35]

From the foregoing typical examples, it is reasonably clear that the major representative bodies, the Party Congress and the Supreme Soviet, do not play a creative role in the formulation of policy on a national scale. In what group, then, does this power lie? It is widely assumed that Stalin, either personally or with the members of the Politburo, exercises the supreme power in the USSR. Though this hypothesis is probably correct, it must be conceded that there is no direct evidence for this conclusion in the Russian sources. Perhaps less is known about Stalin's personal role in the decision-making process, or about the operations of the Politburo, than about any comparable group of men in history. The Politburo is scarcely mentioned at all in the contemporary Soviet press. All of the decisions that have been reached by this body and that are made known publicly are issued in the form of decrees by the Party Central Committee. In international diplomatic circles there is no continuous flow of information about the currents of opinion, personal qualities, and idiosyncracies among the members of the Politburo, corresponding to the lifeblood of diplomatic dispatches concerning the French and British cabinets and in the past the bulk of the diplomatic data on the prewar regimes of Germany and Japan.

The assertion that Stalin represents the apex of the Soviet political pyramid depends, therefore, very largely on indirect evidence. In earlier chapters the various steps were traced by which he rose to power and eliminated his competitors. The purges during the middle and late thirties give good grounds for concluding that ever since the elimination of Trotsky, Bukharin, and a host of others, continuous opposition to Stalin's policies, even in the secret sessions of the Politburo, would be fraught with no little physical danger. All the Soviet leaders of any prominence who have seriously opposed Stalin are either dead, in prison, or have made their peace with him publicly. Together with the evidence concerning the impotence of other bodies in the decision-making process, these facts provide safe grounds for concluding that Stalin, perhaps with a few associates, holds the power of making and remaking policy in the USSR.

Rare and occasional glimpses into the mechanisms by which decisions are reached at the highest level in the Soviet Union indicate that Stalin has the authority to make significant decisions on his own. The German records of the negotiations leading up to the Nazi-Soviet Non-Aggression Pact and continuing to the outbreak of the Soviet-German war, shed some light on the processes of policy formulation at the highest level in the Soviet regime. Although Molotov conducted most of the direct negotiations with the Germans, he appears to have been acting within the bounds of general instructions, since at no time did he introduce any shift in policy during the course of his extended interviews with the German envoys. In at least one instance Molotov changed his position sharply within a half hour after the close of an interview, explaining that in the meantime he had reported to the Soviet Government. It seems very likely, as the German envoy concluded, that in this short space of time Stalin intervened to reverse the original position.[36] On another occasion Stalin on his own authority, and in the presence of the German envoy, altered the draft of a diplomatic note to be sent to the Polish ambassador in order to make it acceptable to the former.[37] In still another instance Molotov announced that he would have to consult Stalin about the draft of a communiqué, whereupon Stalin replied that the original draft was much too frank and wrote out a new version in his own hand.[38] All in all, the relationship between Molotov and Stalin is shown by these documents to be the relationship between an inferior and a superior.

This conclusion agrees with those reached by high American officials who have had protracted negotiations with the Soviet leaders. Former Secretary of State James F. Byrnes, who concedes that he does not know how much the Politburo influences Stalin, concludes that Stalin accepts the recommendations of the Politburo when he has no strong convictions of his own. But Mr. Byrnes is certain that when Stalin has strong convictions of his own, the Politburo supports him. The basis of this assertion is that Stalin was able in conference to make numerous important decisions promptly, without any apparent necessity for consulting his colleagues. Mr. Byrnes recalls, however, two important cases in which Molotov, or perhaps even others, influenced Stalin to change his mind: the German reparations and the rejection by Russia of the offer of a forty-year alliance.[39] General John R. Deane, head of the American military mission in Moscow from 1943 to 1945, who had more continuous contact with the Soviet leaders than Secretary Byrnes, but at a slightly lower level, has no doubts that Stalin was the supreme authority. In General Deane's opinion, based on almost identical grounds with Mr. Byrnes's, there was never the slightest indication that Stalin would have to consult his government about important decisions.[40]

In the Soviet Union itself there has developed over the years an official mythology, composed of two completely contradictory elements, concerning Stalin's role in policy formulation. On the one hand, Stalin is portrayed as merely first among equals. This viewpoint was at one time cultivated by Stalin himself. In commenting on his famous article, "Dizzy With Success" (1930), which reversed temporarily the process of rapid collectivization in agriculture, Stalin asserted that he had been instructed by the Central Committee to warn erring comrades about dangers in the collective-farm movement. He went so far as to add: "Some people think that the article 'Dizzy With Success' was written on

Stalin's personal initiative. That is nonsense of course. It is not for the purpose of permitting anybody, whoever it may be, to exercise his personal initiative in matters of this kind that we have our Central Committee." [41]

On the other hand, there is the myth of Stalin's infallibility, in which he is portrayed as the great leader, responsible for Soviet policy in every phase since the foundation of the regime. The *Short Biography* of Stalin, published in 1944, and the *History of the Communist Party of the Soviet Union,* which together make up the staple elements of indoctrination for Party members, portray Stalin as responsible for the major victories of the Civil War and all subsequent achievements of the regime. In its concluding paragraphs, the *Short Biography* asserts: "In all areas of Socialist construction his orders form the guiding principles of action. The work of Comrade Stalin is exceptionally broad: his energy truly amazing . . . Everybody knows the invincible, crushing strength of Stalinist logic, the crystal clarity of his mind, his steel will, his devotion to the Party, his burning faith in the people and love for the people." [42] On the whole, the picture of Stalin as the infallible leader has tended to replace the picture of Stalin as merely first among equals.

There is evidence that the Politburo takes upon its shoulders the task of deciding a tremendous number of questions of both major and minor import. Kaganovich complained in 1930 that the Central Committee was swamped with requests for information and directives of the most serious political import.[43] As that section of the Central Committee responsible for political matters, the Politburo would be charged with making these decisions. On another occasion Kaganovich revealed that in connection with the Stalingrad tractor factory, the Politburo heard reports on the situation every five days.[44] A refugee from the regime, Alexander Barmine, reports on the basis of his own experience that the Politburo spent several hours discussing a small contract made with the Germans by one of the minor Soviet importing organizations, and that it kept a continuous watch upon the work of this organization.[45] Many other detailed matters are treated in a similar fashion.

It is evident, therefore, that the agenda of the Politburo at any one meeting or series of meetings cover a broad range of subjects, upon which some kind of decision has to be reached rather promptly. In this connection, it is significant to note the way in which the Politburo occasionally stumbles into a decision of major importance. Like many administrative institutions in the United States, the Politburo to some extent meets situations as they arise through a series of small day-to-day decisions, rather than by following a carefully elaborated policy and plan. It is perhaps inevitable that this should be the case where a concentration of power means that a vast number of decisions has to be made in a short period of time. Kaganovich again illustrates this situation for the USSR in his comments on the reform of the educational system. If his account can be accepted as more or less correct—and it fits with the other evidence just mentioned— the reform of the educational system arose from Stalin's discovery that education was proceeding badly in a single school. From there the matter developed into a study of textbooks and the way they were used in the USSR, and then to much broader matters. Kaganovich commented, probably correctly, that he could quote numerous examples to show how very often, out of what at first sight seemed to be a simple question, "a simple communication or letter," a great decision affecting all branches of Soviet activity arose.[46]

No doubt this pattern of reaching decisions upon a host of individual and superficially unrelated matters has an important effect upon the relationship between ideology and action. At first glance, one might anticipate that the procedure of reaching numerous apparently petty decisions would diminish the impact of ideology upon action. In the United States, at any rate, it is a common complaint that high administrative officers never have time to think things through, and that, as a consequence, policy is often made on a short-range basis, resulting in numerous inconsistencies.

At the same time, the study of a series of decisions reached by an administrative group over a period of time frequently reveals an unsuspected and consistent pattern of apparent motivation and goals. This might be said of the American Supreme Court, provided the time span is not too long, or of the State Department, or any important federal agency. The comment also applies with even greater force to any series of decisions made by the Soviet government. The major periods of Soviet history— the era of War Communism, the NEP, the era of large-scale collectivization and industrialization, and the present period—show a great deal of consistency in both foreign and domestic policy.

The presence of such a pattern suggests that the members of the decision-making body were probably operating on the basis of a definite series of ideological assumptions. There seems to be justification for considering this set of assumptions as the effective or operating ideology of the group. Quite naturally all members of the group will not share this set of assumptions to the same degree, although in the case of the present Politburo it is probable that the core of commonly accepted beliefs is considerable. It is necessary to distinguish, of course, between the effective and actually believed ideology and that which is officially promulgated. At times, and perhaps a large proportion of the time, there may be a very marked divergence between official propaganda and the actual beliefs of the ruling elite. But in this problem we are verging on larger questions, whose tentative answer had best be left to the conclusions at the end of this study.

Formulation of local policy

The local units of the Party enjoy a certain amount of freedom in the search for the best ways and means to carry out the policies determined by the top Party leadership. They of course do not have any power to formulate a policy differing from that of the top leadership; nor was it ever intended that they should have such power. The Soviet daily press is full of accounts that encourage the local Party organizations to use their own initiative in solving problems, always remaining within the framework of general directives laid down by the Central Committee. Thus, on June 23, 1943, to cite a typical account, the plenum of the Moscow *oblast'* committee discussed (1) the preparation for sowing and harvesting; (2) the degree of fulfillment of the government plan for livestock breeding in the *kolkhozy* of two *rayons* in the *oblast'*; and (3) the work of the city and *rayon* committee in accepting new Party members during the first five months of 1943.[47] Particularly in the postwar years there have been a number of accounts telling how local Party organizations cleared up some local supply or administrative tangle that had prevented the local factories or farms from operating effectively. These are written in a "booster" tone that would be quite familiar to many Americans.

Though encouraging this variety of local initiative, the Party maintains an elaborate control over the decisions and policies of its constituent units. The protocols of the meetings of each organization are read by the next highest organization, which has the power to annul incorrect decisions. While a good many of the regional Party organizations do not always read the reports in detail, if one may judge from complaints in the Party press, the system on the whole evidently provides tight controls. The Party Central Committee frequently annuls decisions of subordinate units, reprimands them, and directs them to reconsider questions that in its opinion have been improperly handled.[48] Almost every other issue of the Party Central Committee's journal devoted to organizational questions, *Partiinoye Stroitel'stvo* (Party Construction), contains a reprimand along these lines.

It has always been intended that the Party should be a highly centralized organization. It is the local soviets, rather than the Party, which according to Communist theory are intended to provide outlets for the creative initiative of the masses. According to Stalin, the soviets constitute a "school of government for tens and hundreds of thousands of workers and peasants, and in this way bind the masses to the regime." [49] Kalinin considered it a most important task "to construct the organs of power in such a way that they give the maximum opportunity for the collective demonstration of the creative abilities of the peasant and working masses." [50]

The 1936 Constitution gives a broad, if somewhat vague, grant of power to the local soviets for the exercise of this initiative. Article 97 states: "The Soviets of Working People's Deputies direct the work of the organs of administration subordinate to them, ensure the maintenance of public order, the observance of the laws and the protection of the rights of citizens, direct local economic and cultural affairs and draw up the local budgets." There are at present more than 70,000 local soviets with over 1,300,000 deputies.[51]

The city soviets are called upon to administer a broad category of public services, which in Soviet terminology are lumped together under the name of the "communal economy." This includes the management of the local housing fund, the city transportation system, water supply, sewage, baths, laundries, barber shops, electricity, gas, telephone establishments, and a number of other matters bearing on the local appearance and convenience of the city.[52] In addition, they are supposed to manage local industry, assist in the development of the local production of consumers' goods and local trade in such goods, and take steps to ensure the local food supply. All of these functions have to be carried out within the framework of the local five year plan, which in turn is geared in with the general Five Year Plan of the USSR. In the larger soviets there are several subcommissions that deal with each of these special activities. The subsections are expected to draw into their work the more active and interested citizens who show a desire to participate. From this enumeration it is clear that the local soviets handle those aspects of government activity with which the ordinary citizen comes in frequent contact in daily life.[53]

Since the war the press has laid great stress on the efforts made by the soviets to solve their problems with local resources, which of course diminishes to some extent the general strain of reconstruction on the central organs of the economy. Reports from newspapers indicate that the war has had the effect of increasing somewhat the responsibilities and range of activities of the local soviets.

The village or rural soviets (*sel'sovety*) have wider responsibilities than those in the cities and at the same time approach more closely the status of mere administrative agencies of the central government. They have, in addition to propaganda duties, the responsibility for seeing to it that the government's grain collections are carried out promptly and smoothly. They are frequently referred to as the "organizers of the struggle for grain." As the administrative authorities immediately superior to the collective farms, they are held accountable for the effective organization of labor forces at the rush time of the harvest, and for the delivery of grain in good condition, and on time. Furthermore, they are warned by the press, in thinly veiled language, that they must see to it that none of the grain is held back and that the peasants devote the proper amount of time to the collective aspects of collective farming, instead of spending their energies on their privately owned plots.

Despite the widespread range of their activities, there are strong limitations on the autonomy of the local soviets. Their financial independence is extremely limited, since all of their revenues and a considerable portion of their expenditures are determined by higher authorities. The budget of a local soviet travels upward through the hierarchy of soviets, receiving modifications at each stage of the proceedings, until the final figures are determined for the USSR as a whole.[54] Furthermore, in accord with the principles of democratic centralism, the actions taken by the local soviets are subject to review by higher bodies in the soviet hierarchy in the same way that actions taken by local Party organizations are subject to review by higher echelons in the Party. There are occasional complaints in the daily press that the higher levels of the soviet hierarchy have been too free in their habit of annulling the decisions of the lower soviets.[55]

Within the local soviet itself, there is a strong tendency for power and responsibility to become concentrated in the hands of the executive committee. Both before and after the 1947 elections to the local soviets, the daily press carried numerous editorial complaints about the way in which the meetings of the soviets had been postponed or omitted altogether. *Izvestiya* also reported[56] that since 1939 many executive committees had not made reports on their activities before a meeting of their soviet. During 1946, according to another report, the sessions of the *krai* and *oblast'* soviets in the RSFSR were called at the times set by the constitution of this major republic in only seven *oblast's* and one *krai*, out of a total of thirty *oblast's* and six *krais* in the Russian Republic.[57]

No doubt the greatest limitation on the soviets as expressions of the popular will derives from the controls exercised by the Party. Contemporary Soviet writers make no secret of these controls. "The Party," says one legal writer, "directs all organizations of the toilers, including the soviets." This remark is amplified by the statement that "the Party gives the soviets directives that set the political line and direction of their work." [58]

The control is not exercised through majorities, even though the Party representation in the soviets greatly exceeds its proportion to the population. The proportion of Party members in the Supreme Soviet is high; of the 1,339 members of the Supreme Soviet elected in February 1946, 1,085 belonged to the Party, while only 254 were non-Party individuals.[59] Among the local soviets the proportion is much lower, although it has increased considerably since the last election held in 1939. Of the total number of local deputies (766,563), 46.8 per cent in 1947 were Party members or candidates and 53.2 per cent non-Party.[60] In the 1939 elections, only 31.41 per cent of the deputies were Party members or candidates, while 68.59 per cent were non-Party.[61] Because the Party group within a soviet is required by Party discipline to act as a unit on each question that comes before the soviet, the power of the Party is greater than numbers alone would indicate. Finally, since no organized opposition is tolerated, and since the Party controls every aspect of Soviet life from the contents of the daily newspaper to the operations of the local sport club, its power within the soviets is really overwhelming.

Since the completion of agricultural collectivization in the early 1930's, there has been no problem of opposition to Stalin's policies manifesting itself through the soviets. At that time there was a certain amount of opposition, though its strength is difficult to estimate. Soviet sources claim that a number of rural soviets went over to the *kulaks* during the struggle over collectivization.[62] In the thirties the soviets underwent considerable pressure from the Party to cleanse their ranks and reorganize their work. This was soon completed, after which it was possible for the authorities to assert: "The soviets in their very essence must be the organs for bringing to life the general line of the Party, [and] its conductor to the full depths of the toiling masses." [63] Since then there have been no indications that the soviets have offered any form of opposition to the policies of the rulers.

Popular checks on the policy-makers

In the Soviet regime as now constituted there does not appear to be any institutional device which the masses can use as a preventive check on the top policy-makers of the state.[64] Even the rank and file of the Party is now excluded from putting pressure on the Central Committee by the failure to hold Party Congresses and by the rule, included in the 1939 Party statutes, that general discussions of Party policy can be opened only by the Central Committee. The masses are therefore reduced to forms of passive resistance against unpopular policies. After the peasants had been reorganized on a collectivist basis, this possibility was greatly limited. During the past decade and a half there has been no instance in which popular resistance has forced a major policy change upon the top leadership.

At the lower levels of the Party hierarchy, it appears that the rank and file has the opportunity to exercise some influence over the execution of policy. As has already been pointed out in connection with the election meetings of these lower echelons of the Party, unpopular or inefficient local officials may at times come in for severe criticism or replacement.

The Soviet daily press carries at fairly frequent intervals detailed accounts of examples of deviations from inner Party democracy at the level of the *oblast'* committee or lower. In the general pattern of these accounts two features stand out. In the first place, the restoration of democratic processes does not take place from below, but requires the intervention of some higher echelon in the Party hierarchy. In the second place, the restoration of Party democracy is connected in these instances with some major policy that the Party is promoting at that moment. As a rule, the claim is made that the absence of democracy at the local level is causing a "distortion" of Party policy.

One or two illustrations will give the flavor of these incidents. A *Pravda* correspondent who witnessed a gathering of the Rostov *oblast'* committee reported that committee members took up the entire time of the meeting with long-winded speeches, with the result that "self-criticism spoke only in a half-voice." In some cases the chairman shut off speakers who attempted to make critical observations on the work of the committee. Drafts of the resolutions to be discussed were not presented to the participants until the affair was almost over, and the entire session was conducted in a disorganized manner, with many members of the presidium absent during some of the most important reports.[65] In another instance, a *rayon* conference appears to have revolted spontaneously against its leaders and attempted to elect new ones. The next higher Party organization tried to suppress the revolt, annul the elections, and reinstate the old leadership. A major issue appears to have been the crude and domineering personality of one of the local *rayon* Party leaders, who is quoted as saying, "What Jupiter may do, an ox may not do." The *Pravda* correspondent translates the classical allusion for his readers by the phrase, "What one person may do, another may not," and uses the whole event for a piece on the widespread existence of such violations in the Altai section of the Party organization.[66]

Among the local soviets the same pattern of criticism may be observed; this criticism starts off vigorously but tends to die out in many areas until higher authorities step in to galvanize the mechanism into action once more. *Izvestiya* for April 11, 1947, reported that the Council of Ministers of the RSFSR had decided to "activate the local soviets" by requiring the executive committees to make reports to these bodies during the months of January through June. As has been pointed out above, in many cases no such reports had been made during the interval from 1939 to 1947. From the numerous accounts in the press of meetings that have been held, it is clear that the executive and administrative officers undergo some embarrassing questioning and heckling from the deputies. The complaints range over a wide area of problems, from why it is impossible to buy a glass of cold beer in the summertime at the local brewery to disorder in the management of collective farms. As one example among many, at the twenty-second session of the Moscow city soviet, the head of the housing unit of the soviet, who was in charge also of repair work, received a tongue lashing from the deputies.[67] It is not difficult to imagine the vicarious pleasure of many Muscovite citizens at this event, since the chronic Soviet housing shortage has been much more acute since the war. In this fashion the local soviets serve as a means to blow off steam and allay popular discontent.

Several purposes in the Party's efforts to maintain these elements of grass-roots democracy may be suggested. These actions may be directed toward achieving as wide a degree of mass support as possible, by encouraging the sense of participation in the procedures of governing and preventing the local monopoly of power by an unpopular local tyrant. Another apparent purpose is to break up the formation of local cliques, or "protective alliances," between the local Party leader, the head of the local soviet, the local factory director, and the chairman of the collective farm. The growth of these personal cliques deprives the central authorities in Moscow of their ability to control the life of the country. These tendencies toward local independence and autonomy have always been a serious problem in Russia. Both the positive device of the Party and the negative one of the secret police are necessary to check such trends. Yet, when all this has been pointed out, there appears to be a genuine residue of what Western liberals would recognize as democracy at the lower levels of the Party. It operates within the narrow limits of criticizing and suggesting improvements concerning the execution of policy, without touching the policy itself, and in putting forth leaders who can execute Party policy more effectively. Within these limits there appears to be spontaneous action, instead of the dull, cowed obedience portrayed by some anti-Soviet authors. Thus, the retention of the prerevolutionary goal of inner Party democracy, though highly circumscribed, may continue indefinitely as a feature of Soviet ideology. As it is currently practiced, it serves the double purpose of fulfilling certain psychological needs of the masses while at the same time it tends to strengthen the power of the Soviet elite.

12

The Bureaucratic State

Status in the bureaucratic system

mong Lenin's professed goals in 1917 were the destruction of ureaucracy, the performance of official duties at workmen's ages, and the elimination of "official grandeur." Since that time e Soviet regime has become what may be fairly described as e bureaucratic state *par excellence* of modern times. In most rge-scale social units down to the present time, the state has cluded in its activities only a small proportion of the total ctivities of the society. Likewise, the administrative services f the state have been correspondingly restricted to limited areas f social activity, defense, the maintenance of public order, and e provision of certain social services. In the Soviet Union, on the ther hand, the state has taken over a wide sector of human ac-vity. Nearly every employable individual in the USSR today is 1 the position of an employee of the state. The factory worker nd the factory director are directly dependent upon the state for eir income. For all practical purposes, a nearly identical situa-on prevails on the collective farm, though there will be occasion) note certain disintegrating forces at work there which have led) the expansion of the limited area outside the state's control. The cientist and artist in Soviet society are first and foremost servants f the state, and have recently been sharply reminded of this ict.

If we are not to call every working person in the USSR a ureaucrat, and thus lose all meaning for the term, it is necessary) make some distinctions. In Soviet society as a whole one may istinguish four major groups that have their counterparts in any

contemporary industrial society. To some extent these distinctions
like many attempts at classification, are somewhat arbitrary, a
matter about which there is no reason for concern if the classifica
tion serves its purpose. These major groups are (1) the series o
persons who give the orders and make the economic and politica
decisions necessary for the functioning of the regime; (2) th
providers of scientific knowledge and artistic skills; (3) the per
sons who perform the tasks of recording and checking necessary
in a modern industrial society; and (4) the providers of manua
labor. Numerous subdivisions exist, of course, within each group
For the purpose of this analysis, the Soviet bureaucracy may b
said to include the first three groups, on the grounds that they
perform in varying degrees a function of control and regulation

Before presenting any tentative figures on the composition o
these groups, it is desirable to show more clearly the nature o
these distinctions in Soviet society. Perhaps the clearest distinc
tion of all is between manual workers and non-manual workers
that is, in effect, between ordinary workers and bureaucrats
Manual workers are called *rabochie,* and non-manual workers are
called *sluzhashchie,* which might be translated "employees," o
even "desk workers." These terms are used in legal discussion and
census classifications and may be presumed to represent, at leas
roughly, general status distinctions. The distinction between
manual and non-manual workers is, to be sure, not a new one
Originally, the Bolsheviks endeavored to reverse the status posi
tions of these two social groups. By now the superior position o
the desk workers is recognized, although it would not be accurate
to assert that all desk workers enjoy a position superior to tha
of all manual workers. Before the war desk workers had a six-hou
day, while manual workers had a seven-hour day, although both
groups frequently worked much longer hours. Salary scales and
the method of determining salaries distinguish between manua
and desk workers. The latter had special access to rationed sup
plies during the war. Sabotage laws single out the desk worke
for special responsibility. He is also subject to special regulation
about members of the same family working in the same govern
ment office.[1]

Within the category of desk workers there are numerous status grades and distinctions. Merely to discover all of these gradations, together with the formal and informal insignia that set one group off from the others, would require an intensive field investigation and personal experience in the Soviet bureaucratic structure that is out of the question today.

On the basis of Soviet law, it is possible, however, to point out certain major groupings. Although there is controversy in Soviet legal circles over the exact meaning of the term, the Soviets distinguish an officer group (*dolzhnostnoye litso*) within their administrative system. According to one source, the officer group includes the personnel who are given responsibility and power to issue rules and regulations. In other words, the officer group includes those who have power over persons, while it excludes the persons who fulfill purely technical functions. For example, the administration of a factory or other government establishment has, in the person of the director or chief, a number of powers in addition to the obvious one of the general management of the enterprise. These powers include the representation of the organization before other organizations, the right to issue rules and regulations, the right to hire and fire subordinate personnel, the right to inflict disciplinary penalties, authority over credits and bank balances, and the right to sign checks and other financial documents. In a number of branches of the Soviet administration titles, ranks, and grades (the word used is *klassnyi chin,* recalling the divisions of the Tsarist bureaucracy) were introduced for members of the officer group, both before and during the recent war.[2]

Overlapping the so-called officer group is another group, called the "representatives of power" (*predstaviteli vlasti*). The 1944 commentary to the criminal code of the RSFSR, without defining the "representatives of power," enumerates them as including the deputies of law-making organizations, the members of the government, chairmen and members of soviets, court officials, army officers, and officials of the Ministry of Internal Affairs and the Ministry of Government Security (the secret police), insofar as the latter are fulfilling the functions of state power.[3] It is clear

STATUS DIVISIONS IN THE SOVIET BUREAUCRACY [a]

Category	No. of person
A. *Top level*	
Executives of administrative, public health and cultural institutions	450,000
Directors and other executives of state industrial establishments, shops, and departments	350,000
Party leaders [b]	44,000
Total	844,000
B. *Intermediate level*	
Chairmen and vice-chairmen of collective farms, and collective dairy and livestock department superintendents	582,000
Directors of machine and tractor stations and of state farms, and state farm dairy and livestock superintendents	19,000
Heads of producers' and coöperative organizations	40,000
Store managers and department heads	250,000
Managers of restaurants and other public eating places	60,000
Miscellaneous groups of intellectuals (inclusive of the intelligentsia in the armed forces) [c]	1,550,000
Total	2,501,000
C. *Intermediate level, but having little or no power of command over persons*	
Engineers and architects (exclusive of directors and other executives of establishments and factory departments	250,000
Agronomists	80,000
Additional scientific personnel for agriculture (land surveyors and persons specially trained in land improvement, scientific farming, and stock breeding)	96,000
Scientific workers (professors, university faculty members, and others)	80,000
Art workers	159,000
Physicians	132,000
Economists and statisticians	822,000
Judiciary and procurator staffs (judges, procurators, investigators, and others)	46,000
University and college students	550,000
Total	2,215,000

Category	No. of persons
D. *Lower level*	
Intermediate technical personnel (technicians, construction chiefs, foresters, railroad station masters, and others)	810,000
Teachers	969,000
Bookkeepers and accountants	1,617,000
Intermediate medical personnel (first aid practitioners, midwives, and trained nurses)	382,000
Cultural and educational workers (journalists, librarians, club managers, and others)	297,000
Deputies of local soviets [d]	1,281,000
Total	5,356,000
Grand total of all groups	10,916,000 [e]

[a] Unless otherwise indicated, the figures used here have been taken from Molotov's report to the Eighteenth Congress of the Communist Party, *XVIII S'ezd VKP (b)*, pp. 309–310.

[b] Stalin, *O Nedostatkakh Partiinoi Raboty*, p. 28.

[c] This may include the secret police or a portion thereof. Army officers in 1937 constituted only 80,000 persons (White, *Growth of the Red Army*, p. 378).

[d] Denisov, *Sovety*, p. 41.

[e] Rough confirmation of these figures may be obtained in the following way, using the figures given in E. Davidov, "Naseleniye" (Population), *Bol'shaya Sovetskaya Entsiklopediya*, p. 68. In 1939, according to Davidov, the Soviet labor force was about 29 million (figure reached by interpolation). With their families, this group constituted 84.3 million persons (*rabochie* and *sluzhashchie* added together). Dividing 84.3 by 29 gives a figure of 2.9, or the average size of the family. (The estimate of 2.41 given by Lorimer, *Population*, pp. 226–227, appears to be too small on the basis of these data.) Multiplying the grand total of the bureaucratic stratum, 10,916,000, by 2.9 to get the number of persons in this group, including family members, gives the figure of 31,656,400. Since the total number of *sluzhashchie* with family members is only 29,738,484, the grand total of 10,916,000 is probably somewhat too large. 10,000,000 might be a more accurate approximation, since there is probably some overlap in the categories in the table. However, the size of the family in bureaucratic circles is probably smaller than that obtained by averaging the family size of *rabochie* and *sluzhashchie* together. Hence it may be that the conversion factor is somewhat too large. In the absence of better data, I am forced to let the figures stand with a repetition of the warning that they are rough approximations.

from this list that the group called the "representatives of power" contains a rather heterogeneous collection of persons holding widely varying status positions that range from the highest, Stalin himself, to an ordinary agent of the secret police or a member of a village soviet.

Still other distinctions may be made on the basis of a general knowledge of the functions performed by various groups in the Soviet political and economic system, which need not be set out in detail at this point. But an attempt may be made to present the major categories or status divisions in the Soviet bureaucracy, using as the main source of information Molotov's report on the Soviet intelligentsia presented to the Eighteenth Party Congress in 1939. The grouping given below is only a very rough approximation. Changes have undoubtedly taken place as a result of the war, although it is likely that the major result of the war in this connection was merely to swell the ranks of the bureaucracy, without producing far-reaching changes in the proportions of the various status grades. Since truth emerges more readily from error than from confusion, the tentative breakdown on pages 280–281 may serve as a basis for preliminary analysis.

Presumably groups A and B (with the possible exception of the last item in B) belong to the officer group or the "order givers" in Soviet society.

The providers of scientific knowledge and artistic skill fall for the most part in group C. A case could be made for placing the cultural workers of group D in this category also, although it appears that their work is of such routine nature that it would be better to place them in the fourth classification. This fourth category, group D, contains as its core the persons who perform the tasks of recording and checking which are necessary for the operation of a modern complex society.

Members of this bureaucratic stratum, together with their families, constituted in 1939 close to 17 per cent of the total population of the USSR. At first, this figure appears to be a large one, when one reflects that in the United States in the same year the total number of employees of the federal and local governments, including schoolteachers, amounted to only 3,820,000 persons, or a little less than 3 per cent of our population at that time. But it is clear that the large size of the Soviet bureaucracy is also due to the fact that many functions are performed by the Soviet government, either directly or indirectly, which in the United States are left to private enterprise. The Soviets themselves apparently include in their conception of the bureaucracy or controlling apparatus only those persons listed in the A level of the table, together with the large "miscellaneous" group included in the B level. Their own figure for the number of persons working in government establishments in 1937 was only 1,743,300.[4]

The principal remaining group in the Soviet population, the manual workers and their family members, was divided between the collective farmers, with 75,600,000 persons or 44.6 per cent, and the urban and rural workers, with 54,600,000 persons or 32.2 per cent. The rest of the population, 5.7 per cent, was divided into the minor categories of individual peasants, coöperative craft workers, and others that need not concern us here.[5]

Status differences within the bureaucracy are also indicated by means of salary differentials, although there are very little data on this point. Salary scales are set by the Council of Ministers of the USSR, either in the form of a definite scale or as maximum and minimum rates. In the latter case, power is delegated to individual ministers or to the heads of various organizations to set salary rates for specific duties, taking into account the qualifications of the worker, the type of work, and so forth. For certain categories of workers, scales are established in relation to the education or scientific qualifications involved, as well as in relation to the location of the work. A distinction is made between work in the city and work in the country. In the case of famous scientific specialists who are given administrative tasks, special salaries are paid.[6] To some extent these specialist salaries are probably a matter of individual bargaining between the scientist and the administrative agency concerned.

In addition to salary differentials, status distinctions within the Soviet bureaucracy are made clear through such familiar devices as honorary titles, medals, uniforms, grants of living quarters, free railway passes, and the like.[7] As readers of the American newspapers know, the use of uniforms, medals, and titles increased considerably during and after the war. Soviet writers themselves point out that the war brought about an increase in the authority and responsibility of government officials.[8]

To some extent this open recognition of status differentials may reflect the sentiments of power holders who have long been aware of the social distance that separates them from the mass of the population. Glimpses of the actual sentiments of this group may be obtained through official criticism of the bureaucracy. In 1934 Stalin spoke sharply of the type of executive "who rendered certain services in the past, people who have become aristocrats, who consider that Party decisions and the laws issued by the Soviet government are not written for them but for fools." In a typical postwar editorial, *Izvestiya* found it necessary to urge the Soviet official to pay more attention to complaints and declarations that were finding their way in a steady stream into their offices, reminding them that live human beings were behind such pieces of paper.[10]

More important than the personal sentiments of the holders of power as a factor influencing the open acceptance of status differentials is the objective need for such differentials in a modern industrial society. Indeed, even the simplest preliterate societies make use of some types of status distinctions, while a few of them have elaborated such distinctions to an extremely complicated degree. The complex organization of a modern industrial society requires for its functioning that certain persons should hold authority and responsibility, while others should with a minimum of friction, carry out orders and directions. The open recognition of such a need, reinforced by an official ideology of inequality, can do much to reduce such frictions and to contribute to the smooth functioning of the social system. Although the USSR has traveled a long way toward the open acceptance of status distinctions, certain limiting factors, which will be considered shortly, prevent the complete acceptance of a hierarchy of authority.

At various times a number of attempts have been made to systematize the routes and techniques of advancement through

the various status grades of the Soviet bureaucracy. It appears
that all of them have run into the resistance of well-established
informal routes and techniques, and have for the most part
shattered against this resistance. In part, the failure to achieve
such systematization may be the result of the continuing shortage
of administrative skills in relation to the demand for them created
by the Soviet social system. As the experiences of the American
Civil Service during the war indicated, such a demand for skills
makes it difficult to establish by administrative order a pattern
of advancement that will be adhered to, and opens the door for
the individual with the ability to make use of personal contacts
and other informal channels—the "operator" in American bureaucratic slang. Official Soviet complaints speak of the selection of
officials for various posts on the basis of personal ties, "personal
acquaintances and friends, persons from the same place, devoted to an individual and masters at the art of praising their
boss." [11]

The various Soviet ministries have special deputies in charge
of work with cadres, whose task it is to see that the proper man
is selected for each task. But it is found that such work is widely
neglected, or turned over to second-rate officials.[12] So far the
various ministries have had no outstanding success in breaking
up these groupings, according to the Party daily.[13]

There exists now in the Soviet Union a special organization,
similar to the American Civil Service Commission, whose task it
is to introduce systematic arrangements into the Soviet bureaucratic apparatus. On June 5, 1941, the Government Staff Commission (*Gosudarstvennaya Shtatnaya Kommissiya*) was set up
under the Council of People's Commissars and given the task of
working out a general classification of all government jobs and
their corresponding salaries. The Commission was further expected to get rid of "artificially created" sections of the political
and economic administrative machine, and to eliminate duplica-
tion and all kinds of superfluous organizations. It was given
powers of inspection as well as the right to order the dissolution
of any specific section.[14] While it is impossible to evaluate the
work of the Commission accurately without greatly extended

study, the stream of self-criticism in the daily press suggests that it has not wrought any fundamental changes.

Policy execution and the vested interest in confusion

The preceding chapter described the concentration of the decision-making process at the apex of the political system. The consequences of this concentration remain to be considered. In general, the spurs and checks found in a capitalist democracy, which are largely the product of the division of authority and economic competition, are replaced in the Soviet system by pitting the various sections of the bureaucracy against one another. On the whole, the Party acts as a spur or spark plug, while the secret police acts as the main negative check. This description is, however, considerably oversimplified, since both the Party hierarchy and the hierarchy of soviets have developed numerous control organs of their own. For example, the regional units of the Party are supplied with a corps of roving "instructors," who visit the factories and farms in the area under their control in an attempt to learn at first hand the problems faced and the measures taken to cope with them. Good instructors manage to find out what is going on at all levels of the Party and in economic organizations, and to give advice in unraveling knotty problems; poor ones content themselves with superficial conversations with local officials. Thus, in addition to the secret police, the instructors constitute supplementary eyes and ears for the regime.[15]

In this connection there is another dilemma facing the Soviet regime. On the one hand, the system requires for its functioning a definite hierarchy of status positions and an adequate allocation of authority. On the other hand, because of the need for means to check up on the execution of policy decisions, there apparently exists a vested interest in confusion, and particularly confusion in the allocation of authority. This situation may be illustrated in the relationships between Party officers and other foci of authority in the fields of industry, agriculture, and the general administrative services.

In the first two of these fields there are three ladders of authority, the economic ladder, the soviet ladder, and the Party ladder, whose relationship to one another, even on paper, is an extremely tenuous one. Beginning with the situation in industry, the main steps in the economic hierarchy are the *Glavk* or Ministry (formerly called the People's Commissariat), the factory director, and the worker. The hierarchy of soviets also has vague functions of economic supervision. The soviets were recently advised not to take an overly restricted view of their tasks in the economic sphere, at the same time that the factory managers were told not to be perturbed by what at first glance might seem like interference from these organizations.[16] The third ladder of authority is, of course, the Party. Two levels of the Party hierarchy impinge most frequently upon the activities of the Soviet factory director. The regional Party organization (*oblast'*, *krai*, city, or *rayon*) is responsible for nearly everything that takes place within its own area, including the operation of industrial undertakings.[17] In practice, regional Party organizations frequently exert sufficient pressure to be able in effect to discharge and appoint the factory directors, although this task properly belongs to the Ministry. If the regional Party organization is both theoretically and actually superior to the factory director, the primary Party organization, or Party unit within the factory, is supposed to be his helper in raising morale, discipline, and the like.

Conflicts and confusion occur primarily at three points in this set of industrial relationships: between the factory director and the Ministry, between the factory director and the regional Party organization, and between the factory director and the primary Party organization within the factory.

The Ministry supposedly grants to the director a wide degree of autonomy in the making of decisions relating to production. But at the same time it tends frequently to interfere in these decisions by such actions as arbitrarily fixing the plant's manpower and payroll, or by even going so far as to allocate the payroll among the main categories of workers, manual workers, technicians, office workers, and so forth—acts which deprive the director of the necessary flexibility required for maximum productive efficiency.[18]

Likewise, the regional Party organizations have of late been accused of interfering unduly in the area of decision-making supposedly left to the director. However, official advice on the question of the Party's task in industry is quite contradictory. *Pravda* on March 18, 1948, declared in its editorial columns that the Party regional organizations must be freed of the economic and administrative functions that do not belong to them in "order to be able to exercise real control over the work of the economic organs." "The Party leader," *Pravda* continued, "who gets stuck in current details, duplicates and copies the work of the directors, necessarily comes to the mistaken mixing of functions, and propagates irresponsibility among the economic and technical leaders." [19] At the same time, the regional organizations are told that their task is "to reduce the cost of production, diminish the amount of labor, materials, fuel, and electrical energy per unit of output," a task that is, of course, the major one of the director. They are further informed that they should not merely listen to periodic reports from the directors of enterprises within their area, but should get down to the details of actual production. [20]

Confusion of counsel and practice also prevails rather widely in the relationships between the primary organization of the Party in the factory and the factory administration. According to section 61 of the Party statutes, the primary organizations are granted what is called the "right of control." A recent definition of this right of control includes the right to hear the reports of the directors, the right to uncover weaknesses within the organization and functioning of the enterprise, and the right to bring forward their own suggestions for the elimination of these weaknesses. At the same time, the primary Party organization is specifically warned not to interfere with the orders issued by the factory director or factory administration, or to annul the orders of the director. [21]

Accounts of the activities of the primary organizations criticize them for attempting to administer on their own account. Nevertheless, they are praised for investigating and making suggestions about the quality of production, the introduction of new technology, the organization of labor, and general matters of efficiency. They are required to work "through the director," though they have the right to demand that the director elimi- nate any faults that they have uncovered.[22] In a typical case, which took place during the war, a factory director attempted to blame war conditions for his failure to produce up to the plan, pointing to the mountain of telegrams on his desk as proof of his efforts to obtain raw materials. The Party primary organiza- tion, with the help of the Party city committee, investigated the situation and found that the supply division was buried in un- necessary paper work, as a result of which forms showing that the materials had already been received lay around for weeks.[23]

A parallel situation exists in agriculture. The chief agricul- tural unit is the collective farm (*kolkhoz*). The *kolkhoz* is the bottom link in a chain that leads down from the Ministry of Agriculture through the Machine-Tractor Stations. It is also sub- ject to the authority of the District Soviet Executive Committee (*Raiispolkom*) and one of its constituent units, the village soviet, in both political and economic matters.[24] All of these organiza- tions are in one way or another subject to the authority of vari- ous echelons of the Party. In agriculture the function of the pri- mary Party organization is the same as that in industry. How- ever, in relation to the number of collective farms, there are still very few Party primary organizations. Because of this, the Party has organized, alongside the units in the collective farms, what it calls "territorial primary organizations," which bring together Party members working in the village soviet, the coöperative, the school, and *kolkhozy* lacking organized Party units.[25]

In the various government offices, including those of the sovi- ets, a similar system of multiple control exists, though there are important differences to be noted. Each government office is under the supervision of a corresponding echelon of the Party. "Inspection and control over the work of the central, *oblast'* and *rayon* [soviet] establishments is carried out by the Party *oblast'*, city, and *rayon* committees." Party primary organizations in the various administrative and soviet offices (that is, the Party cell in government offices, though the term cell is no longer used) do not have the right of control that the corresponding organizations have in industry and agriculture. In this respect the line of authority would appear to be somewhat clearer. However, in addition to seeing that red tape is kept down and that visitors receive courteous attention, the Party primary organizations are required to "signal the weaknesses of the work of the establishment"—a favorite Soviet phrase—by reporting failures and difficulties to the next higher echelon of the Party, as well as to the administration of the office in which they occur.[26]

The general situation may be summed up by the observation that the Bolsheviks proceed by setting the Party against the soviet and the economic hierarchy, and then setting the secret police to watch over all of them. Clear lines of authority on the whole are lacking. It does not appear that this pattern is in general the product of deliberate creation, although some sophisticated individuals at various levels of the bureaucratic hierarchies are undoubtedly aware of some of the principles by which it operates.

As might be anticipated on the basis of the preceding information, there is a tendency within the bureaucracy for informal groupings to spring up and to serve as a defense against the competitive pressures induced by the system. The role of such informal units in controlling promotion has already been discussed. These protective groupings are called by the picturesque and revealing general term of "familyness" (*semeistvennost'*), which conveys very clearly the conception of protective and friendly relations rather than the system of mutual watchfulness encouraged and approved by the regime.

In industry, for example, there is a tendency for the leadership of the Party primary organization to form a protective alliance with the factory administration. Often this protective alliance is sealed by gifts from the director to the secretary of the primary organization.[27] The formation of these protective groupings need not be attributed solely to the desire to cover up one another's faults. It is also much more efficient, from a purely economic point of view, for the factory director and the head of the Party organization, which is responsible to a large extent for discipline and morale, to have a close working relationship.[28] Furthermore, the factory director nowadays is nearly always a Party member too.

Nevertheless, the Party is well aware that if the primary organization is to serve its purpose of standing watch over the factory administration, it must maintain its independence.[29] The Party does its best, therefore, to discourage the formation of these mutual alliances. Frequent denunciations of the sin of "familyness" are scattered through the daily press, and this problem is attacked in several other ways as well. The recurrence of the problem supports the hypothesis, however, that the periodic growth and destruction of these informal social units are inherent features of the Soviet social order: *Pravda* recently (October 27, 1946) reiterated a 1928 Party decree that attempted to cut the dependence of Party officials on the administrators of economic enterprises.[30]

An almost identical situation is found in agriculture. The Party tries to keep the primary organizations on the collective farms separate from the farm administration, in order that the Party group may act as a stimulant and also as an inspection device in relation to the *kolkhoz* administration. However, it appears that frequently the leadership of the Party primary group and the chairmanship of the collective farm end up in the hands of the same individual.[31] In other words, there is a tendency for status relationships to assume a form that leads to inner group harmony. In part, this may be due to the fact that in many localities there is only one outstandingly energetic and capable person or natural leader. Whatever the causes, the situation reflects the difficulty faced by the Party in its efforts to maintain control by setting one organization to watch another.

For similar reasons, Party members in the administrative services often fail to carry out their obligation to report errors and difficulties.[32] Such a situation arises, it has been said, "because the Party buro or the secretary of the Party organization is afraid to spoil his relationship with the head of the establishment, or doesn't want to 'carry rubbish out of the hut'" (the Russian equivalent of washing dirty linen in public).[33]

There is another reaction to the pressures of the bureaucratic regime, particularly to the pressures of routine and the social demand to "get things done," which affect both the capitalist captain of industry and the Communist administrator. For lack of a better name, this response may be called the affirmation of virtue. Soviet administrative staffs, like their counterparts elsewhere, make "decisions" or adopt resolutions which accomplish nothing, but which may relieve some anxieties about conformance to an expected norm of activity. In this fashion activity becomes an end in itself and a way of avoiding the consideration of serious problems. If a man is able to keep busy enough on inconsequential administrative details, his self-esteem is raised, and there is little danger that he will become depressed by the question of whether this administrative activity is serving its stated purpose or any other. He develops what the Soviets call a blind belief in the effectiveness of directives.[34]

One account, typical of many in the Soviet press, illustrates concretely the nature of these difficulties. According to an editorial in *Izvestiya* on March 4, 1947, the executive committee of a certain city soviet issued almost seventeen hundred resolutions and orders in the course of a year. Sessions and hearings were held regularly. At first glance, *Izvestiya* remarked, one might conclude that these people worked hard and effectively. But complaints made at one session of the soviet revealed that the housing fund of the city had been neglected, streetcars did not work, the public baths were dilapidated, and matters were in a generally sorry state. Whether the authorities of the city could have done anything about this situation is a question that cannot be answered without greater knowledge of local circumstances. It is known, however, that the Soviet system of central economic planning makes it extremely difficult for cities or other social units to obtain materials for projects that are not included in the Plan. In itself, the responsibility of the authorities is not significant. What is significant is the typical reaction of the local officials to a form of frustration combined with the pressure for achievement.

The regime opposes the tendency for informal protective groupings and other "distortions" to grow up within the bureaucratic structure by drawing upon the ideological inheritance of equalitarianism. The argument is put forth, correctly enough, that the growth of these protective associations, the sin of "family-ness," prevents the execution of the Party line. To counteract such development, self-criticism is encouraged and democratic procedures are restored in Party and other organizations that have turned into closed cliques. The resultant situation might be called an open season on bureaucrats, even though it is definitely an open season on minor bureaucrats and not on the top leaders of the regime.

In many cases, the criticism takes the form of scapegoating, in which one official or group of officials is singled out for blame because of problems that are either inherent in the Soviet system as a whole or in other general circumstances. It is a common practice to blame shortages of consumers' goods on the inefficiency of a particular government department, when in fact they are the result of wartime conditions or the necessities of building up heavy industry. A typical example may be cited at random: shortly after the war *Trud,* the trade-union newspaper, asserted that it was necessary to "purge the trading organizations and control and ration card bureaus of all parasites and doubtful workers who are feathering their nests there," and that better public control was needed to put the supply stores, dining rooms, and ration-card bureaus in order.[35] It is not difficult to infer that many exasperated consumers were pleased by such official lashings and relieved by the accompanying promise of an increase in the availability of scarce consumers' goods.

On other occasions the complaints take the form of letters to the editor of the daily press, of which the following is a typical example. A woman architect, who had received authorization to spend her vacation at a tuberculosis sanatorium, arrived at the railroad station nearest the hospital. No further transportation was available, and, despite the heat of the day, she was forced to walk ten kilometers to her destination. There she found that the sanatorium was closed, and was told by the director of the liquidated institution that many other people, evidently less trusting than she had been, had telephoned from the same railroad station to discover this fact. Returning to Moscow, she received no satisfaction from the trade-union officers who had originally issued the authorization. Since they merely shrugged their shoulders and said they knew nothing about the sanatorium's being closed, she went to an officer of the All-Union Central Council of Trade Unions. The latter refused to issue a permit for another sanatorium and put the blame on the original union officers. By this time the woman's vacation was evidently over.[36]

The outcome of this particular complaint is not known, though it is a safe assumption that several uncoöperative bureaucrats got into a good deal of hot water. It is not necessary for such letters to be published to be effective. Many people from all over the Soviet Union continually write to Stalin about their difficulties. Part of the task of Stalin's secretariat is to use these letters as evidence of clogging within the administrative apparatus, particularly in areas and matters that the Politburo considers significant at any given time. This fact is frequently publicized by Soviet leaders, who are fond of asserting that fundamental decisions have been reached on the basis of letters or information from simple peasants or workmen. This device may act as a check on some of the more flagrant forms of obstructionism.

At other times, elected officials may attempt to intervene to straighten out some tangled red tape for their constituents in a manner not unlike that of an American Congressman. *Izvestiya* of May 31, 1947, carried a revealing account of this type of work by a deputy of the Supreme Soviet of the USSR, showing quite clearly the status relationships between members of the Supreme Soviet and more permanent officers of the Soviet bureaucracy. The deputy involved, one I. Panin, reported that he received from his constituents more than a score of letters a day, and that in the course of a year he dealt with the questions and complaints of nearly three thousand constituents. When Deputy Panin tried to reach Soviet officials on the telephone regarding these matters, he found that the secretary usually replied that the official was "in conference." At first he believed the secretaries. Later he learned to give his own name after the secretary had said the official was "out," but before she put the telephone down. The result was that the secretary usually said she would "have a look

o see if he had come back," and as a rule the official was located
nd the business transacted without difficulty. On other occasions,
owever, Deputy Panin ran into outright and repeated refusals
f his requests for an interview, preceded by the secretary's care-
ul ritual of writing down the exact nature of his visit, problems
o be discussed, and so forth. Evidently, certain of the business
olkways of socialism do not differ significantly from those of cap-
talism, both being behavior patterns developed in adaptation to
imilar circumstances.

Consequences

The consequences of the authoritarian and equalitarian pres-
ures, as they work themselves out in the Soviet bureaucracy,
nay be described in the following manner. The competitive situ-
tion is to a large extent the consequence of the extreme central-
zation of authority. The competitive situation provides the chief
nethod for checking up on the execution of policy, which is
cknowledged by the Soviets themselves to be one of the weaker
eatures of the present regime. Equalitarian doctrines and the
radition of "control from below," even if largely abandoned in
he strictly technical sense, continue to play an important politi-
al role in that they are utilized by the top leadership to control
he bureaucratic servants.

In a defensive reaction against these competitive pressures,
rotective nuclei and alliances tend to grow up within the bu-
eaucracy. There is also a tendency for status relationships to
pproach a functional division of power and authority, in which
he man who has responsibility also has power. These protective
uclei are continually being destroyed at the instigation of the top
'arty leadership.

The question may be fairly raised whether this continual
growth and destruction, which wastes an incalculable amount
f human and material resources, is really an inherent feature
f the Soviet social system. Is there anything to prevent the top
eaders from taking advantage of the tendency to develop a func-
ional system of status and authority, from reaping the benefits of
;reater economic efficiency and diminished social friction? Obvi-

ously, something of the sort must take place at the lower levels of the general bureaucratic hierarchy, when, let us say, the regional Party secretary looks the other way at the growth of illegal combinations and groupings. Otherwise, the complaints would not be so continuous.

Once again, such a question cannot be answered definitively in the absence of experimental methods. One must also avoid the temptation to argue that because things are so they cannot be otherwise. Yet it seems very likely that under present conditions the top Party leaders cannot afford to let matters take their course, and that what we have called the vested interest in confusion is an inherent feature of the current regime. If the top Party leadership permitted the continuous growth of combinations between the factory director and the Party primary organization, or between larger units, such as the factory director, the heads of the local soviet, the heads of collective farms, and the local Party officials, it would soon find itself deprived of a valuable means of checking up on the execution of its major decisions. It seems, therefore, that there is a real dilemma between short-run and local interests in efficiency, and the over-all and long-run interests in both efficiency and the maintenance of power.

From another and more long-range point of view, however, there are some grounds for doubting that the so-called vested interest in confusion will remain an essential feature of the Soviet system. In Tsarist Russia the traditions of promptness, accuracy, honesty, obedience, and rationality—in the sense of fitting the most effective means to a given set of ends—were not as highly developed in ruling circles as they were, for example, in the Prussian bureaucracy. In addition, the level of formal education, essential for the recording operations of modern society, was extremely low in comparison with Western Europe. Starting with these conditions, it is understandable that the Bolsheviks would be compelled to improvise all sorts of ways to check up on the execution of a centrally determined policy. This is simply another way of stating the familiar argument that Russia was probably the worst possible place to attempt to introduce socialism.

In Western Europe, if we accept a balance between Max

Weber's views and those of scholars of more materialist leanings, the qualities of promptness, rationality, and the rest were the product of certain features of the Protestant Reformation together with the discipline imposed by the requirements of a machine civilization. In Russia after 1917 the Party constituted the focal point for the diffusion not only of a machine civilization, but also of the qualities that by necessity accompany it. In this process, as has been indicated, the Party had to undergo a considerable transformation itself, eliminating from positions of power the prerevolutionary intellectuals, who could only manipulate symbols, and putting in their places the manipulators of both symbols and men. In the course of the past three decades the impediments imposed by a low level of formal education have been very largely removed. It is safe to assume that, if the present trend continues, these qualities will be more widely diffused among the population at large.[37] There is a possibility then, in the long run at least, that some of the features of the Soviet bureaucracy described in this chapter will in the course of a generation become less important. One may look forward to a partial decline in the elaboration of formal and informal devices utilized for the verification of policy execution. But it is unlikely that the rulers will permit this to go so far as to endanger their power.

13

The Industrial Order: Stalin and Adam Smith

The problem and the Marxist answer

It has been pointed out that any industrial economic system has to find ways and means for making four groups of decisions. First, it is necessary to decide what to produce. In the second place, decisions have to be made concerning the most efficient way of combining labor and resources in order to produce the guns, butter, and other myriad products of a modern industrial order. Thirdly, it is necessary to provide some means for deciding how much economic effort should go into the building of new plants and the replacement of equipment that has become worn out or obsolete. Finally, there have to be devices for ensuring the orderly distribution of the products of the economy among the population.[1]

The answer given to these problems by classical economic theory, and to a lesser extent by capitalist economic practice, is that the free play of the acquisitive impulses of the individual in an atomistic and competitive order of society will result in a maximum flow of goods and services. On the producer's side, the restless search for profit will supposedly lead him to find out what goods the consumer wants. The pressure from his competitors will supposedly compel him to manufacture these goods with a minimum output of labor and resources. Competition also forces the producer to sell his goods at a price that just covers the cost of production, including a return for his own managerial and entrepreneurial skills. On the consumer's side, it is argued that the restless search for gain will send him into the employment that provides a maximum payment for his skills and efforts. Likewise, the acquisitive drives will compel the consumer to spend his earnings in the most efficient manner possible: that is, he will seek to purchase goods and services at the lowest possible price for comparable quality. In this way the consumer controls ultimately the activities of the producer, and the system of theorems is closed.

This system has been under attack ever since its formulation. At least in terms of institutional consequences, Marx and his followers have turned out to be the most important of the attackers. The essence of the Marxist attack lies in the denial of the assumption that the free play of acquisitive impulses among individuals will bring about a maximum of wealth and prosperity for all. Instead, Marx endeavored to show that under the operation of capitalist institutions the free play of such impulses would result in the rich becoming richer and the poor becoming poorer—in the famous "polarization of classes," culminating in the explosion of the class struggle in the proletarian revolution. This doctrine, too, has been subject to critical onslaught ever since it was first propounded.

In addition, Marx anticipated the viewpoint of some anthropologists in his denial that the "laws" of economics were laws in the same sense as the description of universal relationships observed and calculated by the natural scientists. Instead, according to Marx's argument, each type of social organization—slave economy, feudalism, and capitalism—displays economic and social relationships or laws of its own. With the advent of socialism, according to a famous phrase of Engels', man would make the leap from the realm of necessity into the realm of freedom. Marx coined no such phrase, and asserted more cautiously that in a socialist society man would still be subject to some restrictions and limitations, though these would not be the same as in capitalist society.

This denial of the axioms of classical economics was continued and elaborated by Lenin, Trotsky, Bukharin, and Stalin. At the same time, the Communists have taken over and modified

some of the features of capitalist society, such as the utilization
of status differentials and incentives, devices that received an
oblique approval in Marx if not among his lesser followers. As a
consequence of these and other modifications, the hope has been
continually expressed in the West that the Russians were abandoning socialism and adopting capitalism. Every straw has been
seized to prove that their economic system and economic ideology was like our own. Under the pressure of wartime desires to
see our allies in our own image, this discussion reached the point
where a rather turgid restatement of Marxism, indistinguishable
from many others in the Soviet press, was suddenly seized upon
by the American newspapers as evidence that the Russians were
abandoning Marxism.[2] It is well to examine, therefore, at least
in outline form, the basic ideological assumptions, motivating
drives, and institutional structure of the Soviet industrial system.

Who decides what to produce?

The first question raised in the opening paragraph of this
chapter may be used as a starting point: How does the Soviet
system provide for reaching decisions on whether to produce
guns or butter, machinery or knitting needles?

From the available evidence, it is reasonably certain that
the major decisions on the general production goals of the Soviet
economy, including the types of products and quantities of each,
are now reached by the Politburo and embodied in the various
Five Year Plans. This concentration of the decision-making power
on matters of national import in the economic field parallels the
political concentration of power. The present situation differs
markedly from that before Stalin's accession to power. The First
Five Year Plan was itself the product of discussions and small
scale trials that lasted from the November Revolution until 1929.

The highest planning body on economic affairs is the Gosplan
(State Planning Commission). However, as the English economist Maurice A. Dobb, who is not one to emphasize the authoritarian aspects of the Soviet regime, points out, the Gosplan is an
advisory body and "not an executive department of state."[3] It is
a part of the Council of Ministers and, according to Soviet sources,

receives its directives from them and from the Supreme Soviet.[4]

During the war the power to reach economic decisions, as well as supreme political power, was concentrated in the hands of the Government Defense Committee headed by Stalin. In addition to Stalin, this Committee included Molotov, Voroshilov, Malenkov, Beriya, Kaganovich, Mikoyan, and Voznesensky, all, except the last, prominent members of the Politburo.[5] In view of the overlap between the Politburo and the Council of Ministers, as well as between the Politburo and the Government Defense Committee, it is safe to assert that general decisions and directives originated in the Politburo during the war and originate there now.

The procedure by which the Five Year Plans are actually drawn up is quite complicated and need not be considered in detail here, especially since this aspect of the Soviet system has received considerable attention from Western writers.[6] It is sufficient to point out that in formulating the details of a Plan the Gosplan authorities must take careful account of existing capacities and resources, an operation which requires an accurate knowledge of such capacities and resources for the USSR as a whole. In the second place, the planners have to make sure that the plans for each industry and area match one another. For example, in expanding the amount of electric power, the Gosplan has to be sure that there will be available the necessary steel and other equipment for building the new power plants, and that this power in turn will be in a locality where it will be useful to other factories. Thus, it is quite clear that the planners, including not only the technicians but also the political authorities, do not and cannot have a completely free hand in the choices that they make.

The conclusion that the basic decisions concerning what to produce and in what quantities are made in their essentials by the Politburo goes directly counter to the official ideology, according to which the masses participate widely in the planning process and thereby help to control their economic destiny. A recent semipopular Soviet exposition of the planning machinery devotes a whole chapter to the participation of the masses in planning.[7]

An examination of this and other material bearing on this

point throws very severe doubts upon the official contention. What happens, apparently, is that, under the stimulus of the Communist Party, the workers, factory directors, and collective farmers produce counterplans, in which they promise to carry out, or often to overfulfill, the official government plans. In 1947 and 1948 these counterplans have taken the form of long letters to Stalin, printed on the front page of the newspapers, in which groups of workers or farmers set themselves specific production goals that they are pledged to fulfill. Other forms of so-called mass participation in planning are the Stakhanovite movement and "socialist competition," in which various groups of workers or factories as well as collective farms vie with one another for prizes awarded to the group with the greatest output. All of these movements are carefully controlled and stimulated by the Party. There is not the slightest evidence that they can in any way affect the fundamental aims of the Plan. They do not affect such basic decisions as whether the economic resources of the country will be directed into heavy industry or light industry, into war goods or peace goods, consumers' goods or producers' goods, which are the essential decisions of the Plan. They are merely additional stimuli to production that, together with the elaborate apparatus of control, help to take the place of the spurs and checks provided by the market in a capitalist economy.

Position and motivations of the Soviet manager

Once the decision has been reached concerning what goods are to be produced, there remains a host of decisions to be made concerning the most efficient combination of raw materials, factory equipment, and labor necessary to produce them. Under a capitalist system, the profit motive provides the major stimulus for the maximization of efficient production, and the bankruptcy court the chief negative sanction for inefficiency. The capitalist entrepreneur under textbook conditions is free to obtain his supplies of men and materials where he can find them. Actually, he does a great deal of shopping around for them. Likewise, he makes the decision of whether or not to expand his plant by adding new buildings and machines. In practice, these decisions may be greatly influenced or limited by government authorities. The Soviet manager enjoys only a very limited autonomy in the search for supplies, and on his own initiative can do next to nothing about the major aspects of the size and capacity of the plant entrusted to him by the state. This series of graded distinctions in the power to make important economic decisions, and in the motivations behind these decisions, is more important in practice at least than differences in property rights in distinguishing between the Soviet manager and his capitalist counterpart.

As a motivating force to interest the manager in the efficiency of his plant, the Soviets make use of the profit motive in a manner that has certain strong resemblances to familiar capitalist arrangements. The utilization of this device, often regarded as a distinctive feature of capitalism, is openly recognized and accepted in current Soviet doctrine. The Five Year Plan adopted in 1946 aims to "increase the importance of the profit motive and economic accounting as an additional stimulus to production." [8] Nevertheless, the operation of the profit motive is hedged in under the Soviet system by limitations on the opportunities to bargain for supplies, the centralization of decisions concerning plant expansion, and taxation policies that return most of the profit to the state. In this manner it is harnessed to the socialist chariot and prevented from becoming a force that might disrupt Soviet institutions.

To understand the operation of the profit motive and the limitations of the manager's power of decision, the Soviet production process at various points may be examined. Beginning at the point of sale, and working back from there, one may note that the products of a plant are sold at prices fixed by the government. Exceeding these prices is punishable by law. But the prices do not represent the money equivalent of the cost of production. The plant is expected to produce its goods at a cost that is less than the price set by the government. A so-called turnover tax [9] and an amount included as the planned profit are added to the anticipated cost of production. Lowering the quality of the goods to increase the margin between cost of production and selling price is punishable by law. [10] If the manager holds costs below the anticipated amount, the profits of the plant are increased. In 1945 the total profit for the Soviet Union as a whole amounted to 21,051,000,000 rubles.[11]

At earlier stages in the production process, the limitations on the manager's power of decision and the operations of the profit incentive are connected with control over the physical equipment of the plant and over supplies of raw materials. The basic assumption of the Soviet system is, of course, that the manager is not free to buy or sell factories, which are regarded as government property entrusted to him to manage.[12] In the process of spelling this principle out in actual legal and institutional forms, the Soviets have for some time drawn a distinction between what they call basic and circulating resources. Very different possibilities are open to the manager for the utilization of each.

The terms "basic resources" and "circulating resources" derive from the differences Marx believed he saw between the *means* of labor—factory buildings, machines, and so forth—and the *objects* of labor—raw materials, semifinished products, and the like. These differences would exist in any form of society, Marx declared.[13] In general, the means of labor are regarded as the basic resources and the objects of labor as the circulating ones. The distinction between the two types of resources does not depend upon the nature of the object itself, but the purpose for which it is intended. Thus a linotype machine that is the product of a factory that makes them is part of the circulating resources of this factory. When this same machine is transferred to a printing establishment, it becomes part of the basic resources of this plant.[14]

In practice, difficulties soon arose in the application of these distinctions. In 1923 it was decreed that basic resources were those that were not used up or destroyed in a single act of production—buildings, machines, and the like—and that circulating resources were those that could only be used once—fuel, raw materials, and others.[15] In 1936 the definition of circulating resources was broadened to include objects whose useful life was less than a year, independent of their cost, and objects whose cost, independent of their useful life, was less than 200 rubles.[16]

Basic resources cannot be bought or sold again by the individual manager.[17] In other words, the Soviet manager cannot increase or decrease the size and equipment of the plant entrusted to his care through buying and selling operations in the fashion of his capitalist counterpart. However, he does have a voice in the disposal of a small portion of the plant's profits which can be used for expansion. Thus the outlet for the operation of the profit motive is, in this part of the production process, a very small one.

Circulating resources provide the opportunity for the profit motive to serve as a stimulus to production and efficiency. The minimum of supplies necessary for the operation of the plant is determined according to the plan. The flow of supplies to the plant is controlled in different ways for different types of supplies, depending on the scarcity of the commodity concerned. Some of them may be purchased directly from other producers.[18] The production plan for the individual plant includes a certain profit rate, called the planned profit. If the manager makes efficient utilization of his resources, he may exceed the planned rate of profit. Should this take place, the extra profit remains at the disposal of the plant.[19] In 1940, 70 per cent of the cost of production for industry as a whole is reported to have been spent on raw materials, fuel, and other items that come under the definition of circulating resources.[20]

In addition, the manager is permitted to add to his circulating resources through loans from the banks. These loans are supposed to be issued only for strictly defined purposes, though their utilization for purposes other than those defined is deprecated in strong enough terms to suggest that it may occur rather often.[21] Such loans probably increase the leeway available to the manager in the making of production decisions, at the same time providing a further check upon managerial operations in a way that resembles banking control over production decisions in a capitalist society.

The disposition of the profit indicates further its limitations as an incentive. Part of it is taxed and part placed in the Industrial Bank (Prombank) for purposes of capital development within the industry. A third part goes into what is called the

Director's Fund,[22] a slightly misleading name, since it does not appear that this fund is a direct reward for the manager.

The Director's Fund is primarily a way of rewarding the workers for energy and efficiency. Since the way the fund is expended is left partly to the discretion of the director, it is safe to assume that it represents a series of tempting prizes that the manager may distribute to those he chooses. In 1940 the amount distributed through the Director's Fund was 2,600,000,-000 rubles.[23] In some, presumably exceptional plants, individual workers received cash awards of 500 to 1,000 rubles.[24] Though payments into the Director's Fund were replaced by other rewards during the war years, they were revived again in 1946. Under the postwar legislation only 2 to 10 per cent of the planned profits may be credited to the Director's Fund, the percentage varying with different industries. A much larger proportion, between 25 and 50 per cent, of the profits in excess of the plan may be credited to this fund. This arrangement presumably acts as a stimulus toward greater profit on the part of both workers and management. The proceeds of the fund may be spent on improving the housing conditions of the workers and for other amenities, for individual bonuses, trips to rest homes, sanatoria, and the like. While the director has the right to allocate the fund, it does not appear that he may spend any of it upon himself.[25]

On the other hand, salary bonuses for the managers are closely related to profit, though not calculated as a percentage thereof. In coal mining, for each per cent of reduction of real cost of production below planned cost, the manager, assistant manager, chief and assistant engineers obtain a bonus of 15 per cent of their monthly salary. Similar rules prevail in other sectors of heavy industry. On occasion the total bonuses granted to managers and engineers equal or exceed their annual salary.[26]

The Soviets have taken the profit motive of capitalist society and adapted it to the requirements of their own ideology and social system, hedging it in with numerous restrictions so that it may not act as a socially disruptive force. After 1929 they did much the same thing to the capitalist device of competition, which the Webbs described as being, under socialism, the use "of the sporting instinct to augment the wealth of the nation." [27] Socialist competition, as it is known in the USSR, usually takes the form of a race between two or more factories, or shops within factories, to see who can turn out the maximum output. It is thus closely allied to the Stakhanovite movement. The winners receive group publicity in the Soviet press, banners, and other symbols of achievement. During the war there developed, as part of the system of socialist competition, the "200 per cent movement," that is, groups of workers who fulfilled double the requirements of the plan.[28] Whether this type of speed-up leads to an efficient utilization of men and machines is open to doubt, since it often leads to a rapid breakdown of both.[29] It should be noted that socialist competition, directed chiefly toward the quantitative maximization of output, differs sharply from competition in capitalist society, which takes the form of competitive bidding for labor and resources on the side of production, and in competition by price, quality, and services on the side of distribution.

In the light of the foregoing it is safe to conclude, as others have done, that noneconomic incentives and checks play the more important role in producing the desired behavior on the part of the Soviet manager. Chief among these are the possibilities of advancement to positions of greater and greater responsibility and prestige for those who have learned to combine men, machines, and materials in the most efficient manner, and the probabilities of disgrace, or even active physical suffering, for those who fail to measure up to the assigned task. Economic failure is likely to be identified with sabotage, and hence becomes a "sin" in an even stronger sense than is the case in the United States, with severe penalties meted out in this life.

Though large allowances have to be made for the part played by earlier conditions and the relative smallness of the managerial group with which the Soviets began, it may also be concluded that the system has not inculcated through its rewards and penalties the habits of prompt decision-making and accurate attention to detail that are desired by the Soviet leaders. At a meeting of the Supreme Soviet in October 1946, the chairman of the budget commission repeated the typical complaint that many factory directors refuse to look at a balance sheet, to learn the cost of their products, or to eliminate unproductive expenditures.[30] Likewise, the Party press from time to time slashes away at managers who "look for a quiet life and sit with folded arms," paying no attention to cost and quality.[31] While such criticisms cannot be taken altogether at face value, they may be used as evidence for the hypothesis that, together with the historical factors just mentioned, the system of rewards and penalties that apply to the Soviet manager does not yet lead to an efficient combination of men and resources. Still another element in this complex situation is the fact that the Soviet factory manager is under terrific pressure to turn out the goods and probably knows that the penalty for cutting corners on quality and efficiency are less than those for failure to produce at all.[32]

Throughout a considerable sector of the Soviet economy, that directly controlled by the secret police, the incentives provided by profit and competition appear to be almost totally absent. In this area political motivations, the need to eliminate political enemies, covered by euphemisms about the restoration of deviants to society (concentration camps are called "Corrective Labor Camps"), are combined with economic ones and may overshadow them. The extent of these operations remains a state secret that cannot be reliably penetrated from the available fragmentary information. They may be recalled, however, as a reminder that even in the Soviet Union more than one set of rewards and penalties operates within the economy.

The collectivization of thrift

According to classical economic theory, the resources needed for the construction of new plants and the replacement of worn-out machinery come from the sacrifice of present consumption. To a considerable extent they are derived in a capitalist economy from individual savings that are loaned to industry through the purchase of securities. Interest payments have been widely regarded as a form of reward for the sacrifice of present consumption, thus permitting the construction or replacement of capital equipment.

To some extent individual savings are a source of plant construction and replacement in the Soviet Union. The virtues of thrift are recognized there, too. As early as 1926 Stalin himself spoke out in favor of interest payments as the normal way of "mobilizing" individual savings.[33] But they play a much smaller role in the Soviet Union than they do under capitalist conditions.

When the Soviets in the thirties started the drive for socialist industrialization, they could not, for a variety of reasons, afford to rely upon individual thrift alone, or upon voluntary abstention from consumption as a source of real capital investment. Perhaps the most important of these considerations was that the sacrifices required were too great for reliance on voluntary means. Nor could the regime permit people to save money with the idea that they would invest it wherever there was the greatest opportunity for profit. Both socialist doctrine and the requirements of the day demanded that decisions concerning real capital investment be centralized.[34]

For these reasons, capital investment has been, and is, financed very heavily out of the national budget. During the period of War Communism, the economy operated for a time as if Soviet industry were one large factory. Assignments from the budget were the only resources of the individual plant, and all of its monetary income returned to the treasury.[35] This extreme centralization was subsequently abandoned and a number of other schemes tried out. During the thirties between three quarters and two thirds of the amounts devoted to capital construction were derived from the budget, the remaining portion being left to the individual enterprise to reinvest in its own operations, in ways apparently left to the manager's discretion.[36] During the war, and subsequently, this amount has been much smaller.

The relationship between capital investment and the total expenditures of the budget of the USSR may be seen in the following table, compiled from scattered Russian sources. During the period from 1938 to 1940, capital investment constituted nearly one fourth of the budget expenses. This proportion dropped precipitously during the war years, as might be anticipated, and in 1946 formed less than one seventh of the budget.

Plans for the current (Fourth) Five Year Plan call for a total capital investment of 157,500,000,000 rubles, according to one calculation,[37] and according to another, based on estimated 1945 prices, a total of 250,300,000,000 rubles. The difference between the two figures may reflect a price inflation, since most Soviet statistical calculations are based on 1926–1927 prices. Presumably, most of this will come from the budget and may constitute a heavier drain on it than prewar capital investment.

CAPITAL INVESTMENT AND BUDGET OF USSR (1938–1948)
(In millions of rubles)

	1938–40	1942	1945	1946	1947	1948 (proposed)
Total expenses	451,688 [a]	182,800 [c]	298,591 [f, i]	319,424 [j] / 307,500 [n]	361,200 [n]	387,900 [n]
Total capital investment	108,000 [a]	79,000 [d]	40,000.1 [g] / 36,300 [h]	49,400 [k]		
Capital investment from budget			30,300 [g]	41,300 [k]		60,900 [n]
Total income	463,736 [b]	165,000 [c]	302,034 [i]	333,537 [j] / 325,400 [n]	385,200 [n]	428,000 [n]
Income from turnover tax	283,161 [b]	66,000 [e]	123,000 [e]	200,813 [l]	239,900 [n]	280,100 [n]
Income from tax on profits	48,023 [b]	15,300 [e]	16,900 [e]	16,040 [m]		

[a] Plotnikov, in *Finansy SSSR*, pp. 179–180.
[b] *Ibid.*, p. 178.
[c] Voznesensky, *Voennaya Ekonomika SSSR*, p. 132.
[d] *Ibid.*, p. 46. Figure is for the years 1942–1944.
[e] Plotnikov, in *Finansy SSSR*, p. 185.
[f] *Zasedaniya Verkhovnogo Soveta SSSR (Vtoraya Sessiya)*, October 15–18, 1946, p. 15.
[g] Plotnikov, in *Finansy SSSR*, p. 188.
[h] *Zasedaniya Verkhovnogo Soveta SSSR (Vtoraya Sessiya)*, p. 16. Discrepancy unexplained in sources.
[i] *Ibid.*, p. 7.
[j] *Ibid.*, p. 339.
[k] *Ibid.*, p. 16.
[l] *Ibid.*, p. 9.
[m] *Ibid.*, p. 10.
[n] Speech by A. G. Zverev, Minister of Finances, *Izvestiya*, February 1, 1948.

As the table shows, the chief source of budget revenue and hence, indirectly, of capital investment is the turnover tax. It constituted 61.1 per cent of government revenues between 1938 and 1940, and 60 per cent in 1946, although the figure dropped to 40.8 per cent in 1945. This tax, with more than 2,500 individual rates, is imposed on almost all consumption goods at the point where they leave the producing plant and enter channels of distribution. It is the major factor in the difference between the cost of production and the selling price of any article. Even plants that fail to operate at a profit must pay this tax.[38]

A second, and far less important, source of state revenue is the tax on profits. It constituted just over one tenth of the state revenues in the period 1938–1940, and under 5 per cent in 1946. Nevertheless, it sops up most of the profits of industry, taking in 1945, for instance, nearly 17 billion rubles out of the total profit of 21 billion rubles.[39] In a sense, this tax is an unnecessary bookkeeping operation, since both the turnover tax and the tax on profits come out of the difference between the cost of production and the selling price. There is, however, a distinction, in that the turnover tax is levied and collected even if the firm fails to make a profit.

Other taxes are relatively unimportant. Before the war direct taxes on the population, including income taxes, provided only about 5 per cent of the total state revenues. During the war the proportion rose to 14 per cent.[40]

Distribution

In the Soviet system for the distribution of goods to the population at large, one may observe the same mixture of what are commonly considered socialist and capitalist principles as appear in the other aspects of their economic arrangements. The present arrangements for distribution are the product of a long period of trial and error. By the time of the outbreak of the Second World War, the system devised was to sell the products of socialist industry, as well as most of the products of agriculture, through government and coöperative stores at fixed prices.[41] In addition, there is a free market for certain agricultural products, which will be discussed in another connection. In this system the turnover tax provides the means for matching prices to available supplies.[42] With certain relatively minor changes this is the principal arrangement in effect today. Under this system, incentives produced by inequalities in income have their full effect. Additional money income means an additional opportunity to purchase the necessities and good things of life.[43] This situation is in accord with the socialist maxim, "From each according to his abilities, to each according to his work."

However, at various times and under emergency conditions, the Soviet regime, like its capitalist competitors, has found it expedient to resort to other distributive devices. One of these is, of course, rationing, which has existed from time to time, including the period of the Second World War. Wartime rationing was abolished on December 16, 1947, at the same time that consumer demand was checked by a devaluation of the currency. Special stores, where "members of the intelligentsia and highly skilled workers" could obtain various scarce goods, usually at higher prices than those in the regular distribution channels where the goods were often nonexistent, have been another distributive device.[44] Still another has been the organization of special canteens in the factories. During the war the role of these canteens, which often drew their supplies from collective farms that made special agreements with a particular factory, increased sharply. Before the war they accounted for only 4 per cent of the retail turnover in the USSR, while in 1942 they accounted for 28 per cent, and in special areas, such as the Urals, for as much as 45 per cent.[45] Despite these variations, the distribution of consumers' goods has by and large been based on the principle of "come and get it if you can afford it."

Even writers sympathetic to the Soviet Union assert that the system of retail distribution is one of the least successful products of the regime, and the Soviets themselves have denounced it perhaps more frequently than any other feature of their society. Service tends to be disinterested and slow. Little or inadequate attention is paid to local needs and tastes, or to seasonal requirements. "Stores are replenished with merchandise irregularly, and the most necessary goods are lacking." Store staffs are "neither accustomed to nor interested in laying in supplies on time or carefully storing perishable commodities."[46] The Webbs' remark, "There have been not a few occasions when village and even city stores have been clamouring in vain for particular supplies, when these have been lying unopened, and even forgotten at some intermediate point."[47]

These difficulties may be attributed to both ideological and institutional sources. As Yugow argues, the nationalization and centralization of retail trade was undoubtedly premature in Russia, at least from a strictly limited economic point of view. It created an unwieldy and expensive bureaucratic apparatus that paid little or no attention to the habit, customs, and tastes of the people.[48] Of perhaps even greater importance is the fact that while the reigning ideology romanticized the construction of industry, it did not provide motivations and rewards for the distributive side of the economic machine. Stalin recognized some of these difficulties. He endeavored to use his prestige to correct them and to develop a Bolshevik version of the American ideal of "service" in the course of his report to the Seventeenth Party Congress of 1934. His remarks are worth quoting in full as evidence of the difficulties derived from ideology:

> To begin with there is still among a section of Communists a super-cilious, contemptuous attitude towards trade in general, and towards Soviet trade in particular. These Communists, save the mark, look upon Soviet trade as a thing of secondary importance, hardly worth bothering about, and regard those engaged in trade as doomed. Evidently these people do not realize that their supercilious attitude towards Soviet trade does not express the Bolshevik point of view, but rather the point of view of shabby noblemen who are full of ambition but lack ammunition. (*Applause*) These people do not realize that Soviet trade is our own, Bolshevik, work, and that the workers employed in trade, including those behind the counter—if only they work conscientiously—are doing revolutionary, Bolshevik work. (*Applause*) It goes without saying that the Party had to give these Communists, save the mark, a slight drubbing and throw their aristocratic prejudices on the refuse dump.[49]

In their various attempts to ameliorate this situation, the Soviet leaders have borrowed from the capitalist arsenal and endeavored to introduce the competitive incentive into the retail trade. These efforts parallel, though perhaps less successfully, the Soviet introduction of the profit motive into the production side of the economy. On the same occasion cited above, Stalin reported to the Party Congress that the various commissariats had been ordered by the Party to start trade in the goods manufactured by the industries under their control. This led, he claimed, to an extensive improvement in the "competing" coöperative trade and to a drop in market prices.[50]

As happens in many cases of cultural borrowing, only the superficial aspects of an institution were taken over without the essential supporting arrangements, which in this case would have involved a general abandonment of socialist principles in favor of the free play of market forces. It is not surprising, therefore, that the difficulties have continued. Nor is it altogether surprising that the Soviets have continued to try to meet them in the same way. On November 9, 1946, the Council of Ministers again issued a decree that required the coöperatives to compete with the state monopoly of retail trade. Surplus agricultural products, formerly sold by the peasant on a local open-market basis, under the new arrangement are purchased by consumer coöperatives managed by Party officers. These foodstuffs are supposed to be distributed to the city population at prices not exceeding those charged in the special stores for the intelligentsia mentioned above.[51] Producers' coöperatives likewise receive government assistance in the form of supplies and diminished tax burdens, while the prices of their products are set by government authorities.[52]

Some of the ideas associated with the classical doctrine of consumer sovereignty have even been put forth by the Party press, which has warned the manufacturers of consumers' goods that the population will not take whatever goods the producer wants to turn out. "The consumer is a much stricter controller than the technical control section of some factory or other. Entering a store he puts to one side merchandise of poor quality and expresses his preference for the products of that establishment whose trade mark has earned a good reputation." [53] This emphasis on the consumer as the ultimate arbiter is reminiscent of the American slogan, "The customer is always right." In the same issue cited above, *Pravda* warns the various economic ministries and lesser economic units to pay more attention to quality and variety of choice in their products. Now, it is asserted, they spend more time "on the registration of complaints than on correcting mistakes." It is unlikely that these admonitions will have much effect so long as the underlying conditions of centralized control over the decisions about what products are to be made, which is basically independent of consumer pressures, remain a central aspect of the Soviet system. It also appears that these institutional factors would make it difficult for a system of retail distribution, sensitive to the requirements of the population and supported by an ideology of service along American lines, to take effective root in the USSR. It probably will be a long time before "the customer is always right" becomes an accepted Bolshevik slogan.

Summary and conclusions

In order to make their economic system work, the Soviets have arrived by a trial-and-error process at the stage where they have borrowed a number of the motivations of capitalism: inequality of rewards and incomes, the profit motive, and some of the superficial aspects of competition. These borrowings do not provide a warrant for the viewpoint that regards the Soviet system as closely similar to capitalism. They do provide support for the assertion that a modern industrial society implies certain common problems and even certain common solutions. The extreme claim of universal validity for the principles of classical economics is not warranted according to the Soviet evidence. But neither is the extreme claim of cultural or institutional relativism established according to the same evidence.

The motivations generally lumped under the rubric of personal acquisitiveness, which, as Weber points out, are likely to crop up under widely disparate social situations, do not receive the scope and approbation that they do in the United States. The Soviet economic system is one that keeps them hemmed in at every turn and channeled into what are considered socially useful paths. To take their place other motivations and prestige rewards have been developed. Likewise, other justifications for the Soviet system have received wide dissemination: allegations concerning the greater security of the individual, and the system's claimed freedom from the corrosive effects of crises and unemployment.

In this respect Soviet culture is still a materialist culture. The virtues claimed for the system are material virtues. There is none of the contempt for so-called debilitating material comforts displayed, if not practiced, by the leaders of Nazi Germany or Fascist Italy. The Soviet system of values is much closer to the American system in this respect than it is to Western totalitarian ideologies, or to the ascetic ideologies of the East.

In this system of values the conflict between authoritarian and populist elements finds a reflection in economic institutions. The belief that the masses must be led to their salvation played its role in the programs of forcible industrialization and collectivization. It may also be traced in the creation of a highly centralized system for the making of economic decisions. In its present form this highly centralized system is not yet capable of distributing to the people efficiently and courteously the objects it produces. On the one hand, the system emphasizes the desirability of material goods; on the other hand, it is unable to satisfy this demand. The passage of time will reveal, unless an improbable catastrophe intervenes, whether or not this contradiction can be solved.

In general, however, the Soviets have come closer to achieving their original goals in the area of industrial institutions, regarded by their doctrine as crucial, than in any other. They have succeeded in imposing their ideology to a very great extent, yielding only at certain points and borrowing just enough from the capitalist competitors to make their own system function.

14

The Class Struggle in a Socialist Society

Wages and the claim of class peace

It does not require an overly perceptive eye to recognize that a
struggle among various interest groups for power, prestige, and
economic rewards takes place in the Soviet Union, although its
manifestations are not those made familiar by the corresponding
struggle in Western society. The USSR has developed a distinctive set of institutions under which the rights, duties, and expected behavior of the participants in this struggle are defined
with varying degrees of clarity. This chapter will describe in
some detail the rights, duties, and expected and actual behavior
of organized industrial workers as one of the major groups competing for a share in the national income and for the other rewards of Soviet society. The importance of the problem is indicated by the size of the Soviet trade unions. In contrast to other
countries, nearly all the labor force is organized into unions in
the USSR. Before the war, out of a total of 30 million wage earners and salaried employees in all branches of the economy, 25
million belonged to the unions, in which membership is theoretically voluntary. In 1947, according to official Soviet sources,
the figure for union membership was approximately 27 million.[1]

At first glance, it appears that the official ideology simply de-
nies the existence of any struggle between workers and employers, in glaring contradiction to the facts. Closer examination
shows, however, that this denial plays a valuable functional role
in supporting the current system of uneven power relationships
between the managers of Soviet industry and the workers.

As was seen in Chapter 8, Trotsky once put forth the idea that under socialism there could be no such thing as a struggle between the workers and the managers. Attacked at the time by Lenin because of the political circumstances surrounding the introduction of the NEP and the general loosening of Party controls, the same general idea was taken up by Stalin in connection with the reorganization of the unions that formed part of the drive for high-speed socialist industrialization.

In its present form the official denial of a class struggle in the USSR asserts that the working class, together with the whole people, owns the means of production. Therefore, since "the exploitation of man by man" has been ended under socialism, the source of the class struggle has disappeared. The conflicts between employers and workers that do take place are explained as the result of "bureaucratic distortions," or, somewhat less frequently, as the result of personal selfishness and ignorance of the law.[2]

The assertion that there is no power struggle between the workers and the employers in the Soviet Union is justified insofar as there is no open conflict over wages, the principal issue of labor disputes in nonsocialist countries. Soviet writers on labor relations are agreed that wages cannot be set by collective agreement between individual employers and individual unions under a planned economic system, but that instead wages must be fixed by a central authority.[3] The norms of output and the rates of pay are set by the government, either directly by the Council of Ministers (formerly Commissars) and the Central Committee of the Communist Party, or by delegated authority. The government determines salary rates for white-collar workers (*sluzhashchie*) as well. A special commission was established under the Council of People's Commissars on June 5, 1941, for this purpose.[4]

In legal theory, at least, the only decision concerning wages that can be made by the management of a factory concerns what rates apply to a given worker or group of workers according to the qualifications involved.[5] According to a decree of the Council of People's Commissars of June 4, 1938, even the individual commissariats or ministries (including those of the Union Republics) may not alter the rate scales without the permission of the central government.[6]

From the foregoing it is evident that the doctrine of the impossibility of a class struggle under socialism serves among other purposes to support a highly centralized system for the determination of wages. In turn, this highly centralized system of wage determination appears to be an essential feature of the larger social system and of a planned economy. Long-range calculations of cost would be impossible on a national basis if wages in various industries were subject to the vagaries of a shifting power struggle between organized labor and organized management.[7] Thus the regime has to use the numerous resources at its command to prevent the emergence of such a struggle, or better, to keep it within very close limits. There is, however, considerable evidence to indicate that the regime is by no means uniformly successful in this effort.

Complaints about actual practice in the determination of wages strongly suggest that these centralized arrangements tend to break down, and that the local factory administration enjoys considerable autonomy in determining the wages of its workers and employees. Early in 1947 the head of the All-Union Central Council of Trade Unions, V. V. Kuznetsov, complained that rate setting was in a highly disorganized state in the USSR as a whole. Rates based on a rough measurement of output under actual working conditions in the factory (*opytno-statisticheskie normy*, in literal translation, "experience-statistical norms") prevailed widely. This situation, Kuznetsov added, led to the growth of "good" and "bad" rates or jobs from the worker's point of view. The existence of "good" and "bad" rates in turn evidently produced pressure for the equalization of rates and the consequent loss of incentives.[8] More detailed reports confirm and amplify Kuznetsov's description. In the factories producing agricultural equipment, a vital sector of the Soviet postwar economy, output and rates of pay were set "by eye," while earlier experience in "scientific" wage setting was either ignored or forgotten. The rate setters were men of poor education, quite inadequate for the task. Thus the easiest way out appeared to be in the direction of equalization.[9] This pressure for equalization may be compared to the hostile attitude toward "rate busters" and the limitation of output practices that have been the subject of widespread study in American industry. It is a familiar defense reaction against one factor in the competitive pressures of modern industrial society.

Probably under pressure from the Party, which set its face against "petty bourgeois equalization" many years ago, some unions have sought to correct the disorganized system of rate setting and to increase the role of incentives. These actions resemble superficially the pressure on wages typically exercised by trade unions in capitalist countries, but derive from entirely different causes. While the Soviet worker is presumably just as interested as his capitalist brother in raising his wages, the Soviet unions serve primarily as organizations for increasing output. The pressures that they exert are directed toward this end. On this account they frequently demand, at the instigation of the Party, that as many types of work as possible be transferred from payments based on time to piece-rate payments.[10] Likewise the demand, expressed by one writer, for a greater role for the unions in the process of setting wage rates must be interpreted within the general setting of the Party's continuing drive to increase both output and incentives.[11]

Labor-management bargaining in the USSR

Certain additional superficial similarities to labor-capital relationships in capitalist societies may also be found in the Soviet version of collective agreements between unions and management. Collective agreements concerning wages were drawn up at frequent intervals and were the regular practice in Soviet industry during the NEP. With the introduction of widespread planning, they were abandoned between 1933 and 1935.[12] During February and March 1947, the practice of annual collective bargaining was revived.[13]

Wages are, however, specifically excluded as a subject of bargaining in the new collective agreements. The All-Union Central Council of Trade Unions (AUCCTU), in its decree that marked the official revival of these agreements, ordered that wage rates established by the government should be included in the collective agreement. It also ordered the unions to see to it that wage and salary rates not approved by the government should not find their way into the agreement. The unions are at the same time required to do all they can to increase the use of incentive payments by finding out what jobs are paid on a straight time basis and how many of them can be transferred to a piece-rate basis.[14]

The agreements are supposed to contain other matters of definite interest to the workers, such as the amount of housing to be undertaken by the management, construction and repair of dining rooms, factory stores, and the rating of specific jobs.[15] Soviet writers describe the agreements as an important weapon in organizing the masses for the fulfillment and overfulfillment of the Five Year Plan, and for improving the material and cultural position of the workers, salaried employees, and technical personnel.[16] These statements indicate that the main purpose of the agreements is to provide an additional production incentive to the workers by giving them a stronger sense of participation in the determination of working conditions.

The formal procedures by which the agreements are drawn up and ratified could be used by either a strong union or a strong managerial group to impose its will. However, the requirements of economic planning and the watchful eye of the Party provide little room for any contest.

According to the chairman of the All-Union Central Council of Trade Unions, the collective agreements pass through four main stages. First, the ministries and the central committees of trade-union organizations draw up "directive letters" containing the major points of the collective agreement. Then the central committees of the unions involved send out model agreements to the factory committees or locals of their respective unions. After receiving the directive letter, the factory director and the factory committee of the union work out the actual agreement. Disagreements that arise at this point are allegedly settled by the representatives of the union central committee and of the factory director's superiors, that is, the trust or ministry. This agreement is then submitted to the workers for comment and suggestions. Corrections and alterations may, at least in theory, be included after submission to the workers. The Party organizations within the factory and among the workers are supposed to guide the discussions following submission of the agreement. *Pravda* (March 14, 1947) stated that they must play a leading role at this stage of the agreement's formulation. Both the union factory committee and the factory director must be prepared to present to the workers a detailed explanation of why any given suggestion cannot be included in the agreement. After this has been done, the agreement is signed by the factory committee and the director and registered with both the union central committee and the appropriate ministry.[17]

The collective agreement is defined as a form of mutual obligation between the administration of the factory and the factory committee representing the workers, which sets out the rights and duties of each party. The major points in the agreement relate to the obligations of each party in connection with the fulfillment of the plant's task in the current Five Year Plan, and are concerned for the most part with increasing output and eliminating stoppages and breakdowns and similar matters.[18] Perhaps the points that touch the interests of the worker most directly are those concerned with the obligations of the plant to increase the housing facilities of the workers, and those concerned with the introduction and improvement of safety devices. It is on these points, perhaps, that a limited amount of real bargaining may take place.

The unions have been frequently criticized of late for their failure to present their own positions with sufficient vigor. For example, the central committee of the coal miners' union in the western regions of the USSR (the coal ministry is divided into western and eastern divisions) has been blamed for failing to obtain from the ministry an assignment of funds for safety purposes.[19] Another report comments on the widespread failure to introduce safety devices in Soviet industry and to take other measures for protecting the health of the workers. According to the writer, the amount that the factory administration is going to spend on such matters ought to be included in the collective agreement. In addition, he criticizes the unions for not being energetic enough in pressing for such measures.[20]

According to V. V. Kuznetsov, chairman of the All-Union Council of Trade Unions, the new collective agreements should include in black and white the amount of funds the factory administration will devote to housing purposes. The unions are required to watch over the actual execution of these promises. That the housing question is a very sore point among the workers is revealed by Kuznetsov's remark that during 1946 the various ministries completed on the average only 57.9 per cent of their housing plans, while in some cases the percentage was much lower, for example, 46.6 per cent in the case of the Ministry of Heavy Industry, and 37.6 per cent in the case of the Ministry of Agricultural Machinery.[21]

Labor-management relations within the plant

Present-day group relationships between the workers and the administration within the individual factory reveal the same process of creating rules to define the rights and duties of competing groups; but here, too, the existence of such competition is officially denied, just as it is in the larger field of relationships between the unions and the various economic ministries. The factory administration in its efforts to enforce industrial discipline enjoys a large measure of support from the bureaucratic apparatus of the regime, including the secret police. But this support is neither unlimited nor blind. Letters to the editor of the union daily, *Trud,* concerning violations of labor law may precipitate an investigation by the Procurator's office.[22] Or a factory director may be discharged for personal roughness.[23] In general, the Party, which has its eye continually on production, intervenes to check what it considers to be abuses or practices that lower productive efficiency. The chief advantage on the side of the workers in this contest is the general shortage of manpower and the consequent demand for their services.

General rules of internal factory discipline were laid down by the Council of People's Commissars on January 18, 1941. They include such matters as procedures for hiring and firing; the conscientious fulfillment by the worker of his tasks, including the proper care of machinery and socialist property in general and the obligation to work the full working day; and responsibilities of the administration concerning safety devices, and so forth. These general rules may be supplemented by special agreements between the director of the factory and the union committee within the factory.[24]

Unlike the collective farms and coöperatives, disciplinary penalties are applied in industry by the factory administration. The possible infractions and penalties are set out by law. In the case of some heavy industries, the foreman is the individual who metes out the penalty.[25] In legal theory, at least, the worker has the right to appeal to what is known as a conflict commission (RKK—*Rastsenochno-konfliktnye kommissii*, literally "appraisement and conflict commissions") concerning disciplinary penalties imposed by the administration.[26] However, the complaint of a worker in the field of transportation, long a major bottleneck in Soviet economic life, is instead passed through his immediate superior to the individual next above the latter in the hierarchy, who must render a decision within three days of receiving the complaint.[27] It would appear that the worker's opportunity for obtaining satisfaction for even a legitimate grievance is strictly limited under these conditions.

The activities of the conflict commissions have been rarely described in the daily or trade-union newspapers during recent years, though there is evidence that, before the war, management regarded these commissions as thorns in its side. According to a legal textbook, they are composed of representatives of the factory administration and the workers, usually the union factory committee, chosen on an equal basis. In 1933 they lost all power to affect wage rates. Among their asserted present functions is the examination of conflicts that arise from the transfer of a worker from one type of work to another, payments in the case of spoilage or failure to fulfill the required norms, and discharges for incompetence.[28] According to one report, the *oblast'* committee of the union reviews the decisions of the conflict commission that are favorable to the factory administration, since the union factory committee is frequently ignorant of the legal questions involved.[29]

The manpower shortage largely eliminates from the employer's arsenal the possibility of firing a worker for any reason except the grossest forms of incompetence. It is difficult to estimate accurately the significance of this factor in the silent struggle between the workers and the managers, but it is undoubtedly very important. It probably prevents managers from discharging workers on purely capricious or personal grounds. To what extent this advantage is offset by the possibility that a worker may be sent to a concentration camp for fractious behavior constitutes a nearly insoluble puzzle with the information available now. However, Dallin and Nicolaevsky, who cannot be accused of partiality toward the USSR, make no mention of industrial workers in their list of the three main types of inhabitants of the forced-labor camps. Since there is no indication of the specific sources upon which the classification is based, it probably represents the general impression of the authors, based chiefly on scattered accounts by individuals who have managed to get out of the camps. As such the evidence cannot be dismissed, but it is very far from conclusive.[30]

Soviet legislation, together with Soviet comments thereon, throws considerable light on the advantages enjoyed by the worker because of the manpower shortage and the regime's efforts to prevent the workers from exploiting the advantage effectively. The general rules of labor discipline, set forth in the decree of January 18, 1941, did not take up the question of firing a worker for a breach of discipline. For a brief time there was some question in legal circles whether such discharges were possible at all. By a decree of the Supreme Court of the USSR (December 25, 1941) it was decided that disciplinary discharges were possible only under three simultaneous conditions: (1) if the worker repeatedly violated discipline, that is, refused several times to carry out an order of the administration; (2) if the worker had already been penalized or rebuked on some previous occasion for a violation of discipline; (3) if the discharge of such a worker would not bring about a loss in production, but was necessary for strengthening internal discipline.[31] On June 26, 1940, the Supreme Soviet made voluntary absence from work or leaving a job without permission a criminal offense. Although present-day Soviet discussion of this decree considers it a measure of defense and preparation for the conflict with Hitler,[32] the law has not yet been repealed.[33] A decision of the Supreme Court of the USSR on August 15, 1940, defined voluntary absence as absence from work without adequate cause for more than twenty minutes, or for more than three times in one month, or four times in two successive months. Appearance on the job when drunk is also included under absenteeism.[34] Among other fine points in the discussion at this time was whether falling asleep on the job constituted absenteeism. The phrase "without adequate cause" obviously permits a good deal of latitude in applying the law. Although legal attempts to define the circumstances of adequate cause include at least eleven possible combinations, the Soviet Supreme Court on December 12, 1940, tacitly gave up the attempt to enclose them all in the fine meshes of the law by ordering that all relevant facts must be considered in an attempt to determine whether or not such adequate cause existed.[35] These facts suggest that the severity of the law was much mitigated by practical difficulties in its application.

The significance of full employment and the manpower shortage is also revealed by the report that before the decree of June 26, 1940, workers deliberately absented themselves from the job in order to obtain a discharge. Afterward they continued to attempt to obtain such a discharge by other violations of labor discipline.[36] According to the All-Union Central Council of Trade Unions, which supported and helped to promulgate this decree, the attempts to take advantage of the manpower shortage were largely by younger workers and salaried employees new to industry. However, the assertion by the same organization that such practices were limited to 3 or 4 per cent of the workers cannot be considered conclusive evidence as to their extent.[37]

It is worth while to point out that the conclusion, often based on this decree, that Soviet workers and salaried employees have no opportunity to leave their job is incorrect. A worker or salaried employee may leave a specific job by mutual agreement with the employer,[38] although it may be assumed that in the case of a valuable worker or employee the employer's acquiescence is difficult to obtain. Several other possibilities for the worker to change jobs are set forth in the law, including opportunities for the husband or other family members to be transferred to different positions in other parts of the country.[39] The worker may have recourse to the courts if the employer who is obliged to grant such permission to leave the job refuses the permission.[40]

Power relationships within the unions

At the beginning of the Five Year Plans the slight degree of independence that the unions had obtained vis-à-vis the Soviet state was sharply curtailed. Former union leaders were replaced by men who would carry out Stalin's policies of increased productivity and increased incentives. To those aspiring to union leadership it was made clear that the road to advancement lay not in the militant defense of the workers' interests versus their chief employer, the state, but in increasing production for the state.

Even during the NEP period power within the unions had been effectively concentrated in the hands of the leaders despite the unions' democratic organization, as has been clearly shown with abundant evidence in the study by Woldemar Koch.[41] In the subsequent period of the thirties and the war years, this concentration of power in the hands of the union leadership has increased rather than diminished. A fundamental reason for this centralization of power, not only in the unions but in the Soviet state as a whole, was the series of sacrifices demanded of the population in order to make the USSR into a first-class industrial power. To the Kremlin leadership voluntary means, though widely used, did not appear adequate to achieve the required goals.

In this respect the Party faced a dilemma. It had taken power in the name of a material improvement in the condition of the masses. To approach this goal, which demands as its obvious prerequisite military security, the Party had to demand immediate and continued sacrifices and to check not only the unions' autonomy but also much of what remained of the rank and file's power over its leaders. At the same time, after weakening the workers' means of self-defense, the Kremlin could not afford to let the pressure upon the workers grow too great. The reaction to this situation has been a series of "cavalry raids" by the Kremlin for the restoration of union democracy. One finds here the same pattern of continuous search for enthusiastic allegiance expressed through democratic forms as in the soviets, while the same factors prevent the continued operation of these democratic forms. There is a repeated tendency to fall back upon reliance on orders and directives from above, followed by campaigns for "re-democratization," all in a continuing cycle. One of these campaigns took place between 1935 and 1937, in the course of which Stalin ordered the restoration of trade-union democracy, the accountability of union officers to their membership, the reëstablishment of collective bargaining, and similar measures.[42]

Evidence in the present-day press indicates that the abuses denounced at that time continued up until the war and were intensified during it. Early in 1947 the All-Union Council of Trade Unions pointed out that during the war elections and reports of union officers took place infrequently and irregularly, and that coöption of union officials replaced elective practices. Flagrant violations of union democracy still occurred in some places, the Council asserted.[43] Workers and salaried employees are no longer willing to put up with the violations of trade-union democracy that were tolerated during the war, according to the leading editorial of a recent issue of the Council's journal. The editorial goes on to say that an end must be put to the practice whereby union leaders sit in their offices and never visit the factories.[44]

During the postwar years the regime has conducted a widespread campaign for the revival of democratic centralism in the unions. This campaign is closely associated with the revival of a limited form of collective bargaining. The Tenth Trade Union Congress, a general gathering of delegates from all the unions to elect the officials of the All-Union Council of Trade Unions and to settle other organizational matters, was held on April 19, 1949.

Previous to this date, elections had been held in a number of union organizations. In the Moscow area alone, reports to the memberships and elections had taken place in 1160 organizations before June 1947. The work of 195 local units of the unions was declared unsatisfactory at these meetings, and 90 per cent of the membership of the factory committees was replaced.[45] In the USSR as a whole, 70 per cent of the membership of the factory committees and local committees of the unions had been renewed by August 1947.[46]

In only a few instances, however, has the turnover affected the union central committees.[47] This fact strengthens the hypothesis that in the unions, as in other areas of Soviet life, the Kremlin leadership is employing democratic procedures to turn the hostility of the masses against the lower ranks of the bureaucracy, thus deflecting this hostility away from the major sources of power. The operation of this device in connection with both the soviets and the Party has already been noted in earlier chapters. It is also quite clear that the workers may not anticipate any far-reaching changes in policy or leadership. Another editorial in the AUCCTU journal asserts that the persons chosen for leadership in trade-union work must be devoted to the Party of Lenin and Stalin,[48] a qualification for leadership that might indeed be considered axiomatic in the Soviet Union. The same editorial points out that union leaders "are called upon to realize within the unions the decisions of the Party." Elsewhere, the Party's failure to guide union activities is regarded as a fault to be corrected, and it was forecast that the newly elected Central Committee would "under the leadership of the Party organizations" correct the faults of its predecessor.[49]

Despite the qualification that changes in policy and leadership personnel must take place within the general framework of Party control, it appears from the accounts of the election meetings that the rank and file enjoy the opportunity to present some of its real grievances. As in other departments of Soviet political life, the official doctrine regards the occasion of an officer's report to his electors as a serious occasion—an "examination"—when he must take account publicly for his failures as well as for his successes.[50]

The complaints run along a generally similar pattern. Speakers at one meeting criticize sharply the negligent attitude of a factory committee toward social services and the introduction of safety devices.[51] At another, the criticism of the central committee concerns the latter's failure to make more widely available the experience of high-speed and Stakhanovite workers and for inadequate propaganda work. In this instance, the tone and content of the report suggests that the local Party unit dominated the meeting and applied the Party line in a rather mechanical fashion. In another, the familiar complaint is raised that the factory managers and the union leaders together failed to pay adequate attention to the housing and cultural needs of the workers. In still another, the criticism concerns the failure of the union leadership to present the organization's claims with sufficient energy before the ministry concerned, as well as its failure to support the lower union organizations in their legitimate demands upon the managers.[52]

This dependence of the local factory committees upon higher echelons of the union for support is confirmed by other sources. In this particular aspect of the concentration of power, the Soviet unions do not appear to differ significantly from their American or British counterparts. In many affairs concerned with the drawing up and the execution of the collective agreement, the factory committee finds it necessary to call upon the central committee or the *oblast'* committee of the union for assistance.[53] A further indication of the powers of higher union echelons over the factory committee is the right of the *oblast'* committee to call for new elections in the factory committee when the latter's work appears unsatisfactory to the higher authorities.[54]

There are indications that the trend toward a revival of the authority of the lowest levels of the union hierarchy may already have run its course by the end of 1948. In October 1948, the AUCCTU announced the establishment of regional (republic, *krai,* and *oblast'*) union councils for the coördination of union activities.[55] Several explanations were offered for this step. Kuznetsov, the AUCCTU chairman, declared: "Certain central committees of the unions revealed themselves unable to control systematically the *oblast'* union organs, especially in distant ob-

last's. The lack of control brings about among the leaders of certain *oblast'* committees a sense of complacency and self-satisfaction. Deprived of daily leadership on the part of the union central committee, they fall unawares into serious errors and cease to take note of them." [56] The creation of the regional union councils was described as an important step toward the correction of this situation. Elsewhere, the Party has expressed the hope that these councils will strengthen the connection between the local Party and union organizations. In the past, it is pointed out, Party leadership in union matters has been weakened by the absence of a single union center and by the presence of a large number of union branch committees.[57] The third reason, and the one that received the most publicity, was the desirability of a central unit at the regional level for the exchange of experiences among the unions concerning methods for speeding up industrial production.[58]

Conclusions

From this sketch of labor-management relationships in the USSR, it is clear that the unions are not strong, independent centers of power and militant defenders of the industrial workers. There never was any intention on the part of the Soviet leaders that the unions should develop into this type of organization in the Soviet state. It is perhaps equally clear that the Soviet unions are not the cowed hirelings of a ruthless, bureaucratic, industrial management. The workers have the power to bring pressure on the management, and indirectly on the regime, to satisfy some of their needs, even though a substantial case could be made to show that this power is less in the Soviet Union than in the United States. The situation, as a whole, is one in which the state controls both competitors—labor and management—allocating to each that share of rewards which seems empirically necessary to make the economic system function. In this situation the rewards left open by the state to be achieved by competitive economic and political struggle are almost nil. Wages and salaries are directly excluded. The system of strictly limited antagonistic coöperation is supported by a set of ideological formulas that deny or divert the antagonism and stress the coöperation.

15

Revolution from Above: The Transformation of the Peasantry

Collectivization and directed social change

Of the series of crucial problems facing the Bolsheviks upon the seizure of power, their relationships with the peasantry were destined to affect the lives of a larger number of people than any other. In the late twenties and early thirties the Russian Communists found themselves compelled to reorganize the life of the peasants and to introduce a new way of life among the most tradition-bound mass of the population. As the Party itself subsequently acknowledged, this was a revolution carried out from above. For some decades before this undertaking it had been almost axiomatic among many students of human society that such an action could not possibly succeed. "Stateways cannot change folkways," an aphorism based upon Sumner, was accepted as an accurate statement of the possibilities of directed social change. Therefore, the consequences of the collectivization of agriculture in the Soviet Union provide a valuable check upon a major assumption in the social sciences. A survey of official Soviet goals concerning the organization of peasant life, the extent to which these goals are realized, and the factors underlying deviations between official hopes and actual institutionalized behavior, throws considerable light not only upon the Soviet social system as a whole, but also upon more general questions of planned social change.

The Party discussions preceding and accompanying collectivization indicate that with this policy the regime hoped to accomplish several objectives. In the first place, it hoped to assure a reliable and adequate supply of grain for the growing urban and industrial areas of the country. In the second place, it hoped to put an end to the inherent disadvantages of small-scale peasant agriculture, which is unable to make use of modern machinery and scientific methods and can increase its output only by intensifying the labor spent upon the land. Finally, the regime hoped to cut the roots from under the wealthier peasants who were antagonistic to the Soviet regime and to organize the rest of the peasantry in such a way that it would be the Bolsheviks' ally instead of a potential enemy. After trying other forms, the Communist leadership decided that the *kolkhoz* was the organizational form best adapted to serving these ends.[1]

The internal structure of the *kolkhoz* became stabilized in approximately its present form during the year 1935, when the regime finally decided upon a mixed system of socialized and individual property.[2] The *kolkhoz* is a supposedly voluntary union of peasants who have agreed to pool their land and some of their other resources in order to realize the advantages of coöperative agriculture. Actually, the formation of these unions took place only under strong pressure by the Communist Party. According to the Model Statute of 1935, certain means of production, for example, working livestock, ploughs, harrows, seed stocks, and farm buildings, are held in common by the members of the *kolkhoz*. The land is owned by the state, but its use is granted in perpetuity to the collective farm. It may not be bought or sold. The services of agricultural machinery—tractors, threshing machines, combines, and so forth—are provided by the Machine-Tractor Stations (MTS), operated by the Ministry of Agriculture, in return for deliveries of grain.

However, the collective farmers are permitted to retain between one quarter and one half a hectare of land (in special districts an entire hectare or 2.5 acres) for their own personal use. In addition, in the basic farming areas each household may keep one cow, two calves, one or two pigs with their sucklings, up to a total of ten sheep or goats, a maximum of twenty beehives, and an unlimited quantity of poultry and rabbits. Slight variations from these amounts are permitted to suit geographical and cultural conditions. Thus, in nomad regions where agriculture is nonexistent, the household may legally possess eight to ten cows and five to eight camels. By 1938 there were 242,000 *kolkhozy* in the USSR, occupying 99.3 per cent of the sown area of the country.[3] The collective farmers are required to turn over to the government specified quantities of grain and other produce, including that grown on their personal plots. The state itself determines the prices paid for this produce. In the case of the major crops, such as grain and cotton, about 90 per cent of the marketable produce goes to the state in this fashion.[4]

Selection of leadership

According to the official Soviet ideology, the selection of leaders within the *kolkhoz* takes place by democratic methods. A recent textbook on collective-farm legislation declares that *kolkhoz* democracy represents an "inseparable part of Soviet socialist democracy."[5] In other words, *kolkhoz* democracy represents part of the general Communist ideal of voluntary and spirited support for Soviet policies, sparked by the enthusiastic devotees of the Party. The leading officials of the collective farm, its chairman and managing board, are supposed to be chosen by the general gathering of the *kolkhoz* membership. They are theoretically responsible to this body and may be removed by it. The practice of appointment by an external authority is specifically condemned.[6] Thus the control of the collective farm is alleged to be the task of the *kolkhozniki* themselves, "since they alone are the masters of their own farm."[7]

Political necessities have brought about wide departures from the ideal of *kolkhoz* democracy, as defined in the Soviets' own terms. During the first years of collectivization, *kolkhoz* chairmen were usually appointed by the government from the ranks of politically reliable urban workers. As a rule, these men had little or no experience in farming and were generally alien to rural life. Coming from a different cultural background and lacking a knowledge of farming, they were often at the mercy of the peasants' hostility. This situation was reflected in a high rate of turnover in the collective-farm leadership. As late as 1937 only 9.2 per cent of all chairmen and 8.9 per cent of brigade leaders had held their posts for five years or more.[8]

The Party's need to gain control of the peasantry and the bitter conflicts of the thirties also found their reflection in the official doctrine. In 1933 Stalin declared, "the collective farms can be either Bolshevik or anti-Soviet. And if we do not hold the leadership in one or more *kolkhozy,* that means that anti-Soviet elements will lead them." [9] This remark by Stalin points up once more the sharp difference between Western liberal conceptions of democracy and Soviet interpretations. The latter are heavily colored by the crisis-strewn conditions under which they have grown up, by the atmosphere of combat and tension generated ever since Lenin's appearance on the political scene. To a Communist there is nothing contradictory in the statement, "Collective-farm democracy is maintained as indestructible with the full strength of the dictatorship of the working class," or the equally typical remark, "Where there is no Bolshevik leadership, there is no *kolkhoz* democracy, since *kolkhoz* democracy in its essence is a method of Bolshevik leadership in the *kolkhozy.*" [10] Nor is there any overt awareness that such ideas might run counter to the claim, expressed with equal frequency, that the collective farmers are alone the masters of their own affairs.

To date it is evident that the Party in day-to-day practice has not yet been able to get away from the appointment of collective-farm chairmen, even though the practice is frowned upon in the highest circles. As recently as September 1946, a decree issued over Stalin's signature revealed that chairmen of *kolkhozy* were often removed by local soviet and Party organizations without even informing the *kolkhoz* membership.[11] The Party is still also troubled by the high rate of turnover among collective-farm leaders. In a speech before the Party Central Committee, A. A. Andreev, a Politburo member and trouble shooter in farming matters, pointed out in 1947 that 38 per cent of the *kolkhoz* chairmen had been in their jobs for less than a year, 34 per cent between one and three years, and only 28 per cent for more than three years.[12]

The problem of obtaining adequate leadership may in time be eased somewhat, since the Party has greatly increased its membership in the rural areas during and since the war. In 1947 there were 61,211 Party primary organizations in the collective farms, a very marked increase over the 1941 figure of 29,723.[13] However, there were, according to Andreev's report, 222,000 *kolkhozy* in 1947, which would mean that on the average there would be only one Party unit for each three or four *kolkhozy*. In addition, frequent remarks in the Soviet press indicate that the new recruits to the Party are far from thoroughly indoctrinated. Therefore, they do not as yet constitute a reliable corps of leaders.

Formulation and execution of policy

In a nonsocialist society the individual farmer makes his decisions on what to plant, how to grow it, and how to market his produce within the framework of the state of the market (which may be affected by government policies), climate and weather, and local custom. In other words, the major decisions of the individual farmer are strongly influenced by factors that are beyond the individual's control.

Within a very different institutional setting the same is true of the chief agricultural unit, the collective farm, in the socialist society of the USSR. The *kolkhoz* must operate within the institutional framework of a socialist planned economy. This means that the basic decisions on what to grow are determined by the government, a requirement that conflicts with the official doctrine that the *kolkhoz* is a democratic social unit which is the master of its own fate. According to the Model Statute and legal textbooks, the first obligation of the *kolkhoz* is to execute its part in the general government plan for agriculture and industry, and to turn over to the government its share of agricultural produce. In theory, the *kolkhoz* has its own production plan, which is geared in to the general plan of the country as a whole, and which is worked out and confirmed by the *kolkhoz* membership.[14] The plan comes down the hierarchy to the *kolkhoz* by way of the *rayon* executive committee, the local organ of the soviet with which the *kolkhoz* has a number of other important connections. Supposedly the *kolkhoz* may make alterations in the plan and send it back to the *rayon* executive committee. The latter has the legal power to change the plan only if it does not guarantee the execution of the general government program.[15] Actually, it is unlikely that the collective farm can make any serious alterations in the plan, though there are no doubt a number of upward revisions of planned production suggested by local Party members and other activists.

The ways in which the government has attempted to control agricultural production and secure its share of farm output have varied a great deal since the establishment of the collective farms. The continual search for new methods, whether forceful or voluntary, indicates that the problem is by no means satisfactorily solved as yet. We need mention only some of the more recent developments. Before 1939 the government attempted to allocate to each *kolkhoz* individually the type and quantity of grain to be produced. In 1939 individual allocation was abandoned, and the collective farms were permitted to vary the amount and types grown so long as general government plans were fulfilled. In 1940 a new incentive arrangement provided that the amounts to be delivered would be based upon the amount of arable land available for each *kolkhoz*.[16] In February 1947 a central government inspection service was set up for determining the amount of the harvests. Among the reasons advanced for establishing this service was the assertion that collective farmers were in the habit of underestimating the amount of their crops. Therefore, the inspectors were to be removed from local "anti-governmental" influences.[17] These frequent changes suggest that the regime has not yet found a satisfactory way of gearing the farms into the machinery of planning and of overcoming local centrifugal forces.

Such a system of planned agricultural production requires a large and complex administrative machine, whose activities necessarily limit the power of the *kolkhoz* to determine its own affairs. Several sectors of the Soviet bureaucracy compete with one another in the field of agricultural administration. The executive committees of the local (*rayon*) soviets are charged with important supervisory functions. They transmit to the *kolkhoz* the government's plans and assigned tasks. They supervise the *kolkhoz's* estimates of income and expenditure. Finally, they bear the primary responsibility for seeing that the *kolkhoz* carries out its promised deliveries to the state.[18] At harvest time the Soviet press is full of exhortations to the local soviets to make sure that the deliveries are carried out on schedule.

The network of Machine-Tractor Stations forms another channel of Party control. Today the political assistant to the director of the MTS is a Communist who has the function of general trouble shooter in the area.[19] In addition to other duties, the MTS is required by its contract with the collective farm to give the latter help in setting up its production plan, organizing crop rotation, arranging an efficient distribution of tasks among the *kolkhoz* membership, and supervising the distribution of income among them.[20]

Finally, the Party *rayon* committees are supposed to be in charge of all Party work, including that of the MTS, within the area under their jurisdiction.[21] Since the Party guides, directly or indirectly, the work of all the above organizations, it may be assumed that the competition among them is kept to a minimum. The difficulties that do arise appear to be those of divided responsibility, since there are frequent complaints in the press about a passive attitude on the part of all of these organizations.

As the preceding information has suggested, the types of decisions that can be made within the *kolkhoz* are in practice of a distinctly secondary nature. This fact automatically limits the effective area of *kolkhoz* democracy and internal decisions to a very narrow range.

According to the Model Statute of 1935, the managing board of the *kolkhoz* has the important responsibility of working out the norms of payment for each task in the form of "labor days." Afterward the norms are supposed to be confirmed by a general gathering of the membership.[22] The labor day is the unit used for measuring the amount of work and skill required to complete a specific job. Thus a day's work on one job may be rated at less than a labor day, while a day's work on another job may be rated at more than a labor day. In addition, the managing board is responsible for the allocation of labor to the different tasks of plowing, sowing, caring for the stock, and so forth, within the *kolkhoz*,[23] although the MTS may provide assistance in this internal administrative task. The managing board is also responsible for discipline on the farm. In practice, the chairman tends to usurp these functions from both the managing board and the general assembly, and to make decisions on his own about rates of pay and the allocation of labor.[24]

In theory, the general gathering of the *kolkhoz* membership controls the use of the farm's funds. The gathering is supposed to approve the estimates of income and expenditure in both monetary and natural form. It is likewise supposed to determine the actual value of the labor day, that is, to determine the quantity of natural produce and money that may be distributed at the end of the year to the members in accord with the number of labor days they have earned. These tasks, too, are frequently usurped by the *kolkhoz* chairman.[25] The theoretical functions of the *kolkhoz* assembly also include the election of *kolkhoz* officers. *Pravda* has found it necessary, however, to use its editorial columns to remind overzealous Party members that the *kolkhozniki* must make full use of their right to nominate candidates and to vote down those whom they disapprove.[26]

In the collective farms, as elsewhere in the Soviet social system, the repeating cycle of alternating authoritarian and democratic procedures may be observed. The political necessity for strict control combined with the necessities for control inherent in a planned economic system bring about an extension of authoritarian practices, a multiplication of orders, directives, and the like, while democratic procedures and the rights of the rank and file fall into abeyance. This situation in turn produces a diminution of the enthusiasm upon which the regime depends. It may create outright opposition or, in other cases, intensify existing opposition. At such a point the regime typically engages in a campaign of re-democratization, in which the democratic aspects of its ideology are given not only lip service but receive additional realization in practice. In the collective farms this stage was reached again early in 1947, when the Party ordered that general gatherings of the rank-and-file membership be held in all of the *kolkhozy* of the Soviet Union before February 15 of that year.[27] This action parallels the re-democratization campaigns carried out in the soviets, the trade unions, and to a somewhat lesser extent in the Party itself. It is part of a larger pattern of postwar political activity in the Soviet Union.

Incentives and status differentials

The Communist leaders of Russia have endeavored to introduce into the collective farms a system of incentive arrangements and organized inequality similar to that which prevails in industry. On February 28, 1933, the Commissariat of Agriculture issued a model scale of payments, which rated different types of farming tasks into seven grades, with different payments for each. According to this scale, the man who completes the daily norm of accomplishment for a task in grade seven receives a credit of two labor days. The man who completes the daily norm of accomplishment for a task in grade one receives only a half day's credit.[28] On April 21, 1940, additional premiums in cash, based on the annual income of the farm, were decreed for the farm chairmen in the eastern sections of the USSR.[29]

As in industry, there are indications that a significant number of the farmers have successfully resisted the application of these competitive pressures. The Party has complained that the norms of accomplishment are frequently set too low, and that the local organs of authority pay little attention to their application.[30] In a similar vein Andreev has attacked the practice of petty-bourgeois equality (*uravnilovka*) in the collective farms and the failure to relate payments to the amount harvested.[31]

In order to indicate the responsibility of the individual for an assigned task, as well as to arouse individual interest, collective-farm organization provides for a minute division of labor. Collective farmers are divided into brigades, and within the brigades into detachments. So far as possible each brigade and each detachment is kept at the same task for a full season. Each brigade is responsible for a specified portion of the collective-farm property, which is supposed to be described in an exact list and registered with the farm chairman. The brigade is supposed to retain the same responsibilities for a full production cycle, that is, a year in the case of most crops, and not less than three years in the case of livestock.[32] The brigadier is responsible for the organization of work within the brigade, and for recording the number of labor days with which each individual under his command is credited. His position is roughly that of a rural foreman.[33]

In 1947 and 1948 the system of individual incentives was developed even further. By a decree of the Council of Ministers of April 19, 1948, which elaborated on an earlier Party decision published on February 28, 1947, the "recommendation" was made to the collective farms to make payments in labor days to the brigades and detachments directly dependent upon the fulfillment of the Plan. For each per cent by which the Plan was overfulfilled, the brigades and detachments should receive an additional credit of 1 per cent in labor days. For each per cent of underfulfillment, there should likewise be subtracted 1 per cent in labor days from the payments made to the brigades and detachments, down to a maximum deduction of 25 per cent.[34]

Special problems occur in connection with the differential rewards to be offered agronomists and other technical specialists. Owing to the general shortage of qualified administrative personnel in the USSR, there are strong pressures pushing scientifically trained personnel into administrative rather than scientific work. Some idea of the enormous number of people in administrative work connected with the *kolkhozy* may be gleaned from the fact that in 1941, for the 27,000 *kolkhozy* of the eastern Ukraine, there were over 29,000 responsible officials in control agencies.[35] Allegedly at Stalin's personal suggestion, an attempt was made in the decree of February 27, 1947, to diminish the flow of scientific skill toward administrative work and to direct the bureaucrat technicians into the field by reducing the salary of those who held desk jobs by 25 per cent.[36]

Since so much of the collective farm's produce is taken by the

government, there are limitations on the operation of personal
incentives in the collective-farm system. It is estimated that between 1937 and 1939 only about 40 per cent of the produce and
55 per cent of the cash income was distributed among the collective farmers themselves.[37] Another writer reports Soviet figures
showing that in 1938 only 26.9 per cent of the gross yield of grain
was distributed to the farmers in payment of labor days. More
than 90 per cent of the grain that reached the market was sold to
the state at prices fixed by the latter.[38]

The operation of the system of incentives, together with wide
variations in fertility and natural resources, has apparently produced a much wider range of differences in wealth among *kolkhozy* than within a single *kolkhoz*. In 1937, in all the USSR, there
were 610 *kolkhozy* with a money income of a million rubles or
over. These millionaire *kolkhozy* constituted only 0.3 per cent
of the total *kolkhozy*. The medium-sized *kolkhozy*, 75 per cent of
the total, had an average income of only 60,000 rubles a year. At
the bottom of the scale were the farms, comprising 6.7 per cent
of the total, with an annual income of only 1,000 to 5,000 rubles.[39]
In the absence of free movement from one farm to another, these
differences cannot operate as incentives. Significant as the variations in wealth are, it would be rash to predict that they will be
a source of social tension. The millionaire farms are in most
instances those that produce raw materials for industry, fruit,
tea, and medicinal plants. Most of them are in Central Asia; only
thirty of them are in the Ukraine. Therefore, the type of sharp
contrast that might give rise to envy is probably infrequent.

Divisive tendencies and evaluation

Within the present institutional framework of the collective
farms, certain divisive tendencies which the government has been
forced to combat may be observed. The series of decrees from
1932 onward that endeavor to protect collective cultivation
against encroachments from various sources, and particularly
against the expansion of the privately owned plots, contradicts the
official claim that through the collective farms the USSR has
succeeded in harmonizing the interests of the individual farmer
with those of the state.

While the decree of August 7, 1932, merely spoke in general terms about the need for "strengthening socialist property," [40] that of May 27, 1939, concerned primarily the tendency of the *kolkhoznik's* private plot to expand at the expense of the collectivized sector.[41] A survey of the private plots which was carried out at that time revealed that the total land under such allotment amounted to 2,500,000 hectares in excess of the regulations.[42] Since the sown area in private plots amounted to only 5,300,000 hectares the year before,[43] it is safe to conclude that nearly half the existing allotments prior to the war were illegal. Over Stalin's signature the Party complained in the 1939 decree that the homestead plot had frequently become the private property of the *kolkhoznik,* who either kept it for his own use or rented it out, even when he did no work for the *kolkhoz*. The homestead plot, the complaint continued, had lost its character as a subsidiary undertaking and had become a basic source of income for the collective farmer, who gave a major part of his time to it. Generally similar decrees attempting to put an end to this expansion were issued again after the war on September 19, 1946, and February 27, 1947.[44]

The basic factor in the expansion of the private plots at the expense of the collectivized sector is, according to one thorough student, that the collective farms do not produce enough foodstuffs for the city population. They produce the grain, cotton, sugar, flax, and other raw materials, but fail to yield a sufficient amount of other foodstuffs to supply the cities through official channels. This function is largely taken over by the private plots, from which come the meat, dairy products, eggs, poultry, vegetables, and other important consumption items.[45] In 1932 the government permitted the organization of open markets in which the collective farmers and individual peasants might sell the produce of their farms direct to the consumer at whatever prices were formed by the interplay of supply and demand.[46] While not all of the produce sold on the open market in this fashion comes from the private plots, it is very likely that a high proportion comes from this source.

Another reason for the expansion of the private sector at the expense of the collective sector may be the *kolkhoznik's* need and opportunity to supplement the income received in payment for labor days. According to the estimate of an English economist, the collective farmer's income from labor days in 1937 accounted for only a small proportion of his money income, while a larger share came from the sale of surplus dividends in kind and surplus produce from the private allotments.[47] Since, as we have seen, only a limited proportion of the *kolkhoz* produce is available for distribution in the form of dividends, the significance of the private plot, whose produce is directly dependent on the individual's own efforts, is considerable.

It is perhaps on this account that the Party has found it necessary to put continued pressure on the farmers to work a minimum number of days on the collective farm. In 1932 and 1933 over 50 per cent of the members did less than 30 days of *kolkhoz* work a year. A study made in 1937 showed that, on the average, members worked for the *kolkhoz* only 46.6 per cent of the time. While the decree of May 27, 1939, asserted that the majority of collective farmers earned from 200 to 600 labor days a year, it pointed to the existence of evaders who worked no more than 20 or 30 days, and raised the required minimum number to 60, 80, and 100 days, depending on the local conditions. Under war conditions, on April 13, 1942, these figures were again raised to 100, 120, and 150 days, respectively.[48] After the war Party authorities still pointed out that a considerable portion of the collective farmers did not work the required minimum number of labor days. In several areas the number of such individuals reached 20 to 25 per cent of the able-bodied members of the *kolkhoz*.[49]

War conditions aggravated the divisive tendencies within the collective farms, although such tendencies were kept firmly in check by the authorities. The large-scale emission of funds to pay for war production had the effect, as the Soviets themselves concede, of increasing the prices of food products available on the *kolkhoz* market. In 1943 these prices were between twelve and thirteen times as high as in the prewar year 1940, although by 1945 they had dropped to a little less than half the 1943 peak.[50] This inflation provided a tremendous incentive to the peasants to devote their energies to their private plots, whose produce they could sell at uncontrolled prices. There are indications that many profited thereby. Before the war the income tax on peasants was progressive on incomes up to 4,000 rubles a year, after which the rates remained constant. During the war the tax was made progressive on incomes up to 10,000 rubles a year, for the specific purpose, said the Soviets, of taxing those *kolkhozniki* and individual peasants who derived high incomes from their subsidiary activities.[51] Thus the postwar decrees directed toward the curbing of the private plots (September 19, 1946), the absorption of surplus agricultural products and their transfer to the market through the coöperatives (November 9, 1946), the devaluation of the ruble and the abolition of bread rationing (December 14, 1947) represent a concerted attack on a single basic problem.[52]

Encroachments on the collective lands of the *kolkhoz* also derive from sources other than the expansion of the private plots. There are some indications that they may be more important sources of weakness in the *kolkhoz* system than those just discussed. A general explanation may be found in two related factors, which can be presented only as hypotheses because of the limited nature of the supporting data.

One hypothesis is that the prohibition on the sale of land by the collective farm has acted as an economic strait jacket, which the farm administration has sought to escape by legal and quasi-legal devices. One such device was for the *kolkhoz* to arrange with an industrial establishment for the latter to plant and make use of land unused by the *kolkhoz* itself. In part, these arrangements may have been made to supply agricultural products used in industry, and in part as a way of obtaining food for the factory canteens, which played an important role during the war.[53] On April 7, 1942, the government granted permission to the *kolkhozy* to conclude agreements with industrial establishments for the utilization of unused *kolkhoz* land. This permission was rescinded by the decree of September 19, 1946.[54] Further indications that the prohibition on the sale of land is a source of difficulty comes from scattered complaints in the Soviet press that the *kolkhoz* chairmen treat the farm as their own property, carrying on a lively trade in land as well as in its produce.[55]

The second hypothesis, which helps to explain the absorption of collective-farm lands by industrial units, as well as the growth of informal clique relationships among the heads of collective farms, factory directors, and local administrative officials, may be expressed in the following terms.[56] In the USSR the centralized machinery of production and distribution in both industry and agriculture works by fits and starts and with numerous local shortages. Therefore, there is a widespread tendency for farming and manufacturing organizations in the same locality to make individual trade arrangements with one another that at times conflict sharply with the patterns of distribution and production that the central authorities attempt to impose. The more grain and manufactured goods that are diverted into these local channels, the smaller are the quantities available for general distribution. In this manner, extreme centralization of the economy tends to generate its own antithesis.

Figures have been published which indicate clearly the extent of the various divisive tendencies in the collective farms and permit a rough estimate of the importance of each. During the war period the amount of land lost to collective farming was more than double that which had been lost by 1939. *Pravda* for September 19, 1947, reveals that by this date 5,780,000 hectares of collectivized land had been returned to the collective farms, all of which had been illegally taken out of collective cultivation. Andreev, the Politburo member selected as chief trouble shooter in collective-farm matters, issued in March 1947 a preliminary breakdown of these figures from a report made earlier to the Party Central Committee.[57] Inspections, carried out on 90 per cent of the farms, uncovered 2,225 cases of encroachment on collective property; in other words, on 1 per cent of the farms examined. In itself this figure is strong testimony to the regime's ability to keep the divisive tendencies under control.

At the time of the survey, 4,700,000 hectares of land had been returned to the *kolkhozy*. This figure represents about 4 per cent of the total area (117,200,000 hectares) under cultivation in 1938.

4,000,000 were returned by "various organizations and establish-ments." Most of the land was probably returned by the various industrial establishments whose activities have just been de-scribed. The *kolkhozniki* themselves returned 521,000 hectares, presumably from overexpanded private plots. "Other persons," who received no further identification in Andreev's report, turned back 177,000 hectares.[58] These figures are sufficient to contradict any allegations that the system of collective farming underwent a widespread collapse in the Soviet Union under the stress of the war.[59] They also prevent hasty conclusions that the system of collective farming suffers from internal strains that will even-tually bring about its collapse. At the same time, these strains are inherent in the Soviet collectivistic system and are likely to pro-duce difficulties with which the Party will have to cope in times to come.

In evaluating Soviet experience with the *kolkhoz* as a test of the proposition that legislation cannot change the mores, one is compelled to conclude that the Soviet regime has unquestionably succeeded in imposing a new form of social organization upon practically the entire mass of the Russian peasantry. A new insti-tutional pattern, resembling the socialist latifundia suggested by Kautsky and taken up by Lenin,[60] has definitely come into being. On this basis it seems necessary to abandon the proposition, at least in this crude and absolute form.

The evidence will not warrant, however, the opposite conclu-sion: that legislation may alter customary patterns in any way desired by the legislator. The *kolkhoz* does not possess on any significant scale the characteristics of autonomy or internal de-mocracy, defined in the Soviets' own terms, that were and remain part of the officially expressed Soviet ideal. This aspect of their goal has not been achieved, largely because it conflicts with other goals more important to the Communists. These may be stated as the retention of power by the Communist elite and the success-ful operation of a planned economy.

The data indicate that there is an important residue of truth in the *laissez-faire* doctrine. It may be expressed in the general-ization that it is impossible to achieve mutually incompatible goals. The history of the Bolshevik regime can be written around this theme and the sacrifices of one set of objectives in order to attain or come closer to attaining another set. It is well to point out again in this connection that the sacrifices are sometimes temporary ones, and that the subordinated goals may remain latent, to emerge and influence policy under more favorable circumstances. The adoption and later abandonment of the NEP illustrate this process. It does not seem likely that a general list of mutually incompatible goals, applicable for all groups and all times and places, can be drawn up. To determine whether or not two or more goals are incompatible is an empirical problem that can be solved only with a knowledge of the relevant circumstances.

In the conflict of goals associated with the *kolkhozy,* the official ideology plays a dual role. In the first place, it conceals the existence of this conflict. In the literature known to me there is no evidence of any overt awareness among the Communists that there is a conflict of aims in their policies related to collective farming. A convinced Communist would certainly deny the existence of any such conflict to an outsider, though he might conceivably admit it in confidence to another Party member. A second role played by the official doctrine is to smooth over the contradictions between the major goal of retention of power by the Communist elite and the minor one of Soviet democracy on the collective farms. The way in which this takes place is characteristic of the relationship between ideology and behavior in other parts of the Soviet system. The device, probably used unconsciously for the most part, is to assert that the realization of the subordinate goal, *kolkhoz* democracy, will take place in the very near future. In numerous discussions in the Party press the recurrent theme is: "One more campaign—one more effort—and the objective will be won." Reform groups often display a similar pattern of thinking in the United States, saying in effect, "Throw the rascals out, and our troubles will be over." In both America and Russia the sources of difficulty are located in the errors made by individuals, even though the Communists may color this with vague references to the "relationship of class forces." By declaring that the realization of the goal lies in the immediate future, present difficulties are smoothed over and made to appear transient phenomena, which makes allegiance to the goal easier to maintain. It would be rash to assert that this device cannot be used over considerable periods of time. Quite possibly it can be used indefinitely.

16

The Pattern of Soviet Foreign Policy

General considerations

In Robert E. Sherwood's account of Molotov's visit to President Roosevelt, there is reproduced a snatch of conversation that serves as a vivid reminder of one prominent feature of Soviet foreign policy: its ability to reach agreements with anyone, if the agreement promises advantages. Roosevelt asked Molotov for his personal impressions of Hitler. Motolov replied that, after all, it was possible to arrive at a common understanding with almost anyone. But he had never met two more disagreeable people to deal with than Hitler and Ribbentrop.[1]

Soviet Russia's participation in the pact with the Nazis, as well as its alternating periods of friendship and hostility toward the Western democracies, are sometimes considered enigmatic and mysterious. However, sudden changes from friendship to hostility are familiar features of international relationships and are by no means confined to the diplomatic history of the Soviet Union. This chapter will endeavor to show that the main outlines of Soviet foreign policy, with its shifts from one camp to another, are typical reactions to alterations in the distribution of political power in the world at large. To the extent that such is the case, there is no difference between Soviet foreign policy and that of any other state. However, there is more to the story than this.

In the same general fashion that democratic ideology influences American reactions to world situations, the Russian Marxist intellectual tradition plays an important part in Soviet adaptation to the changing balance of power. The Marxist tradition consists of a specifically defined goal, the proletarian revolution, and a way of looking at political events which emphasizes the clash of economic interest groups. Both of these aspects play a definite role in Soviet responses to changes in the international balance of power.

The revolutionary goal can be reconciled with the promotion of Russian national interests through the familiar argument that any act which strengthens the proletarian fatherland automatically contributes to eventual proletarian victory throughout the world. What non-Communists or ex-Communists may regard as the sacrifice of Communist Parties outside the USSR to Russian national interests can be explained by the Soviets as a necessary peripheral sacrifice to strengthen the fortress of revolution. The Marxist analysis of political events abroad stresses some facts, while it ignores or plays down others.[2] Thus the Marxist interpretation of events affects the Soviet reaction to the events.

Although Soviet foreign policy is distinguished from that of other states by the presence of this Marxist ingredient, it is not necessarily true that the Marxist component is the most important one. The structure of international relationships itself imposes certain forms of behavior upon the participants. The penalty for failure to conform, for unwillingness to engage in balance-of-power politics, is national disaster. Such factors appear to have been the significant determinants of Soviet foreign policy, as well as that of other modern states. At the same time, the way in which each individual state may react to an international situation will differ considerably according to its specific historical background, cultural tradition, and prevailing ideology or series of ideologies.

Quite justifiably, international relations has been compared to a quadrille, in which the dancers change their partners at a definite signal. But no two dancers execute the steps in precisely the same fashion. Some, who are new to the steps, may try to stop the dance altogether, or call for a new tune. For this they may be sent to the corner (behind a *cordon sanitaire*), to emerge later as seeking and sought-after partners. Or, conceivably at least, they might bring the dance to a halt. There is more than illustrative metaphor behind this comparison. International relationships, like the dance or any other pattern of organized human relationships, are composed of a series of formally patterned requirements for the participants. Those who participate will do so in an individual fashion, and may on occasion seek to alter the general pattern.

Power politics calls the tune

The major developments in the international field that faced the Soviet Union after the establishment of Stalin's internal leadership were the rise of Germany and Japan as expansionist states. The relations of these powers to each other, to the USSR, and to the other major powers, England, France, and the United States, constituted the focal problems of Soviet foreign policy from the 1930's until the defeat of the Axis in 1945.

At first the Soviet leaders, like those in other countries, were slow in recognizing the danger to their country implicit in German National Socialism. This lag may be related to factional struggles within the Russian Communist Party, centering around differing evaluations of the political situation abroad as well as more personal rivalries, and hence indirectly to the influence of Marxist ideological factors.

There are strong indications that within the Russian Communist Party and the Communist International as well there was a group, probably led by Bukharin, that wished to reach some kind of working agreement with the German Social Democrats and representatives of gradualist socialism in other countries in order to combat the rising danger of fascism.[3] This group was not successful in imposing its point of view. Instead, Stalin turned on Bukharin and his followers, accusing them in a vitriolic speech of failing to see the necessity for purging the Communist Parties of conciliationist tendencies.[4]

Stalin's explanation of the current political situation claimed that both the Nazis and the Social Democrats served the reactionary purposes of the bourgeoisie. The official interpretation of the world depression, which had become acute at that time, and its political consequences was that the bourgeoisie would seek the solution of its difficulties by way of fascism, an argument that in itself has considerable plausibility in the light of subsequent events. In resorting to fascism, said Stalin, the bourgeoisie would make use of "all reactionary forces, including social democracy." [5] Another reason for Communist hostility to the Social Democrats was derived from Lenin's fundamental point that the "democratic illusions," propagated among the working class by the Social Democrats, prevented an influential stratum of the proletariat from realizing that its "true" interests could be served only by the destruction of capitalism. For this reason it was possible for the German Communists to declare, "A Social Democratic coalition government, standing over a disabled, split, and bewildered proletariat, would be a thousand times worse evil than an open fascist dictatorship that stood over a class-conscious proletariat, unified and decided upon battle." [6] The working policies employed by the Communist Party in Germany, under pressure from the Soviet leaders, followed fairly closely the lines set forth in the official doctrine. The Communists opposed the Nazis, but devoted a large part of their energies to attacks upon the Social Democrats. [7]

In addition to the preceding considerations, derived from Marxist ideology, there were others, based less upon Marxist doctrine than upon an evaluation of Russian national interests, that prevented the USSR from aligning itself against Germany even after the Nazi coup. Germany was a useful counterweight in the balance of power against England and France, and the Soviets did not manifest any haste in abandoning the policy they had followed almost without exception from Rapallo onward. They seem to have hoped that the Nazis would limit their anti-Communist policies to domestic matters, while remaining on good terms with the Soviet Union in foreign affairs. Goering gave some grounds for such hopes in his statement to the Dutch press that the extirpation of Communism in Germany had nothing to do with friendly German-Russian relations. [8] The Soviets' long record of hostility to the Versailles Treaty and to the League of Nations was indeed objectively in alignment with certain features of proclaimed Nazi foreign policy.

Thus Litvinov, although he was one of the first Soviet statesmen to point out publicly the potential danger of Nazism to the USSR,[9] adopted a conciliatory tone toward the Nazis. His first major speech on this question following the Nazi victory said in effect that the Soviets were perfectly willing to sacrifice the German Communist Party, provided the Germans maintained friendly relations with the Soviet Union. "We certainly have our own opinion about the German regime," he said. "We certainly are sympathetic towards the suffering of our German comrades; but it is possible to reproach us Marxists least of all with permitting our sympathies to rule our policy. All the world knows that we can and do maintain good relations with capitalist governments of any regime including fascist. That is not what matters. We do not interfere in the internal affairs of Germany or of other countries, and our relations with her are determined not by her domestic but by her foreign policy." [10] A few weeks later, at the Seventeenth Party Congress, Stalin voiced the same theme. Denying the German allegation that the Soviet Union had become a supporter of the Versailles Treaty because of the Nazi victory, he went on to say, "Of course we are far from being enthusiastic about the fascist regime in Germany. But fascism is not the issue here, if only for the reason that fascism in Italy, for example, has not prevented the USSR from establishing the best relations with that country." [11]

The Soviet reaction to Japanese expansionism in its beginning stages followed a similar pattern. In 1925 Soviet-Japanese relations reached the friendliest point of many years, owing in part to parallel interests in internal Chinese affairs. Afterward the friendship declined. The outbreak of hostilities in Manchuria on September 19, 1931, was interpreted in the Soviet press as the preliminary for an attack on the Soviet Union. However, Soviet suspicions of the Western capitalist states, strongly expressed by Stalin the year before at the Sixteenth Party Congress, for a time helped to prevent the Russians from aligning themselves with Japan's opponents. The Russian leaders remained skeptical and antagonistic toward the League of Nations and the efforts of the Lytton Commission to settle the conflict, accusing the Japanese of trying to promote a "Red scare" to cover Japanese antagonism toward the Commission. A further reason, according to later statements by Maxim Litvinov, was that the Russians did not want the League to embroil the USSR in a war with Japan. On December 31, 1931, Litvinov broached the subject of a nonaggression pact to the Japanese without success.

Not until the spring of 1932 were the first steps taken toward the improvement of relations between the Soviet government and Chiang Kai-shek, and in this case the initiative came primarily from the Chinese side. On December 12, 1932, diplomatic relations with China were reëstablished, although they were somewhat strained by the Soviet proposal of May 12, 1933, to sell the Chinese Eastern Railway to Japan, a move dictated by the desire to avoid further involvement with Japan in Manchuria. Thus, as in the German case, the Russians attempted to ward off a threatened attack through the offer to continue friendly relations with their main antagonist. Since this did not appear to be overly successful, the Russians soon found themselves seeking allies or being sought as an ally. The balance-of-power mechanism had begun to operate once more according to its familiar pattern. To this the Soviets adapted themselves, if slowly and reluctantly.[12]

The search for allies

The first step toward meeting the danger of German and Japanese expansion were taken through the instrument of the Communist International, instead of through regular diplomatic channels. There are several indications that the impetus behind the change came not so much from Moscow as from within the ranks of the European Marxist parties, and that it was transmitted to Moscow by Western Communists in touch with rank-and-file sentiment. Hitler's crushing defeat of the left made many of the rank and file in both the Communist International and gradualist Marxist parties impatient with what seemed to them finespun wrangling over how the world should end, when it was ending before their eyes in terror and concentration camps. To many the lesson of the Nazi victory seemed obvious: the split in the working class had enabled fascism to triumph in Germany and would enable it to triumph elsewhere, if the split were not healed. Socialist and Communist leaders, however, remained skeptical of each other's intentions.

Some of the pressures to abandon the fratricidal conflict appeared when a German Social Democratic publication broached the possibility of reaching an agreement just before Hitler suppressed the Party.[13] It was in France, however, where fears of a possible fascist coup played an important part in producing cooperation among the lower echelons of the Communist and Socialist Parties, that a formal agreement was first reached. This took place on July 27, 1934, a year and a half after the Nazi victory in Germany.[14] The new policy was endorsed by the presidium of the Communist International during the same month. In the spring of the previous year the French leader, Maurice Thorez, had been called to Moscow. Probably the situation was discussed with the Russian leaders at that time.[15]

Despite the 1934 agreement between the French Socialists and Communists, it is clear that the Russians had not yet given up the hope of coming to an agreement with Nazi Germany. As on other occasions, the Soviets gave evidence of trying to keep two strings for their bow. In his report to the Seventh Congress of Soviets on January 28, 1935, Molotov gave a broad hint that the USSR was still willing to reach some kind of agreement with Germany. On this occasion he repeated Stalin's theme that the Soviet Union sought for the development of good relations with all countries, "not excluding countries with a fascist regime," citing once more Italo-Soviet relations as proof of the possibility of coöperation between countries with completely contrary social systems.[16]

The change in Communist tactics involved in the search for allies among the working class did not become fully apparent until the highly publicized Seventh and last World Congress of the Communist International, held in Moscow during the summer of

1935. This body declared: "In the face of the towering menace of fascism . . . it is imperative that unity of action be established between all sections of the working class, irrespective of what organisation they belong to, even before the majority of the working class unites on a common fighting platform for the overthrow of capitalism and the victory of the proletarian revolution." [17]

From this point until the Nazi-Soviet Non-Aggression Pact of August 23, 1939, anti-fascism became a dominant note in both Soviet and Comintern propaganda. In addition, the Communists in each country attempted to pose as the true defenders of national interests against the onslaught of fascism. In the new anti-fascist bloc, as conceived by the Soviets, former enemies on the left, and even middle-class groups with anti-fascist sentiments, were welcomed as allies. In France, in the summer of 1935, the united front was extended to become the popular front by the inclusion of the Radical Party (despite its name a middle-of-the-road group that provided many of the leaders of the Third Republic) under Daladier, whose last ministry the Communists had helped to overturn in February 1934.[18]

Similar events took place at a later date in the Far East. In August 1936 the Chinese Communists abandoned, under the pressure of the Japanese advance, their hostility to Chiang Kai-shek. In December of the same year, following the famous Sian incident in which Chiang was kidnapped and released by a Kuomintang leader anxious for a more vigorous policy against Japan, relations between the two groups improved, though a formal agreement was not reached until after the Japanese attack on the Marco Polo Bridge in 1937. By this time the united front was extended to the Far East.[19]

Throughout this search for allies the Soviets were faced with a problem that recurs continually in the history of the Communist movement. To gain assistance against one enemy it was necessary to make programmatic concessions to another enemy, to soften or disguise ultimate objectives. Failure to make such concessions might obviously result in sectarian impotence, or even destruction. At the same time, sentiment was strong against any apparent betrayal of ideals. Communist ethics permit and even encourage one to admit the existence of compromises over methods and means. But to admit openly a compromise over ends is extremely difficult, indeed nearly impossible, before an outsider.

In fashioning the popular front of the middle thirties, Russian and foreign Communists tried to resolve the conflicting pressures for expediency and doctrinal consistency by conceding once more the postponement of the proletarian revolution, while reaffirming it as their ultimate objective. The Seventh World Congress of the Communist International still spoke about the "transformation of the maturing political crisis into a victorious proletarian revolution," [20] a phrase that was hardly likely to reassure non-Marxist allies. Dimitrov, the new general secretary of the Comintern, told the same gathering: "Comrades! We have purposely thrown out of the speeches and Congress resolutions *high-sounding phrases* about revolutionary perspectives." Then, as if failing to heed his own words, he went on to proclaim that the present rulers of the capitalist world were but temporary figures, and that the proletariat was the true ruler who would soon "take up the reins of government in every country, the entire world." [21] Communist adherence to revolutionary symbolism did not help to reduce the suspicions that continually endangered the united front. Such statements as André Marty's, that the interests of French imperialism and the Soviet Union in the maintenance of peace covered entirely different ultimate objectives, were hardly reassuring to potential non-Communist followers.[22]

Even without such statements, it was frequently clear that the Communists owed their general allegiance to the Soviet Union, and that they supported a particular cause at a particular moment merely because the two interests happened to coincide. At every point and by a wide variety of techniques they tried to capture the leadership of trade unions, political pressure groups, intellectuals' gatherings, and the like in order to bend them to Soviet purposes. They demanded coöperation, but insisted on maintaining their own organization intact, continuing to criticize in vitriolic terms those who questioned their policy. For all these reasons, united front and popular front agreements were highly unstable and in continuous danger of disintegration.

In their search for protection against Germany and Japan, the Soviets did not confine themselves to the instrument of the Communist International. On September 18, 1934, the Soviet Union became a member of the League of Nations.[23] Having castigated this organization for some years as a pious front for the Anglo-American imperialists, the Soviet leaders evidently now considered that it might serve Soviet purposes. Between 1934 and 1938 the Soviets were among the strongest supporters of the League, though they were often critical of its unsuccessful attempts to check Axis expansion.[24] On May 2, 1935, the Franco-Soviet Treaty of Mutual Assistance was signed by Laval and the Soviet representative. The terms of the pact obligated the two governments to assist one another in case either of them were subject to an unprovoked attack.[25] One consequence of the new Franco-Soviet rapprochement was that the French Communists, after a public statement by Stalin approving French rearmament, immediately dropped their campaign against the lengthening of the period of military service.[26] On May 16, 1935, a mutual assistance pact between the Soviets and Czechoslovakia was signed in Prague. Though its provisions were identical with those of the Franco-Soviet pact, its protocol of signature provided that the provisions for mutual assistance should come into force only if France came to the assistance of the country attacked.[27] This provision was probably a reflection of the Soviet suspicion, frequently voiced later, that the ties with the West might simply be utilized to drag Russia into the war to serve Western purposes. A treaty of nonaggression with Italy, signed on September 2, 1933; recognition by the United States, achieved on November 16, 1933; the reduction of tension with England over the question of the Dardanelles through the Montreux Convention of July 20, 1936; and the conclusion of a nonaggression pact with China on August 28, 1937, constituted the remaining diplomatic ramparts erected by the Soviet Union against potential dangers.

Suspicions among allies

By 1939 this system of paper ramparts lay in ruins, and the Russians found it expedient to ally themselves, at least temporarily, with Nazi Germany, their major diplomatic antagonist. To consider all of the reasons for the collapse of these defenses is a task that would take us far afield. But a few may be mentioned for the light they throw on the general problems of Soviet foreign policy.

In the first place, many influential groups in the powers connected with the USSR by its system of alliances were suspicious of Soviet aims and intentions. They argued that the Communist assumption of the democratic mantle and the Soviet alignment with the Western democracies were tactical maneuvers designed to further Soviet ends. In several chancelleries the ends were assumed to be the original ones of world revolution and the establishment of the Soviet system in the major power centers of the world. Those less fearful of a world-wide upheaval still feared that the Soviet Union, since it lacked a common frontier with Germany, might take control of Eastern Europe and thereby undermine the status quo. Still others suspected that the Soviets might embroil them in a war with Germany, thereby avoiding the main burden of fighting to gather the fruits of social upheaval. A number of influential persons argued that the trials and purges had so weakened the USSR that its military contribution would be insignificant. Thus, many European leaders were torn between their fears of the Axis and their fears of the Soviet Union. The Spanish Civil War, in which it seemed for a time that the Communists might gain a dominant position in a corner of Western Europe, increased the dilemma of those who wished neither for an extension of Soviet influence nor for continued fascist expansion.

On the Soviet side there were frequent expressions of the suspicion that the Western powers were not really interested in peace and security, but were merely anxious to divert Germany and Japan against the USSR. Stalin, as we have seen, expressed these ideas in his report to the Party Congress of 1934, at which he held out the possibility of a rapprochement with Nazi Germany. In his speeches before the League of Nations, Litvinov continually reproached France and England with failure to take active steps to halt aggression.

There are also strong indications that the distrust of *all* capitalist powers remained an influential factor in Soviet policy. In a report to a plenary session of the Central Committee in 1937, Stalin drove home the theme of a united capitalist world, waiting hungrily to attack the USSR. "Capitalist encirclement—that's no empty phrase, that's something real and unpleasant. Capitalist encirclement—that means that there is one country, the Soviet Union, that has established for itself a socialist system; and there are, besides that, many countries, bourgeois countries, which continue to carry on a capitalist way of life and which surround the Soviet Union, waiting for the opportunity to attack it and plunder it, or in any case—to undermine its power and weaken it." [28]

To some extent Stalin's speech, and others of the same tenor, must be discounted as part of a deliberate attempt to create an atmosphere of spy hysteria for the purpose of destroying the remnants of domestic enemies, since the speechmaking took place during the 1936–1938 purges. Yet it is hardly likely that Stalin would have used these symbols if he did not believe they would strike a responsive chord among his listeners in the Party Central Committee.

Thus, strong mutual suspicions, at least partly justified on both sides, contributed to the collapse of efforts to create an effective bloc of powers against Axis expansion. It might be argued that these suspicions could have arisen independently of the Marxist-Leninist tradition in Russia, and that they could have been based on mutual suspicions concerning the territorial and political aims of both the Russian and the Western states. But in this particular case, it is at least reasonably clear that Western suspicions of the specifically revolutionary intentions of the USSR contributed to the collapse. It is likewise equally clear that Soviet suspicions of the West were increased by viewing the world through Marxist lenses.

If any single incident can be selected as the key point in the collapse of the anti-Axis coalition, that incident is the Munich Conference of September 29, 1938.[29] At this conference, to which the Soviets were not invited, the French and British leaders attempted to "appease" Hitler and to avoid war by granting his demands in regard to the Sudeten areas of Czechoslovakia.

New partners

The results of the Munich Conference evidently raised once again serious questions in the Kremlin concerning the desirability of continuing its opposition to Germany. At the Eighteenth Party Congress in March 1939, Stalin referred caustically to the Anglo-French retreat before the military bloc of Italy, Germany, and Japan. In his explanation of the retreat, he laid less emphasis on the fear of revolution as a motivating factor in Anglo-French policy, and more upon their alleged policy of encouraging German and Japanese aggression against the USSR.[30] Dimitry Manuilsky, speaking as the Party's representative in the Comintern, put the matter in somewhat more Marxist terms. The plan of the English reactionary bourgeoisie, he claimed, was to sacrifice the little countries of Europe to fascism and turn Germany against the USSR. By such a counterrevolutionary war they hoped to prevent the further success of socialism and the victory of communism in the Soviet Union, at the same time that they used the "arms of the USSR to pull the teeth of German imperialism" and maintain for themselves the ruling position in Europe.[31]

Shortly after the 1939 Party Congress, the Kremlin leaders initiated a policy of playing the Anglo-French combination off against the Germans in an effort to force both groups to make the highest possible bid for a minimum of Soviet support. That this was a deliberate and consciously employed technique is indicated by the fact that on the same day that the Russians proposed a Franco-British-Soviet defense pact against fascist aggression (April 17, 1939), the Soviet ambassador in Berlin gave a broad hint to the German foreign office that the USSR wished to reach an agreement with Germany.[32]

It is worth noting that in the course of their negotiations with the Germans the Soviets repeatedly made the point, emphasized in public speeches by Stalin some years before, that the internal nature of the Nazi regime and its anti-Communist policies should not prevent friendly relations between the German and Soviet states. On one occasion during the negotiations, the Soviet chargé in Berlin remarked to a German official that in Moscow the authorities had never been able to understand why the Nazis sought the enmity of the Soviet Union, although "they always had full understanding for the domestic opposition to Communism." [33] In addition to the revealing sidelight these remarks throw upon the attitude of the Russian policy-makers toward the Communist Parties abroad, they indicate that at all times during the thirties there was a group among these policy-makers who believed in the possibility of good relations with the Nazi regime.

Nevertheless, this group was by no means dominant, and it would be rash to conclude that the Russians had no intention at any time of coming to an agreement with the Anglo-French representatives. As late as August 4, 1939, less than three weeks before the conclusion of the Nazi-Soviet Pact, the German ambassador in Moscow reported to his government, after a conversation with Molotov, "My over-all impression is that the Soviet Government is at present determined to sign with England and France if they fulfill all Soviet wishes." [34]

To the astonishment of many, agreement was reached between the Germans and the Russians, formalized in the famous Non-Aggression Pact of August 23, 1939. Whether or not the Russian action was a blunder in terms of balance-of-power politics is an arguable question. It is clear from the record of the conversations preceding the pact that Stalin and Molotov knew that this act would be the prelude to war. That the war might lead to a rapid expansion of German influence is a factor Stalin and Molotov must have considered. It is doubtful, however, that they foresaw, or could have foreseen, the rapidity of the German conquest. Stalin told Ribbentrop that "England, despite its weakness, would wage war craftily and stubbornly," and that France had an army "worthy of consideration." [35] Furthermore, the Russians could believe that in signing the pact they had achieved four major objectives, which figured prominently in the negotiations leading up to the pact and in the public speeches of Soviet leaders. The treaty, so it seemed, secured Russia from a German attack and at the same time prevented the Soviet Union from being drawn into a general European war to serve Anglo-French interests. Likewise, the Russians obtained a diminution of Japanese pressure on their Eastern flank, while they gained simultaneously an opportunity for territorial adjustments in the West.[36] In the light of the information available at this time, it does appear, therefore, that the Soviet adherence to the pact was a rational action in terms of contemporary power politics.

Soviet behavior, following its adherence to the pact, also followed the standard pattern of maintaining one's own strength vis-à-vis an associate that might some day become an enemy. Most of the important Russian actions during the brief period of the pact may be accounted for by the hypothesis that the Soviets were endeavoring to place themselves in as advantageous a position as possible in relation to Germany, while at the same time they tried to avoid any action that would precipitate an outright break. As matters turned out, these two policies were mutually incompatible, since Russian defensive measures sharpened German suspicions and eventually contributed to the Nazi invasion. Although the two policies were incompatible, they are easy to understand, since the Soviets had good reason to fear that the Germans might turn on them no matter what happened.

At first the strains imposed on the Nazi-Soviet alignment by Soviet actions were minor. Russian participation in the partition of Poland, the Soviet military pacts with the Baltic States (September–October 1939), the Soviet war against Finland (December 1939–March 1940), and the virtual annexation of the Baltic States at the height of German military successes against France (June 1940) produced no more overt signs of strain than occasional warnings by the German foreign office to its staff abroad, cautioning them to avoid anti-Soviet statements in their conversations with foreigners.[37] The first sign of coolness on the Russian side appeared in connection with the Axis guarantee to Rumania that her frontiers, following the Vienna award, would be inviolate. On August 31, 1940, Molotov told the German ambassador that this action was a violation of the Non-Aggression Pact.[38]

Acute difficulties arose in connection with Molotov's visit to Berlin in November 1940. In the discussions that accompanied and followed this visit, Molotov's demands revealed a series of territorial aims, and a willingness to engage in classical *Realpolitik*, that is strongly reminiscent of Tsarist expansionist policy. While this was far from an altogether new element in Soviet foreign policy, it appeared on this occasion in an especially clear form, unencumbered by Marxian messianic phraseology.

Hitler offered Molotov the opportunity for the Soviet Union to join the Axis and share in the new division of the world. Molotov replied that Soviet participation in the Axis appeared to him "entirely acceptable in principle," provided that the USSR "was to coöperate as a partner and not be merely an object." [39] During the course of several conversations with Hitler and Ribbentrop, Molotov insisted on a precise recognition of Russian interests in Finland, the Balkans, and Turkey as a prerequisite to Soviet participation in the Tripartite Pact. On his return to Moscow he informed the German ambassador that the Soviet government would join the Axis under four conditions: (1) German troops would have to be withdrawn from Finland; (2) Bulgaria would have to conclude a mutual assistance pact with the USSR and grant the USSR a base for land and naval forces within range of the Bosporus and the Dardanelles; (3) the area south of Batum and Baku in the general direction of the Persian Gulf would have to be recognized as the "center of the aspirations of the Soviet Union"; (4) Japan would have to renounce her concession rights for coal and oil in northern Sakhalin.[40] It is hardly necessary to point out that these objectives, which represent a continuation of Tsarist aims, have formed highly significant elements in Soviet foreign policy since this date. Hitler's reaction to their exposition was to order his generals to prepare in utmost secrecy for a knockout blow against the Soviet Union.[41]

How much the Soviets learned about the German preparations is far from clear, though the impending attack became common diplomatic gossip in Moscow. The British ambassador even predicted correctly the date of the invasion.[42] Stalin told Harry Hopkins in 1941 that he had believed Hitler would not strike, but that he had taken all precautions possible to mobilize his army.[43] Diplomatic precautions were taken as well, of which the most important was the neutrality pact with Japan (April 23, 1941), diminishing the probability of a two-front war for the Soviets. As part of the price of agreement, the Japanese exacted from the Russians the recognition of the territorial integrity of Manchukuo.[44] For the Russians this symbolic recognition of the existing situation was a small price to pay for the advantages gained.

The Nazi-Soviet attempt at collaboration failed, not because the Kremlin leaders had any objections "in principle" to coöperation with the Axis, but because the Nazis felt they could not permit the Russians the degree of security against their Nazi partners that the Kremlin leaders demanded. Well-grounded mutual suspicions brought about its collapse, just as similar suspicions had contributed to the collapse of Soviet collaboration with the Western democracies.

Old partners

The march of the Nazi legions, begun on June 22, 1941, automatically made the Soviet Union the ally of the Western democracies once more. In the light of the historical record, it is clear that this alignment had little if anything to do with ideological or "democratic" affinities.

In the new anti-Axis coalition, the Soviets pursued the same basic policy of protecting themselves against allies, as well as enemies, that they had followed in previous years and alliances. Throughout the war Soviet policy was directed not only toward a military victory, but also toward emerging from the conflict in as strong a position as possible in relation to both allies and current enemies.

Both the Soviets and their allies feared that their partners might conclude a separate peace with Germany. The Russians in particular had grounds for fearing that the British and the Americans might stand aside in the hope that Germany and the Soviet Union would exhaust themselves in a mutual bloodletting. This hope was openly expressed by a member of the British government in the first days of the German attack, and even his prompt dismissal could not have been altogether reassuring. Hence the Soviets sought through official and unofficial channels to engage the Anglo-American forces in the second front.[45] Churchill, as is widely known, opposed the second front and in its place proposed a Balkan and Mediterranean campaign, probably with the aim of checking Soviet postwar expansion into Eastern Europe. At Teheran in 1943 Stalin resisted successfully all of Churchill's oratorical arguments in favor of this plan.[46]

As early as September 1941 Stalin gave the Beaverbrook-Harriman mission to Moscow a "rough time" by raising a number of political issues, and by showing only moderate mollification when these two men promised abundant military supplies. Even at this date it appears that Stalin was entertaining dreams of empire. When the first Nazi attack had spent itself and the Russians had recaptured Rostov, in the beginning of winter, 1941, Stalin insisted on continuing detailed political discussions, whose range reflected the extent of Soviet interests. The discussions concerned the borders between the Soviet Union and Finland, Poland, and Rumania; the status of the Baltic States; and more distant matters such as the future of the Rhineland, Bavaria, East Prussia, the restoration of the Sudeten area to Czechoslovakia, and territorial adjustments affecting Greece and Turkey. The situation became so tense that it was necessary to send Anthony Eden to Moscow, where he arrived just before the Japanese attack on Pearl Harbor.[47]

Difficulties arose over the future status of Poland almost at once. On December 4, 1941, Stalin indicated to the leader of the Polish government in exile, whose headquarters were in London, that he wished certain changes in Poland's postwar frontiers.[48] Early in 1943 it became apparent that the Russians had in mind the Curzon Line as the future boundary between the two countries, an idea which the London group refused to accept.[49] When, in April of the same year, it became clear that the London group could not be prevailed upon to accept the Soviet proposals, the Kremlin seized upon Polish accusations that the Russians had murdered a number of Polish officers as diplomatic justification for breaking off relations.[50] Afterward the Russians intensified their efforts to create around a Communist nucleus a Polish group of their own, capable of taking power and governing Poland in a manner amenable to Soviet interests. Although the Soviets at various times before and after the establishment of this regime indicated a willingness to incorporate into this group of Soviet-sponsored leaders certain individuals from the London government in exile, their efforts to broaden its base of popular support in this fashion did not succeed.

A similar pattern of events unfolded in Yugoslavia. The Soviets supported Tito, a Communist, in opposition to the Serbian guerrilla leader Mihailovich, who in turn enjoyed for a time the indirect support of London. In October 1944, on the occasion of Churchill's visit to Moscow, the Soviets agreed to a merger between Tito's forces and the Royal Yugoslav Government, whose quarters were in the British capital. Subsequently, Tito and his followers managed to eliminate opposition leaders and establish a near monopoly of political power in their own hands. Until Tito's defection from the ranks of Soviet supporters, it seemed that Russian influence might extend to the shores of the Adriatic.

In June 1944, apparently at the initiative of the British, the attempt was begun to resolve existing conflicts through an old-fashioned agreement on spheres of influence. At that time the United States had not yet begun to display any great interest in the postwar distribution of power, although it would be forced at a later date to take over from Britain the role of chief diplomatic antagonist to the USSR. The British suggested that Rumania and Bulgaria should be treated as part of the Soviet zone of influence, and that Greece, vital to British Mediterranean interests, should belong to the British zone. Stalin agreed, thereby giving the British a free hand to deal with the Greek left as best they could, while the British gave Stalin a free hand to eliminate in his own way the opponents of the Soviets in their zone.[51] The Russians are sometimes credited with keeping to their part of the bargain, since the Soviet press failed to give any support to the Greek rebels in the first stages of the British attempt to reëstablish a parliamentary regime. However, one cannot be certain that the prolonged rebel resistance was not to some extent aided, directly or indirectly, by the Soviets.

Neither this attempt nor the more formal discussions at Teheran, Yalta, and Potsdam succeeded in eliminating the sources of present and future tension among the allies. Each of these conferences ended in high hopes because the Anglo-Americans managed to extract some promise from Stalin that the Russians would alter their policy. Disenchantment set in afterward as the Soviets continued their efforts to consolidate and extend their power position.

The foregoing does not imply that these conferences failed to produce significant political decisions. At the Yalta Conference the Soviets achieved important diplomatic gains, particularly in the Far East. At the time, however, the agreement may well have seemed, even to its signers, to be a diplomatic compromise without serious gains or losses for either side. The Soviets promised to enter the war against Japan and agreed to conclude a pact of friendship with the Nationalist Government in China, which implied repudiation of the Chinese Communists. In return, the USSR received, among other things, promises that the southern part of Sakhalin would revert to Russia, that the Kurile Islands would be turned over to her, and that the Soviets might lease Port Arthur as a naval base. In addition, the agreement, by recognizing the existing situation in Mongolia, legalized its detachment from China and its dependence on the Soviet Union.[52] These Soviet actions were probably directed toward neutralizing American power in the Far East, whether based upon the occupation of Japan or exercised more indirectly through China.

During the war Soviet actions were by no means limited to efforts at checkmating the Anglo-American powers in case of a postwar struggle. There are clear indications that the Kremlin authorities also feared a revival of German and Japanese expansionism at some future date. At Teheran in 1943, Stalin on more than one occasion expressed the belief that Germany would be able to recover its power completely in fifteen or twenty years, and requested strong safeguards against this possibility.[53] It was primarily as a safeguard against the resurgence of Germany and Japan that the Soviets displayed an interest in the proposal for a United Nations organization. The Soviet leaders in both their programmatic speeches and diplomatic discussions with other powers treated the United Nations as a continuation of the wartime coalition under peaceful conditions.[54] Even before the end of the war, however, Soviet leaders began to express the fear that the new instrument of collective security, like its predecessor the League of Nations, might turn out to be nothing more than a thinly veiled instrument of one set of powers directed against another. The United Nations, the Soviets apparently suspected, might be transformed from the Big Three into an Anglo-American bloc directed against the USSR.[55] Subsequent Soviet actions, largely dictated by the postwar distribution of political power, have contributed toward the realization of these fears, although the Soviets, by remaining in the United Nations, have managed to prevent it from taking effective action against the USSR.

New patterns of power

After victory over the Axis, a new configuration of world politics rapidly emerged. Germany and Japan were eliminated as independent sources of power; England was greatly weakened; and France and Italy were weakened even more. For these reasons the only effective threat to Soviet interests in the postwar world would have to come from the United States, and vice versa. This new situation has often been referred to as the polarization of power in the postwar world.

As some writers have suggested, there may be nothing inherent in a two-power system that inevitably generates conflicts between these powers.[56] But if the conflicts are already present, they have a tendency to become aggravated. Each "defensive" measure taken by one power calls forth a corresponding action by the opposite one. President Roosevelt's wartime policy was directed toward preventing the United States from initiating such conflicts, for which he has been subsequently criticized. However, as has been pointed out, during the war the Russians were busily engaged in maximizing their potential advantages, and the British were not altogether behindhand in such activities. With the conclusion of hostilities, latent conflicts among the Big Three came out into the open. Sharp competition soon ensued for the control of those portions of the world that were actual or potential sources of political power. On this account, the remaining lesser powers have tended to associate themselves, in widely varying degrees of dependence, with either Washington or Moscow.

Along with this polarization of power there has been a powerful resurgence of Marxist-Leninist doctrine in the USSR. The first signs appeared in 1943, when Soviet arms were about to turn from defense to attack. From 1944 onward, the reaffirmation of Marxism-Leninism-Stalinism increased sharply. A number of special schools were established for the training of local leaders in Marxist theory. The *Short Course in the History of the Communist Party*, which gives the official Stalinist version of the lessons of Bolshevik experience, was revived as a basic text.[57] By the winter of 1944–45, Soviet propaganda was already directed against the United States and Great Britain. Also, Soviet troops were told by those responsible for political indoctrination that they should not let themselves be fooled by the existing alliance with these capitalist states.

On February 9, 1946, Stalin made an important speech which summed up and gave official blessing to the changes that had taken place. He declared that it would be a mistake to think that the Second World War arose by accident, or because of the errors of political leaders—an interesting indication that some such idea may have been circulating in the Party. "Actually," said Stalin, "the war arose as the inevitable result of the development of world economic and political forces on the basis of modern monopoly capitalism." His analysis of the future was a nearly verbatim restatement of the Leninist thesis that the uneven development of capitalism usually leads to violent disturbances and war between capitalist states.[58]

In the course of repeated restatement since the war, these ideas have become transformed into the stereotype of world capitalism versus Soviet socialism. Thus Voznesensky, while still a member of the Politburo, wrote in a book on the war economy of the Soviet Union: "Fattening on the blood of people during the period of the Second World War, American monopoly capitalism now stands at the head of the imperialist and anti-democratic camp and has become the advance guard of imperialist expansion in all parts of the world . . . As long as capitalist encirclement exists, we must keep our powder dry. As long as imperialism exists, there remains the danger of attack upon the USSR, the danger that a new third world war may come." [59]

Similar statements constitute the stock-in-trade of the Soviet press. They are, however, from time to time qualified by remarks to the effect that Marxism does not preclude the possibility of the peaceful coexistence of two social systems during a given historical epoch. Such statements are occasionally found in even the most savage attacks on the West.[60] This qualification is an indication that the Soviet leaders do not reject outright the possibility that a diminution of the tension between Moscow and Washington might promote Soviet interests under current conditions.

Another feature, which distinguishes the current revival of Leninist doctrines from earlier similar statements, is that the Soviet leaders now refrain from drawing any revolutionary conclusions. Although they state over and over again that capitalism is undergoing extreme difficulties, they do not take the next step, so heavily emphasized by Lenin, and predict that the proletarian revolution is in the offing. Even ritual obeisances toward this revered symbol are rare and take the form of predictions about the "final liberation of mankind from the capitalist yoke." [61]

The revival and vigorous restatement of Marxism-Leninism cannot be wholly attributed to the persistence of old beliefs. As part of an over-all development in both domestic and foreign affairs, it also forms one aspect of the attempt to strengthen the hold of the top Party leadership on the country and to correct, in relatively minor ways, certain weaknesses in the Soviet political and economic structure that were revealed during the war. To some extent the Soviets find it necessary to create capitalist bogeymen in order to make the Communist version of socialism function, though it is not always easy to determine the line at which deliberate deception begins. Finally, the revival of the Leninist explanation of international politics, which was never wholly abandoned during the war, provides an illustration of the way in which ideology may be adapted to explain a new situation, in this case the postwar polarization of power between the United States and the USSR. Since the United States happens to be a capitalist power, it is not difficult for the Soviets to fit the facts of the contemporary distribution of power into a not altogether implausible version of Marxism.

In the actual behavior of the Soviets, the revival of Leninist doctrines makes itself apparent in Soviet policy toward the areas of Europe liberated and occupied by the Red Army. Communist control over these areas was established by stages. After the Nazis had been driven out, coalition regimes, in which the Communists did their best to obtain strategic posts (such as the control of the police), were established. These regimes set themselves the task of nationalizing industry and distributing among the peasantry the land taken from the few remaining large estates. The local Communists, presumably in agreement with the makers of Soviet policy, followed a variety of popular-front policy. In their propaganda they made a considerable attempt to obtain nonproletarian, and particularly peasant, support. For a time some disinterested observers expressed the hope that the Communists might be losing some of their doctrinaire intransigence and that the countries in the Soviet orbit might be permitted to work out a social and economic solution to their problems that would combine features of Eastern and Western democracy. Such hopes were destined to severe disappointment. In the period from 1946 to 1948 the Communist Parties destroyed or absorbed the older traditional parties by means of a series of skillfully executed bureaucratic maneuvers and palace revolutions, and managed to obtain a near monopoly of political power. Though enjoying a certain degree of mass support, these coups were predominantly "revolutions from above." [62]

A superficially plausible explanation of the course of events in the "new democracies" can be obtained through the hypothesis that the Soviets began with the Leninist plan of collaborating with their future opponents and then eliminating them one by one. Suitable quotations can be found in abundance in Lenin's writings to "prove" that such were the tactics he originally advocated. But such an explanation confuses Communist hopes with Communist foresight. An explanation that does not rely so heavily on long-range planning is probably more in accord with the facts. Certain Communists themselves have admitted that they were unaware of the nature and direction of the changes taking place in the course of the struggle to eliminate the opposition. "At most we were feeling our way in the right direction," a Hungarian leader said at a gathering of his Party's prominent officers. "The Party didn't possess a unified, clarified, elaborated attitude in respect to the character of the People's Democracy and its future development." [63]

A number of factors in the domestic and international situation very probably impelled the local Communist Parties and their Soviet advisers to follow an increasingly intransigent, and in some respects doctrinaire, policy. The social systems established in the early postwar period were highly unstable. The ruling groups, largely identified with the Nazis, had been heavily discredited by the latter's defeat. Many of those persons who had not fled with the retiring Germans were anxious to regain some semblance of power. From a more purely economic point of view, large-scale rural underemployment, which can only be solved temporarily by a redistribution of the land, was an endemic feature of much of Eastern Europe. Industrialization under a planned economy, together with some form of coöperative farming, appears on objective grounds to be about the only solution in this area. It is significant in this connection that the form of collective agriculture, undertaken so far on a small but nevertheless increasing scale, is not the Soviet *kolkhoz* but a producers' coöperative, in which the individual peasant household retains title to the land.[64] Still another important factor is the absence of a strong parliamentary tradition in several of the East European states, although Czechoslovakia constitutes a significant exception in this respect. For these and other reasons the trend toward socialist forms in the "new democracies" cannot by any means be considered purely a matter of external pressures by the Soviets or their agents, the Communist Parties.

The impact of Russian Marxist ideology may be discerned in the following aspects of the situation. In the first place, it is difficult for trained Communists to belong to a coalition without seeking to dominate the situation. To a certain extent this is true of any political grouping that coöperates with another for limited ends when their general goals are dissimilar. But it applies more strongly to Communists than to those who have absorbed even a small portion of the Western liberal tradition. The conception of a "loyal opposition" is utterly alien to the Communist viewpoint. In the second place, when Communists do get power, it is not within the framework of their doctrine to establish an open society composed of competing interest groupings. Instead, they attempt to eliminate opposition groups as rapidly as possible without endangering their own position, always with the argument that they are acting in the interests of the broad masses of the population. Still another aspect of Leninist ideology may be noted in the fact that the Soviets have continually endeavored to alter the social and economic structure of areas over which they have gained control in a way that will strengthen their own position. Their behavior is such that it suggests very strongly that influential Soviet leaders still think in terms of the simpler Marxist categories of class interest. The ruling groups are apparently (and often justifiably) assumed to be hostile to Soviet interests, as are large portions of the middle classes. The peasants have to be "neutralized" or their support won by certain immediate concessions; the industrial workers, a small group in Eastern Europe now as in Russia in 1917, are evidently regarded as the most reliable base for Soviet power.

One need be no mystical believer in the inevitability of trends to observe that in this combination of men, ideas, and circumstances there is an inner logic that urges the Communists toward an increasingly doctrinaire application of their views. The existence of opposition to the Communists makes it necessary for them to be increasingly systematic in stamping out what appears to them as the economic roots of such hostility. It is from this viewpoint, rather than that of an unchanging goal grimly pursued by master tacticians, that we may perhaps gain an understanding of the role of the Leninist tradition in shaping Soviet policy toward Eastern Europe.

Although the clearest examples of the role of Marxist doctrines occur in the satellite states, their influence may also be observed in Germany and China, areas whose eventual fate will be far more crucial in determining the outcome of the present struggle. In these areas the employment of such Marxist techniques as the transformation of the existing social structure has been intertwined with other policies designed to promote Russian national interests. There may be noted in this process a series of conflicts between policies adopted in pursuit of immediate short-range objectives and policies designed for long-range ends. The net impression obtained from examining Soviet actions is one of flexible empiricism in the pursuit of power objectives.

One of the recurring features of the balance of power is the attempt by the victors, when they fall out among themselves, to gain the assistance of the vanquished against their erstwhile allies. Since Germany, whose industry was not as thoroughly destroyed by bombing as was supposed in some American circles during the war, remains one of the major bases of political power, the struggle between the East and the West for the *de facto* control of Germany has been an acute one. Only a few of the highlights need be mentioned here to draw attention to some of the main features of Soviet policy.[65]

Soviet policy within Germany has revealed two somewhat contradictory tendencies. On the one hand, there is an obvious effort to get as much out of Germany in the way of material goods and services as possible. On the other hand, there is the attempt to control and direct German social and political development to serve larger Soviet aims in relation to the Soviet conflict with the Western powers. Both policies have been pursued simultaneously, and at times have tended to nullify one another.

The first or exploitative policy is reflected in the Soviet proposal at Yalta that 80 per cent of all German industry should be confiscated, carried away physically, and used as reparations payments. On this occasion the Soviets made a strong but unsuccessful effort to persuade the British and Americans to agree to a total reparations bill of twenty billion dollars, of which half should go to the USSR.[66] During the early part of the Soviet occupation, according to widespread press reports, the Russians did indeed confiscate and remove all sorts of equipment. Later this policy was at least superficially reversed, when in January of 1947 the Soviet-supported Socialist Unity Party promised for the Soviet zone an economic level above that of Potsdam.[67] However, on March 17, 1947, Molotov again asked for ten billion dollars' worth of reparations from Germany.[68] Soviet insistence on reparations of such great magnitude was one of the major issues that brought about the collapse of this attempt by the former allies to reach a settlement of the German question.

The second policy—which might be called a policy of reconciliation—found its first sharp expression in Molotov's speech of July 10, 1946, at the Paris Council of Foreign Ministers. In this speech Molotov asserted that feelings of revenge ought not to be a guide in the framing of a treaty with Germany, and that it would not be in the interests of the world's economy or the tranquillity of Europe to destroy the German state, or to destroy her major industries and convert her to an agricultural nation. Germany should instead be given the opportunity for a wider industrial development, which should merely be guided along peaceful lines and in the direction of serving the peaceful requirements of the German population, including those of trade with Germany's neighbors. Before a peace treaty was actually signed, Molotov continued, a single German government, democratic, peace-loving and sufficiently responsible to be able to carry out its obligations to the allies, ought to be created.[69] The American response to this bid for German support was not long in coming. In his famous Stuttgart speech of September 6, 1946,

Secretary of State Byrnes made similar comments concerning the economy of Germany and, more important, announced that the United States did not regard the Polish acquisition of East German territory as final.[70] This pair of speeches by Byrnes and Molotov might be regarded as the unofficial funeral of the Potsdam agreement and the overt beginning of a race for Germany between the Western powers and the USSR, though the roots of the split can be traced back to the divergent policies of the various powers from the first days of the occupation.

The contradiction between the exploitative and conciliatory aspects of Soviet policy toward Germany may perhaps be resolved in the light of general Soviet purposes. By demanding and taking high reparations, the Soviets ease the task of reconstruction in the USSR and simultaneously keep German industrial power out of Western hands. Such objectives help to clarify Molotov's demand at Potsdam, as well as on later occasions, for Soviet participation in the control of the Ruhr. Finally, by their exploitative technique the Soviets may hope, as they frequently assert, to destroy the economic and social basis of German militarism. At the same time, through their efforts to promote a high level of economic activity in their zone, the Soviets aim at increasing the quantity of materials available to the USSR and also winning German support for Soviet goals.[71]

The over-all result of these forces has been the partition of Germany. Each side has devoted considerable energy to the incorporation of the territory under its control into its larger political strategy. The more important steps taken by the West have included the internationalization of the Ruhr, the inclusion of Western Germany in the Marshall Plan, the slowing of decartelization, and the formation of a Western German state, which, it was hoped, might act as a magnet upon the Soviet zone. Soviet tactics have included the effort to force the Western allies out of Berlin, an attempt they were forced to abandon in the spring of 1949, and the formation of their own "independent" state, under Communist auspices, in Eastern Germany. In this area their efforts have been centered upon promoting a political and economic pattern guaranteeing their own hegemony, similar to that adopted in the new democracies. At the same time, they have encouraged the expression of German nationalist sentiments in the hope that the new East German state will attract more support than its Western counterpart. In this tug of war the technique of many German leaders has been to use the concessions granted by either the Soviets or the Western powers as a lever to extract further concessions from the opposite power. However, this policy has not been very successful thus far, since neither the Soviets nor the Western powers seem willing to relax their hold on Germany. Both are reluctant to abandon this hold for fear that their antagonist might gain control of all Germany. While future moves cannot be predicted in detail, it is safe to conclude that both sides will continue to try to strengthen their own position and make inroads upon that of their opponents. Although Eastern and Western techniques may differ, the power struggle for control of Germany is not likely to diminish.

Since Europe, and especially Germany with its important industrial base, constitutes the major locus of power conflicts, it has received the largest amount of public attention and, in the United States at least, the largest amount of attention by responsible policy-makers. Nevertheless, events have taken place in the Far East which, in terms of power potentialities, may have more far-reaching consequences. Although the Soviets were balked in their efforts to extend their influence into Japan,[72] the march of events has led to a great extension of Soviet influence on the Asiatic mainland, and to a corresponding diminution of Western power. In part, this has been the result of Asiatic attempts to throw off Western capitalist influences, a long-term movement upon which the Soviets have attempted to capitalize without success until most recently. If in the Asiatic arena they succeed in making long-term social trends serve their power interests, they may achieve a fundamental victory in the struggle with the United States.

There is evidence that the top Soviet policy-makers up until the end of 1946 may have overestimated the strength of the Chinese Nationalist regime, as well as the amount of assistance the United States would be able to render Chiang Kai-shek. In 1944 Molotov told two representatives of President Roosevelt that the United States should take the lead in unifying and strengthening China.[73] In a similar vein, Stalin at Potsdam spoke of Chiang Kai-shek as the only possible leader for China.[74] Both Stalin and Molotov denied that the Chinese Communists were real Communists, owing any allegiance to the Soviet Union, a denial that is no more significant in itself than numerous similar statements by Soviet leaders concerning the alleged independence of Communist Parties elsewhere outside the USSR. At this time the Soviet leaders did not urge the formation in China of a coalition regime to include the Communists, perhaps because this point then formed a major objective in American policy.

In the early postwar years the Soviets adopted the policy, already familiar in Eastern Europe, of verbal adherence to the principles of Allied coöperation, while striving to obtain as much for themselves as possible. By the Sino-Soviet Treaty of August 14, 1945, the Soviets recognized Chiang Kai-shek, and not the Communists, as the legal ruler of China. Article 5 of the treaty contained the usual phrases about mutual undertakings to refrain from interference in each other's internal affairs. This was reaffirmed in December of the same year, when the British, American, and Soviet chiefs of the respective foreign offices announced their agreement "upon the necessity of a united and democratic China under the control of the National Government."[75]

Nevertheless, by the Sino-Soviet agreement the Russians gained effective control of the Chinese Eastern Railway and the South Manchurian Railway (renamed the Chinese Changchun Railway) and the ports of Dairen and Port Arthur. By this maneuver the Russians recaptured the former outposts of Tsarist Russia in the Far East. Likewise, as the result of a plebiscite agreed upon between the USSR and China, Outer Mongolia obtained "full independence" from China and fell even more definitely than before into the Soviet orbit.[76]

At the same time, the Red Army took a number of steps that enabled the Chinese Communists to seize power temporarily in a few of the more important Manchurian cities and to entrench themselves rather firmly in neighboring areas. Among the more significant Russian actions was their refusal to permit the Nationalists to use Dairen as a port of entry for their troops.[77] The entrenchment of the Communists was further facilitated by the fact that the Chinese National Government on two occasions requested the Soviets to prolong their stay in China. Soviet troops were not finally withdrawn from China until May 3, 1946.[78]

Since American efforts to produce a reconciliation between the Nationalist and Communist forces in China ran up against increasing obstacles, the Soviets evidently considered the possibility of giving diplomatic support to the Communist cause. At the Moscow Conference of March 10, 1947, when the Chinese Communists had already adopted a strongly anti-American position, Molotov attempted to bring up the Chinese question for settlement among the great powers. In this move, however, he was rebuffed by the Americans.[79]

The subsequent sweep of the Chinese Communists to the banks of the Yangtze and beyond can probably be accounted for on the basis of internal conditions in China. The disintegration of the Kuomintang, whose weaknesses had been apparent at a much earlier date, and the fact that the Communists had a program with stronger appeal to the peasant masses, are probably more important factors in the Nationalist debacle than surreptitious Soviet assistance to the Communists. Partly in order to avoid arousing American antagonism, which might have resulted in greater support for the Nationalist cause, the Soviets followed a policy, at least at the visible level, of extreme diplomatic correctness toward the collapsing Nationalist regime. When the Communists captured Peiping, Tientsin, and Shanghai, the Russians closed their consulates, declaring that a new regime, not recognized by the Soviet government, had come to these cities.[80]

As soon as the Communists had gained control over enough territory to put forth the claim that they were the legitimate rulers of China, the Soviets abandoned this façade of neutrality. On October 2, 1949, the day following the proclamation of the

Chinese People's Republic, the Soviets granted diplomatic recognition to the new regime. Not long afterward the claim began to appear in the Soviet press that the Chinese Communists owed their success in large measure to the "support of the forces of the world democratic camp, headed by the Soviet Union, the sole defender of democracy and national independence." [81]

The significance of the recognition and subsequent press comment does not lie in their very slight value as evidence concerning the Soviet role in the Chinese civil war. If the new Republic is a success from the Soviet viewpoint, Stalin will probably receive the credit, no matter what the facts were. The significance lies rather in the indication given by these actions that the Soviets will now give open support to the Communist regime, at the same time that they endeavor to bring it under Soviet control. Since the Chinese Communists have built up their Party organization on a power base among the peasantry, which in the past at least was very largely independent of Soviet support, hopes have been expressed that the Chinese Communists may follow the course taken by Tito. However, with the rapid expansion of Chinese Communist influence, great opportunities are now opened up for Soviet intrigue within the Chinese Party, which may enable the Russians to subordinate it effectively to their own interests.

Certainly the difficulties facing any Soviet-directed effort toward welding China into an integrated political unit and creating an industrial base for effective power on the international scene are enormous. But if the Soviets succeed, the time may come when their success will be regarded as the greatest disaster ever faced by the United States. [82]

The several phases of Soviet foreign policy in Europe and Asia represent in their essentials a single, continuous pattern. In this pattern the Marxist-Leninist-Stalinist tradition has had, at each stage, varying degrees of influence upon the specific way in which the Soviet Union has reacted to the shifting distribution of power in international politics. Sooner or later, however, the Soviets have danced the power political quadrille, throwing the weight of their force against any grouping of powers that showed signs of threatening their security. They have always aligned themselves against their "natural" antagonist in the balance of power at a given time. The choice of antagonist or allies has been determined not primarily by ideological factors, but by the structure of the balance-of-power system itself.

17

The Relations of Ideology and Foreign Policy

The impact of experience on behavior and doctrine

The rapid adjustment to the ways of international politics executed by Lenin in 1918 has been continued by Stalin down to the
present day. So far, however, there are few if any signs of the
development in the Soviet Union of an overt tradition that recognizes the role played by the balance of power in Soviet foreign
policy. For the most part, the major shifts in the international
distribution of power have continued to find their explanation
in the familiar Leninist categories, at least insofar as the public
speeches and writings of prominent Soviet leaders are concerned.
The enemy of the moment has always been showered with
strong Marxist invective concerning the evils of monopoly capitalism and imperialism. First, the major recipients were the Anglo-
French plutocracies. Later, Nazi Germany held the limelight, to
be replaced after the war by the United States. Intertwined with
these Marxist themes have been others of a more strictly nationalist nature, which came to the fore after about 1934 and
were most prominent during the years of war against Germany.
Even then, as has sometimes been asserted, the Soviet Union
did not fight the war under strictly nationalist slogans. Stalin's
major wartime speeches had strong Marxist overtones, as in
his references to Hitler and Himmler as the "chained dogs of the
German bankers," [1] his references to Nazi imperialism, and his
distinction, based on Lenin, between aggressive wars and wars
of liberation. [2]

Perhaps the most striking modification of Communist doctrine concerning international relations is the sharp toning down of revolutionary optimism. It is necessary to go back to 1929 to find any statement by a top Soviet leader to the effect that the proletarian revolution would take place in the near future. In that year Stalin spoke of strengthening the Comintern to help the working class prepare "for impending revolutionary battles," [3] although the Third International had actually adopted a defensive policy by this time. Some five years later, in 1934, Stalin declared that, as a result of the economic tendencies of imperialism, war "for a new redivision of the world" was the order of the day, and drew the conclusion that the coming conflict was "sure to unleash revolution" and to "jeopardize the existence of capitalism." [4] But by this time the expression of revolutionary optimism was very much less. Stalin conceded that the "masses of the people have not yet reached the stage when they are ready to storm capitalism," though he did add, somewhat lamely perhaps, that "the idea of storming it is maturing in the minds of the masses—of that there can hardly be any doubt." [5]

From this time onward Stalin refrained from making revolutionary predictions. Only relatively minor figures continued on rare occasions to make such statements. In 1939, at a Party Congress, L. Mekhlis, head of the Red Army's political indoctrination and control apparatus, spoke about the "liquidation of capitalist encirclement" and remarked that, should "the second imperialist war turn its point against the first socialist state in the world," the Red Army would carry the war to the enemy and "fulfil its internationalist obligations and increase the number of Soviet Republics." [6] Such remarks, moreover, were confined to Party circles, while the propaganda directed to the country at large adopted a more nationalistic and patriotic tone. [7]

The mention of the Red Army as the chief instrument of revolution indicates that the Soviets had begun to doubt very seriously that "spontaneous" proletarian revolutions, even if assisted by Moscow, would succeed in parts of the world over which the Soviets exercised no direct control. The experience of the years following the Second World War may have confirmed this viewpoint. In the course of acrid correspondence with Tito before the Soviet-Yugoslav break became public, the Central Committee of the Russian Party declared: "It is also necessary to emphasize that the services of the French and Italian CPs [Communist Parties] to the revolution were not less but greater than the CPY [Communist Party of Yugoslavia]. Even though the French and Italian CPs have so far achieved less success than the CPY, this is not due to any special qualities of the CPY, but mainly because . . . the Soviet army came to the aid of the Yugoslav people . . . Unfortunately the Soviet army did not and could not render such assistance to the French and Italian CPs." [8]

"Historicus," the anonymous author of a widely publicized article, "Stalin on Revolution," [9] has made an exhaustive study of Stalin's writings and cites no prediction of revolution made later than 1934. Nevertheless, as he points out, many of the earlier documents with their fire-eating passages are reprinted and circulated widely today with the cachet of authority. From this fact, however, the conclusion cannot be drawn that the older ideas are still accepted as the basis for policy, since a number of Lenin's more equalitarian writings, which are no longer taken seriously as a basis for policy, also receive wide circulation. Nor is it necessarily correct to assume that the Soviet leaders believe in some kind of regular ebb and flood in the revolutionary situation, since the ebb of revolutionary optimism in Soviet statements is much more marked than the flood. Even the present Marxist revival fails to draw overt revolutionary conclusions. However, the continued circulation of the older revolutionary symbolism, even though it does not appear in current statements, may well be an indication that this point of view remains a latent one, which could reappear in a modified form under favorable circumstances. Such a recurrence of latent and temporarily discarded ideas has taken place under favoring circumstances on other occasions, such as in the years of forced collectivization and industrialization following the relaxation of the NEP.

The evidence concerning changes in officially promulgated doctrine is abundant; that concerning the actual beliefs of Soviet policy-makers is highly fragmentary. Nevertheless, enough data are available to permit tentative inferences.

There are several indications that the Leninist theses concerning imperialism, war, and revolution underwent skeptical scrutiny in high Soviet quarters as a consequence of the experiences of World War II. Stalin on several occasions during the war expressed complete disenchantment with the German working class, formerly the apple of the Comintern's eye, and was particularly bitter about its support of the Nazi attack on the Soviet Union. It is worth noting that this represents a wartime shift in Stalin's expressed opinions, since at the outbreak of the conflict he had told the Soviet people that they could count on allies among the German people.[10]

Other evidence on this point is contradictory. The contradictions may be accounted for by two hypotheses: first, that the Soviet leaders themselves were not sure of their position; and secondly, that they tried to maintain the appearance of consistency before outsiders and even moderately high officials in their own bureaucratic hierarchy. In other European Communist Parties there was lively discussion during the war about whether or not capitalism was really aggressive and expansionist.[11] It is unlikely that the Soviets, despite their generally stricter controls, could avoid raising the question among themselves.

The American correspondent, Edgar Snow, reports that the late Alexander Shcherbakov, Vice-Commissar of Defense and an alternate member of the Politburo, agreed in private conversation that capitalist assistance to the USSR constituted a "profound deviation from the development of history as foreseen in Lenin's work *Imperialism*."[12] Snow also reports that P. F. Yudin, a prominent Russian economist and head of the State Publishing House, told him, "It is proved that there is nothing in Marxism which need prevent progressive capitalist countries from co-operating closely with the Soviet Union in the economic and cultural spheres."[13] The report is significant in suggesting the possibility that the "deviation of the economists," for which Eugene Varga was to suffer at a later date, owes its origin to the experience of the war. Yudin's remark, if reported correctly, goes much further than any statement for which Varga was later attacked.

It is also worth noting that such "subversive" ideas were the chief targets of attack in the closed wartime indoctrination meetings of Party bureaucrats, if Victor Kravchenko's account of such affairs may be accepted. Ironically enough, Yudin turns up in Kravchenko's report as one of the attackers. He is quoted by the Soviet exile as telling the assembled Party officials that the Soviet "war partnership with the capitalist nations must not breed illusions . . . The two worlds of capitalism and Communism cannot forever exist side by side. *Kto kogo?* who will conquer whom?—remains the great question now as always. It represents the chief problem of the future." [14]

Such reports need not be dismissed because they are superficially contradictory. They agree on the point that is significant: that "illusions" concerning the possibilities of collaboration with capitalism existed. And it is also understandable that Yudin, in the light of his position, should be given the task of laying down the line to those at the lower levels of the Kremlin hierarchy. [15]

Though there may have been a certain amount of questioning of accepted doctrines during the war, subsequent events have revealed that the top Soviet policy-makers, as early as 1944, became convinced of the necessity of making a strong effort to reimpose at least outward conformity to the Leninist theories of imperialism. The energy with which this has been done and the extent to which it has been carried might be a further reflection of the degree to which these doctrines were questioned during the war. After the war a process of ideological purification was carried out in the natural sciences, philosophy, economics, and the arts. The Leninist view of the world was repeated with much energy and little variety.

The polarization of world power into the two major centers, Washington and Moscow, together with the resulting competition between the Soviet Union and the United States, has created a situation in which doctrinaires on both sides of the Iron Curtain can easily find justification for their views. It is highly likely that certain Soviet leaders who retained their suspicions of the West during the war, but whose influence was partly diminished by the necessities of coöperating against a common enemy, found their advice taken more seriously as the postwar tensions became more serious. One may even guess that Zhdanov may have been the spearhead of this anti-Western revival in private, as he was in public. Among other reasons for the postwar ideological purification may be fear on the part of the Soviet leaders that the events of the war, including widespread personal contact of Russian occupation forces with nonsocialist cultures, have undermined mass belief in official doctrines and hence threatened support of the Communist elite. Such fears might even be tinged with worries about the effectiveness of one of the chief competing doctrines, the American version of liberalism. Stalin in 1941 told Harry Hopkins that Roosevelt and the United States had more influence with the common people of the world than any other force.[16] Although it is unlikely that he considers President Truman an equally charismatic force, Stalin may retain traces of his original attitude.

While it is reasonably certain that doubts have continued to arise in Kremlin circles concerning the applicability of specific points of Marxist doctrine, just as they arose in the past during the days of open polemics, it is probable that the top leaders have not abandoned the Marxist-Leninist categories for the ordering of experience. Foreign affairs are in all likelihood still seen through the Marxist prism, even though the reddish hues may not take up so prominent a portion of the spectrum. On general grounds, it might be anticipated that one consequence of political responsibility would be to produce among the Soviet leaders a cynical and manipulative attitude toward their own public symbolism. In the history of Nazi-Soviet relations between 1939 and 1941 there are a number of striking illustrations of this attitude. It is worth noting, however, that this evidence gives no clear indication of a cynical attitude toward any of the central assumptions of Leninist doctrine.

One of the incidents concerns Soviet efforts to construct a communiqué justifying the Nazi-Soviet partition of Poland in 1939. According to the German records, both Molotov and Stalin concerned themselves personally with this apparently minor task, an indication of the serious attention given by the Politburo to the proper manipulation of words and symbols. At one point Molotov wished to give a presentable motive for Soviet actions by the argument (among others) that the Soviet Union "considered itself obligated to intervene to protect its Ukrainian and White Russian brothers and make it possible for these unfortunate people to work in peace." In discussions with the Germans, Molotov conceded that the projected argument contained a note jarring to German sensibilities, but asked that the Germans overlook this trifle in view of the difficult situation in which the Soviet government found itself. "The Soviet Government," the report of Molotov's conversation continued, "unfortunately saw no possibility of any other motivation, since the Soviet Union had thus far not concerned itself about the plight of its minorities in Poland and had to justify abroad, in some way or other, its present intervention." [17] The next day the German ambassador submitted a draft of the joint communiqué to Molotov for approval. Stalin, when called on the telephone by Molotov, stated that he could not entirely agree to the German text, "since it presented the facts all too frankly," and instead wrote out a new draft in his own hand.[18]

Stalin's willingness to cast overboard old symbols and adopt new ones as the occasion requires is shown by his reported remarks at the meeting with Ribbentrop and Molotov on the night of August 23, 1939. The German account reads: "In the course of the conversation Herr Stalin spontaneously proposed a toast to the Führer, as follows: 'I know how much the German nation loves its Führer; I should therefore like to drink to his health.' " [19] Few other Communists at home or abroad were able to make the change with a lighthearted toast.

The impact of doctrine on behavior

Even though the Soviet Union has been compelled by the structure of international power relations to adopt a diplomacy closely resembling that of any other modern state, there remain a number of individual characteristics attributable to the Marxist-Leninist tradition. The familiar comparison between the behavior of states under balance-of-power conditions and the dance has already been referred to. It might be added that the Marxist-Leninist tradition affects the way in which the Russian bear hears the music, and hence the way it executes the steps. It must be realized, of course, that we are dealing here with groups rather than individuals, and that a group's composition, in the widest sense of the word, including its specific ideology, affects the way in which it responds to situations facing it. Though the similarities are greater than the differences, the United States, England, and other great powers exhibit their own special traits in their responses to the ever-changing balance of power.

The role of Marxist-Leninist ideology can be observed in the Soviet response to the danger presented by German National Socialism, particularly in its beginning stages. As has been seen, this factor helped to delay the Soviets in adopting a policy hostile to the Nazis. Similar factors were at work in slowing up the Soviet response to Japanese expansionism in the early thirties. Marxist ideas also contributed to the series of mutual suspicions that broke up the first anti-Nazi coalition with the Western powers at Munich. They played a part in the difficulties and frictions connected with maintaining the wartime coalition of the Big Three, and contributed to its subsequent disintegration. Furthermore, an important part of Soviet diplomatic technique—the utilization of the Communist Parties and the promotion of a specific type of economic and social transformation of society—is clearly derived from the Leninist tradition as modified by subsequent experience.

It is not possible to determine with mathematical precision, of course, the exact contribution of Marxist ideology to Soviet behavior in Russia's relations with other powers. The evidence seems to indicate that Marxist doctrine has not made the Soviet Union join any coalition or abandon any alliance that it would not have joined, or abandoned, on grounds of simple national self-interest. Yet there are clear indications that in some cases Marxist ideology retarded the shift, while in others it speeded up the change.

To Marxist ideology may also be attributed some portion of

that dynamic expansionism that has been characteristic of Soviet policy since 1939. The important question, however, is how much?

Russian expansion can be explained very largely without reference to Marxist ideological factors. For the most part, each step in Soviet expansion can be considered a logical move to counter a specific actual or potential enemy. The absorption of part of Poland, the Baltic States, and the Rumanian portion of Bessarabia, and the war against Finland were part of Soviet efforts to keep pace with Germany's growing power and were directed specifically against the German threat. In the Second World War the Soviets could scarcely have permitted their Anglo-American partners to extend Western influence into all sections of the power vacuum created by the Axis defeat. It is clear, of course, that the Russians never had any such intentions, and they did their best to emerge from the conflict in as strong a position as possible, a policy also followed by Great Britain and at a somewhat later date by the United States. American expansion in both Europe and Asia has often been hesitant and reluctant. Nevertheless, the war ended with an American general in Berlin and another in Tokyo. This the Soviets could hardly afford to neglect. They enlarged and consolidated their own sphere of influence by ways that are made familiar in the daily headlines. In rivalries of this type, it is futile to argue which contestant has aggressive intentions and which has peaceable aims, since each move in the struggle calls out its countermove from the opponent.

What, then, is there left for the Marxist ideological factor to explain? This much at least: the Marxist-Leninist tradition has made it very difficult to reach a *modus vivendi* with the Soviets, which the Americans have been genuinely anxious to do. A belief in the inherently aggressive tendencies of modern capitalism obviously excludes any agreement except an armed truce of undetermined duration. Likewise, the acceptance of Leninist theory makes it almost impossible to believe in the friendly intentions of American leaders. Even though the Soviets may accept the personal honesty of individual American leaders, as seems to have been the case in Stalin's relations with Harry Hopkins, they are likely to feel that this is a matter of little consequence, since objective factors will push any capitalist state into warlike adventures. By heightening their suspicions, the Marxist-Leninist tradition makes the Soviets much more prone to take the protective steps just reviewed and hence to aggravate existing tensions.

The role of ideology in Soviet expansionism may also be examined from a slightly different standpoint. With the victory of Soviet arms there has been a sharp resurgence of statements about the superiority of the Soviet version of socialism as a way of life. Although such statements serve specific domestic purposes, it would be rash to disregard them as evidence of a continuing belief that the Soviet system represents the wave of the future. It is probably a belief only distantly related to immediate tactical problems of everyday diplomacy. When Soviet diplomacy was on the defensive, such ideas were relatively unimportant. Now that the situation has altered so tremendously in favor of the USSR, it is highly probable that such beliefs have been imbued with new life. While it is difficult to point to specific incidents and illustrations, this aspect of Marxist doctrine may account for the persistence with which the Soviets search for weak spots in the positions of their diplomatic opponents. At the very least, it has probably helped them to refuse to admit defeat when their fortunes are low, and to press every advantage home when their fortunes are high.

As was seen in connection with other aspects of Leninist doctrine, under the impact of political responsibility, goals and tactics, means and ends, have become jumbled up with one another and have often tended to change places. The familiar thesis that the Soviets have pursued a single aim through flexible tactics will not withstand the test of comparison with the historical record. Even though the proletarian revolution may still be a latent goal in Soviet policy, after the victory of November 1917 it was increasingly regarded as a technique, and only as one technique among many, for strengthening the socialist fortress. Soviet policy in the satellite states has been a very care-

fully modulated effort to effect a social and economic transformation of these countries in order to render them more amenable
to Soviet interests. Isaac Deutscher, Stalin's recent biographer,
has pointed out how the instruments of revolution, the secret
police and the army, have in these areas assumed the leading
role, and has contrasted the new movement with the original
revolutionary impulse that created these instruments.[20] The contrast reveals in concrete and dramatic form the transformation
of revolution from a goal into a technique. The change is, to be
sure, not a complete one. Soviet leaders acquire Communist virtue by extending the influence of the Kremlin to foreign lands,
no matter how this is done. If there is any central goal behind
the policy of the Soviet leaders, it is the preservation and extension of their own power, by any means whatever, rather than
the spread of a specific social system or the realization of a
doctrinal blueprint.

Some prospects

During the postwar years the hostilities and tensions between East and West have increased, with but few and transient
interruptions. Each measure taken by one of the contestants to
strengthen its position has been rapidly followed by counter-
measures on the other side in a continuing vicious circle. For
those who value peace and the major question is an obvious one:
can the vicious circle be broken at any point? Is there any possibility of achieving a reduction in tension or in stabilizing the
present distribution of power?

Before this question can be answered, it is necessary to know
the answers to certain others. For example, it is necessary to
know whether the Soviets are impelled by the dynamism of the
vicious circle alone, or whether there are important internal
forces in Russian society that by themselves, and independent
of the balance of power, work to produce expansionist tendencies.
In other words, has Soviet expansion during the past decade
been primarily defensive, and would it come to rest if external
threats were removed? Or is the world now witnessing a special
variety of expansionism: Communist imperialism? The same gen-

eral series of questions would have to be answered about the United States, but the analysis in this study must necessarily be confined to the Russian side of the equation.

Four considerations enter into the conclusion advanced by many that the Soviet system contains a number of internal expansionist forces impelling it to seek one conquest after another. It is often said that, because the USSR is an authoritarian state, its rulers need a continuous series of triumphs in order to maintain their power. The rulers of a dictatorship, it is claimed, cannot afford to rest on their laurels. Occasionally this type of argument is supported by a neo-Freudian chain of reasoning. It is asserted that the frustrations imposed upon the individual in modern society, especially under a dictatorship, tend to produce socially destructive impulses that have to be channeled outward against an external enemy if the society is not to destroy itself. The second line of argument, at a different level of analysis, emphasizes the indications of a strong power drive in Stalin's personality. Parallels can be drawn on this basis between his urge for new worlds to conquer and the political aspirations of Napoleon, Hitler, and others. A third line of reasoning points to various indications in Soviet statements and actions of an old-fashioned interest in territorial expansion that shows strong resemblances to traditional Tsarist policy. The latter argument draws its reasoning from the facts of geography and history, emphasizing traditional Russian interest in warm-water ports, the long drive to the South and East, and similar matters. Under the fourth type of argument, Marxist-Leninist ideology is selected as a separate expansionist force. Persons who hold this view point out the Messianic qualities of Marxist doctrine and the continuous need for struggle and victory that it generates.

Each of these arguments and hypotheses represents some portion of the truth. It might even be possible to reduce them to a single theoretical scheme—a task, however, that lies outside the scope of the present work. And before such a task could be undertaken, it is necessary to break the arguments down even more and point to a number of additional considerations and factors that operate to prevent further Soviet expansion. This may be done by examining the validity of each of the four arguments presented above.

Concerning the first point, that authoritarian states tend to be expansionist ones, it is necessary to express reservations and doubts on both general and specific grounds. The connection between the internal organization of a society and its foreign policy is a complex question that cannot yet be answered on the basis of simple formulas. Athens engaged in foreign conquest perhaps more than did warlike Sparta, and the Japanese, despite the militaristic emphasis of their society, lived in isolation for centuries until the time of their forced contacts with the West. To show that the authoritarian structure of any state is a source of expansionist tendencies, one would have to show the way in which these pressures make themselves felt upon those responsible for foreign policy. At this point the argument often breaks down, though there are cases where it can be shown that the rulers have embarked on an adventurous policy to allay internal discontent. But those at the apex of the political pyramid in an authoritarian regime are frequently freer from the pressures of mass discontent than are the responsible policy-makers of a Western democracy. They can therefore afford to neglect much longer the dangers of internal hostilities. Furthermore, modern events reveal the weakness of the argument that a warlike policy is the result of hostilities toward outsiders among the individuals who make up the society. In the days of total war it is necessary to use all sorts of force and persuasion, from propaganda to conscription, to make men and women fight. To regard war as primarily the expression of the hostilities of rank-and-file citizens of various states toward one another is to fly in the face of these facts.

In the case of the Soviet Union, the Nazi-Soviet Pact of 1939 shows that the rulers of modern Russia had no difficulty in disregarding the hostilities to Nazism that had been built up during preceding years, and that in this respect they enjoyed greater freedom for prompt adjustment of disputes than did other countries. Both totalitarian partners were able to keep mass hostility under control as long as it suited purposes and plans based on the configuration of international power relationships.

In addition, those who conclude that external expansion is necessary for the survival of the Soviet leaders overlook the fact that war places a severe strain on the Party's control over Russian society. War tends to raise the role of the military forces and to diminish by comparison the power of the Party. While no insoluble problems arose in this respect in the last war, these considerations have to be taken into account. The past war showed that Party doctrines had to give way, at least in part, to nationalist slogans and other viewpoints of a somewhat disruptive nature. To be sure, the situation would be different in a war in the near future, since the Soviets would not be troubled with capitalist allies and would undoubtedly pose as the victim of imperialist attack. Nevertheless, to win internal support unwanted concessions might have to be made.

An acceptable modification of the argument that the authoritarian nature of the present Soviet regime is a source of an aggressive and expansionist foreign policy may be found along the following lines. It is probable that a certain amount of hostility toward the outside world is an essential ingredient in the power of the present rulers of Russia. Without the real or imagined threat of potential attack, it would be much more difficult to drive the Russian masses through one set of Five Year Plans after another. Yet it does not seem likely that this hostility is in turn a force that reacts back on the makers of Russian foreign policy. Their power can be more easily maximized by the threat of war than by war itself—a precarious enough situation. Nor is there evidence that mass hostility is in any way cumulative or sufficient to force the Soviet leaders into an aggressive policy. There are a number of devices for draining off internally generated hostility into channels other than those of external expansion. Military and combative sentiments, aroused for specific purposes, can be and have been directed into the socially productive channels of promoting a conquest of the physical environment.

There are good grounds for concurring in the conclusion that a drive for power in Stalin's personal make-up has been and will remain a very significant element in Soviet policy as long as his leadership is maintained. Although biographical data on Stalin are scanty, it is probable that conclusions concerning this trait will stand the test of further impartial investigation. The way, however, in which this trait displays itself has important implications. It is difficult to accuse Stalin of being rash or foolhardy. One has but to contrast the bombastic speeches and writings of Hitler with the cold pedantic logic of Stalin, illuminated by rare flashes of heavy sarcasm, to get important clues to the differences in their personalities. Stalin has nearly always managed to keep his aggressive impulses and his drive for power under rigid control, for which he has been well rewarded in the defeat of his domestic and foreign enemies. He has arrived at his most important decisions cautiously and empirically, testing the political ground at each step of the way. The major decisions of collectivization and industrialization were reached only after numerous tentative trials. Once decisions have been reached by Stalin, he has not failed to display sufficient energy to carry them through. And like Lenin, though in a lesser degree, he has shown the ability to back out of an impossible situation without serious damage to his forces. Thus it is unlikely that Stalin would plunge the Soviet Union into war when the chances of victory were highly problematical.

Those who emphasize the continuity of the Russian historical tradition and the importance of Russia's geographical position in the determination of Soviet foreign policy are correct insofar as Russia's place on the globe and her past relations with her neighbors set certain limitations and provide certain readily definable opportunities for Russian foreign policy. In other words, an expansionist Soviet foreign policy can follow only certain well-defined lines of attack. It may have Persia, China, or Germany as its major object of infiltration, but Latin America and the Antarctic are much more remote objectives.

The reappearance of old-fashioned Russian territorial interests in various parts of the globe has been associated with the revival of Russian strength from the low ebb of revolution, intervention, and civil war. It may be suspected that the early idealist statements of the Bolshevik leaders about the abandonment of Tsarist imperialism were inspired not only by Marxist doctrine but were also made on the grounds that they were the only possible tactics to follow in Russia's weak condition. Now that the proletarian revolution has a territorial base, it is understandable that attempts should be made to combine the interests of the two, and that some of the results should show marked similarities to Tsarist policy. Furthermore, the possibility may readily be granted that the present rulers of Russia are somewhat influenced by the model of Tsarist diplomacy. But the driving forces behind any contemporary Soviet expansionism must be found in a contemporary social situation. Historical and geographical factors may limit the expression of an expansionist drive. They cannot be expansionist forces in their own right.

Turning to the ideological factor, it has already been noted that the Messianic energies of Communism can be, and at times in the past have been, very largely directed toward tasks of internal construction. The "creative myth of Leninism," to use Sorel's suggestive term, involves the building of factories in desert wastes and the creation of a more abundant life for the inhabitants of the Soviet Union. One must agree, however, that a creative myth, if it is effective, is usually an article for export as well as for domestic consumption. Those who really believe in socialism usually believe it is necessary for the world as a whole, just as do the more emotional believers in the virtues of democracy and the four freedoms. There remains, however, another important aspect of Soviet doctrine, which sets at least temporary limits to its expansionist qualities. It is a cardinal point in the Leninist-Stalinist doctrine that a retreat made in good order is not a disgrace. The Soviet creative myth does not have a "victory or death" quality—there is no urge to seek a final dramatic showdown and a *Götterdämmerung* finale. When faced with superior strength, the Soviets have on numerous occasions shown the ability to withdraw with their forces intact. Although the withdrawal may be followed by a renewal of pressures elsewhere, it may be repeated once more if superior forces are again brought to bear.

The foregoing considerations are enough to suggest the complexity of the problem of interpreting the expansionist forces contained in the Soviet system. They should make us wary of dramatically pessimistic conclusions to the effect that the Soviet leaders, propelled by forces beyond their control, are marching to a world holocaust. But they give many more grounds for pessimism than for optimism concerning the probability of preventing a further increase in tension in the power relationships of Moscow and Washington. Even though Soviet expansionism of the past decade may be explained as primarily an adaptation to the changing balance of power, such an explanation by no means precludes the possibility, perhaps even the probability, that the series of adaptations and "defensive" measures taken by the United States and the USSR may culminate in war.

The situation in which the two major powers stand at uneasy guard, carefully watching each other's activities and countering one another's strengthenings in all portions of the globe, contains internal forces of its own that could lead to a violent explosion. That it has not done so already is an indication that both sides are still making their political calculations largely in defensive terms, inasmuch as neither antagonist is committed by its own system of values to war for war's sake.

The resurgence of another major power, such as Germany or Japan, that constituted a threat to both the United States and the Soviet Union could bring about a drastic alteration in this situation. There is nothing in recent Russian actions to indicate that the Soviet Union would be unwilling to seek once more a common alliance with the West to ward off threatened danger. But the present polarization of power itself makes any such alliance an improbable eventuality. The struggle between Washington and Moscow has as one of its consequences the partition of Germany and American control of Japan. So long as this struggle continues, it is not unlikely that either Germany or Japan can regain the semblance of an independent foreign policy. Nor is it likely, so long as modern warfare requires a powerful industrial base, that some other state will emerge in the near future to challenge the two giants of today. Should there be indications that some weak state might be developing a technology with which it would be possible to become a power in its own right, steps would probably be taken at once to gain control of this new resource by one or both of the existing great powers. In this manner the existing balance of power tends to inhibit any change in its structure or destructive potentialities.

If the prospects of fundamental improvement in American-Russian relations are dim indeed, they are not necessarily hopeless. One of the few warrants for hope is the Communist tradition that retreat from a situation that threatens the power of the leaders is no defeat. If, as seems most likely, neither side is yet actively seeking war, there is still room for the reduction of tension through the familiar devices of highly skilled diplomacy. To succeed, this diplomacy would have to part company with the parochial moralism that has characterized much American negotiation and free itself from the miasma of dogmatic suspicion likely to become chronic on the Russian side. Whether modern diplomats can escape from the pressures engendered by their own societies remains to be seen.

18

Conclusions and Implications

Major features of ideological and social change in the USSR

Our original task, in its simplest form, was to discover which prerevolutionary Bolshevik ideas have been put into effect in the Soviet Union, which have been modified or abandoned, and for what reasons. The answers to these questions, tentative though they may be, have certain implications concerning the limits and possibilities of directed social change in modern industrial society, and concerning the general relationship between changing belief systems and changing social institutions.

The idea that inequalities of authority are necessary in human society, that is, that some must command and others must obey, received very little recognition in the prerevolutionary Bolshevik ideology of ends. When Bolshevik theory began to show signs of developing beyond the goals of a bourgeois democratic republic, the new goals emphasized the sharing of the masses in the power of the state. The dictatorship of the proletariat was conceived of as a dictatorship of the many over the few. Through the device of the soviets the many would be able to share in this transitory phase, which would be far more representative of the will of the masses than any regime previously known by man.

On the other hand, the Bolshevik ideology of means laid heavy stress upon the need for authority and discipline. Lenin wanted the Party, which was to be the instrument of the liberation of Russia and eventually of the human race, to be a strictly centralized, highly disciplined organization, responding to the orders of its leaders like a well-trained orchestra to a wave of the conductor's baton. In the prerevolutionary period this discipline was very much weaker than it became later.

With the assumption of political responsibility in 1917, the Bolshevik ideology of means played a greater role in the determination of behavior than the ideology of ends. Partly because of the series of crisis situations faced by the regime, the original ideas concerning the need for discipline and authority continued to come to the fore and to serve as a justification for the establishment of sharp inequalities of power. After Lenin's death, and after severe internecine struggles, his goals of discipline and hierarchical subordination have come close to their realization. The means have been largely realized, but the end of control by the masses over their political and economic destiny seems about as far away as ever.

In this process the original anti-authoritarian ideas, and the practices that flowed from them, have undergone a sea-change, with the result that they now serve as justifications and additional supports for an authoritarian regime. The safeguards of democratic centralism and self-criticism have been modified in such a way that they do not act as a check upon the power of the top Party leaders. Instead, they serve as devices to strengthen this power by directing the hostility of the masses against local nodules of power in the lower levels of the bureaucratic system, which would otherwise nullify the policies and decisions taken by the central authorities. Criticism is deflected away from policy itself to the execution of policy. Elections serve either to correct weaknesses in the execution of policy or, perhaps more frequently, as public demonstrations and directed affirmations of loyalty to the leaders.

The result which has emerged is a curious amalgam of police terror and primitive "grass-roots" democracy. The coexistence of these two elements no doubt leads to occasional soul-searchings in high quarters that may play a role in the repetitive cycles of increasing bureaucratic and authoritarian rigidity followed by vigorous campaigns of "re-democratization," which form a continuing feature of Soviet political life. These cycles may also, as we have seen, be explained on more general sociological grounds. The present political and economic system requires for its successful operation strong central control and the issuing of orders from above, which in turn results in a loss of enthusiasm and initiative at the lowest levels of the bureaucracy and among the population at large. This loss of initiative and enthusiasm then tends to encourage various breakdowns in the system, which the leaders try to correct by the restoration of democracy in the Party, the soviets, the trade unions, the collective farms, and elsewhere. Re-democratization cannot be carried too far, however, for fear of undermining the central controls. Likewise, motives of self-preservation among those responsible for the bureaucratic and police controls probably prevent too great a swing in an anti-authoritarian direction. One reason why the system does not break down is that the democratic elements in both ideology and practice have acquired the doubly useful function of furnishing support for the authority of the top leaders and checking the recurrent growth of elements hostile to these leaders.

The ideal of equality of rewards, as distinguished from equality of authority, played a significant role in prerevolutionary Bolshevik thinking, even though Marx himself had considered such a goal impractical. For some years after the establishment of the Bolshevik regime, pressures continued in the direction of putting this ideal into practice, although most of the force of the pressures was spent before 1921. Coincident with the efforts to build an industrial society and to establish a new social organization in the countryside, the ideal of equality of rewards was specifically and openly repudiated. A system of incentives, closely related to output, has gradually evolved for industrial workers and farmers. By a system of bonuses, a similar device was applied to managerial personnel in industry.[1] The claim of consistency was not altogether violated, since the repudiation took the form of a denial that the goal of equality of rewards had ever formed a part of Marxist doctrine.

In the area of relations with other states, the Bolsheviks came to power with an interpretation of their own concerning the forces behind international relations, summed up in Lenin's theory of imperialism. Though the new Soviet state was forced to abandon, at least temporarily, its highest hopes at Brest-

Litovsk, revolutionary ideas continued to play an influential role in subsequent Soviet policy. The instrument of the Communist International was created and various attempts made to achieve the goal of proletarian revolution. The failure of these attempts forced the Soviets to fall back increasingly upon more traditional balance-of-power techniques. However, since the proletarian revolution had obtained a territorial base, these traditional techniques, such as alliances with one set of capitalist powers against another, could be rationalized as efforts to strengthen the heartland of the revolution. But the new doctrine, first expounded by Lenin at Brest-Litovsk, was not entirely a rationalization devoid of influence upon the actions of the new rulers of Russia. Soviet policy during and after the Second World War has shown several indications of attempts to utilize the new power base and its instruments, the Red Army and the secret police, for the expansion of the Soviet system.

On the whole, however, Soviet policy has been characterized by a series of adjustments to the existing structure of international relationships, which the USSR has been unable to overthrow and replace by a new world community of toilers' states. These accommodations to changes in the international distribution of political power have on several occasions been markedly influenced by the Marxist-Leninist viewpoint and interpretation of political affairs in foreign countries. While the original goals are no longer openly proclaimed, they may remain latent influences in Soviet policy that could recur in a modified form under favorable conditions.

Implications for modern industrial society

The successes and failures of Leninist doctrine, and the modifications that have been made in this doctrine, contain a number of implications for the nature of modern industrial society. This study has refrained from the outset from any analysis of the political and social "realities" faced by the Bolsheviks, but in concluding it seems permissible to draw attention to the way in which Bolshevik doctrine was reformulated in adaptation to problems that are common to any industrial society. On the basis of the Bolshevik experience, it may be suggested that certain features of modern industrial society are inherent aspects that cannot be eliminated without the destruction of the entire system, while other features can be more readily altered or even omitted. In this respect the word "utopian" can perhaps be given some objective meaning and cease to be merely a partisan epithet.

One difficulty in such an analysis is that the failures and successes of Bolshevism were due not only to the inherent requirements of constructing a modern industrial society, but also to the peculiar problems that derived from Russia's past. This difficulty is part of the more general one produced by the impossibility of utilizing experimental methods in many areas of inquiry into human affairs. Nevertheless, it is possible to make crude statements concerning the relationships of various social phenomena.

The Bolshevik experience, it is suggested, reveals the need for inequalities of power in an industrial society. At the same time, it reveals the needs for a functional division of labor and for inequality of rewards. All of these requirements add up to the necessity of a system of organized social inequality.

If this conclusion is correct, one may infer legitimately enough that widespread demands for social equality are in a broad sense utopian. In this respect, familiar conservative pleas against moving in this direction may be regarded as being based in part on social necessities. Yet this argument can by no logical means be twisted into a justification for any particular system of inequality as it exists in any particular society at the present time. It certainly will not serve to justify in scientific terms the inequalities of wealth and property in capitalist society (though these might be justified, of course, on other scientific grounds), since Soviet society shows clearly that an industrial order can function without them.

Whether the existence of social classes, or what may be more broadly defined as inequalities of opportunity, can be inferred as a social necessity on the basis of Soviet experience is more difficult to decide. With the disappearance of extreme equalitarianism, the ideal concerning rewards has been that the latter should be distributed on the basis of merit alone. Such an ideal has also been extremely influential in Western capitalism and particularly in the United States. In the Soviet Union, however, the concept of merit has, from the beginning, included political loyalty to the Bolshevik leadership. This requirement has excluded considerable sectors of the population at all times, and still excludes in effect the inhabitants of the concentration camps, although these men and women theoretically have the opportunity to rehabilitate themselves. The inhabitants of concentration camps seem to form an inevitable bottom stratum in twentieth-century authoritarian societies.

At the other end of the scale, high officials transmit to their children a number of tangible and intangible advantages: superior education, nutrition, clothing, and above all acquaintance in the circles that hold power. It is difficult to see how the transmission of these advantages can be avoided without destroying the family as a primary social unit, which the Soviets, for other reasons, have long since decided they could not do. Nevertheless, the near absence of any opportunity to obtain and transmit a claim on the output of a large sector of the economy, comparable to the industrial dynasties perpetuated by trust funds under capitalism or the landed properties of feudalism, indicates that the transmission of certain economic advantages will probably remain much less secure in the USSR.

To determine whether the absence of hereditary fortunes plus the existence of concentration camps means greater or fewer inequalities of opportunities than the reverse situation (as, for example, in the United States) is a question that cannot be answered at present. A tentative conclusion, however, is that through the device of the bureaucratic and authoritarian state men may be able to diminish the inequalities of opportunity characteristic of other societies and ages. At the same time, there does not seem to be any possibility of eliminating them altogether. Furthermore, it seems that a successful authoritarian state in modern times may produce a new type of stratification, derived in part from the transmission of certain advantages referred to above and from the system of political differentiation as a basis for status.

It may also be inferred, on the basis of the Soviet experience, that some variety of competitive stimulus is a necessary ingredient in a modern industrial society. The transfer of the means of production to the state has, in the Soviet case at least, failed to eliminate the need for this stimulus, which the Bolsheviks have applied in a number of ingenious ways to industrial workers, managers, and farmers. It is worth noting that, for this stimulus to be effective, there must also be opportunities to rise for at least a short distance in the economic hierarchy. If keeping up with the Joneses is to be an effective motivation, there must be the opportunity to overtake and surpass the Joneses.

Likewise, the Soviets have not been able to do away with certain other conceptions of the dismal science of economics, such as that the costs of production have to be met out of receipts, that capital investment means the postponement of present satisfactions, and that there are efficient and inefficient ways of combining labor and capital to turn out finished products.

In the international sphere, the record of Soviet relations with the rest of the world indicates that the Russians have been compelled to adapt themselves to the pattern of world politics prevailing in the twentieth century, many of whose features have existed in other times and places. While adding some new twists of their own, the Communist rulers of Russia have depended to a great extent on techniques that owe more to Bismarck, Machiavelli, and even Aristotle than they do to Karl Marx or Lenin. This pattern of world politics has been widely recognized as a system of inherently unstable equilibrium, described in the concept of the balance of power. Its chief behavioral principles are that one should oppose the strongest power, or the power that in growing stronger threatens one's own security, and that in so doing one should seek allies where they can be found, independently of cultural and ideological affinities. The Soviets have behaved as if this were their maxim, though not as if it were their exclusive maxim, with only highly infrequent overt statements to this effect. The same has been true of the behavior of the other great powers. It seems very likely, therefore, that the structure of world politics imposes a certain form of behavior on states that is independent of the social and economic structure of these states.

If this conclusion is correct, or even approaches the truth, there is a strong need to relate the study of the structure of international relationships to the study of domestic determinants of behavior on the international scene. In recent years there has been a large amount of research directed toward showing that the behavior of various states in international affairs is primarily determined by specific peculiarities in the society of these states, particularly by the type of personality produced through child-rearing techniques, and similar factors. This approach is a sophisticated revival of the idea of national character. It is not altogether dissimilar to the Marxist analysis, which seeks the springs of international behavior in the clash of class and group interests within each society, though the two schools have differing emphases on causal factors and widely differing remedies for the ills they profess to see in modern society. The weakness of these two approaches is that they take but little cognizance of the structure of the international arena in which the clash of national interests takes place. The difficulty is the same as that which beset psychology when it tried to explain human behavior by studying the individual *in vacuo,* without perceiving the society in which the individual lived. For certain purposes it is of course legitimate and desirable to study as independent entities either the balance of power or the domestic determinants of political behavior in a particular state. But to understand international politics, an approach is necessary that will combine the two areas of inquiry and assign a correct weight to the conclusions drawn from each of them.

In closing this portion of the discussion, we may point to the apparent necessity that any set of beliefs be at least in part above and beyond rational criticism if the society is to avoid disintegration. Sumner used the term "pathos" in this somewhat unusual sense to describe the way in which a protective barrier was set up to fend off criticism from symbols and ideas to which social allegiance was deemed important.[2] Without some degree of pathos and unquestioning belief, the social relationship of leader and follower would be most difficult to maintain. And without these relationships, which are found in even the simplest equalitarian and preliterate societies, society as a whole cannot function. A purely atomistic society, composed of rational, calculating beings, whose only connections with one another are based upon enlightened self-interest—a type posited by classical economic theory—never has existed and probably never will.[3]

Although Marxism makes the claim, especially in its Communist version, that it represents a set of scientific beliefs that can be modified by scientific evidence, it is unlikely that it could have become the ideology of any important ruling group if such were actually the case. Even among scientists an attitude of suspended judgment, finely shaded degrees of doubt and acceptance, ready to be modified or abandoned in the face of new evidence, is largely a myth. It cannot form the bond that holds a political unit together. The revisions that have been made in Marxist theory by the Communists have been political readjustments in adaptation to the requirements of political survival and then dressed in the language of science.

Up to this point in this analysis, it has been noted that the Soviets have been forced to take over and modify for their own purposes certain beliefs and behavior patterns that had already become familiar features of industrial society elsewhere. A system of organized social inequality, the use of the competitive stimulus and other weapons from the capitalist arsenal, and an adherence to the prevailing pattern of international world politics might be postulated as basic requirements for the survival of an industrial society.

On the other hand, it is quite clear from the Soviet experience that an industrial society can function without private property in the means of production. A certain doctrinaire blindness in the West for a long time inhibited the development of awareness to this fact, just as doctrinaire blindness in the USSR inhibited for a time the growth of any awareness of the necessities outlined in the preceding paragraph.

The transfer of the means of production to the community as a whole represents the closest congruence between prerevolutionary anticipations and post-revolutionary facts of any aspect of Bolshevik doctrine and behavior. The implications of this achievement are not all that the Bolsheviks hoped for. While it is claimed that the transfer of the means of production to the state has ended the exploitation of man by man, such a claim cannot be measured by objective criteria. Exploitation is a term used according to slippery subjective standards which cannot be brought out into the open. But no matter how severely the present regime may treat its labor force, its existence and survival in war reveals that it is a viable social system. Whether it is productive of happiness is a much more difficult question to answer, although it is the question most amateurs on both sides of the Iron Curtain are readiest to answer. The answer to this question is, incidentally, far from the most important factor determining the development and outcome of competing social systems. The most viable social system in a world of competing national states is not necessarily the one that provides the greatest amount of happiness to its constituent members.

The fact that the Soviet Union has been able to dispense with private property in the means of production indicates that there is some variety possible in the ways in which a modern industrial society can meet the familiar needs of self-maintenance. In the same way, the fact that other countries have been able to industrialize without resort to a totalitarian political system illustrates the variety of roads that lead to approximately similar goals. While recognizing that the variety exists, it is equally necessary to recognize that limitations also exist. Under the influence of anthropological discoveries, there has been in the recent past somewhat of an overemphasis upon the plasticity of human nature and the freedom of choice supposedly open to any society in the development of its own institutions. Once the major goals are chosen, there seems to be only a limited number of ways by which these goals can be reached.

For example, it is at least conceivable that certain of the equalitarian goals, particularly those relating to equality of rewards, might have been brought closer to achievement if the Communists had been willing to forego the goal of industrialization. Likewise, more political power could perhaps have been left in the hands of the masses if the Bolshevik rulers had been willing to postpone or discard the general goals of the Stalinist Revolution.

Furthermore, it can hardly be maintained that the choice of goals and values is a free and open one in any society. It is doubtful that any serious student of human affairs would today hold to the extreme rationalist position that a group of men can sit down and determine whether it will establish a democratic or some other form of society. Organized human beings do not present a *tabula rasa* upon which one can work one's will in any fashion whatsoever. To this extent it is possible to agree with Sumner's position. The goals of society, and of groups within society, are in a sense given—determined by tradition, by past historical circumstances, by the requirements of organized life in society and group survival, and a host of other factors. Some of these conditions can be directly modified by deliberate rational actions, but others are highly resistant to any form of interference.

In a sense these remarks go to the heart of the problem posed in this book. If the goals of a social group are given, is not ideology *ipso facto* determined by other social factors and hence a purely superficial phenomenon that plays no role itself in social causation? I do not see the problem in this fashion. Once an ideology has been determined, it enters in as a determining factor in its own right in subsequent social situations. It has an effect, sometimes slight, sometimes considerable, on the decisions taken by those who hold it. In its turn, it is modified, sometimes slightly and sometimes considerably, by the impact of subsequent considerations.

Are there limits to ideological change?

Are there limitations, however, to the permutations and modifications that any given system of goals, beliefs, and interpretations of the external world may undergo? Does a given *Weltanschauung* commit its holders, within broad limits of course, to a distinctive and recognizable type of behavior? Is there a point beyond which modifications and reinterpretations cannot go, when the entire system of beliefs and perhaps a whole section of society suffers disintegration rather than undertake a further modification of its belief system?

Intellectual historians have often tended to give positive answers to these questions, perhaps without always being aware that they had raised them. They stress the continuity of intellectual traditions, seeing in Franklin D. Roosevelt the "logical culmination" of Jeffersonian ideas, and in Adolf Hitler the "logical culmination" of earlier authoritarian currents in German thought. We are not concerned, of course, with the merit of these specific conclusions, but with the general approach to such problems that such conclusions exemplify.

Perhaps in a rather gross sense these contentions are correct. It is difficult to see how a firm belief in the divine right of kings could be reconciled with an equally firm belief in the principle of *vox populi, vox dei,* although the English have managed to combine elements of both in their political and social system, perhaps because they refused to have any firm beliefs in first principles.

It may well be that some types of ideological traditions do exclude certain viewpoints. If such is the case, the exclusion would take place on grounds that extend beyond the realm of formal logic. Political ideologies are seldom if ever stated in such a form that they can be subjected to rigorous logical manipulation. Nevertheless, they may make easy the acceptance of one set of conclusions and render difficult the acceptance of an opposite set. For example, the acceptance of Leninist doctrine does not exclude the potential conclusion that capitalism and socialism can exist on the same planet for an unspecified period of time. Yet it does place some barriers in the way of accepting such a conclusion. On the other hand, the acceptance of Euclidean postulates completely excludes the possibility of concluding that the hypotenuse is the shortest side of a right-angle triangle. Though the difference in the flexibility of the two systems of ideas just cited is one of degree rather than an absolute and qualitative distinction, it is nevertheless a clear difference.

Among the causes for a certain lack of flexibility in ideological systems is the tendency of various groups within a political organization to develop strong emotional attachments to a system of doctrine. This group of emotional adherents, the doctrinaires, has to be controlled, and at times even eliminated, if a political organization is to retain sufficient flexibility to maneuver successfully in the struggle to obtain and retain power. The problem of controlling the doctrinaires has been a recurrent one in the Soviet Union down to the most recent times. Lenin faced it even before the seizure of power, as shown in several prerevolutionary controversies. It became acute again with each major change of policy after the November Revolution: the adoption of the Brest-Litovsk Treaty, the change from War Communism to the NEP, and the shift from the NEP to the Stalinist Revolution. After the Second World War the problem recurred in a different form. At that time it was reflected in the struggle to reimpose an orthodoxy that had been ever so slightly set aside in the course of the war with the Axis. It is perhaps significant that the postwar battle for the restoration of orthodoxy was not accompanied by the blood bath that followed the Stalinist Revolution. Altogether, these facts reflect the existence of strong and continuing pressures to adhere as closely as possible to the original sources of the doctrine.

Examining the problem of the elasticity of ideologies from another viewpoint, one finds frequently in historical and literary accounts the statement that a particular doctrine has "lost its vitality" or begun to suffer from old age. When the biological metaphor is dropped, such statements usually mean that a certain doctrine is no longer useful in explaining or justifying a new and different social situation. The failure of symbols to serve a new social situation may come about for a number of reasons. Perhaps certain social groups do not wish the symbols to be reinterpreted and are strong enough to prevent readjustment. This appears to have been the case in Tsarist Russia, where the arch-conservatives were at least strong enough to slow up the transition of Russia from an autocratic state to a constitutional monarchy. In other cases, the failure of readjustment may take place because no group of persons has the ability or the motivation to readapt the symbols to a new situation. In still other instances, it may perhaps be that the symbols themselves are incapable of readaptation. It seems that the anthropologist, A. L. Kroeber, has this phenomenon in mind when he speaks of the "exhaustion" of a cultural pattern. There comes a time when all possible solutions to a problem within the framework of a given cultural pattern seem to have been tried out, and further innovations have to come from within an entirely new variety of approach.[4]

Students of language have pointed out how the structure of a language may make it difficult to understand—that is, to make the desired responses to—concepts that have originated in another language and culture.[5] To realize these difficulties, one has only to think of the obstacles involved in undertaking a problem in long division with the use of Roman numerals alone. On these grounds, it is at least a reasonable hypothesis that a set of ideas, or a system of political notation, such as Marxism-Leninism, would make certain types of political responses difficult, or perhaps even impossible, whereas it would make others relatively easy. Although the limits of a system of political notation are probably not as definite as those in the linguistic and mathematical symbol systems, it seems a very probable inference that such limits do exist.

Since we cannot isolate with laboratory techniques the variables in the study of a social movement, it is impossible to point to unarguable cases in which ideology has limited or inhibited the political responses of the Bolsheviks to a given situation. But one can indicate the difficulties that have occurred on numerous occasions when the Bolsheviks have felt themselves forced to act in contradiction to their previous doctrinal statements. Likewise, one can refer to the various returns to policies arising from original doctrine and suggest that more than mere expediency was involved in these returns. In particular, the Stalinist return to a modified form of Leninism, which resolved the social tensions created by the policies of the NEP, goes quite contrary to a policy of mere ideological adjustments to the circumstances that existed at that time.[6] Furthermore, the failure of the Chinese revolution of the twenties seems to have come about in part from an inability to break with familiar stereotypes and to develop a fresh approach to an admittedly difficult situation. Perhaps the Tito incident may also reflect a similar doctrinal sterility.

On the whole, one is likely to be more impressed with the flexibility of Communist doctrine than with its rigidity. Its elasticity has proved its value in the ideology of that strange alloy of authoritarian and populist practices, the Soviet Union itself, as well as in its adaptive forms in the Soviet satellite states and, at the hands of other than Stalin, in agrarian China. With certain shifts of emphasis, Communist doctrine would be congruent with the institutions and practices of Western democracy, as the Stalin Constitution of 1936 reveals. The undoubted fact that Communism does not mean exactly the same thing in each of the Communist areas illustrates its flexibility as a system of symbols. (The same generalization may, of course, be made to apply to the flexibility of Western democratic doctrines.)

Within the Communist system of symbols, as in others, resilience and the opportunity for perpetuation come from the fact that it is often possible to make far-reaching social changes with only a minimum reinterpretation of the doctrine. The way in which the populist and democratic aspects of the original Leninist theory have been reinterpreted and reutilized to support the power of central Party leadership is a case in point. As a rule, it is easier to bring about a fundamental alteration of any social system within the framework of the symbols than in opposition to them. It is a commonplace observation that many religious revolutions take place under the flag of orthodoxy. Lenin's interpretation of Marx and Stalin's interpretation of Lenin both lay claim to orthodoxy in the strongest possible fashion.

Flexibility and resilience also come about from the mechanics of doctrinal transmission. No system of ideas is ever transmitted in exactly the same form from one person to another, as many a teacher has observed to his chagrin. Errors and inaccuracies always arise. Sometimes the errors are deliberately introduced by one of the transmitters, as has been the case in the transmission of much Party history and doctrine in the Soviet Union. At other times they are unconscious distortions by the receiver. In both cases the adaptations usually take the form of serving new wine in old bottles.

As Pareto has shown in abundance, it is possible for organized social groups to profess, and even to hold to, a wide variety of contradictory beliefs. When political circumstances require the incorporation of new and contradictory ideas into a reigning ideology, some intellectuals can usually be found to perform the task in a passable fashion. The task is made easier when the reigning system of ideas receives emotional allegiance and is on this account felt to be beyond rational criticism. It may also be made easier by the fact that different sets of ideas tend to be held at different levels of overt awareness.

To an outsider there seems to be a contradiction in Marxism-Leninism between the belief in a special variety of historical determinism and an equally strong belief in the necessity for vigorous action to bring about the inevitable. Psychologically, these ideas probably tend to reinforce one another, rather than to arouse skepticism and similar difficulties. Greater, but not insuperable, difficulties occur when ideas are taken over in order to appeal to wavering or hostile groups in the population: witness the fact that during the war the banner of the hammer and sickle could incorporate Russian nationalist symbols and even some of those of the orthodox church.

In earlier irreverent days, when Leninism had already received a number of opportunist accretions, it was once said to be "like Uncle Sasha's store—you can get everything you want there." This impatient remark is, however, somewhat of an exaggeration. In Communist doctrine, accretions in the form of concessions to various interest groups have a way of disappearing when there is no longer a need to conciliate these groups. Ideological and practical concessions made to the peasantry in 1921 and subsequent years were withdrawn in the collectivization campaigns, and, following the war, various writers and intellectuals were reprimanded for "bourgeois nationalist deviations." One may observe the tendency to revert to a common doctrinal core, which undergoes slower modifications than the shifting "Party line."

In recent years experimental psychology has uncovered a number of the mechanisms that explain both the retention of certain symbolic formulations and their occasional abandonment.

Studies of perception in human beings have shown a tendency to exclude what is inimical or irrelevant; the person sees what he wants or expects to see. These expectations are in part determined by past experience. This is true so long as the situation is not too threatening or too exacting. But in threatening situations the perceptive response takes a more vigorous account of reality; the human organism, again in a selective fashion, will become aware of aspects of the environment that represent danger.[7] This helps to explain the way in which certain Soviet doctrines have been thrown overboard in times of acute danger (the Treaty of Brest-Litovsk, the NEP, the Nazi-Soviet Pact), as well as Soviet attempts to meet new situations in terms of familiar stereotypes.

Information of this type provides a valuable underpinning because it shows how certain types of reaction are possible, but it does not relieve the student who operates at the more general level of the study of group behavior from explaining matters in his own terms. It is necessary, therefore, to turn to a survey of the possible forms an ideology may take in response to circumstances, or what might be considered the natural history of a doctrine of protest.

The natural history of a successful protest movement

The tendency of protest movements to develop different types of doctrines within their own ranks at various stages of their growth has an important bearing on the more general questions of the nature of ideological and social change. On the basis of the Bolshevik experience, it is possible to draw up a schematic series of stages of ideological and institutional growth. The schematic nature of the following sketch should be understood clearly. Its purpose, as suggested by Max Weber, is merely to draw attention to potentially significant relationships that are not limited to a series of historically unique events. While parallels with the development of Christianity and other religious protest movements may occur to the reader, it should be clear that any scheme of this type is a theoretical construct which may not correspond exactly with empirical historical realities at any one point. Its utility is merely to draw attention to potentially important matters that might otherwise escape beneath a welter of historical detail.

A new ideology is likely to be formed or, perhaps more frequently, to be borrowed from external sources, as was the case with Russian Marxism, in a period of rapid institutional change. Under conditions of rapid social change the relationship of the various parts of society to one another, often precarious in any case, tends to break down. In the case of Russia during the nineteenth century, tremors were sent out from the economic field into the areas of politics, law, religion, and family relationships, though there is no reason to assume, as Marx did, that the tremors always begin in the economic institutions of society. With this partial disintegration of the social fabric, new frustrations are felt that are not readily accepted, and old ones are felt more keenly. New ideas arise concerning the legitimate level of expectations among various sections of the population. There is, one might say, a new cultural definition of wants in different parts of the society. In Russia the urban middle classes, the peasants, and the industrial workers all showed signs of wanting to improve their political and economic position, while the landed nobility at the same time tried to prevent this, or even to strengthen their own position. Under such conditions there tends to arise in a number of different groups some kind of analysis of what the source of the trouble is, some notion of what to do about the situation, and some organized effort to bring about a change in the desired direction. Both "reactionary" and "radical" groups are apt to coalesce into formal organizations in protest against the existing situation. It is at this point, especially before the development of formal organizations has proceeded very far, that the level of sincere belief in an ideology is likely to be close to its highest level.

As the organization develops, and as leaders emerge, a process of differentiation begins to take place in the ideology. If the group is to win power and influence, if it is going to accomplish anything, it must take power factors into account. The dilemma between means and ends raises its head. The ways chosen to

achieve power may contradict the ultimate goals that the organization wishes to achieve. In the case of the Bolshevik movement this dilemma was especially acute. Some persons are inclined to lay heavy emphasis on the means to power, while others
continue to stress the ultimate goals. At crucial moments before
and after the November Revolution, splits on this point threatened to disintegrate the Bolshevik Party.

By the time a protest group has become well organized it may
contain several ideologies at once. One may distinguish the informal or operating ideology of the leaders, a series of fundamental and often unstated assumptions upon which they all more
or less agree. This is likely to represent a compromise between
means and ends or, to put it in another way, between power considerations and original doctrines. In the second place, one may
distinguish the formal or official ideology, which consists of publicly stated or printed programs and pronouncements of goals
and means, phrased in the symbols common to the original doctrine or to its officially sanctioned adaptations. In the third place,
there is the wide variety of beliefs, shadings, interpretations, and
even misunderstandings, held by the rank and file of the organization. If the protest organization succeeds in obtaining power, the
strains and stresses and forces for both ideological and institutional change are, as we have seen, considerably increased.

The relationship between the official ideology of an organization and the operating ideology of its leaders is a complex matter, and the discussion here will be limited to the considerations
that apply in the Soviet case alone. It is often thought that the
top Soviet leadership is a group of purely cynical manipulators,
and that on this account there is no relationship whatever between
the operating ideology of the top Communist elite and officially
promulgated doctrines. On several grounds it would appear
that this conclusion must be modified in important respects.

The current relationship between the operating ideology and
officially promulgated doctrines in the Soviet system is in a large
measure governed by the fact that the invention of alternative
solutions to pending problems is almost entirely limited to the
very top of the political pyramid. This leads to a situation in

which conflicting opinions on any topic of major national importance are concealed from the general public. The development and maturation of a new policy takes place behind closed doors and appears suddenly when the final decision has been reached at the highest level. Only occasionally, as in the publication of confidential diplomatic documents, does the investigator have the opportunity to observe the process at work directly. It is this element of secrecy which sometimes gives to Soviet policy an air of unpredictable and Machiavellian shiftiness. After a new policy has been decided upon, the Party line is readjusted, and the propaganda machinery of the state puts all of its resources to work in promulgating the new doctrine. In this manner shifts in the operating ideology of the elite produce changes sooner or later in the officially promulgated doctrine. The new program ideology may in some instances contain fairly candid statements of the reasons for a revision of the Party line. In other cases, the considerations that motivated the change must be inferred from the surrounding circumstances.

Cases in which the program ideology corresponds fairly closely to the operating assumptions of the leaders are likely to occur when the leaders find it necessary to deal with an important political problem by efforts to change the official doctrine. For example, the official repudiation of former Communist goals concerning the desirability of equality of rewards was a practical move designed to increase incentive differentials and provide motivation for greater economic production. In a situation of this sort it is safe to assume that there is a fairly close agreement between a new official or program ideology and the ideas current in the ruling group that influence the reaching of decisions.

It is obvious, however, that although the informal ideas of the leaders and the official doctrines may overlap in part, they will not always be identical. In still other situations, such as Lenin's concessions to the peasantry, the official ideology may be deliberately and consciously manipulated for purposes of strengthening the power of the rulers. But even in such cases, as the career of Bukharin shows, there is a tendency for some of the top leaders to take the official doctrine seriously, or for the operating ideology and the official doctrine to approach one another.

Cases undoubtedly do occur when the leaders manipulate the official doctrines without in the least believing them. One instance of this type may be the simultaneous negotiations with the Anglo-French bloc and the Nazis in 1939, which had very little to do with the officially proclaimed goal of putting a stop to war and fascism. Since, as a rule, the goals proclaimed in the official ideology have received implementation in behavior, it appears that cynical manipulation of this type is relatively rare in Soviet behavior so far. With the passage of time it may become more common.

In order to avoid confusion on this point, it should also be noted that there is nothing un-Leninist in the use of deception for political purposes. It is perfectly possible for the leaders to adhere quite strictly in their private beliefs to Leninist doctrines and to put forth an official ideology that has very little to do with such doctrines. In fact, this is what many people assume to be the case, without much factual support for their assumptions. On the whole it appears to be the least likely assumption, since the operating ideology of the leaders is more sensitive to environmental factors and the influence of success and failure than is an organized system of overtly expressed doctrine.

After a protest ideology has become established, there are at least five different fates that may befall the original doctrine or various portions of it.

The first possibility is that of outright repudiation. Certain parts of a doctrine may be repudiated if they go counter to other goals that the carriers of this ideology deem more important. This question is not one of formal logical consistency, but of contradictions between the social effects of some portion of the doctrine—for example, the goal of equality of rewards—and other goals, such as the maximization of power and the establishment of a large-scale industrial technology.

Another possibility is the continuation and incorporation of old symbols that still evoke a favorable emotional response un-

der new and very different social conditions. The incorporation
of the anti-authoritarian and populist symbols of early Leninist
theory into the ruling doctrines of the contemporary authoritarian Soviet state provides an illustration of this type of adaptation.

The postponement to an increasingly indefinite future of goals
that cannot be realized represents the third form of adjustment
to the situation of political responsibility. The proletarian revolution appears to be a goal that has undergone this fate.

Postponed goals may also return as active ingredients in
policy-making when the leaders find themselves in a dilemma, or
when circumstances judged favorable for their achievement recur. The goals may return in a slightly modified but easily recognizable form. This is particularly apt to happen after the leaders
have been following without success a policy that represents a
deviation from earlier doctrines. Then the cry can be raised that
failures have been due to the fact that the original doctrines
were not adhered to. The clearest illustration of this type of con-
catenation of circumstances may be found at the time of the end
of the NEP, when the leaders returned very largely, though by
no means entirely, to earlier ideas and solutions in both domestic
and foreign policy. The elimination of private capitalism in industry, the collectivization of agriculture, and the return to
uncompromising hostility toward non-Communist leftist groups
at the Sixth Congress of the Comintern all belong to the same
pattern of thinking. To some extent the same situation holds true
today. The failure of attempted collaboration with the West, because of the polarization of world politics, has led to a recrudes-
cence of doctrinaire othodoxy.

It is worth noting that an indefinite future does not necessarily mean a distant future. Elusive goals that are just around
the corner may serve the sociological and psychological function
of maintaining group cohesiveness and faith in a doctrine even
better than distant goals. For a long time the proletarian revolution was treated as an event that was just around the corner.
Only about 1934 did signs appear that it was being postponed to
the Greek calends. At the present time the elimination of "bu-

reaucratic distortions" and the realization of "true Soviet democracy" are often treated as goals to be achieved in the immediate future. Thus they serve the purpose of smoothing over immediate contradictions in the social system. As Sorel pointed out, men sometimes work more effectively for impracticable goals than for practicable ones. As one final instance, one may mention the goal of a communist, as opposed to a socialist, society. For some persons this goal may be one that is to be realized in the very near future. As recently as July 1939 the Soviet economist Varga declared, "The material basis for the transition from socialism to Communism has been laid." [8] For others it is probably a goal to be achieved in a very distant future.

A concomitant feature of the postponement of goals is their ritualization. Upon state occasions various ideals are brought out for public reaffirmation, although few persons if any take them seriously as guides to policy. Nevertheless, reaffirmation of these goals is somehow reassuring, an indication that nothing has changed after all, that the leaders are trustworthy bearers of tradition, and that the world will soon be put to rights. Loyal followers are likely to be disturbed if this ritual attention fails to take place at the appropriate time and place. If the President of the United States, to use an American example, failed to utter certain symbolic platitudes at the time of his inauguration, there would be a vague feeling of uneasiness in many parts of the nation. Likewise, if the Soviet leaders failed to reaffirm their loyalty to the principles of Lenin on the anniversary of the Revolution, many good Communists might feel that the heavens were about to collapse.

The simplest, and perhaps the rarest, fate to befall any portion of the doctrines of a protest movement is their continuation and application in practice. The transfer of the means of production to the society as a whole is the only aspect of Marxist-Leninist doctrine about which one can say with considerable plausibility that the goal has been achieved. For many Marxists this was not an important goal in itself, but a means to the end of creating a society free from the oppressions believed to be inherent in the capitalist system. Some of the Marxist-Leninist ends appear to have been achieved, particularly the elimination of recurring cycles of unemployment with their corrosive effects on human personality. Yet it would be difficult to maintain that the other goals of liberation have been won.

Notes

Notes

Shortened titles have been used whenever possible; for fuller identification see the Bibliography. No Russian titles have been translated here when full translations occur in the Bibliography. In general, it has been my custom to retain familiar English transliterations of Russian words and names. In addition, Russian *e* when preceded by a vowel has been transliterated *ye*, except in those cases in which by so doing the standard Russian pronunciation is misrepresented.

INTRODUCTION

1. The limitations of a case-study approach to this problem are stressed in Parsons, "The Role of Ideas in Social Action," *Essays in Sociological Theory*, chap. vi.

2. For a critical analysis, see Merton, *Social Theory*, chap. viii.

3. Marx and Engels, *German Ideology*, pp. 7, 13. This work, completed in the summer of 1846, represents the earliest and most comprehensive exposition of Marx's views on the role of ideas.

4. *Ibid.*, pp. 13–14.

5. *Ibid.*, p. 14.

6. *Ibid.*, p. 28.

7. From a letter by Engels to Joseph Bloch, in Marx, *Selected Works*, I, 381–383.

8. Northrop, *Meeting of East and West*, p. 12.

9. *Ibid.*, p. 246. Italics in original in this and other quotations unless otherwise noted.

10. On this question see, for one side of the case, Trotsky, *Stalin School of Falsification*. Nearly all the accusations are directed against misrepresentation in Soviet secondary accounts, though there is one essay, "The Lost Document," devoted to the suppression of one of Lenin's speeches.

11. Compare Stalin, *October Revolution*, p. 30, and his *Sochineniya*, IV, 154.

12. For a recent discussion of the political functions of the Soviet press, see Inkeles, *Public Opinion*, chaps. ix–xiv.

CHAPTER 1: HOW AN IDEOLOGY EMERGED

1. Trotsky, *My Life*, p. 337.

2. See Trotsky, *Our Revolution*, pp. 73–93, and a much more fully developed analysis by the same author in his *Geschichte der Russischen Revolution*, I, 15–27. The thesis is very cogently argued by

Dan, *Proiskhozhdeniye Bol'shevizma*, esp. pp. 20–31. Dan was a prominent Menshevik leader who later became reconciled to Stalinist policy, though remaining in exile. Souvarine, *Staline*, chap. ii; Rosenberg, *Geschichte des Bolschewismus*, chaps. i and ii; and Borkenau, *Communist International,* chaps. i–iv, present the same thesis with many suggestive insights. Of these three, only Souvarine has command of the Russian sources. With the exception of Dan, all are strongly anti-Stalinist. Likewise Berdyaev, a former Marxist, in his *Origin of Russian Communism* (p. 113), argues that "Communism was the inevitable fate of Russia," because social circumstances forced liberalism in Russia to become utopian. Completely convincing proof or disproof of such arguments is, of course, impossible.

3. *The Great Retreat.*
4. Miliukov, *Ocherki,* I, 192–202. Figures on p. 195.
5. Berlin, *Russkaya Burzhuaziya,* pp. 235–236.
6. *Ibid.,* pp. 287–290.
7. Miliukov, *Rossiya na Perelome,* I, 31–32; Berlin, *Russkaya Burzhuaziya,* p. 150.
8. Berlin, *Russkaya Burzhuaziya,* p. 286.
9. Robinson, *Rural Russia,* p. 147.
10. Vernadsky, *History of Russia,* p. 179.
11. Robinson, *Rural Russia,* pp. 144–145.
12. *Ibid.,* pp. 128, 138–139, 196, 203.
13. *Ibid.,* pp. 160–162, 170–174.
14. *Russia in Flux,* pp. 108–109.
15. Robinson, *Rural Russia,* p. 144.
16. Maynard, *Russia in Flux,* p. 87.
17. *Ibid.,* p. 89.
18. Robinson, *Rural Russia,* pp. 226–227.
19. Maynard, *Russia in Flux,* pp. 89–90.
20. *Rossiya na Perelome,* I, 39–41.

21. Dan, *Proiskhozhdeniye Bol'shevizma,* chap. v and p. 106. See also Gurian, *Bolshevism,* pp. 12–24, for valuable observations on the Russian intelligentsia and the social tensions produced by the diffusion of Western culture. Berdyaev's entire study, *Origin of Russian Communism,* is concerned with the intelligentsia's reaction to the impact of the West.
22. Quoted by Wolfe, *Three Who Made a Revolution,* pp. 93–94.
23. Dan, *Proiskhozhdeniye Bol'shevizma,* pp. 262–263.
24. *VKP(b) v Rezoliutsiyakh* (3d ed.), pp. 16ff.
25. *Ibid.,* p. 2.
26. *Ibid.,* p. 33.
27. Plekhanov, *Sochineniya,* XII, 418–419.
28. Dan, *Proiskhozhdeniye Bol'shevizma,* p. 363.
29. Lorimer, *Population,* p. 22.
30. Lenin, "Two Tactics of Social Democracy," July, 1905, *Selected Works,* III, 72.
31. *Ibid.,* p. 75.
32. *Ibid.,* p. 82.
33. See the Bolshevik proposals to the Sixth Congress, Stockholm, 1906, in *VKP(b) v Rezoliutsiyakh* (3d ed.), pp. 50–54. The proposals were not adopted.
34. See Chapter 2.
35. Souvarine, *Staline,* pp. 85–86, gives a valuable account of the tactical disagreements in the evaluation of the 1905 revolution.
36. "Two Tactics," p. 100.
37. *Ibid.,* p. 101.
38. "Neskol'ko Tezisov" (Some Theses) in *Sochineniya* (2d ed.), XVIII, 312, published in *Sozial Demokrat,* October 13, 1915.
39. "Nabrosok Tezisov 17 Marta 1917" (Rough Draft of Theses, March 17, 1917) in *Sochineniya* (2d ed.), XX, 9–11.

40. For a brief characterization of this Cabinet, see Chamberlin, *Russian Revolution*, I, 88–89.

41. Lenin, "Nabrosok Tezisov," p. 12.

42. "O proletarskoi militsii" (On a Proletarian Militia), in "Letters

from Afar," letter 3, March 24, 1917, *Sochineniya* (2d ed.), XX, 33, 34.

43. "The Tasks of the Proletariat in the Present Revolution," April 20, 1917 (also referred to as the "April Theses"), *Selected Works*, VI, 23.

CHAPTER 2: LENIN'S PLANS

1. *Sochineniya* (2d ed.), XXVII, 398–401. The article was printed in *Pravda*, May 30, 1923.

2. *State and Revolution* in *Selected Works*, VII, 44.

3. *Ibid.*, p. 18.

4. *Ibid.*, p. 51.

5. "Can the Bolsheviks Retain State Power?" October 21, 1917, *Selected Works*, VI, 278.

6. *State and Revolution*, p. 29.

7. "Can the Bolsheviks Retain State Power?" p. 262.

8. *Ibid.*, p. 264.

9. *Ibid.*, p. 263.

10. "Political Parties and Tasks of the Proletariat," *Selected Works*, VI, 81.

11. *Ibid.*, pp. 271–273.

12. *State and Revolution*, p. 42.

13. "Can the Bolsheviks Retain State Power?" pp. 264–265.

14. *State and Revolution*, p. 47.

15. *Ibid.*

16. *Ibid.*, p. 42.

17. "Can the Bolsheviks Retain State Power?" p. 266.

18. *Ibid.*, p. 269.

19. *Ibid.*, p. 265.

20. *Ibid.*, p. 267.

21. *Ibid.*, p. 270.

22. *State and Revolution*, p. 48.

23. *Ibid.*, pp. 88, 89.

24. See *Leninskii Sbornik* (1932 ed.), XIX, 27–85. The *Leninskii Sbornik*, still in the process of publication, is a many-volumed collection of Lenin's notes, notebooks, rough drafts of articles and speeches, tele-

grams, letters, and similar informal materials.

25. Kautsky's assertions to this effect were heavily underscored by Lenin. See *Leninskii Sbornik*, XIX, 71.

26. "The Agrarian Programme of Social Democracy in the First Russian Revolution, 1905–1907," written in November and December 1907, *Selected Works*, III, 279–280.

27. *Ibid.*, pp. 258, 280.

28. *Ibid.*, XII, 324, with full quotations from Marx. For some reason, Lenin's article is divided between volume III and volume XII of the *Selected Works*, perhaps because the latter volume is entirely given over to Lenin's theoretical writings on agricultural matters.

29. *Ibid.*, XII, 330. The statement is by Lenin and attributed to Marx.

30. *Ibid.*

31. *Ibid.*, p. 326.

32. *Ibid.*, p. 305.

33. "Materials Relating to the Revision of the Party Program," submitted to the All-Russian Conference of the RSDLP, May 7–12, 1917, *Selected Works*, VI, 123.

34. "The Agrarian Programme of Social Democracy," XII, 333.

35. *Ibid.*, p. 334.

36. *Die Agrarfrage* (2d ed.), p. 300.

37. *Leninskii Sbornik*, XIX, 62.

38. *Ibid.*, p. 42.

39. "To the Rural Poor, An Explanation of What the Social Demo-

crats Want," 1903, *Selected Works*, II, 293.

40. "Materials Relating to the Revision of the Party Program," p. 123. The text of the 1903 program is given on the same page.

41. See *VKP(b) v Rezoliutsiyakh* (3d ed.), p. 182.

42. "Two Tactics," pp. 96–97.

43. "The Stages, Trends and Prospects of the Revolution," written at the beginning of 1906, *Selected Works*, III, 135.

44. Dan, *Proiskhozhdeniye Bol'-shevizma*, pp. 293–294, 390.

45. Trotsky, "Prospects of a Labor Dictatorship," a partial translation of *Itogi i Perspektivy* (Past Achievements and Prospects), in *Our Revolution*, p. 85. The original brochure was written in 1906.

46. *Ibid.*, pp. 95–96.

47. *Ibid.*, pp. 100–101.

48. *Ibid.*, pp. 103–108.

49. *Ibid.*, pp. 136–137.

50. *Ibid.*, p. 139.

51. *Ibid.*, p. 140.

52. *Leninskii Sbornik* (1931 ed.), XII, 416.

53. *Ibid.*, pp. 424ff.

54. *Ibid.*, p. 408.

55. As copied by Lenin, the passage reads: "Wo es auch kein System, keinen Wahrheitsapparat giebt, da giebt es doch eine Wahrheit, und dies wird dann meistens nur durch ein geübtes Urtheil und den Takt einer langer Erfahrung gefun-

den. Giebt also die Geschichte hier kiene Formeln, so giebt sie doch hier wie überall *Übung des Urtheils.*" *Leninskii Sbornik*, XII, 420.

56. *Imperialism, the Highest Stage of Capitalism*, in *Selected Works*, V, 81, 88–89, 109–110.

57. *Ibid.*, pp. 116–117.

58. "Defeat of One's Own Government in the Imperialist War," written in 1915, *Selected Works*, V, 142.

59. The Manifesto was drafted in September 1914 and sent to members of the Central Committee who were in Russia, as well as to other responsible Party leaders there. After receiving their approval, it was published on November 1, 1914. See the editor's note to the Manifesto in *RKP(b) v Rezoliutsiyakh*, p. 165, and the text of the Manifesto itself on the following pages. The refusal to vote war credits is mentioned in the Manifesto and also by Souvarine, *Staline*, p. 133.

60. "A Few Theses," October 1915, *Selected Works*, V, 157.

61. *Ibid.*

62. "The Aims of the Revolution," October 9–10, 1917, *Selected Works*, VI, 244. For the offer to Germany, see L. Fischer, *Soviets in World Affairs*, I, 128.

63. "The Aims of the Revolution," pp. 244–245.

CHAPTER 3: DILEMMA OF MEANS AND ENDS

1. Dan, *Proiskhozhdeniye Bol'-shevizma*, p. 288.

2. *Ibid.*, p. 181.

3. Quoted, *ibid.*, p. 281; see also p. 273.

4. *What Is To Be Done?* written in 1902, *Selected Works*, II, 53.

5. *Ibid.*, pp. 62–63.

6. *Ibid.*, p. 64.

7. *Ibid.*, p. 62.

8. "A Dual Power," April 22, 1917, *Selected Works*, VI, 29.

9. See, for example, "The Bolsheviks Must Assume Power," a letter to the Central Committee and

to the Petrograd and Moscow Committees of the RSDLP, September 25–27, 1917, *Selected Works*, VI, 215–217.

10. *Ibid.*, p. 217.

11. See "The Tasks of the Proletariat in the Present Revolution," Lenin's April Theses, *Selected Works*, VI, 23.

12. *What Is To Be Done?* p. 147.

13. *Ibid.*, p. 150.

14. *Ibid.*, pp. 138, 152.

15. *VKP(b) v Rezoliutsiyakh* (3d ed.), p. 46.

16. "Pis'mo k tovarishchu o nashikh organizatsionnykh zadachakh" (Letter to a Comrade about Our Organizational Tasks), *Sochineniya* (4th ed.), VI, 224.

17. *Ibid.*, p. 209.

18. *What Is To Be Done?* p. 154.

19. "Pis'mo k tovarishchu," p. 213.

20. *Ibid.*, pp. 222–223.

21. "Proyekt rezoliutsii ob otnosheniyakh rabochikh i intelligentov v S–D organizatsiyakh" (Draft of a Resolution on the Relationship between Workers and Intellectuals in Social Democratic Organizations), *Sochineniya* (4th ed.), VIII, 377.

22. *VKP(b) v Rezoliutsiyakh* (3d ed.), p. 46.

23. "Tasks of the Proletariat," p. 22.

24. Quoted by Chamberlin, *Russian Revolution*, I, 183.

25. *Protokoly Shestogo S'ezda RSDRP(b)*, pp. 165–166.

26. *VKP(b) v Rezoliutsiyakh* (3d ed.), p. 3.

27. "Pis'mo A. A. Bogdanovu i S. I. Gusevu" (Letter to A. A. Bogdanov and S. I. Gusev), *Sochineniya* (4th ed.), VIII, 124.

28. Such statements may be found in Lenin's writings as early as the summer of 1904. See "Chego my dobyvaemsya?" (What Are We

Aiming At?), written in July 1904, *Sochineniya* (4th ed.), VII, 418. This stands in sharp contrast with his famous "One Step Forward, Two Steps Backward," written in May of the same year.

29. "Doklad ob ob'edinitel'nom s'ezde RSDRP, Pis'mo k Peterburgskim rabochim" (Report on the Unity Congress of the RSDLP, Letter to the Workers of St. Petersburg), *Sochineniya* (4th ed.), X, 348. The pamphlet was written in May 1906.

30. "Svoboda kritiki i edinstvo deistvii" (Freedom of Criticism and Unity of Action), May 1906, *Sochineniya* (4th ed.), X, 408–409.

31. "Doklad ob ob'edinitel'nom s'ezde RSDRP," pp. 348–349.

32. *VKP(b) v Rezoliutsiyakh* (3d ed.), p. 258.

33. "The Boycott," written in September 1906, *Selected Works*, III, 392–400.

34. "Doklad ob ob'edinitel'nom s'ezde RSDRP," p. 349.

35. "Svoboda kritiki," p. 409.

36. "Sotsial-demokratiya i vybory v Peterburge" (Social Democracy and the Elections in St. Petersburg), written January 26–27, 1907, *Sochineniya* (4th ed.), XI, 396. The English term "referendum" is used by Lenin.

37. "Where to Begin," *Selected Works*, II, 17.

38. "Can the Bolsheviks Retain State Power?" *Selected Works*, VI, 269.

39. Souvarine, *Staline*, pp. 56, 104.

40. Chamberlin, *Russian Revolution*, I, 289.

41. Lenin, "The Crisis Has Matured," *Selected Works*, VI, 232, and notes, p. 584, where the text of Kamenev's resignation is included.

42. The text of the resolution is

given in Lenin, *Selected Works,* VI, 303.

43. Chamberlin, *Russian Revolution,* I, 293–294. Lenin, *Selected Works,* VI, 595 (notes).

44. *Selected Works,* VI, 331.

45. Additional material on the differences of opinion between Kamenev and Zinoviev on the one hand and Lenin on the other may be found in *Kamenev i Zinoviev v 1917 g. Fakty i Dokumenty* (Kamenev and Zinoviev in 1917, Facts and Documents). This book, published at the time of later factional struggles, when both of these men were allied with Trotsky, consists of reprints of their newspaper controversies with Lenin during 1917.

46. The texts of these bylaws are included in the collection of Party resolutions, of which there are several editions.

47. Piatnitsky, *Memoirs of a Bolshevik,* p. 159.

48. *Ibid.,* p. 116.

49. *Ibid.,* pp. 162–163.

50. A full account of Malinovsky's career, based on a careful study of the sources, may be found in Wolfe, *Three Who Made a Revolution,* chap. xxxi. Scattered through Wolfe's book is a large amount of additional information on the Party's relations with the police.

51. Piatnitsky, *Memoirs,* p. 19.

52. *Ibid.,* p. 179, note.

53. *Ibid.,* pp. 76–77.

54. *Ibid.,* p. 163.

55. Quoted in Spiridovich, *Istoriya Bol'shevizma,* p. 52.

56. Spiridovich, *Istoriya Bol'shevizma,* pp. 103–104. Souvarine, *Staline,* p. 73, credits the revolt to the Mensheviks.

57. Spiridovich, *Istoriya Bol'shevizma,* p. 142.

58. White, *Growth of the Red Army,* chap. i.

59. Souvarine, *Staline,* pp. 91, 93ff. For a different interpretation, see Trotsky, *Stalin,* p. 105.

60. Souvarine, *Staline,* p. 120.

61. *Ibid.,* p. 91.

62. Spiridovich, *Istoriya Bol'shevizma,* pp. 50–51.

63. Wolfe, *Three Who Made a Revolution,* chap. xxii.

64. Trotsky, *Stalin,* p. 104, lists the sections of the Party opposed to further expropriations.

65. *VKP(b) v Rezoliutsiyakh* (3d ed.), p. 95.

66. Spiridovich, *Istoriya Bol'shevizma,* p. 265. This statement may have been motivated by personal and bureaucratic rivalries within the police organization.

CHAPTER 4: VICTORY CREATES DILEMMAS

1. The name was changed from Russian Social Democratic Labor Party to Russian Communist Party (Bolsheviks) at the Seventh Congress in March 1918. Following the formation of the USSR in 1922, the Fourteenth Congress in 1925 changed the name to All-Union Communist Party (Bolsheviks). However, it has become customary in English to use the less clumsy name of Communist Party of the Soviet Union.

2. See the theses of the Left Communists of April 20, 1918, from *Kommunist,* no. 1, reproduced in Lenin, *Sochineniya* (2d ed.), XXII, appendix, esp. pp. 569–570. Dobb, *Russian Economic Development,* pp. 52–53. This account is very

valuable, not only for its interpretation of the early problems faced by the Bolsheviks and the alternate solutions presented, but also for its wide use of quotations from Russian sources not easily accessible in the United States.

3. Dobb, *Russian Economic Development*, pp. 53–60.

4. On the period of War Communism, see Dobb, *Soviet Economic Development*, chap. v. This is a new and revised version of his *Russian Economic Development*. Larin and Kritzmann, *Wirtschaftsleben*, provide a brief sketch of some of the major developments from the point of view of two left-wing economists.

5. See Dobb, *Soviet Economic Development*, pp. 122–123.

6. "Speech Delivered at the First All-Russian Conference on Work in the Rural Districts," November 18, 1919, *Selected Works*, VIII, 190–191.

7. *Protokoly VIII S'ezda RKP (b)*, pp. 36, 38.

8. *Ibid.*, p. 39.

9. Prokopovicz, *Russlands Volkswirtschaft*, p. 250.

10. *Ibid.*, p. 100.

11. Baykov, *Development of the Soviet Economic System*, pp. 26–27.

12. Trotsky, *My Life*, pp. 463–464.

13. Liberman, *Building Lenin's Russia*, p. 93.

14. *Kommunist*, no. 1, as reproduced in Lenin, *Sochineniya* (2d ed.), XXII, 567.

15. For the Workers' Opposition, see "Theses of the Workers' Opposition for the Tenth Congress of the Communist Party," Russian text in Lenin, *Sochineniya* (2d ed.), XXVI, 563–569, and Dobb, *Russian Economic Development*, pp. 156–157. The platform of the Group for Democratic Centralism may be found in *Pravda*, January 25, 1921.

16. Lenin's more important speeches on the NEP are collected in vol. IX of his *Selected Works*.

17. "On Cooperation," January 4–6, 1923, *Selected Works*, IX, 408.

18. *Ibid.*, p. 405.

19. Lorimer, *Population*, p. 30.

20. Baykov, *Development of the Soviet Economic System*, p. 121.

21. *Ibid.*, p. 136. Prokopovicz, *Russlands Volkswirtschaft*, p. 109. The figures are from the latter source.

CHAPTER 5: ALTERNATIVE SOLUTIONS

1. Trotsky, *K Sotsializmu*, pp. 38–39.

2. *Ibid.*, p. 57.

3. *Ibid.*, pp. 26–27.

4. *Dvenadtsatyi S'ezd RKP(b)*, pp. 315–316.

5. *Ibid.*, pp. 318–319.

6. *K Sotsializmu*, p. 49.

7. *Dvenadtsatyi S'ezd RKP(b)*, p. 312.

8. *K Sotsializmu*, p. 6.

9. *Ibid.*, pp. 18–19.

10. For a summary of his views, see Dobb, *Soviet Economic Development*, pp. 183–184, citing E. Preobrazhensky, "The Fundamental Law of Socialist Accumulation," in *Vestnik Komm. Akademii*, VIII, 59ff., 69–70, 78ff. A fuller discussion may be found in Erlich, "Preobrazhenski and the Economics of Soviet Industrialization," *Quarterly Journal of Economics*, no. 1 (February 1950), pp. 57–88.

11. *K Sotsializmu*, p. 20.

12. See *Erklärung der Fünfhundert;* see also *Mitteilungsblatt*, no. 3, February 1, 1927. The latter

publication later assumed the title of *Fahne des Kommunismus*. The various platforms and documents of the Left Opposition received only clandestine circulation in Russia and were published abroad.

13. Trotsky, *Real Situation*, p. 68. According to Trotsky's translator, this document was a project for a Party platform introduced into the Central Committee by thirteen opposition members in September 1927 in preparation for the Fifteenth Party Congress. This project was allegedly suppressed by Stalin.

14. *XV S'ezd VKP (b)*, p. 56.

15. The articles were gathered into a brochure, published under the title *Novyi Kurs* (Moscow, 1924).

16. Trans. by John G. Wright (New York, 1937).

17. *K Sotsializmu*, p. 57; see also pp. 59–61.

18. Trotsky, *Permanentnaya Revoliutsiya*, p. 167. This conception represents a development of his 1905 ideas that the inherent dynamics of revolution would prevent it from stopping at the so-called bourgeois-democratic stage.

19. *Mitteilungsblatt*, no. 3, February 1, 1927.

20. Cf. Trotsky, *Revolution Betrayed*.

21. The text of this document is included as an appendix in Trotsky's *Real Situation*, as well as in pamphlet form, *On the Suppressed Testament of Lenin*. Though there is some question concerning the genuineness of this document, I accept as evidence of its authenticity Stalin's reference to it in *International Press Correspondence* of November 17, 1927, quoted in the foreword of the pamphlet version.

22. Bukharin, *Put' k Sotsializmu* (4th ed.), pp. 64–66.

23. *Ibid.*, p. 68.

24. He also proposed such a policy for the Communist International. See Bukharin, *Über die Bauernfrage*.

25. Speech by Kamenev, *XIV S'ezd VKP(b)*, pp. 269–270.

26. Speech by Bukharin in *Trudy Pervogo Vsesoiuznogo Soveshchaniya Sel'sko-khozyaistvennykh Kollektivov*, p. 258.

27. Speech by Bukharin, *ibid.*, p. 261.

28. Speech by Bukharin, *ibid.*, p. 257.

29. Bukharin, *Put' k Sotsializmu*, pp. 56–57.

30. L. Fischer, *Men and Politics*, pp. 96–98. Mr. Fischer had access to some of the clandestine opposition documents and refers to various incidents about which the Party Central Committee complained at a later date; his account, therefore, may be considered highly reliable. A more detailed account, apparently based on similar materials, though they are not identified in his extensive bibliography, may be found in Souvarine, *Staline*, pp. 444–450.

31. Many of his polemical articles against Trotsky are collected in *K Voprosu o Trotskizme*.

32. September 30, 1928.

33. Resolution approved on April 23, 1929. See *VKP(b) v Rezoliutsiyakh* (6th ed.), II, 317.

34. *Pravda*, June 30, 1929.

35. Bukharin, *Ergebnisse des VI. Kongresses der KI*, pp. 23–24.

36. Clues to his probable line of reasoning may be found in his pessimistic appraisal at the Fifteenth Party Conference of the possibilities of increasing the rate of capital investment. See *XV Konferentsiya VKP(b)*, pp. 108–113.

37. *VKP(b) v Rezoliutsiyakh* (6th ed.), II, 314.

38. *Ibid.*
39. *Ibid.*, p. 316.
40. For Bukharin's version, see his *Probleme der Chinesischen Revolution.*
41. Borkenau, *Communist International,* chap. xx.
42. "Teoreticheskie vyvody tov. Bukharina," *Kommunisticheskii Internatsional,* nos. 34–35 (August 31, 1929), p. 15.
43. *Ergebnisse des VI. Kongresses der KI,* p. 39.
44. For Stalin's version, see his "The Right Deviation in the CPSU(b)," excerpt from a speech delivered at the Plenum of the Central Committee of the CPSU(b), April 1929, in *Problems of Leninism,* pp. 248–249.
45. *XIV S'ezd VKP(b),* pp. 28, 49, 958.
46. From his report to the Fourteenth Congress of the Party, in Stalin, *Sochineniya,* VII, 315.
47. Stalin, *Ob Industrializatsii Strany,* pp. 43–44.
48. Baykov, *Development of the Soviet Economic System,* p. 155. For an outline of the various plans presented, see Dobb, *Soviet Economic Development,* pp. 230–237. The discussion among the economists and other experts was public; that among those who made the real decision was secret.
49. See his speech of October 23, 1927, in Stalin, *Ob Oppozitsii,* pp. 738–739.

50. *XV S'ezd VKP(b),* pp. 55ff.
51. *Ibid.,* pp. 1207–1216.
52. *Ibid.,* pp. 1061–1062.
53. *Ibid.,* p. 56; see also p. 59.
54. A decree of the Party Central Committee, "On the Tempo of Collectivization and Measures of Government Assistance in Collective Farm Construction," January 5, 1930, is usually regarded as the opening gun in this campaign. Text in *Direktivy VKP (b) po Khozyaistvennym Voprosam,* pp. 662–664. The Communists deny that collectivization was forced upon the peasants, although this is the opinion of most observers.
55. See the remarks on Georg von Vollmar, a German Socialist who adopted strong gradualist views around the turn of the century, in Florinsky, *World Revolution,* p. 148, n. 13.
56. "The Political State of the Republic," speech of October 27, 1920, in *October Revolution,* p. 31.
57. "Foundations of Leninism," April 1924, in *Problems of Leninism,* p. 26.
58. Later he changed this opinion and modified subsequent editions of his speech. But the early version may be found quoted in an article dated January 25, 1926, "On the Problems of Leninism," *Problems of Leninism,* p. 153.
59. See "Foundations of Leninism," pp. 27–28.

CHAPTER 6: POLITICAL DYNAMICS

1. "The Anniversary of the Revolution," speech delivered at the Sixth Extraordinary Congress of Soviets, November 6, 1918, *Selected Works,* VI, 495.
2. *Sochineniya* (2d ed.), XXIII, 318, 319.

3. *Ibid.,* p. 322.
4. *Ibid.,* p. 320.
5. Chamberlin, *Russian Revolution,* I, 365.
6. "Speech on the Agrarian Question," delivered at the Extraordinary Congress of Soviets of Peas-

ants' Deputies, November 27, 1917; press report, *Selected Works*, VI, 422.

7. "The Elections to the Constituent Assembly and the Dictatorship of the Proletariat," published December 29, 1919, *Selected Works*, VI, 464.

8. Trotsky, *Stalin*, p. 343.

9. *Ibid.*

10. *Sochineniya* (2d ed.), XXII, 186.

11. Lenin, speech of December 4, 1917, *ibid.*, p. 97.

12. Lenin, "Speech Delivered at the Second All-Russian Congress of Peasants' Deputies," December 15, 1917, *Selected Works*, VI, 430, 638 (note).

13. It should be pointed out that these measures were perfectly compatible with the "democratic stage" of the Bolshevik scheme of social development and with the measures that they had advocated for this stage. See Lenin's letter to *Pravda*, "An Alliance Between the Workers and the Toiling and Exploited Peasants," December 1, 1917, *Selected Works*, VI, 425–427, and his speech of November 6, 1918, *Selected Works*, VI, 491.

14. Chamberlin, *Russian Revolution*, I, 354.

15. Trotsky, *Stalin*, p. 337.

16. Chamberlin, *Russian Revolution*, II, 54.

17. Chamberlin, *ibid.*, I, 355, describes some of the anti-Bolshevik organizations existing after the November coup, and in vol. II, pp. 49–57, recounts the gradual elimination of the competing political parties. See also Trotsky, *Stalin*, p. 339, for further details.

18. Complete text in Chamberlin, *Russian Revolution*, II, 495–496. See also his account of the revolt, pp. 440–445.

19. *VKP(b) v Rezoliutsiyakh* (6th ed.), I, 464–465.

20. *Ibid.*, II, 105.

21. *Russian Revolution*, I, 341.

22. Texts of the declarations reprinted in appendix of Lenin, *Sochineniya* (2d ed.), XXII, 551–552.

23. Chamberlin, *Russian Revolution*, I, 358–359; II, 64–66.

24. *VKP(b) v Rezoliutsiyakh* (6th ed.), I, 285.

25. *Selected Works*, VIII, 67.

26. *Russian Revolution*, II, 75. He rejects as a wild exaggeration the figure of 1,700,000 victims of the Red Terror.

27. *Ibid.*, p. 79.

28. Liberman, *Building Lenin's Russia*, p. 62.

29. *Sochineniya* (2d ed.), XXVII, 139–140.

30. *Selected Works*, VII, 113–217.

31. *Defence of Terrorism.*

32. Speech of November 27, 1918, *Sochineniya* (2d ed.), XXIII, 309.

33. From the account of Boris Sapir, a former inmate with wide experience, in Dallin and Nicolaevsky, *Forced Labor*, p. 176.

34. *Sochineniya* (2d ed.), XXVII, 296 and notes.

35. For a valuable discussion of these points see Schlesinger, *Soviet Legal Theory*, *passim* and esp. pp. 75, 76, 106, 112, 208–209, 237–238.

36. Text and commentary from Glebov, *Nash Osnovnoi Zakon*. The exclusion of nonproletarian elements from these soviets was justified on the grounds of the present struggle between the proletariat and the exploiters.

37. In section 31 of the Constitution, the All-Russian Central Executive Committee is described as the

"highest law-giving, administrative, and controlling organ of the RSFSR." As real political power passed from the Congress of Soviets to the All-Russian Central Executive Committee, then to the Council of People's Commissars, and finally to the Politburo, this section for a while corresponded to actual political practice and then too became a vestigial declaration of intentions.

38. Glebov, *Nash Osnovnoi Zakon*, p. 27.

39. Chamberlin, *Russian Revolution*, I, 342.

40. For details, see Batsell, *Soviet Rule*, pp. 55ff. This seems to me to be the best book in English for the political and administrative details of the period under consideration. It contains innumerable valuable references to original texts and many important documents in translation. Though Batsell has a keen eye for political realities, his interpretation is on occasion emotionally anti-Soviet.

41. Text in Lenin, *Sochineniya* (2d ed.), XXII, 570.

42. *Sovetskoye Gosudarstvennoye Ustroistvo*, pp. 137–138.

43. *VKP(b) v Rezoliutsiyakh* (6th ed.), I, 306.

44. Article by Sorin in Pashukanis (ed.), *15 Let Sovetskogo Stroitel'stva*, p. 144.

45. Quoted by Batsell, *Soviet Rule*, pp. 478–480, from the Stenographic Report of the Congress, pp. 55, 56.

46. Stuchka, *Ucheniye o Gosudarstve*, p. 259.

47. Adoratsky, "Diktatura," *Entsiklopediya Gosudarstva i Prava*, I, 935.

48. *S'ezdy Sovetov SSSR v Postanovleniyakh i Rezoliutsiyakh*, pp. 89–90.

49. *XIV Konferentsiya RKP(b)*, p. 38.

50. *VKP(b) v Rezoliutsiyakh* (6th ed.), II, 105.

51. *Ibid.*, pp. 104–105.

52. *XIV Konferentsiya RKP(b)*, p. 26.

53. *Sovetskoye Gosudarstvennoye Ustroistvo*, p. 141; Levin and Suvorov in Pashukanis, *15 Let Sovetskogo Stroitel'stva*, p. 433.

54. *XIV S'ezd VKP(b)*, p. 68. His figures are given on pp. 65–66.

55. Levin and Suvorov in Pashukanis, *15 Let Sovetskogo Stroitel'stva*, p. 434.

56. *Ibid.*, p. 439.

57. Resolution of the Plenum of the Party Central Committee of July 14–23, 1926, *VKP(b) v Rezoliutsiyakh* (6th ed.), II, 108.

58. Levin and Suvorov in Pashukanis, *15 Let Sovetskogo Stroitel'stva*, p. 433.

59. *Ibid.*, p. 457.

60. *Ibid.*, p. 473.

61. Rivkin, "Uchastiye Mass v Rabote Sovetov," *Sovetskoye Stroitel'stvo*, no. 12 (December 1928), p. 85.

62. *Ibid.*, p. 12.

63. Levin and Suvorov in Pashukanis, *15 Let Sovetskogo Stroitel'stva*, p. 427.

64. *Ibid.*, p. 436.

65. *Ibid.*, p. 458.

66. *Ibid.*, p. 459.

67. *Ibid.*, p. 461.

68. See, for example, S. and B. Webb, *Soviet Communism*, I, 27, where the authors quote the account and conclusions of Karl Borders, *Village Life Under the Soviets* (New York, 1927), pp. 111–115.

69. *Sovetskoye Gosudarstvennoye Ustroistvo*, p. 166.

70. Levin and Suvorov in Pashu-

kanis, *15 Let Sovetskogo Stroitel'-stva*, pp. 426, 428.

71. *Sovetskoye Gosudarstvennoye Ustroistvo*, pp. 168–169.

72. *Ibid.*, p. 166.

73. Prokopovicz, *Russlands Volkswirtschaft*, p. 7.

74. *XIV Konferentsiya RKP(b)*, p. 21.

75. *VKP(b) v Rezoliutsiyakh* (6th ed.), II, 447.

76. *Ibid.*, p. 449.

77. Quoted by Levin and Suvorov in Pashukanis, *15 Let Sovetskogo Stroitel'stva*, p. 487.

78. *Ocherednye Zadachi Partraboty*, pp. 26, 27.

79. Levin and Suvorov in Pashu-

kanis, *15 Let Sovetskogo Stroitel'-stva*, pp. 470–471.

80. *Ibid.*, p. 498.

81. *Ibid.*, pp. 425, 480.

82. *Ocherednye Zadachi Partraboty*, pp. 23, 24.

83. *Dvenadtsatyi S'ezd RKP(b)*, pp. 41–42.

84. Chamberlin, *Russia's Iron Age*, p. 153. Although somewhat opposed to the Soviet regime by this time, Chamberlin possessed the advantages of direct observation and experience developed in a decade of previous residence.

85. S. and B. Webb, *Soviet Communism*, II, 577.

CHAPTER 7: TRANSFORMATION OF RULERS

1. "Demokraticheskii Tsentralizm," *Bol'shaya Sovetskaya Entsiklopediya*, XXI, 236–238.

2. This set of statutes was adopted at the Eighth All-Russian Conference of the Party, December 2–4, 1919. Text in *VKP(b) v Rezoliutsiyakh* (6th ed.), I, 318–323.

3. Still another set was adopted in 1939; this set will be considered in Part III.

4. *VKP(b) v Rezoliutsiyakh* (6th ed.), II, 592.

5. *Protokoly TsK RSDRP*, p. 101. This volume consists of the texts of summary notes made upon the meetings of the Central Committee, August 1917–February 1918.

6. *VKP(b) v Rezoliutsiyakh* (6th ed.), I, 304.

7. See editor's interpolation in Trotsky, *Stalin*, p. 345.

8. See table in Towster, *Political Power*, pp. 159–160.

9. *Protokoly Devyatogo S'ezda RKP(b)*, pp. 14, 17.

10. For the nature of topics dis-

cussed, see *VKP(b) v Rezoliutsiyakh* (6th ed.), II, 100, 275–276.

11. *XIV S'ezd VKP(b)*, p. 508.

12. For some interesting figures see Towster, *Political Power*, p. 155, n. 51, and p. 159, n. 2.

13. *Protokoly Devyatogo S'ezda RKP(b)*, p. 17.

14. *Leninskii Sbornik* (1945 ed.), XXXV, 304.

15. The text may be found in *Izvestiya*, January 1, 1922, and in Kliuchnikov and Sabanin, *Mezhdunarodnaya Politika*, part III, section i, pp. 157–160.

16. Trotsky, *My Life*, p. 334.

17. The details of Brest-Litovsk are given from a detached point of view in Chamberlin, *Russian Revolution*, I, 397–408. They may also be found in the *Protokoly TsK RSDRP, passim*.

18. The case of Kamenev and Zinoviev, who broke with the Party leadership over the issue of the seizure of power as well as over the question of agreements with other political parties, has already been

mentioned. In both cases what particularly angered Lenin was the fact that they revealed their disagreements with the Party leadership to the outside world.

19. Trotsky, *My Life*, p. 424.

20. *Ibid.*, p. 459.

21. "Once Again on the Trade Unions, the Present Situation, and the Mistakes of Comrades Trotsky and Bukharin," January 25, 1921, *Selected Works*, VIII, 78.

22. From his report at the Tenth Congress of the Party, March 8, 1921, *Selected Works*, IX, 90.

23. *VKP(b)* v *Rezoliutsiyakh* (6th ed.), I, 364–366.

24. "Party Unity and the Anarcho-Syndicalist Deviation," report delivered at the Tenth Congress of the Communist Party, March 16, 1921, *Selected Works*, IX, 130.

25. *Protokoly TsK RSDRP*, p. 175.

26. January 26, 1921.

27. Report to the Tenth Congress of the Party, *Selected Works*, IX, 91.

28. *Protokoly VIII S'ezda RKP(b)*, pp. 165–166, 168.

29. *Protokoly Devyatogo S'ezda RKP(b)*, p. 57.

30. Editor's interpolation in Trotsky, *Stalin*, p. 350.

31. *VKP(b)* v *Rezoliutsiyakh* (6th ed.), I, 368.

32. "Kontrol'nye Kommissii," *Malaya Sovetskaya Entsiklopediya*, IV, 166.

33. Investigative units were approved at the Eleventh Congress, according to the *VKP(b)* v *Rezoliutsiyakh* (6th ed.), I, 442. The reference to the "Chekist type" may be found in the *Malaya Sovetskaya Entsiklopediya*, IV, 167.

34. *Malaya Sovetskaya Entsiklopediya*, IV, 168.

35. *VKP(b)* v *Rezoliutsiyakh* (6th ed.), II, 402.

36. *History of the CPSU(b)*, p. 268. This book was published shortly after the treason trials and attempts to show that Trotsky, Bukharin, and others were at all times traitors to the Party. As a historical source it is almost completely useless.

37. *Ibid.*, pp. 262, 269. There does not appear to be any reason why these figures should have been tampered with.

38. Kaganovich, *Ocherednye Zadachi Partraboty*, pp. 30, 38.

39. *Dvenadtsatyi S'ezd RKP(b)*, p. 133.

40. *Ibid.*, pp. 92–93.

41. See Stalin's speech at the Plenum of the Central Committee and the Central Control Commission, October 23, 1927, in his *Ob Oppozitsii*, pp. 725–727.

42. *History of the CPSU(b)*, p. 285.

43. Stalin, *Ob Industrializatsii Strany*, p. 45. At first Stalin used a figure of 6,000. Someone from the floor shouted "10,000," the figure Stalin then used. It is perhaps significant that this speech is not included in the collection *Problems of Leninism*.

44. *Pravda*, no. 292, 1920, as quoted in "'Demokraticheskogo Tsentralizma' Gruppa," *Bol'shaya Sovetskaya Entsiklopediya*, XXI, 242.

45. *Ibid.*

46. Trotsky, "The Lost Document," *Stalin School of Falsification*, pp. 114, 116. "The Lost Document" refers to a report of the Session of the Petersburg Committee of the RSDLP of November 14, 1917, which Trotsky alleges was destroyed on Stalin's orders because of the favorable references to Trotsky's

behavior that were made by Lenin on that occasion.

47. Trotsky, *Novyi Kurs*, pp. 22–23. For the circumstances under which this was written, see the editor's notes in Trotsky, *Stalin*, p. 371.

48. *Novyi Kurs*, pp. 25–26.

49. *Ibid.*, p. 3.

50. *Ibid.*, p. 82.

51. *Ibid.*

52. Text of their statement in Lenin, *Sochineniya* (2d ed.), XXII, 571.

53. Editor's note, Trotsky, *Stalin*, p. 371.

54. Bukharin, *Nieder mit der Fraktionsmacherei*, p. 7.

55. *VKP(b) v Rezoliutsiyakh* (6th ed.), I, 542.

56. *Diskussionnyi Sbornik.*

57. *Ibid.*, p. 60.

58. *Ibid.*, p. 58. The speech was prophetic, more so than Stalin or anyone at the time could realize. Both within and without the monolithic Party, discussion of such practical matters as cleaning seeds to raise agricultural production has remained free and vehement. It has perhaps become in fact even more vehement as other subjects became taboo, and as intellectual energies were more and more directed away from general philosophical and political problems into scientific and practical administrative matters under the Stalinist regime.

59. "Eshchë Raz o Sotsial-demokraticheskom Uklone v Nashei Partii" (Once Again on the Social Democratic Deviation in Our Party), speech at the Eighth Plenum of the Executive Committee of the Communist International, December 7–13, 1926, in *Ob Oppozitsii*, pp. 442–445.

60. *Russian Peasant*, p. 218.

61. *Ob Industrializatsii Strany*, pp. 52–53.

62. "Some Questions Concerning the History of Bolshevism," letter to the editors of *Proletarskaya Revoliutsiya*, in *Problems of Leninism*, p. 389.

63. "Trotskyism or Leninism?" speech of November 19, 1924, in *October Revolution*, p. 76.

CHAPTER 8: MYTHOLOGY OF STATUS

1. See Lenin, "Draft Statutes on Workers' Control," November 8–13, 1917, *Selected Works*, VI, 410–411.

2. Maynard, *Russian Peasant*, p. 109.

3. Koch, *Die Bol'sevistischen Gewerkschaften*, pp. 152, 154. This little-known work is an excellent study of the political aspects of labor-management relations, with abundant references to the Russian sources.

4. Bienstock, Schwarz, and Yugow, *Management*, p. 32.

5. *Desyat' Let Sovetskoi Diplomatii*, p. 4.

6. Maisky, *Vneshnyaya Politika RSFSR*, pp. 21–22.

7. *Desyat' Let Sovetskoi Diplomatii*, p. 6.

8. Bukharin, *Oekonomik*, pp. 78–79. The original Russian edition appeared in 1920.

9. *Ibid.*, p. 81.

10. *Ibid.*, p. 82.

11. *Selected Works*, VIII, 39.

12. *Ibid.*, IX, 369.

13. *Ibid.*, p. 364.

14. Alimov and Studenikin in Pashukanis, *15 Let Sovetskogo Stroitel'stva*, p. 255.

15. *Ibid.*, p. 256.

16. Lebed', "Biurokratiya," *Bol'-*

shaya Sovetskaya Entsiklopediya, VIII, 485, reports that in 1926 half the office workers in Soviet trading establishments were former workers or peasants, the remaining half being mostly members of the new intelligentsia, and only an insignificant portion former Tsarist officials. The Pashukanis figures are both more comprehensive and for a later period.

17. *XIV S'ezd VKP(b)*, p. 73.

18. Lebed' in *Bol'shaya Sovetskaya Entsiklopediya*, VIII, 488.

19. Koch, *Die Bol'ševistischen Gewerkschaften*, p. 159.

20. Maynard, *Russian Peasant*, p. 109.

21. Bukharin and Preobrazhensky, *Azbuka Kommunizma*, p. 180. The original edition, from which the one cited was reprinted without change, was published in 1919.

22. Amfiteatrov and Ginzburg in Pashukanis, *15 Let Sovetskogo Stroitel'stva*, p. 334.

23. Dobb, *Russian Economic Development*, pp. 106–107.

24. Tomsky, "Zadachi Professional'nykh Soiuzov" (The Tasks of the Trade Unions), Theses for the Ninth Congress of the Communist Party, *Ekonomicheskaya Zhizn'* (Economic Life), no. 54, March 10, 1920, reproduced in Lenin, *Sochinenya* (2d ed.), XXV, 544 (appendix). Also N. Osinsky, T. Sapronov, V. Maksimovsky, "Tezisy o Kollegial'nosti i Edinolichii" (Theses on Collegial Management and Individual Responsibility), *Ekonomicheskaya Zhizn'*, no. 68, March 28, 1920, in Lenin, *Sochineniya* (2d ed.), XXV, 548.

25. *Selected Works*, VIII, 92.

26. "Rech' na III Vserossiiskom s'ezde sovetov narodnogo khozyaistva 27 yanvarya 1920 g." (Speech at the Third All-Russian Congress of Soviets of the National Economy, January 27, 1920), *Sochineniya* (2d ed.), XXV, 17.

27. *VKP(b) v Rezoliutsiyakh* (6th ed.), I, 333.

28. See the valuable discussion in Towster, *Political Power*, pp. 288–293.

29. Thesis nine of Tomsky's views on the trade-union question, *Ekonomicheskaya Zhizn'*, no. 54, March 10, 1920, as reproduced in Lenin, *Sochineniya* (2d ed.), XXV, 544.

30. Koch, *Die Bol'ševistischen Gewerkschaften*, pp. 164–165.

31. *VKP(b) v Rezoliutsiyakh* (6th ed.), I, 339–340.

32. *Ibid.*, p. 420.

33. Koch, *Die Bol'ševistischen Gewerkschaften*, p. 175.

34. See the study, based on an investigation by the Central Control Commission of the Party, by Il'insky, in *Sovetskoye Stroitel'stvo*, nos. 5–6 (May–June 1928), pp. 54–55.

35. Quoted from *Pravda*, March 11, 1937, in Bienstock, Schwarz, and Yugow, *Management*, pp. 43–44.

36. *XII S'ezd RKP(b)*, pp. 131–132.

37. *Ibid.*, p. 113.

38. *Ibid.*, pp. 42–43.

39. Koch, *Die Bol'ševistischen Gewerkschaften*, pp. 211–212.

40. Speech by Yakovlev, *XIV Konferentsiya VKP(b)*, pp. 220–221.

41. *VKP(b) v Rezoliutsiyakh* (4th ed.), I, 581.

42. *Ibid.*, p. 646.

43. *XVI S'ezd VKP(b)*, p. 79.

44. Dobb, *Russian Economic Development*, pp. 133–134.

45. Alimov and Studenikin in Pashukanis, *15 Let Sovetskogo Stroitel'stva*, p. 257.

46. For a Soviet discussion of the problem of checking up on decisions in the period under discussion, see *ibid.*, pp. 279ff.

47. Liberman, *Building Lenin's Russia.*

48. White, *Growth of the Red Army*, pp. 88–89, 209, 231, 236, 329.

49. Trotsky, *My Life*, p. 479.

50. "The New Economic Policy and the Tasks of the Political Education Departments," *Selected Works*, IX, 274.

51. *XVI Konferentsiya VKP(b)*, pp. 212–216.

52. Lebed' in *Bol'shaya Sovetskaya Entsiklopediya*, VIII, 480–481.

53. "A Letter to J. V. Stalin on Drawing Up Regulations for the Workers' and Peasants' Inspection," January 24, 1920, *Selected Works*, IX, 457. The absence of workers in the administrative apparatus can hardly, however, have been the cause of the regime's difficulties, since according to Lenin's own figures, taken from a government economic report of 1920, workers comprised 61.6 per cent of the higher administrative bodies of the state. See Lenin, "Once Again on the Trade Unions, the Present Situation, and the Mistakes of Comrades Trotsky and Bukharin," January 25, 1921, *Selected Works*, IX, 60.

54. *Novyi Kurs*, pp. 16–18.

55. *VKP(b) v Rezoliutsiyakh* (4th ed.), II, 785.

56. *XVI Konferentsiya VKP(b)*, p. 231.

57. Pashukanis, *15 Let Sovetskogo Stroitel'stva*, p. 29.

58. See *XVI S'ezd VKP(b)*, pp. 67ff.; also Alimov and Studenikin in Pashukanis, *15 Let Sovetskogo Stroitel'stva*, pp. 267ff.

59. Decree of March 16, 1930, *VKP(b) v Rezoliutsiyakh* (4th ed.), II, 793–795.

60. "Rech' na zasedanii kommunisticheskoi fraktsii VTsSPS" (Speech at a Session of the Communist Fraction of the All-Union Council of Trade Unions), March 15, 1920, *Sochineniya* (2d ed.), XXV, 84.

61. Il'insky, "Predely Uprochneniya Apparata," *Sovetskoye Stroitel'stvo*, nos. 5–6 (May–June 1928), pp. 37–40.

62. "K Perevybornoi Kampanii Sovetov," *Sovetskoye Stroitel'stvo*, no. 11 (November 1928), p. 10.

63. *VKP(b) v Rezoliutsiyakh* (4th ed.), II, 631.

64. Alimov and Studenikin in Pashukanis, *15 Let Sovetskogo Stroitel'stva*, p. 285.

65. "How We Should Reorganize the Workers' and Peasants' Inspection," a proposal to the Twelfth Party Congress, *Selected Works*, IX, 384. This may be contrasted with his proposal, made three years before, to encourage illiterate peasants to participate in this work.

66. *Diskussionnyi Sbornik*, p. 53.

67. Bukharin and Preobrazhensky, *Azbuka Kommunizma*, p. 193, comment on the destruction of capitalist discipline and assert that it is impossible to think of Communist construction without new discipline, similar to that of the Red Army.

68. "How to Organize Competition," January 7–10, 1918, *Selected Works*, IX, 417.

69. "Doklad na II Vserossiiskom s'ezde professional'nykh soiuzov" (Speech at the Second All-Russian Congress of Trade Unions), January 20, 1919, *Sochineniya* (2d ed.), XXIII, 490–491.

70. "Report of the Central Committee at the Ninth Congress of the Russian Communist Party (Bolsheviks)," *Selected Works*, VIII, 93.

71. See Lenin, *Sochineniya* (2d ed.), XXIII, 591 (notes), where the resolution is quoted.

72. *VKP(b) v Rezoliutsiyakh* (4th ed.), I, 398.

73. Trotsky, "Rech' na III Vserossiiskom s'ezde professional'-nykh soiuzov" (Speech at the Third All-Russian Congress of Trade Unions), *Sochineniya*, XV, 198.

74. *Ibid.*, p. 180.

75. *Ibid.*, p. 181.

76. *Ibid.*, p. 201.

77. Gordon, *Workers Before and After Lenin*, pp. 81–82; Trotsky, *My Life*, pp. 464–466.

78. "The Trade Unions, the Present Situation and the Mistakes of Comrade Trotsky," *Selected Works*, IX, 9–10.

79. *Ibid.*, pp. 4–7.

80. *VKP(b) v Rezoliutsiyakh* (4th ed.), I, 495.

81. Lenin, *Sochineniya* (2d ed.), XXVII, 515 (notes).

82. *Ibid.*, pp. 148–149; see also p. 150.

83. *VKP(b) v Rezoliutsiyakh* (4th ed.), I, 496.

84. *XVI S'ezd VKP(b)*, p. 63.

85. *Ibid.*

86. *Ibid.*, p. 646.

87. *VKP(b) v Rezoliutsiyakh* (4th ed.), II, 662.

88. Bukharin and Preobrazhensky, *Azbuka Kommunizma*, p. 193.

89. *VKP(b) v Rezoliutsiyakh* (4th ed.), I, 329–330.

90. *Ibid.*, p. 337.

91. Bergson, *Structure of Soviet Wages*, p. 181.

92. See Tomsky's theses for the Ninth Party Congress. Text in Lenin, *Sochineniya* (2d ed.), XXV, 546, from *Ekonomicheskaya Zhizn'*, no. 54, March 10, 1920.

93. *VKP(b) v Rezoliutsiyakh* (4th ed.), I, 389.

94. "The New Economic Policy and the Tasks of the Political Education Departments," October 17, 1921, *Selected Works*, IX, 265.

95. Bergson, *Structure of Soviet Wages*, p. 10.

96. *Ibid.*, p. 227, table.

97. *Ibid.*, p. 70.

98. Rosenberg, *Geschichte des Bolschewismus*, p. 229, citing Nagler, *Die Finanzen und die Währung der Sowjet-Union* (Berlin, 1932), p. 40, and *Zeitschrift der Handelsvertretung*, Nr. 16 (1930), pp. 53ff.

99. Decree, "On the Regulation of Working Activity and Income of Communists," *Izvestiya TsK VKP(b)*, no. 13 (May 15, 1929), p. 28. There is some question about whether or not the maximum was subsequently abolished by a secret Party directive. It was never included in the Party bylaws, as implied by the Webbs. Writing in 1935, the Webbs still attributed much force to the Party version of the vow of poverty. See their *Soviet Communism*, I, 348–350.

100. Dobb, *Russian Economic Development*, pp. 326–327, 392.

101. *XV Konferentsiya VKP(b)*, p. 284.

102. *Ibid.*, p. 802.

103. Bergson, *Structure of Soviet Wages*, p. 187.

104. "The Tasks of Business Executives," speech delivered at the First All-Union Conference of Managers of Socialist Industry, February 4, 1931, in *Problems of Leninism*, p. 359.

105. "New Conditions—New Tasks in Economic Construction," speech

delivered at a conference of business executives, June 23, 1931, in *Problems of Leninism*, p. 368.

106. *Ibid.*, pp. 371–372.

107. "Communism strives for equality of incomes." Bukharin and Preobrazhensky, *Azbuka Kommunizma*, p. 196.

CHAPTER 9: REVOLUTION AND WORLD POLITICS

1. Modern analyses of the balance of power may be found in Morgenthau, *Politics Among Nations*, parts IV, VII; Lasswell, *World Politics*, chap. iii; Spykman, *America's Strategy in World Politics*, part I.

2. Perhaps the clearest statement by Lenin on projected post-revolutionary tactics may be found in "The United States of Europe Slogan," written in 1915, *Selected Works*, V, 141. See also Chapter 2 above.

3. Decree of Peace, November 8, 1917, text in Barbusse (ed.), *Soviet Union and Peace*, pp. 22–25.

4. Fainsod, *International Socialism*, p. 167.

5. *Ibid.*, pp. 168–171. On the strike, see also Borkenau, *Communist International*, pp. 91ff.

6. "War and Peace," report delivered to the Seventh Congress of the Russian Communist Party, March 7, 1918, *Selected Works*, VII, 297.

7. Quoted by Lenin in "Speech in Reply to the Debate on the Report on War and Peace," delivered at the Seventh Congress of the Party, March 8, 1918, *Selected Works*, VII, 307.

8. From a declaration to the Central Committee of the Party by a group of its members and People's Commissars, February 23, 1918, reproduced from the archives of the Central Committee in Lenin, *Sochineniya* (2d ed.), XXII, 558–559.

9. "War and Peace," p. 291.

10. *Ibid.*, p. 303.

11. "Speech in Reply to Debate on War and Peace," p. 310.

12. L. Fischer, *Soviets in World Affairs*, I, 62.

13. *Ibid.*, p. 128.

14. "Doklad o vneshnei politike na ob'edinennom zasedanii VTsIK i Moskovskogo soveta" (Speech on Foreign Policy at a Joint Session of the All-Russian Central Executive Committee and the Moscow Soviet), May 14, 1918, *Sochineniya* (2d ed.), XXIII, 4, 5.

15. *Ibid.*, pp. 13–14.

16. "Rech' o mezhdunarodnom polozhenii 8 noyabrya 1918 goda" (Speech on the International Situation of November 8, 1918), *Sochineniya* (2d ed.), XXIII, 261.

17. Trotsky, "Mezhdunarodnaya obstanovka" (The International Situation), *Kak Vooruzhalas' Revoliutsiya*, I, 372.

18. *Ibid.*, p. 370.

19. Joffe boasted publicly of these actions. See L. Fischer, *Soviets in World Affairs*, I, 75–76.

20. Borkenau, *Communist International*, p. 150. The radio message to the Munich regime may be found in *Communist International*, no. 1 (May 1, 1919), p. 90.

21. See "Letter from Comrade Béla Kun to Comrade Lenin," *Communist International*, no. 2 (June 1, 1919), p. 225; also the account in Borkenau, *Communist International*, chap. vi.

22. L. Fischer, *Soviets in World Affairs*, I, 268–270.

23. Zetkin, *Erinnerungen an Lenin*, pp. 20–21.

24. See Kliuchnikov and Sabanin, *Mezhdunarodnaya Politika*, part III, section i, p. 30.

25. Lenin's criticisms of the programmatic statements and actions of the European Communist Parties in the appendix to his famous "Left Wing Communism, An Infantile Disorder," published in May 1920, throw much light on the loose Party relations of that time and Lenin's objections thereto. See his *Selected Works*, X, 148–158.

26. *II Kongress KI*, p. 193.

27. "Left Wing Communism," *Selected Works*, X, 58.

28. *Ibid.*, p. 60. See also *II Kongress KI*, pp. 57, 63.

29. Text of the Twenty-One Conditions in *II Kongress KI*, pp. 560–567. They have since been frequently republished.

30. For a detailed analysis of Comintern policy and statements, using statistical procedures, see chapters xi and xii by Nathan Leites and I. de Sola Pool in Lasswell and others, *Language of Politics*. Chapter x, by Sergius Yakobson and Lasswell, deals with the May Day slogans of the Communist Party of the Soviet Union in a similar manner.

31. *IV Vsemirnyi Kongress KI*, pp. 37, 28.

32. *Ibid.*, pp. 31–32.

33. The clearest illustration of the actual procedure from the point of view of an insider may be found in Clara Zetkin's record of her conversations with Lenin in 1921. See her *Erinnerungen*, pp. 24ff.

34. See the account in Borkenau, *Communist International*, pp. 214–220, and that of a participant, Ruth Fischer, *Stalin and German Communism*, pp. 174–178, as well as

Protokoll des III. Kongresses der KI, esp. p. 555, where Karl Radek is accused of initiating the revolt. The other accounts attribute the initiative to Béla Kun.

35. See "The Political Activities of the Central Committee," report delivered at the Tenth Congress of the Russian Communist Party, March 8, 1921, *Selected Works*, IX, 95, 97; Zetkin, *Erinnerungen*, p. 31.

36. "Report on the World Economic Crisis and the New Tasks of the Communist International," in Trotsky, *First Five Years of the CI*, I, 254.

37. *Ibid.*, p. 223.

38. *Ibid.*, pp. 208, 206.

39. *Ibid.*, pp. 174, 176, 224, 260.

40. *Ibid.*, p. 224.

41. "The International and Internal Position of the Soviet Republic," report delivered at a meeting of the Communist fraction of the All-Russian Congress of Metal Workers' Union, March 6, 1922, *Selected Works*, IX, 306.

42. "Political Report of the Central Committee to the Eleventh Congress of the Russian Communist Party," March 27, 1922, *Selected Works*, IX, 327.

43. Rubinshtein, *Sovetskaya Rossiya i Kapitalisticheskie Gosudarstva*, p. 298. In general, this source must be used with extreme caution, since it is careful to avoid mentioning the role of any Soviet diplomats who later became identified with Trotsky. Joffe and Rakovsky are not referred to at all.

44. *Soviets in World Affairs*, I, 331.

45. *Ibid.*, pp. 320, 326, 327.

46. *Ibid.*, p. 464.

47. From the text of Chicherin's speech in Kliuchnikov and Sabanin, *Mezhdunarodnaya Politika*, part III, section i, p. 170.

48. See the account in Miliukov, *La Politique Extérieure des Soviets*, pp. 92, 101, 102, and L. Fischer, *Soviets in World Affairs*, I, 337, 339–342.

49. Quoted by L. Fischer from the *Berliner Tageblatt*, October 2, 1925, in *Soviets in World Affairs*, II, 593.

50. L. Fischer, *Soviets in World Affairs*, II, 595–596.

51. *Ibid.*, pp. 600–601.

52. *Ibid.*, pp. 608–609.

53. Miliukov, *La Politique Extérieure des Soviets*, chap. xi. On Persia, see Lenczowski, *Russia and the West in Iran*, pp. 52–59, and chap. iv; on Turkey, L. Fischer, *Soviets in World Affairs*, I, 400–410, and II, 729.

54. See Barbusse, *Soviet Union and Peace*, parts III and IV.

55. Litvinov's proposal at the Moscow Disarmament Conference, December 2, 1922, *ibid.*, p. 115.

56. *Godovoi Otchet Narodnogo Kommissariata po Inostrannym Delam za 1924 g.*, p. 5.

57. *IV Vsemirnyi Kongress KI*, pp. 195–196.

58. The evidence of Politburo control is clear. According to Stalin, the German Commission of the Comintern, including Zinoviev, Bukharin, Trotsky, Radek, and himself, reached a number of concrete decisions concerning "direct help to the German comrades in the matter of the seizure of power." See Stalin, "Po povodu 'zayavleniya' oppozitsii ot 8 avgusta 1927" (On the Occasion of the "Declaration" of the Opposition of August 8, 1927), speeches at the sessions of the Combined Plenum of the Central Committee and the Central Control Commission of the CPSU, August 5 and 9, 1927, first published with some abridgments in his *Ob Oppozitsii*,

p. 685. Further evidence may be found in the account of a former German Left Communist, who participated in some of the preliminary discussions in Moscow; see R. Fischer, *Stalin and German Communism*, pp. 321 and 325, the latter page giving a revealing telegram of instructions. Nevertheless, Moscow did not dictate the decisions, but gave interpretations and suggestions which the Germans were under considerable pressure to follow.

59. Zinoviev, *Probleme der Deutschen Revolution*, pp. 95–96.

60. Some of the details of the negotiations may be found in the papers of the chief of the Reichswehr, Hans von Seeckt. See von Rabenau, *Seeckt*, pp. 305–320.

61. See the letter by Stalin quoted in R. Fischer, *Stalin and German Communism*, p. 306.

62. See *Ob Oppozitsii*, p. 685.

63. R. Fischer, *Stalin and German Communism*, p. 321.

64. Text in *Russian Information and Review*, published by the information Department of the Russian Trade Delegation (London, October 20, 1923), p. 243.

65. Dallin, *Rise of Russia in Asia*, chap. vii.

66. Quoted by Yakhontoff, *Chinese Soviets*, p. 71. This book gives a strictly pro-Soviet account of events, but has a great deal of valuable material from inaccessible Soviet printed sources.

67. *XV S'ezd VKP(b)*, p. 601.

68. Trotsky, *Problems of the Chinese Revolution*, pp. 28, 48–59. This is a collection of contemporary opposition documents and statements by Trotsky and others.

69. *Ibid.*, p. 70. See also *Anglo-Sovetskie Otnosheniya*, sections XI and XII. China figures more promi-

nently in the Soviet communications than in the British ones.

70. The leftward steps in Comintern policy may be traced in *Kommunisticheskii Internatsional v Dokumentakh*, pp. 621–623, 671–673, 719–728. See also Stalin, "O perspektivakh revoliutsii v Kitae"

(On Perspectives of Revolution in China), speech of November 30, 1926, to the Executive Committee of the CI, *Sochineniya*, VIII, 357–374.

71. Borkenau, *Communist International*, pp. 319, 321–322, and Yakhontoff, *Chinese Soviets*, p. 77.

CHAPTER 10: THEORY OF EQUALITY

1. These contacts are mentioned in Ciliga, *Au Pays du Grand Mensonge*, p. 171. Ciliga is a former Yugoslav Communist who became disillusioned with the Soviet regime and was imprisoned for opposition activities.

2. See the remarks in *Iubileinaya Sessiya Akademii Nauk*, p. 121, where it is said: "Our epoch has received a general scientific explanation . . . and its laws have been formulated in the works of Joseph Vissarionovich Stalin."

3. "The Results of the First Five Year Plan," January 7, 1933, *Problems of Leninism*, p. 437.

4. *Problems of Leninism*, p. 518.

5. *Ibid.*, p. 571.

6. *Ibid.*, p. 569.

7. *Ibid.*, pp. 578, 579.

8. *Ibid.*, p. 579.

9. See, for instance, *Osnovy Sovetskogo Gosudarstva i Prava*, p. 199.

10. "Report to the Eighteenth Congress of the CPSU(b)," *Problems of Leninism*, p. 662.

11. "Speech at the First All-Union Conference of Stakhanovites," November 17, 1935, *Problems of Leninism*, p. 552.

12. "Report to the Seventeenth Congress of the CPSU(b)," *Problems of Leninism*, pp. 506–507.

13. *Pravda*, September 21, 1946.

14. "Report to the Seventeenth Congress of the CPSU(b)," p. 537.

15. "Speech at the First All-Union Conference of Stakhanovites," November 17, 1935, p. 553.

16. Schlesinger, *Soviet Legal Theory*, p. 208.

17. *O Nedostatkakh Partiinoi Raboty*, a pamphlet containing Stalin's speech and concluding remarks at the Plenum of the Central Committee of the CPSU(b), March 3–5, 1937, p. 33.

18. *VKP(b) v Rezoliutsiyakh* (6th ed.), II, 672–677.

19. Schlesinger, *Soviet Legal Theory*, p. 238.

20. For a valuable general study of this aspect of political ideologies and its relationship to childhood experiences, see De Grazia, *Political Community*.

21. Many examples of such materials from the Soviet press may be found in Bazili, *Rossiya pod Sovetskoi Vlast'iu*, pp. 156–166. English and French translations of this little-known and very useful work are available.

22. It is worth noting that these admissions, referring to Stalin's position in favor of mere pressure on the Provisional Government before Lenin's return in April 1917, are reprinted in a postwar collection of Stalin's writings and speeches. See Stalin, " 'Trotskizm ili Leninizm'?" speech at the Plenum of the Communist Fraction of the All-Union Council of Trade Unions,

November 19, 1924, *Sochineniya*, VI, 333. Yet no Soviet writer of history would dare to bring this incident out today in a report of these events. The official Party history, published for the first time in 1938, in whose writing Stalin is said to have participated, gives an exactly opposite account, placing Stalin and Molotov on the same side of the fence as Lenin. See the account of the April 1917 Party Conference in *History of the CPSU(b)*, p. 183. The same is done in the official biography of Stalin published toward the end of the Second World War. See the anonymous *Stalin, Kratkaya Biografiya*, p. 24.

23. *Report of Court Proceedings in the Case of the Anti-Soviet Trotskyite Centre*, p. 85.

24. *O Nedostatkakh Partiinoi Raboty*, p. 21.

25. *XIV S'ezd VKP(b)*, p. 502.

26. *History of the CPSU(b)*, p. 305. Italics in original.

27. *O Nedostatkakh Partiinoi Raboty*, p. 43.

28. Speech of March 2, 1930, *Problems of Leninism*, p. 338.

29. "Demokraticheskii Tsentralizm," *Kratkaya Sovetskaya Entsiklopediya*, p. 423.

30. *Osnovy Sovetskogo Gosudarstva i Prava*, p. 29.

31. "Samokritika" (Self-criticism), *Kratkaya Sovetskaya Entsiklopediya*, p. 1280. See also Inkeles, *Public Opinion*, chap. xiv.

32. *Osnovy Sovetskogo Gosudarstva i Prava*, p. 28.

33. Zhdanov, *Izmeneniya v Ustave VKP(b)*, pp. 31–34.

34. *O Nedostatkakh Partiinoi Raboty*, p. 42.

35. *Problems of Leninism*, pp. 550–551.

36. Mosca, *Ruling Class*, p. 139.

37. Among the more illuminating analyses are the following: Dallin, *The Real Soviet Russia*, chaps. vi-xi, anti-Soviet but with numerous shrewd hypotheses; Timasheff, *Great Retreat*, chap. x, whose conclusions are at times more precise than the data warrant; Yugow, *Russia's Economic Front*, chaps. ix and x, for data on economic aspects of the problem; Bienstock, Schwarz, and Yugow, *Management*, chap. ix, on factory managers; S. and B. Webb, *Soviet Communism*, II, 795–796, for standard pro-Soviet interpretation; Yvon, *L'U.R.S.S.*, with much firsthand cultural data, though anti-Soviet, *passim;* Trotsky, *Revolution Betrayed*, esp. pp. 102, 125, 133–134, 155–156, where naïve equalitarianism is combined with curious insight into social relationships.

38. Ashby, *Scientist in Russia*, pp. 63–64. On the state labor reserves, see also Shore, *Soviet Education*, pp. 212–214.

39. Bergson, *Structure of Soviet Wages*, pp. 109–111, 113–114. For texts of the decrees on tuition fees and labor reserves, see pp. 234–235, 236–238.

40. See Ashby, *Scientist in Russia*, pp. 71–73; Bienstock, Schwarz, and Yugow, *Management*, pp. 111–112.

41. See Chapter 8.

42. "Report to the Seventeenth Congress of the CPSU(b)," *Problems of Leninism*, pp. 521–522.

43. "Address to the Graduates from the Red Army Academies," *ibid.*, p. 543.

44. *Ibid.*, p. 544.

45. *Pravda*, September 24, 1947, carries pictorial reproductions of the various insignia.

46. *Pravda*, September 19, 1947.

47. *Problems of Leninism*, p. 521.

48. Stalin, "On the Draft Con-

stitution of the USSR," report delivered at the Extraordinary Eighth Congress of Soviets of the USSR, November 25, 1936, *Problems of Leninism*, pp. 564–565; "Sotsializm i Kommunizm" (Socialism and Communism), *Kratkaya Sovetskaya Entsiklopediya*, pp. 1367–1371.

49. *Problems of Leninism*, p. 581. The argument that the intelligentsia is not a class is not confined to Leninist or Communist doctrine.

50. Kovalev, "Intelligentsiya v sovetskom gosudarstve," *Bol'shevik*, no. 2 (January 1946), p. 33.

51. "SSSR, Naseleniye" (USSR, Population), *Kratkaya Sovetskaya Entsiklopediya*, p. 1382. The total population of the USSR, according to these figures, was 169,500,000.

52. *XVIII S'ezd VKP(b)*, p. 310. His statement includes breakdown by categories.

53. *Problems of Leninism*, p. 572.

54. See Littlepage and Bess, *Soviet Gold*, pp. 7, 8, 13.

55. "Trud" (Labor), *Kratkaya Sovetskaya Entsiklopediya*, p. 1561.

56. "Speech at the First All-Union Conference of Stakhanovites," *Problems of Leninism*, pp. 548–549.

57. Yugow, *Russia's Economic Front*, p. 228.

58. *Problems of Leninism*, p. 549.

59. One interesting, though not conclusive, attempt to measure such changes in industry is by Schwarz in Bienstock, Schwarz, and Yugow, *Management*, chap. ix. Without stating his specific sources, the author concludes (p. 122) that manual workers no longer have significant prospects of rising to industrial leadership.

60. "Narodnoye obrazovaniye" (Popular Education), *Bol'shaya Sovetskaya Entsiklopediya*, pp. 1228, 1232, 1233. "Iz zakona o pyatiletnem plane vosstanovleniya i razvitiya narodnogo khozyaistva SSSR na 1946–1950 gg." (From the Law on the Five Year Plan for the Restoration and Development of the National Economy of the USSR for 1946–1950), *Direktivy VKP (b) o Narodnom Obrazovanii*, I, 76.

61. *Au Pays du Grand Mensonge*, p. 89.

62. For numerous similar observations, see also the account of a Swiss schoolteacher who lived for many years in Siberia: Jucker, *Erlebtes Russland*.

63. Some good observations on these points may be found in Yvon, *L'U.R.S.S.*, pp. 162–163. An amusing but revealing incident in a modern Soviet play reflects the manner in which Marxist-Stalinist doctrine may justify status differences. When a girl comments on the luxury of the appointments in the apartment of a promising architect, he replies, "Excuse me, what sort of luxury is that? From each according to his abilities, and to each according to his labor" ("Uspekh" [Success], in Yal'tsev, *Malen'kie P'esy*).

CHAPTER 11: ORGANIZATION OF AUTHORITY

1. White, *Growth of the Red Army*, p. 388, citing V. Nikolsky, "Velikii razgrom" (The Great Destruction), *Chasovoi* (The Sentinel), February 1, 1939. Nikolsky's figures may be an underestimate. A comparison of the Central Committee memberships at the Seventeenth and Eighteenth Congresses shows that fifty-five of the names given in the first list do not occur in the second. However, at least three of these

persons, Kirov, Ordzhonikidze, and Lenin's widow, Krupskaya, died of causes other than the purge.

2. See sections V and VI and the Party statutes. According to *Pravda,* September 26, 1946, the Party was composed of the following units: 15 Party organizations of the Union Republics; 6 *krai* organizations; 154 *oblast'* organizations; 11 *okrug* organizations; 489 city organizations; 514 city *rayon* organizations; 4,238 village *rayon* organizations; over 250,000 primary organizations.

3. See, for instance, the account by Nazarov, secretary of Sokol'nicheskii *rayon* committee of Moscow, "*Otchetnost',*" *Partiinoye Stroitel'stvo,* no. 9 (May 1, 1938), pp. 48–49.

4. Rodionov, secretary of the Gorky *oblast'* committee of the CPSU, "Otchety i vybory," *Partiinoye Stroitel'stvo,* nos. 5–6 (March 1940), p. 50.

5. "Nekotorye itogi vyborov," *Bol'shevik,* no. 10 (May 15, 1937), p. 6.

6. Borisov, "Mestnye organy gosudarstvennoi vlasti," *Sovetskoye Gosudarstvo i Pravo,* no. 12 (1947), p. 18.

7. Mandelshtam, Rebrov, and Tumanov, *Vybory v Mestnye Sovety,* pp. 50, 51.

8. *Ibid.,* p. 51.

9. "Beseda tovarishcha Stalina s . . . gospodinom Roy Govardom," *Bol'shevik,* no. 6 (March 15, 1936), p. 8.

10. Maynard, *Russian Peasant,* p. 437.

11. Kalinin, *Stat'i i Rechi,* p. 271.

12. *Pravda,* January 7, 1948.

13. *Pravda,* December 27, 1947.

14. Embassy of the USSR, *Information Bulletin,* March 12, 1946.

15. Mandel, "Democratic Aspects of Soviet Government Today,"

American Sociological Review, June 1944, p. 262.

16. Zhdanov, "Doklad na plenume TsK VKP(b)," *Bol'shevik* nos. 5–6 (March 15, 1937), p. 12.

17. *Ibid.,* p. 14.

18. *Problems of Leninism,* p. 533.

19. *XVIII S'ezd VKP(b),* p. 30. *Partiinoye Stroitel'stvo,* no. 13 (July 1939), p. 6. The best study in English of the cadres problem is Nemzer, "The Kremlin's Professional Staff," *American Political Science Review,* March 1950, pp. 64–85, which appeared when this book was in press.

20. *Partiinoye Stroitel'stvo,* nos. 19–20 (October 1938), p. 78.

21. *Pravda,* August 23, 1946.

22. Speech by Malenkov in *XVIII S'ezd VKP(b),* p. 149.

23. Kaganovich, "O vnutripartiinoi rabote," *Bol'shevik,* no. 21 (November 15, 1934), p. 10.

24. A recent discussion of the general entrance requirements may be found in *Pravda,* September 9, 1946.

25. *SSSR Strana Sotsializma,* p. 94, for 1936 figures.

26. See the extremely careful and detailed study by White, *Growth of the Red Army,* pp. 367–368.

27. *XVIII S'ezd VKP(b),* p. 515.

28. *Ibid.*

29. Speech by Shatalin at the Eighteenth Party Conference, in *Bol'shevik,* nos. 3–4 (February 1941), p. 56.

30. *Pravda,* September 9, 1946.

31. *Zasedaniya Verkhovnogo Soveta SSSR (Pervaya Sessiya),* March 12–19, 1946, pp. 39, 30.

32. *Pravda,* January 30, 1939, and February 1, 1939, contain the theses.

33. "Obzor predlozhenii k tezisam doklada tov. Zhdanova," *Partiinoye Stroitel'stvo,* no. 5 (March 1939), p. 45.

34. *Zasedaniya Verkhovnogo Soveta SSSR (Pervaya Sessiya)*, March 12–19, 1946, pp. 82–84, 328–334.

35. *Zasedaniya Verkhovnogo Soveta SSSR (Vtoraya Sessiya)*, October 15–18, 1946, pp. 272–288.

36. *Nazi-Soviet Relations*, p. 65.

37. *Ibid.*, p. 96.

38. *Ibid.*, p. 99.

39. Byrnes, *Speaking Frankly*, p. 281.

40. Deane, *Strange Alliance*, p. 43.

41. "Reply to Collective Farm Comrades," April 3, 1930, *Problems of Leninism*, pp. 346–347.

42. Stalin, *Kratkaya Biografiya*, p. 74.

43. Kaganovich, "Ob Apparate TsK VKP(b)," *Partiinoye Stroitel'stvo*, no. 2 (February 1930), p. 10.

44. *Socialism Victorious*, p. 235.

45. Barmine, *One Who Survived*, pp. 212, 218, 228.

46. *Socialism Victorious*, pp. 239ff.

47. *Pravda*, June 25, 1943.

48. For the general operations of this system, see *Partiinoye Stroitel'stvo*, nos. 23–24 (December 1940), pp. 71–72, and no. 21 (November 1940), p. 67.

49. As quoted in *Izvestiya*, June 15, 1947.

50. Quoted in *Izvestiya*, June 7, 1946.

51. Borisov, "Mestnye organy gosudarstvennoi vlasti," *Sovetskoye Gosudarstvo i Pravo*, no. 12 (1947), p. 12.

52. "Kommunal'noye Khozyaistvo" (Communal Economy), *Kratkaya Sovetskaya Entsiklopediya*, p. 670.

53. *Pravda*, January 16, 1948, gives a good description of the functions of the local soviets.

54. Maynard, *Russian Peasant*, pp. 451–452.

55. *Izvestiya*, July 17, 1947.

56. July 17, 1947.

57. *Izvestiya*, June 15, 1947.

58. Borisov, "Mestnye organy gosudarstvennoi vlasti," *Sovetskoye Gosudarstvo i Pravo*, no. 12 (1947), pp. 10–11.

59. *Zasedaniya Verkhovnogo Soveta SSSR (Pervaya Sessiya)*, March 12–19, 1946, pp. 30, 39.

60. *Pravda*, December 27, 1947.

61. Denisov, *Sovety*, p. 41.

62. Abramov and Aleksandrov, *Partiya*, p. 101.

63. *Ibid.*, p. 100.

64. Professor Timasheff points to what seems to be the last instance of a popular check on the makers of policy, when the Seventeenth Party Congress of 1934 reduced the sights for the next Five Year Plan. See his *Great Retreat*, p. 369.

65. *Pravda*, August 9, 1946.

66. *Pravda*, July 11, 1946.

67. *Izvestiya*, June 18, 1947.

CHAPTER 12: BUREAUCRATIC STATE

1. Evtikhiev and Vlasov, *Administrativnoye Pravo*, p. 47.

2. *Ibid.*, pp. 49–50.

3. *Ibid.*, p. 52.

4. Davidov, "Naseleniye," *Bol'shaya Sovetskaya Entsiklopediya*, p. 68. American figures are based upon *Historical Statistics of the U.S.*, pp. 26, 295.

5. *Kratkaya Sovetskaya Entsiklopediya*, p. 1382. What proportion of the manual laborers is made up by forced labor or the inhabitants of the Soviet concentration

camps it is almost impossible to say. Dallin has estimated that the total is somewhere between 7,000,000 and 12,000,000, or about 16 per cent of all adult males. See Dallin and Nicolaevsky, *Forced Labor*, pp. 86–87. While the lesser of these two figures is at least a distinct possibility, it would seem that even this figure may be too large, since it represents a very heavy deduction from the free population, which is economically much more productive than the inhabitants of the labor camps.

6. Evtikhiev and Vlasov, *Administrativnoye Pravo*, p. 43.

7. *Ibid.*, p. 63.

8. *Ibid.*, p. 57.

9. "Report to the Seventeenth Congress of the CPSU(b)," *Problems of Leninism*, p. 531.

10. April 27, 1946.

11. *Izvestiya*, August 11, 1946.

12. *Ibid.*

13. *Pravda*, December 27, 1946.

14. Evtikhiev and Vlasov, *Administrativnoye Pravo*, p. 41.

15. Many details on the operations of the "instructors" can be found in Khmelevsky, "O nekotorykh voprosakh raboty apparata partiinykh komitetov," *Bol'shevik*, no. 23 (December 15, 1948), pp. 32–41. For a brief survey of Party and soviet control organs, see Towster, *Political Power*, pp. 169–175.

16. *Izvestiya*, May 24, 1946. See also issue of June 11, 1946, for the relationship in practice between the local soviets and an enterprise operated by an All-Union Ministry on their territory.

17. On this point see my article, "CPSU: 1928–1944," *American Sociological Review*, June 1944, p. 271. According to *Pravda*, December 14, 1946, "The local organs of

the Party—republic, *krai, oblast'*, city and *rayon*—are the most important link in the Party's leadership. These are the organs that direct, unite, and control the entire work in the republic, *krai, oblast'*, and *rayon*."

18. Bienstock, Schwarz, and Yugow, *Management*, pp. 9–10.

19. Identical complaints are made in the editorial columns of *Pravda*, March 4, 1948.

20. From a report of the combined *oblast'* and city conference of the Leningrad Party organization, *Pravda*, December 25, 1948.

21. *Pravda*, October 27, 1946.

22. A detailed article on the activities of the primary organization may be found in *Pravda*, January 16, 1949.

23. From my article, "CPSU: 1928–1944," pp. 274–275, where several additional cases are given.

24. Bienstock, Schwarz, and Yugow, *Management*, p. 152.

25. *Pravda*, October 27, 1946. For further data on the social organization of the *kolkhoz*, see Chapter 15.

26. *Pravda*, October 27, 1946.

27. *Ibid.*

28. Scott, *Behind the Urals*, pp. 80–81, 152, describes the situation in the great steel plant of Magnitogorsk on the basis of firsthand observation. There the plant director was "supreme commander" and relations with the local Party organization were harmonious.

29. *Pravda*, August 29, 1946.

30. Concerning this problem during the earlier period of the regime's history, see Chapter 8.

31. *Pravda*, September 12, 1946.

32. *Pravda*, August 7, 1946.

33. *Ibid.*

34. Khmelevsky, "O nekotorykh voprosakh raboty apparata par-

tiinykh komitetov," *Bol'shevik,* no. 23 (December 15, 1948), p. 36.

35. Quoted in *New York Times,* November 21, 1946.

36. *Pravda,* June 14, 1947.

37. On the efforts to introduce these qualities via the school system there is much valuable information in Raskin, *Vospitaniye Distsiplinirovannosti,* a teachers' handbook issued by the Ministry of Education of the RSFSR.

CHAPTER 13: INDUSTRIAL ORDER

1. We follow here with some variations the argument of Knight, *Economic Organization.*

2. See *Political Economy in the Soviet Union.* The translator of this work is not responsible for the misinterpretations in the American press. For a postwar restatement of the Marxist view with special attention to the limitations and necessities imposed by socialism, see Leont'ev, "K voprosam politicheskoi ekonomii sotsializma," *Planovoye Khozyaistvo,* no. 6 (1947), pp. 47–61.

3. Dobb, *Soviet Economic Development,* p. 341.

4. Sorokin, *Sotsialisticheskoye Planirovaniye,* p. 84.

5. *Ibid.;* "Gosudarstvennyi Komitet Oborony" (Government Defense Committee), *Kratkaya Sovetskaya Entsiklopediya,* p. 373.

6. Among the most useful works are Bienstock, Schwarz, and Yugow, *Management,* chap. iv; Bettelheim, *La Planification Soviétique,* chap. iii; Baykov, *Development of the Soviet Economic System,* chap. xx; and Prokopovicz, *Russlands Volkswirtschaft,* pp. 255–283.

7. Sorokin, *Sotsialisticheskoye Planirovaniye,* chap. v.

8. V. D'yachenko, "Khozraschet kak metod planovogo rukovodstva sotsialisticheskim khozyaistvom" (Business Accountability as a Method of Planned Management in a Socialist Economy), *Izvestiya,* April 4, 1946.

9. A tax applied when goods enter consumption channels. See pp. 310–311 for further details.

10. *Izvestiya,* April 4, 1946.

11. *Zasedaniya Verkhovnogo Soveta SSSR (Vtoraya Sessiya),* October 15–18, 1946, p. 10.

12. Venediktov, *Gosudarstvennaya Sotsialisticheskaya Sobstvennost',* pp. 363–364.

13. *Ibid.,* p. 368, citing the Russian edition of Marx's *Collected Works,* XVIII, 168, 239–240.

14. Venediktov, *Gosudarstvennaya Sotsialisticheskaya Sobstvennost',* pp. 370–371.

15. *Ibid.,* p. 372.

16. *Ibid.,* p. 375.

17. *Izvestiya,* April 4, 1946. More details on the degree of control exercised by the individual plant over basic resources may be found in Venediktov, *Gosudarstvennaya Sotsialisticheskaya Sobstvennost',* p. 378.

18. Bienstock, Schwarz, and Yugow, *Management,* pp. 58–59.

19. *Izvestiya,* April 4, 1946.

20. Vladimirov, "Za rentabel'nuyu rabotu predpriyatii," *Voprosy Ekonomiki,* no. 8 (1948), p. 27.

21. *Izvestiya,* April 4, 1946.

22. Dobb, *Soviet Economic Development,* p. 354.

23. Vladimirov, "Za rentabel'nuyu rabotu predpriyatii," p. 30.

24. Bogolepov, *Sovetskaya Finansovaya Sistema,* p. 13.

25. *Sobraniye Postanovlenii,* no. 14 (December 27, 1946), section

272. The decree itself is dated December 5, 1946.

26. Bienstock, Schwarz, and Yugow, *Management*, pp. 94–95.

27. S. and B. Webb, *Soviet Communism*, II, 740.

28. "Sorevnovaniye Sotsialisticheskoye" (Socialist Competition), *Kratkaya Sovetskaya Entsiklopediya*, pp. 1365–1366.

29. For complaints about this in the Soviet press, see Gordon, *Workers Before and After Lenin*, pp. 406–408.

30. *Zasedaniya Verkhovnogo Soveta SSSR (Vtoraya Sessiya)*, October 15–18, 1946, p. 32.

31. "Peredovaya—rezhim ekonomii," *Bol'shevik*, nos. 23–24 (December 1946), p. 7. Since *Bol'shevik* is the organ of the Party Central Committee, its unsigned editorial introductions carry special significance.

32. Bienstock, Schwarz, and Yugow, *Management*, conclude (p. 75) that "the difference between Soviet labor efficiency and that of England and Germany is diminishing, although Soviet is still very far from American efficiency." While it is not possible with the available data to separate managerial from labor efficiency, it is likely that the conclusion applies to the former as well as to the latter. As partial evidence for their conclusion, the writers point to the fact that the annual output of coal in tons per basic worker in 1929 and 1937 was respectively 179 and 370 in the USSR, 323 and 435 in Germany, 844 and 730 in the United States. Likewise, the annual output of pig iron per blast furnace worker in 1929 and 1937 was respectively 240 and 756 tons in Russia, and 1729 and 1620 tons in the United States. Improved managerial techniques no doubt played a role in the increase in Soviet output per worker.

33. Quoted by L. Valler, "Sberezheniya naseleniya v SSSR" (The Savings of the Population in the USSR), *Finansy SSSR*, p. 301.

34. For a study of the consequences in terms of physical output and a comparison of rates of industrial growth in Tsarist times, see Gerschenkron, "Rate of Industrial Growth," *Journal of Economic History*, supplement VII (1947), pp. 144–174.

35. K. Plotnikov, "Gosudarstvennyi biudzhet Sovetskogo Soiuza" (The Government Budget of the Soviet Union), *Finansy SSSR*, p. 140.

36. Dobb, *Soviet Economic Development*, p. 381. According to a *New York Times* report of March 11, 1949, the proposed 1949 budget allotted 79 billion rubles for capital investment, in addition to which 25 billion rubles would be derived from the enterprises' own funds.

37. *Zasedaniya Verkhovnogo Soveta SSSR (Pervaya Sessiya)*, March 12–19, 1946, p. 58.

38. Bienstock, Schwarz, and Yugow, *Management*, p. 85.

39. *Zasedaniya Verkhovnogo Soveta SSSR (Vtoraya Sessiya)*, October 15–18, 1946, p. 10.

40. G. Mar'yakhin, "Nalogovaya sistema sovetskogo gosudarstva" (Tax System of the Soviet Government), *Finansy SSSR*, pp. 273, 288.

41. Yugow, *Russia's Economic Front*, pp. 84, 85, reports that nearly all of the manufactured articles were distributed through the government stores and through the coöperatives, which were in effect controlled by the government through the Party. More than 70 per cent of the agricultural products went through the same system. City trade was in the hands of the government stores;

rural trade was assigned to the consumer coöperatives.

42. Dobb, *Soviet Economic Development*, p. 373. See also Voznesensky, *Voennaya Ekonomika SSSR*, p. 122.

43. Dobb, *Soviet Economic Development*, pp. 351–352.

44. Voznesensky, *Voennaya Ekonomika SSSR*, p. 129. These stores were also abolished on December 16, 1947.

45. *Ibid.*, p. 124.

46. Yugow, *Russia's Economic Front*, p. 89.

47. S. and B. Webb, *Soviet Communism*, I, 324.

48. Yugow, *Russia's Economic Front*, pp. 90–91.

49. "Report on the Work of the Central Committee to the Seventeenth Congress of the CPSU," January 28, 1934, *Problems of Leninism*, p. 512.

50. *Ibid.*, p. 513.

51. The effect of the abolition of these stores is not known.

52. *Pravda*, November 11, 1946; *Izvestiya*, November 12, 1946.

53. *Pravda*, March 1, 1948.

CHAPTER 14: CLASS STRUGGLE

1. N. Ritikov, "Sovetskie profsoiuzy" (Soviet Trade Unions), *Bol'shaya Sovetskaya Entsiklopediya*, pp. 1753–1754.

2. *Sovetskoye Trudovoye Pravo*, pp. 121, 310. This volume was approved by the *Sovnarkom* (Council of People's Commissars) committee on higher education for use as a textbook. Similar statements occur from time to time in the Soviet press.

3. *Ibid.*, p. 126. Moskalenko, "Pravovye voprosy kollektivnogo dogovora," *Professional'nye Soiuzy*, no. 8 (August 1947), p. 16.

4. *Sovetskoye Trudovoye Pravo*, pp. 212–213.

5. *Ibid.*, p. 217.

6. *Ibid.*, p. 212.

7. On this point and on earlier practices in the setting of wage rates, see Dobb, *Soviet Economic Development*, pp. 409–410.

8. V. V. Kuznetsov, "O zakliuchenii kollektivnykh dogovorov na 1947 god," *Professional'nye Soiuzy*, no. 2 (February 1947), p. 6.

9. Il'in, "O normirovanii truda i organizatsii zarabotnoi platy," *Professional'nye Soiuzy*, no. 1 (January 1947), pp. 14–18.

10. Amelin, "Posle otchetno-vybornykh sobranii," *Professional'nye Soiuzy*, no. 6 (June 1947), p. 20.

11. Moskalenko, "Rol' profsoiuzov," *Professional'nye Soiuzy*, no. 4 (April 1947), p. 21.

12. *Sovetskoye Trudovoye Pravo*, p. 203.

13. A Tass announcement in *Trud*, February 19, 1947, reported that the Council of Ministers of the USSR "approved, according to the example of previous years, the suggestions of the All-Union Central Council of Trade Unions [AUCCTU] concerning the conclusion in 1947 of collective agreements between the administration of enterprises and the factory committees of the unions."

14. Decree of the Presidium of the AUCCTU, *Trud*, March 16, 1947.

15. A recent decree of the AUCCTU, not differing in any essentials from the first one, which sets out the types of questions to be included in the agreement, may be found in *Trud*, January 26, 1949.

16. Al. Kuznetsov, "Kollektivnyi dogovor v deistvii," *Professional'nye Soiuzy*, no. 12 (December 1947), p. 12.

17. V. V. Kuznetsov, *Professionl'nye Soiuzy*, no. 2 (February 1947), pp. 8–9.

18. *Ibid.*, pp. 3–4.

19. Amitin, "Uluchshit' okhranu truda," *Professional'nye Soiuzy*, no. 6 (June 1947), p. 17.

20. Gaisenok, "Voprosy okhrany truda," *Professional'nye Soiuzy*, no. 2 (February 1947), pp. 14–16. See also *Trud*, January 16, 1949.

21. V. V. Kuznetsov, *Professional'nye Soiuzy*, no. 2 (February 1947), p. 7.

22. See *Trud*, May 21, 1946.

23. *Trud*, April 1, 1947.

24. *Sovetskoye Trudovoye Pravo*, pp. 264–265, 268.

25. *Ibid.*, pp. 268, 269.

26. *Ibid.*, p. 270.

27. *Ibid.*, p. 274.

28. *Ibid.*, pp. 313–319. See also the discussion by Harold Berman in *The Challenge of Soviet Law*, part III (in press; Harvard University Press).

29. Kachnova, "O nekotorykh voprosakh rukovodstva fabkomami," *Professional'nye Soiuzy*, nos. 9–10 (September–October 1946), p. 38.

30. See Dallin and Nicolaevsky, *Forced Labor*, pp. 4–6.

31. *Sovetskoye Trudovoye Pravo*, pp. 296–297.

32. *Ibid.*, p. 277.

33. On December 26, 1941, voluntary absence from work in a war industry was classed with desertion. See *ibid.*, p. 278.

34. *Ibid.*, p. 279.

35. *Ibid.*, pp. 280–281.

36. *Ibid.*, p. 297.

37. *Ibid.*, p. 300.

38. *Ibid.*, p. 301.

39. *Ibid.*, p. 303.

40. *Ibid.*, p. 326.

41. *Die Bol'ševistischen Gewerkschaften*, chaps. ii–v.

42. A good brief outline of these events, though with a strong anti-Stalinist bias, may be found in Gordon, *Workers Before and After Lenin*, chap. xv.

43. From the resolutions of the Sixteenth Plenum of the AUCCTU, in *Professional'nye Soiuzy*, no. 5 (May 1947), p. 13. Similar complaints are scattered through the 1949 issues of the AUCCTU daily, *Trud*, prior to the Tenth Trade Union Congress.

44. *Professional'nye Soiuzy*, no. 8 (August 1947), p. 4.

45. Amelin, in *Professional'nye Soiuzy*, no. 6 (June 1947), p. 19.

46. Editorial in *Professional'nye Soiuzy*, no. 8 (August 1947), p. 4.

47. That is, the case of the Uzbek teachers' union, mentioned by Dneprovoi, "Pochemu s'ezd priznal rabotu TsK profsoiuza neudovletvoritel'noi," *Professional'nye Soiuzy*, no. 9 (September 1947), p. 13; and the notes in "Na s'ezdakh profsoiuzov," *Professional'nye Soiuzy*, no. 6 (June 1947), p. 46, where, despite some strong criticism, the work of the central committees of the three unions was declared satisfactory.

48. *Professional'nye Soiuzy*, no. 9 (September 1947), p. 7.

49. Dneprovoi, *ibid.*, p. 16.

50. *Trud*, January 8, 1949.

51. Amelin, in *Professional'nye Soiuzy*, no. 6 (June 1947), p. 19. A very similar account is in *Trud*, January 11, 1949.

52. "Na s'ezdakh profsoiuzov," p. 46.

53. For some details on how this works out in actual practice, see Pavlik, "Uroki vypolneniya odnogo koldogovora," *Professional'nye*

Soiuzy, no. 12 (December 1947), pp. 22, 23.

54. Kachnova, in *Professional'nye Soiuzy,* nos. 9–10 (September–October 1946), p. 36. Strictly speaking, the right of the *oblast'* committee appears to be limited to putting the question of calling for

new elections before the union membership.

55. *Pravda,* October 15, 1948.
56. *Pravda,* October 16, 1948.
57. *Pravda,* October 17, 1948.
58. *Pravda,* October 15–17, 1948, and January 10, 1949.

CHAPTER 15: TRANSFORMATION OF PEASANTRY

1. See Chapter 5 and my study, "The Influence of Ideas on Policies," *American Political Science Review,* August, 1947, pp. 733–743.

2. See *Primernyi Ustav Sel'skokhozyaistvennoi Arteli.* This was originally published in *Izvestiya,* February 18, 1935, and also in the *Sobraniye Zakonov SSSR,* no. 11 (1935), paragraph 82.

3. Yugow, *Russia's Economic Front,* p. 46.

4. Baykov, *Development of the Soviet Economic System,* p. 311.

5. Mikolenko and Nikitin, *Kolkhoznoye Pravo,* p. 139.

6. *Ibid.,* p. 140.

7. *Ibid.,* p. 139.

8. Bienstock, Schwarz, and Yugow, *Management,* pp. 179–181.

9. Quoted by Mikolenko and Nikitin, *Kolkhoznoye Pravo,* p. 139.

10. *Ibid.,* pp. 140–141, 139–140.

11. Text in the major Soviet newspapers, September 20, 1946.

12. *Pravda,* March 7, 1947.

13. *Pravda,* March 13, 1947. Altogether there were, in 1947, 139,434 primary Party organizations in rural areas.

14. Mikolenko and Nikitin, *Kolkhoznoye Pravo,* p. 61.

15. *Ibid.,* p. 64.

16. *Ibid.,* p. 62.

17. *Pravda,* June 2, 1947.

18. Mikolenko and Nikitin, *Kolkhoznoye Pravo,* pp. 37–39.

19. *Pravda,* May 13, 1947; August 17, 1947.

20. Mikolenko and Nikitin, *Kolkhoznoye Pravo,* p. 159.

21. A description of their tasks may be found in *Pravda,* July 4, 1947.

22. *Primernyi Ustav,* paragraph 15; Mikolenko and Nikitin, *Kolkhoznoye Pravo,* p. 119.

23. Mikolenko and Nikitin, *Kolkhoznoye Pravo,* p. 145.

24. See *Izvestiya,* August 21, 1946; *Pravda,* February 3, 1947.

25. *Izvestiya,* August 21, 1946; *Pravda,* February 3, 1947.

26. January 13, 1948.

27. *Izvestiya,* January 25, 1947.

28. Mikolenko and Nikitin, *Kolkhoznoye Pravo,* p. 119.

29. *Ibid.,* p. 125.

30. *Pravda,* June 21, 1947.

31. *Pravda,* March 7, 1947.

32. Mikolenko and Nikitin, *Kolkhoznoye Pravo,* p. 114.

33. *Ibid.,* p. 115.

34. The date of the decree is mentioned in *Izvestiya,* January 6, 1949, and some of the provisions described. Curiously enough, the decree is not published in the official gazette of the Council of Ministers, *Sobraniye Postanovlenii,* nor is it available in the press. The provisions mentioned are taken from *Pravda,* February 25, 1948. A few additional details, including the title

of the decree, may be found in *Pravda*, December 16, 1948. Secret statutes are discussed from a general point of view in Gsovski, *Soviet Civil Law*, I, 228–229. There is abundant evidence of their existence.

35. Bienstock, Schwarz, and Yugow, *Management*, p. 155.

36. Decree in *Pravda*, February 28, 1947; Stalin's role is mentioned by Andreev in *Pravda*, March 7, 1947.

37. Bienstock, Schwarz, and Yugow, *Management*, p. 167.

38. Baykov, *Development of the Soviet Economic System*, p. 311.

39. Yugow, *Russia's Economic Front*, p. 67.

40. Mikolenko and Nikitin, *Kolkhoznoye Pravo*, p. 26.

41. Text in *VKP (b) v Rezoliutsiyakh* (6th ed.), II, 769–773. Reprinted also in *Pravda*, September 20, 1946.

42. Baykov, *Development of the Soviet Economic System*, p. 314.

43. *Ibid.*, p. 327. The sown area of the collective farms was 117,200,-000 hectares.

44. Full texts in the Soviet press on the days following issuance of the decrees.

45. Yugow, *Russia's Economic Front*, p. 71.

46. Hubbard, *Economics of Soviet Agriculture*, p. 201.

47. *Ibid.*, pp. 218–219.

48. Mikolenko and Nikitin, *Kolkhoznoye Pravo*, pp. 112–113; Bienstock, Schwarz, and Yugow, *Management*, p. 150.

49. Karavaev, "O dal'neishem ukreplenii sel'skokhozyaistvennoi arteli," *Bol'shevik*, no. 8 (April 30, 1948), p. 39.

50. Voznesensky, *Voennaya Ekonomika SSSR*, p. 129. The author attributes the drop in prices between 1943 and 1945 to the opening of the commercial stores which sold food products at higher than rationed prices to a selected clientele.

51. G. Mar'yakhin, "Nalogovaya sistema sovetskogo gosudarstva" (The Taxation System of the Soviet Government), *Finansy SSSR*, p. 290. No figures are given on the actual tax rates or on the numbers of persons at different income levels.

52. Texts of the decrees may be found in the Soviet press with the exception of that of November 9, 1946. Except for a brief mention of personnel changes, this decree was also omitted from the official gazette of the Council of Ministers. Extensive explanation of its provisions may be found in *Pravda*, November 11, 1946, and *Izvestiya*, November 12, 1946.

53. On the factory canteens, see Voznesensky, *Voennaya Ekonomika SSSR*, p. 124. Reference has already been made to the fact that before the war they accounted for only 4 per cent of the retail trade in the USSR, while in 1942 they accounted for 28 per cent thereof. In part, this rise was due to a sharp curtailment in retail trade.

54. *Izvestiya*, October 5, 1946.

55. See, for example, *Pravda*, September 23, 1946.

56. Typical complaints about these clique relationships may be found in *Pravda*, July 4, August 24, August 29, and September 1, 1946. See also Chapter 12.

57. *Pravda*, March 7, 1947.

58. *Ibid.*

59. While Andreev's report indicates that by January 1, 1947, there were 20,000 fewer *kolkhozy* in the expanded territories of the USSR than there were in 1938

(222,000 in 1947 and 242,000 in 1938), this decrease may have been due to reëstablishing larger collective-farm units in areas occupied by the Germans, as well as elsewhere in the USSR.

60. See Chapter 2.

CHAPTER 16: PATTERN OF FOREIGN POLICY

1. Sherwood, *Roosevelt and Hopkins*, p. 565. The author reproduces verbatim the account of one of the interpreters.

2. The same is of course true of any viewpoint, including those which claim the highest degree of scientific objectivity. This does not mean that some viewpoints do not involve greater distortions than others.

3. For Bukharin's position, see Chapter 5. In his report to the Sixteenth Party Congress, Molotov referred briefly to the ejection of such elements. See *XVI S'ezd VKP(b)*, pp. 423, 425.

4. Stalin, "The Right Deviation," excerpt from a speech delivered at a plenum of the Central Committee of the CPSU(b), April, 1929, *Problems of Leninism*, p. 246.

5. *XVI S'ezd VKP(b)*, pp. 22–23; see also Molotov's speech, p. 419.

6. Quoted from *Die Internationale*, XIV, 499, in Flechtheim, *KPD*, p. 166.

7. Beloff, *Foreign Policy*, I, 62–69.

8. *Ibid.*, p. 68.

9. Speech of December 29, 1933, in Litvinov, *Vneshnyaya Politika SSSR*, p. 69.

10. *Ibid.*, p. 70.

11. "Report to the Seventeenth Congress of the CPSU(b)," January 26, 1934, *Problems of Leninism*, p. 484.

12. Detailed accounts of the events in the Far East, with numerous quotations from the Soviet sources, may be found in Beloff, *Foreign Policy*, I, chap. vi, which does its best to remain objective. An interpretation hostile to the Soviets may be found in Dallin, *Soviet Russia and the Far East*, chap. i, and a pro-Soviet one in H. L. Moore, *Soviet Far Eastern Policy*, chap. ii.

13. Walter, *Parti Communiste Français*, p. 245.

14. *Ibid.*, pp. 276, 281.

15. *Ibid.*, pp. 268, 278.

16. Molotov, *Otchetnyi Doklad o Rabote Pravitel'stva VII S'ezdu Sovetov SSSR*, pp. 54, 50. Italy's dispute with Abyssinia had already come before the League at this time. Later the Soviets opposed the Italians on this issue.

17. "Resolution on the Report of Comrade Dimitrov, Adopted on August 20, 1935," *Report of the Seventh World Congress of the CI*, p. 7. The pages are not consecutive in this volume, and the table of contents lists the sequence of the separate sections incorrectly.

18. Walter, *Parti Communiste Français*, p. 287; Borkenau, *Communist International*, p. 383.

19. Dallin, *Soviet Russia and the Far East*, pp. 131–132, 138; H. L. Moore, *Soviet Far Eastern Policy*, pp. 77–79.

20. "Resolution on the Report of Comrade Pieck, Adopted on August 1, 1935," *Report of the Seventh World Congress of the CI*, p. 39.

21. Speech of August 20, 1935, in Dimitrov, *V Borbe za Edinyi Front*, pp. 99, 100.

22. Speech at the Seventh Congress of the Communist International, *Report,* p. 11.

23. Taracouzio, *War and Peace,* p. 193.

24. *Ibid.,* pp. 187–208, and for the period down to 1936, Beloff, *Foreign Policy,* I, chap. xiii.

25. Beloff, *Foreign Policy,* I, pp. 152–153.

26. *Ibid.,* p. 156. The statement was made on the occasion of Laval's visit to Moscow and antedates the turn in the Communist line made at the Seventh World Congress.

27. *Ibid.,* p. 155.

28. Stalin, *O Nedostatkakh Partiinoi Raboty,* p. 9.

29. A well-documented outline of the major events and the positions taken by the powers concerned may be found in Beloff, *Foreign Policy,* II, 120–166.

30. "Report to the Eighteenth Congress of the CPSU(b)," March 10, 1939, *Problems of Leninism,* pp. 624–626.

31. The stenographic report of Manuilsky's speech to the Congress is printed in many places. The above is taken from *Sputnik Agitatora,* no. 6 (March 1939), p. 5.

32. The proposal of the Franco-British-Soviet Pact was in reply to British inquiries concerning Soviet guarantees to Rumania and Poland. It is mentioned in Potemkin (ed.), *Istoriya Diplomatii,* III, 674. Potemkin was a Deputy Commissar of Foreign Affairs and for many years played an important role in Soviet diplomacy. The German version of the Soviet ambassador's conversation may be found in *Nazi-Soviet Relations,* pp. 1–2. Though the documents are of German origin, it is safe to assume that they represent Soviet statements with considerable accuracy, since foreign offices are meticulous in their summaries of conversations, interviews, and the like, when the documents are for the use of their own officials and not for public consumption.

33. *Nazi-Soviet Relations,* p. 35.

34. *Ibid.,* p. 41.

35. *Ibid.,* p. 74.

36. These territorial adjustments were included in the secret protocol added to the pact, and may be found in *Nazi-Soviet Relations,* p. 78.

37. *Ibid.,* pp. 127–128, 154. Dallin's book, *Foreign Policy,* is a very useful study of this period. Many of Dallin's hypotheses have been verified by the subsequent publication of the German documents.

38. *Nazi-Soviet Relations,* pp. 180–181.

39. *Ibid.,* p. 233.

40. *Ibid.,* pp. 258–259.

41. *Ibid.,* pp. 260–261. There are strong indications that Hitler had reached the decision to attack the USSR several months earlier. Molotov's statements in Berlin may have merely confirmed the decision. See Beloff, *Foreign Policy,* II, 339.

42. *Nazi-Soviet Relations,* p. 330.

43. Sherwood, *Roosevelt and Hopkins,* p. 335.

44. Dallin, *Foreign Policy,* p. 345.

45. See Deutscher, *Stalin,* p. 475. At the end of May 1942, Molotov in his visit to Roosevelt asked directly for a Western front, according to Sherwood, *Roosevelt and Hopkins,* pp. 387–388, 563.

46. Deane, *Strange Alliance,* pp. 40–45. General Deane was head of the United States Military Mission in Moscow from 1943 to 1945.

47. Sherwood, *Roosevelt and Hopkins,* p. 401. See also Deane, *Strange Alliance,* p. 88.

48. Mikolajczyk, *Rape of Poland,* p. 23.

49. *Ibid.,* p. 27.

50. The principal Soviet statements may be found in the collection of documents, *Vneshnyaya Politika,* I, 348–359.

51. Deutscher, *Stalin,* pp. 515–516, citing the accounts of Cordell Hull and James F. Byrnes.

52. The texts of the Yalta, Potsdam, and Teheran agreements were published in the *New York Times,* March 25, 1947. See also the account of former Secretary of State Byrnes, *Speaking Frankly,* chap. ii.

53. Sherwood, *Roosevelt and Hopkins,* pp. 787, 798.

54. See Stalin's speech of November 6, 1944, in Stalin, *O Velikoi Otechestvennoi Voine,* pp. 153–154; Byrnes, *Speaking Frankly,* pp. 36–37.

55. See Molotov's remarks at San Francisco on April 26, 1945, in Molotov, *Voprosy Vneshnei Politiki,* pp. 11–12.

56. See, for example, Morgenthau, *Politics Among Nations,* pp. 285–286.

57. Curtiss and Inkeles, "Marxism in the USSR," *Political Science Quarterly,* September 1946, pp. 354–356.

58. *Pravda,* February 10, 1946.

59. Voznesensky, *Voennaya Ekonomika SSSR,* pp. 189–190.

60. As in Zhdanov's speech on the formation of the Communist Information Bureau, *Pravda,* October 22, 1947. Stalin made similar statements in his reply of May 17, 1948, to an open letter from Henry Wallace. Text in *Bol'shevik,* no. 10 (May 30, 1948), pp. 1–2.

61. Khrushchev, "Bol'sheviki Ukrainy," *Bol'shevik,* no. 3 (February 15, 1949), p. 38.

62. An account of the major events may be found in Gyorgy, *Governments of Danubian Europe.*

63. Revai, "On the Character of Our People's Democracy," as translated in *Foreign Affairs,* October 1949, p. 147.

64. See Warriner, "Economic Changes in Eastern Europe," *International Affairs,* no. 2 (April 1949), pp. 157–167.

65. A detailed study of Soviet policy in Germany may be found in Neumann, "Soviet Policy in Germany," *Annals of the American Academy of Political and Social Science,* May 1949, pp. 165–179.

66. Byrnes, *Speaking Frankly,* p. 26; Stettinius, *Roosevelt and the Russians,* pp. 130–131, 263–266, 272.

67. *New York Times,* January 19, 1947.

68. Molotov, *Voprosy Vneshnei Politiki,* pp. 370–371.

69. *Ibid.,* pp. 60–66.

70. Text in *New York Times,* September 7, 1946. In *Speaking Frankly* (p. 192), Byrnes explains his actions by saying that the Stuttgart speech "made it impossible for the Soviets to continue talking one way to the Poles and another way to the Germans. Forced to choose they announced they would support Poland's claim to the territory." Subsequently, according to Byrnes, the German support of the Communist cause began melting away.

71. According to Soviet sources, the removal of capital equipment and the payment of reparations from current production largely ceased in 1947. The level of industrial production in the Soviet zone had reached 52 per cent of the 1938 figure, it was claimed, while that of the Anglo-American zone was only 35 per cent of the 1938 amount. Cartels and syndicates had allegedly been broken up and workers placed in control of more than 38 per cent of the plants. The large estates were dis-

tributed among the peasantry, and economic planning was introduced in industry. See Gertsovich, "Vosstanovleniye mirnoi ekonomiki," *Voprosy Ekonomiki*, no. 1 (1948), pp. 93–101. This somewhat rosy picture should probably be taken as an indication of Soviet goals rather than of achievements. No doubt the situation deteriorated after the imposition of the blockade in the summer of 1948. Nevertheless, the assumption of widespread economic distress in the Soviet zone, frequently stated as a generally known fact in the American press, lacks detailed substantiation. Even Neumann ("Soviet Policy in Germany," p. 178), concedes that the deterioration cannot be measured, and does not present very strong evidence on this matter.

72. See Byrnes, *Speaking Frankly*, pp. 93, 216.

73. *U.S. Relations with China*, p. 72.

74. Byrnes, *Speaking Frankly*, p. 228.

75. Text in *Pravda*, April 7, 1947.

76. See Atkinson, "Sino-Soviet Treaty," *International Affairs*, no. 3 (July 1947), pp. 360–361, 364.

77. On August 27, 1945, Stalin told Harriman that the Red Army had not yet come across Chinese Communist guerrilla units. By March 1946 the Chinese guerrillas were moving into Manchuria in large numbers. On these events, see *U.S. Relations with China*, pp. 119, 145–162; Dallin, *Soviet Russia and the Far East*, pp. 251–255.

78. Atkinson, *International Affairs*, no. 3 (July 1947), p. 362.

79. *U.S. Relations with China*, pp. 232–233.

80. *New York Times*, May 30, 1949.

81. Perevertailo, "People's Republic Established in China," *New Times*, no. 41 (October 5, 1949), p. 5.

82. For varying interpretations on future developments in China, see Fairbank, *U.S. and China*, and Leites and Rowe, "Choice in China," *World Politics*, April 1949, pp. 277–307.

CHAPTER 17: IDEOLOGY AND FOREIGN POLICY

1. Speech of May 1, 1942, in Stalin, *O Velikoi Otechestvennoi Voine*, p. 48.

2. Speech of November 6, 1941, *ibid.*, pp. 25, 31.

3. "The Right Deviation," *Problems of Leninism*, p. 252.

4. "Report to the Seventeenth Congress," *Problems of Leninism*, pp. 476, 478.

5. *Ibid.*, p. 477.

6. *XVIII S'ezd VKP(b)*, p. 273.

7. White, *Growth of the Red Army*, p. 414.

8. *Soviet-Yugoslav Dispute*, p. 51.

9. *Foreign Affairs*, January 1949, pp. 175–214.

10. Speech of November 6, 1941, *O Velikoi Otechestvennoi Voine*, p. 14; Sherwood, *Roosevelt and Hopkins*, p. 782. In August 1942 Stalin told Churchill, according to Sherwood (*Roosevelt and Hopkins*, p. 617), that German homes as well as factories should be bombed. Churchill replied that though civilian morale constituted a military objective, hits on workers' homes were merely by-products of misses on factories.

11. See the report by the Yugo-

slav, Edward Kardelj, in *Pravda,*
December 5, 1947. Kardelj later became a supporter of Tito.
12. Snow, *People on Our Side,*
p. 241.
13. *Ibid.*
14. Kravchenko, *I Chose Freedom,* p. 424.
15. There is at least one report
of disbelief in the official doctrine
from more recent times. According
to the *New York Times,* March 28,
1948, James Carey, the anti-Communist secretary of the Congress of
Industrial Organizations, asked Va-
silii Kuznetsov, the Soviet trade-
union leader, whether or not the
latter believed that the European
Recovery Program was the creation
of agents of reaction and supporters
of Wall Street. Kuznetsov's reply
was—in Carey's words—that "he
didn't believe the stuff and knew
those charges to be untrue."
16. Sherwood, *Roosevelt and
Hopkins,* pp. 342–343.
17. *Nazi-Soviet Relations,* p. 95.
18. *Ibid.,* p. 99.
19. *Ibid.,* p. 75.
20. *Stalin,* pp. 534, 554.

CHAPTER 18: CONCLUSIONS

1. There seems to be only a very
limited awareness among the Soviets
that factors other than wage scales
may be extremely important in their
effect on output. Nor is there any
systematic study of these factors,
such as that which has engaged the
attention of sociologists and anthropologists in the United States for
some twenty years.
2. Similar ideas may be found in
the writings of Mosca, Sorel, and
Pareto. De Grazia, *Political Community,* gives the most detailed explanation, couched in terms of the
life cycle of the individual, for the
development of belief systems
which, to be socially effective, must
be above rational criticism.
3. A modern industrial democracy is about as close as one can
expect to come to such a social
order. In such a society there is at
least a strong probability that for
each question the society faces
there is some person or group of
persons whose task it is to think
about this problem in a manner
freed of the shackles of traditional
answers provided by ideology and
culture. But it is quite obvious that
even a democracy, while it may be
willing to permit untraditional thinking about political and social matters, is reluctant to permit its practi-
tioners to practice.
4. Kroeber, *Configurations of
Culture Growth,* pp. 91, 763.
5. Whorf, "Science and Linguis-
tics," in *Readings in Social Psychology,* pp. 210–218; Lee, "A Linguistic Approach to a System of
Values," in *Readings in Social Psychology,* pp. 219–224.
6. See chapter v.
7. Bruner and Postman, "An Approach to Social Perception," in
Dennis (ed.), *Current Trends in
Social Psychology,* pp. 71–118.
8. Varga, *Two Systems,* p. 241.

Bibliography

Bibliography

Books and Pamphlets

Abramov, Ark., and A. Y. Aleksandrov, *Partiya v Rekonstruktivnyi Period* (The Party in the Period of Reconstruction). Moscow, 1934.

Anglo-Sovetskie Otnosheniya: So Dnya Podpisaniya Torgovogo Soglasheniya do Razryva 1921–1927 gg., Noty i Dokumenty (Anglo-Soviet Relations: From the Day of the Signing of the Trade Agreement to the Break, 1921–1927, Notes and Documents). Moscow, 1927.

Ashby, Eric, *Scientist in Russia*. London, 1947.

Barbusse, Henri (editor), *The Soviet Union and Peace*. London, n.d.

Barmine, Alexander, *One Who Survived*. New York, 1945.

Batsell, Walter Russell, *Soviet Rule in Russia*. New York, 1929.

Baykov, Alexander, *The Development of the Soviet Economic System*. London, 1946.

Bazili, N. A., *Rossiya pod Sovetskoi Vlast'iu* (Russia Under the Soviet Power). Paris, 1937.

Beloff, Max, *The Foreign Policy of Soviet Russia, 1929–1941*. Vol. I, London, 1947. Vol. II, London, 1949.

Berdyaev, Nicolas, *The Origin of Russian Communism*. Second edition, London, 1948.

Bergson, Abram, *The Structure of Soviet Wages*. Cambridge: Harvard University Press, 1944.

Berlin, P. A., *Russkaya Burzhuaziya v Staroye i Novoye Vremya* (The Russian Bourgeoisie in Old and New Times). Moscow, 1922.

Bettelheim, Ch., *La Planification soviétique*. Paris, n.d.

Bienstock, Gregory, Solomon M. Schwarz, and Aaron Yugow, *Management in Russian Industry and Agriculture*. New York, 1944.

Bogolepov, M. I., *Sovetskaya Finansovaya Sistema* (The Soviet Financial System). Moscow, 1945.

Bol'shaya Sovetskaya Entsiklopediya (Large Soviet Encyclopedia). 65 vols. Moscow, 1926–1939. A special volume was published in 1948: *Bol'shaya Sovetskaya Entsiklopediya: Soiuz Sovetskikh Sotsialisticheskikh Respublik*. Moscow.

Borkenau, Franz, *The Communist International*. London, 1938.

Bukharin, N. I., *Ergebnisse des VI. Kongresses der Kommunistischen Internationale*. Moscow, 1929.

Bukharin, N. I., *K Voprosu o Trotskizme* (On the Question of Trotskyism). Moscow-Leningrad, 1925.

—— *Nieder mit der Fraktionsmacherei.* Hamburg, 1924.

—— *Oekonomik der Transformationsperiode.* Trans. by Frida Rubiner. Hamburg, 1922.

—— *Die Probleme der Chinesischen Revolution.* Hamburg-Berlin, 1927.

—— *Put' k Sotsializmu i Raboche-Krest'yanskii Soiuz* (The Road to Socialism and the Worker-Peasant Union). Fourth edition, Moscow, 1927.

—— *Über die Bauernfrage; Rede vor der Erweiterten Executive, April, 1925.* Hamburg, 1925.

Bukharin, N. I., and E. Preobrazhensky, *Azbuka Kommunizma* (The ABC of Communism). New York, 1921.

Byrnes, James F., *Speaking Frankly.* New York, 1947.

Chamberlin, William Henry, *Russia's Iron Age.* Boston, 1935.

—— *The Russian Revolution, 1917–1921.* 2 vols. New York, 1935.

Ciliga, A., *Au Pays du Grand Mensonge.* Paris, 1938.

Communist International, *see* Kommunisticheskii Internatsional.

Communist Party of the Soviet Union (Bolsheviks), *see* Vsesoiuznaya Kommunisticheskaya Partiya (b).

Dallin, David J., *The Real Soviet Russia.* New Haven, 1944.

—— *The Rise of Russia in Asia.* New Haven, 1949.

—— *Soviet Russia and the Far East.* New Haven, 1948.

—— *Soviet Russia's Foreign Policy 1939–1942.* New Haven, 1942.

Dallin, David J., and Boris I. Nicolaevsky, *Forced Labor in Soviet Russia.* New Haven, 1947.

Dan, F. I., *Proiskhozhdeniye Bol'shevizma* (The Origin of Bolshevism). New York, 1946.

Deane, John R., *The Strange Alliance.* New York, 1947.

De Grazia, Sebastian, *The Political Community: A Study in Anomie.* Chicago, 1948.

Denisov, A., *Sovety—Politicheskaya Osnova SSSR* (Soviets—The Political Basis of the USSR). Moscow, 1940.

Dennis, Wayne (editor), *Current Trends in Social Psychology.* Pittsburgh, 1948.

Desyat' Let Sovetskoi Diplomatii; Akty i Dokumenty (Ten Years of Soviet Diplomacy; Papers and Documents). Moscow, 1927.

Deutscher, Isaac, *Stalin: A Political Biography.* New York and London, 1949.

Dimitrov, G., *V Borbe za Edinyi Front Protiv Fashizma i Voiny: Stat'i i Rechi 1935–1937* (In the Struggle for a United Front Against Fascism and War: Articles and Speeches 1935–1937). Moscow, 1937.

Diskussionnyi Sbornik, Voprosy Partiinogo Stroitel'stva (Discussion Collection, Questions of Party Construction). Moscow, 1923.

Dobb, Maurice, *Russian Economic Development since the Revolution.* New York, 1928.

—— *Soviet Economic Development Since 1917.* London, 1948.

Entsiklopediya Gosudarstva i Prava (Encyclopedia of Government and Law). 3 vols. Moscow, 1925–1927.

Erklärung der Fünfhundert; Flugschrift des Verlags der Fahne des Kommunismus. N.p., n.d.

Evtikhiev, I. I., and V. A. Vlasov, *Administrativnoye Pravo SSSR: Uchebnik dlya Iuridicheskikh Institutov i Fakul'tetov* (The Administrative Law of the USSR: A Textbook for Juridical Institutes and Faculties). Moscow, 1946.

Fainsod, Merle, *International Socialism and the World War.* Cambridge: Harvard University Press, 1935.

Fairbank, John K., *The United States and China.* Cambridge: Harvard University Press, 1948.

Finansy SSSR za XXX Let 1917–1947 (The Finances of the USSR for Thirty Years, 1917–1947). Moscow, 1947.

Fischer, Louis, *Men and Politics.* New York, 1941.

—— *The Soviets in World Affairs.* 2 vols. London, 1930.

Fischer, Ruth, *Stalin and German Communism.* Cambridge: Harvard University Press, 1948.

Flechtheim, Ossip K., *Die KPD in der Weimarer Republik.* Offenbach a. M., 1948.

Florinsky, Michael T., *World Revolution and the USSR.* New York, 1933.

Glebov, N., *Nash Osnovnoi Zakon, Raz'yasneniye Konstitutsii Rossiiskoi Sotsialisticheskoi Federativnoi Sovetskoi Respubliki* (Our Fundamental Law, An Explanation of the Constitution of the Russian Socialist Federated Soviet Republic). Moscow, 1918.

Godovoi Otchet Narodnogo Kommissariata po Inostrannym Delam za 1924 g. (Annual Report of the People's Commissariat for Foreign Affairs for 1924). Moscow, 1925.

Gordon, Manya, *Workers Before and After Lenin.* New York, 1941.

Grazhdanskii Protsessual'nyi Kodeks: Ofitsial'nyi Tekst s Izmeneniyami na 1 Sentyabrya 1947 g. i s Prilozheniyem Postateinosistematizirovannykh Materialov (The Code of Civil Suits: Official Text with Changes up to September 1, 1947, and with an Appendix of Materials Systematized by Paragraphs). Moscow, 1948.

Gsovski, Vladimir, *Soviet Civil Law.* 2 vols. Ann Arbor, 1948.

Gurian, Waldemar, *Bolshevism: Theory and Practice.* Trans. by E. I. Watkin. New York, 1932.

Gyorgy, Andrew, *Governments of Danubian Europe.* New York, 1949.

Historical Statistics of the United States, 1789–1945. A supplement to the Statistical Abstract of the United States. Department of Commerce, Washington, 1949.

History of the Communist Party of the Soviet Union (Bolsheviks) Short Course. New York, 1939.

Hubbard, Leonard E., *The Economics of Soviet Agriculture.* London, 1939.

Inkeles, Alex, *Public Opinion in Soviet Russia.* Cambridge: Harvard University Press, 1950.

Iubileinaya Sessiya Akademii Nauk SSSR (Jubilee Session of the Academy of Sciences of the USSR). Moscow-Leningrad, 1943.

Jucker, Ernst, *Erlebtes Russland.* Bern, 1945.

Kaganovich, L. M., *Ocherednye Zadachi Partraboty i Reorganizatsiya Partapparata* (The Next Tasks in Party Work and the Reorganization of the Party Apparatus). Moscow, 1930.

Kalinin, M. I., *Stat'i i Rechi 1919–1935 gg.* (Speeches and Articles, 1919–1935). Moscow, 1936.

Kamenev i Zinoviev v 1917 g., Fakty i Dokumenty (Kamenev and Zinoviev in 1917, Facts and Documents). Second edition, Moscow, 1927.

Kautsky, Karl, *Die Agrarfrage.* Second edition, Stuttgart, 1902.

Kliuchnikov, Iu. V., and A. V. Sabanin, *Mezhdunarodnaya Politika Noveishego Vremeni v Dogovorakh, Notakh i Deklaratsiyakh* (International Politics of Modern Times in Treaties, Notes, and Declarations). 3 parts. Moscow, 1925–1929.

Knight, Frank H., *The Economic Organization.* Chicago, 1933.

Koch, Woldemar, *Die Bol'ševistischen Gewerkschaften.* Jena, 1932.

Kommunisticheskii Internatsional (Communist International). Summary notes, selected reports, and stenographic reports:

—— *Pervyi Kongress Kommunisticheskogo Internatsionala, Protokoly zasedanii v Moskve so 2 po 19 marta 1919 goda* (First Congress of the Communist International, Protocols of the Meetings in Moscow, March 2–19, 1919). Petrograd, 1921.

—— *Vtoroi Kongress Kommunisticheskogo Internatsionala, Stenograficheskii Otchet* (Second Congress of the Communist International, Stenographic Report). Held in Petrograd, July 19–August 6, 1920. Petrograd, 1921.

—— *Protokoll des III. Kongresses der Kommunistischen Internationale.* Held in Moscow, June 22–July 12, 1921. Hamburg, 1921.

—— *IV Vsemirnyi Kongress Kommunisticheskogo Internatsionala, Izbrannye Doklady, Rechi i Rezoliutsii* (Fourth World Congress of the Communist International, Selected Reports, Speeches, and Resolutions). Held in Petrograd, November 5–December 3, 1922. Moscow-Petrograd, 1923.

—— *Pyatyi Vsemirnyi Kongress Kommunisticheskogo Internatsionala, Stenograficheskii Otchet* (Fifth World Congress of the Communist International, Stenographic Report). Held in Moscow, June 17—July 8, 1924. 2 vols. Moscow, 1925.

—— *La Correspondance internationale, compte rendu sténographique du VIe Congrès de l'Internationale Communiste, Moscou, 17 juillet–septembre 1928.* No. 69, July 26, 1928–No. 149, December 11, 1928.

—— *Report of the Seventh World Congress of the Communist International.* Held in Moscow, July 25–August 20, 1935. London, 1936.

—— *Kommunisticheskii Internatsional v Dokumentakh 1919–1932* (The Communist International in Documents 1919–1932). Edited by Béla Kun. Moscow, 1933.

Kratkaya Sovetskaya Entsiklopediya (Brief Soviet Encyclopedia). Moscow, 1943.

Kravchenko, Victor, *I Chose Freedom.* New York, 1946.

Kroeber, A. L., *Configurations of Culture Growth.* Berkeley and Los Angeles, 1944.

Larin, I., and L. Kritzmann, *Wirtschaftsleben und wirtschaftlicher Aufbau in Sowjet-Russland, 1917–1920.* Hamburg, 1921.

Lasswell, Harold D., *World Politics and Personal Insecurity.* New York, 1935.

Lasswell, Harold D., and others, *Language of Politics.* New York, 1949.

Lenczowski, George, *Russia and the West in Iran 1918–1948.* Ithaca, 1949.

Lenin, V. I., *Selected Works.* 12 vols. New York, n.d.

—— *Sochineniya* (Collected Works). 30 vols. Second edition, Moscow-Leningrad, 1926–1932.

—— *Sochineniya* (Collected Works). Several vols. Fourth edition, Moscow, 1941—.

Leninskii Sbornik (Leninist Collection). Several vols. Moscow, 1925—. Second and third editions, Moscow, 1925—.

Liberman, Simon, *Building Lenin's Russia.* Chicago, 1945.

Littlepage, John D., and Demaree Bess, *In Search of Soviet Gold.* New York, 1937.

Litvinov, M. M., *Vneshnyaya Politika SSSR, Rechi i Zayavleniya 1927–1935* (Foreign Policy of the USSR, Speeches and Statements, 1927–1935). Moscow, 1935.

Lorimer, Frank, *The Population of the Soviet Union: History and Prospects.* Geneva, 1946.

Maisky, Ivan, *Vneshnyaya Politika RSFSR 1917–1922* (The Foreign Policy of the RSFSR, 1917–1922). Moscow, 1923.

Malaya Sovetskaya Entsiklopediya (Small Soviet Encyclopedia). 10 vols. Moscow, 1928–.

Mandelshtam, L., N. Rebrov, and P. Tumanov, *Vybory v Mestnye Sovety Deputatov Trudyashchikhsya* (Elections of Workers' Deputies to the Local Soviets). Moscow, 1939.

Marx, Karl, *Selected Works*. 2 vols. New York, n.d.

Marx, Karl, and Friedrich Engels, *The German Ideology*. Edited by R. Pascal. New York, 1939.

Maynard, Sir John, *Russia in Flux*. London, 1941.

—— *The Russian Peasant and Other Studies*. London, 1943.

Merton, Robert K., *Social Theory and Social Structure*. Glencoe, Illinois, 1949.

Mikolajczyk, Stanislaw, *The Rape of Poland*. New York, 1948.

Mikolenko, Y. F., and A. N. Nikitin, *Kolkhoznoye Pravo* (Collective Farm Law). Moscow, 1946.

Miliukov, P., *La Politique extérieure des Soviets*. Paris, 1936.

—— *Ocherki po Istorii Russkoi Kul'tury* (Essays on the History of Russian Culture). 2 vols. Fourth edition, St. Petersburg, 1900.

—— *Rossiya na Perelome* (Russia in Upheaval). 2 vols. Paris, 1927.

Molotov, V. M., *Otchetnyi Doklad o Rabote Pravitel'stva VII S'ezdu Sovetov SSSR, 28 Yanvarya 1935 g.* (Report on the Work of the Government to the Seventh Congress of Soviets of the USSR, January 28, 1935). Moscow, 1935.

—— *Voprosy Vneshnei Politiki, Rechi i Zayavleniya, Aprel' 1945 g.– Iiun' 1948 g.* (Questions of Foreign Policy, Speeches and Declarations, April 1945–June 1948). Moscow, 1948.

Moore, Harriet L., *Soviet Far Eastern Policy, 1931–1945*. Princeton, 1945.

Morgenthau, Hans J., *Politics Among Nations: The Struggle for Power and Peace*. New York, 1948.

Mosca, Gaetano, *The Ruling Class*. Trans. by Hannah D. Kahn. New York, 1939.

Nazi-Soviet Relations, 1939–1941: Documents from the Archives of the German Foreign Office. Edited by Raymond J. Sontag and James S. Beddie. Department of State, Washington, 1948.

Northrop, F. S. C., *The Meeting of East and West: An Inquiry Concerning World Understanding*. New York, 1946.

Osnovy Sovetskogo Gosudarstva i Prava (The Foundations of the Soviet State and Law). Moscow, 1947.

Parsons, Talcott, *Essays in Sociological Theory*. Glencoe, Illinois, 1949.

Pashukanis, E. (editor), *15 Let Sovetskogo Stroitel'stva* (Fifteen Years of Soviet Construction). Moscow, 1932.

Piatnitsky, O., *Memoirs of a Bolshevik*. New York, n.d.

Plekhanov, G. B., *Sochineniya* (Collected Works). 24 vols. Second edition, Moscow, 1923–1927.

Political Economy in the Soviet Union. Trans. by Emily A. Kazakevich from *Pod Znamenem Marksizma* (Under the Banner of Marxism), Nos. 7–8, July–August 1943. New York, 1944.

Potemkin, V. P. (editor), *Istoriya Diplomatii* (History of Diplomacy). 3 vols. Moscow, 1945.

Primernyi Ustav Sel'skokhozyaistvennoi Arteli (Model Statute of the Agricultural Artel). Moscow, 1938.

Prokopovicz, S. N., *Russlands Volkswirtschaft unter den Sowjets.* Zürich, 1944.

Rabenau, Friedrich von, *Seeckt: Aus seinem Leben 1918–1936.* Leipzig, 1940.

Raskin, L. E., *Vospitaniye Distsiplinirovannosti* (Education in Discipline). Moscow, 1946.

Readings in Social Psychology. Edited by T. M. Newcomb, E. L. Hartley, and others. New York, 1947.

Report of Court Proceedings in the Case of the Anti-Soviet Trotskyite Centre: Heard before the Military Collegium of the Supreme Court of the USSR, Moscow, January 23–30, 1937. Verbatim report. Moscow, 1937.

Robinson, Geroid T., *Rural Russia under the Old Regime.* London and New York, 1932.

Rosenburg, Arthur, *Geschichte des Bolschewismus.* Berlin, 1932.

Rubinshtein, N., *Sovetskaya Rossiya i Kapitalisticheskie Gosudarstva v Gody Perekhoda ot Voiny k Miru 1921–1922* (Soviet Russia and the Capitalist States in the Years of Transition from War to Peace, 1921–1922). Moscow, 1948.

Russian Communist Party (Bolsheviks), *see* Vsesoiuznaya Kommunisticheskaya Partiya (b).

Russian Social Democratic Labor Party, *see* Vsesoiuznaya Kommunisticheskaya Partiya (b).

Schlesinger, Rudolf, *Soviet Legal Theory: Its Social Background and Development.* London, 1945.

Scott, John, *Behind the Urals.* Boston and New York, 1942.

S'ezdy Sovetov SSSR v Postanovleniyakh i Rezoliutsiyakh (The Congresses of Soviets of the USSR in Decrees and Resolutions). Edited by A. Y. Vyshinsky. Moscow, 1939.

Sherwood, Robert E., *Roosevelt and Hopkins: An Intimate History.* New York, 1948.

Shore, Maurice J., *Soviet Education.* New York, 1947.

Snow, Edgar, *People on Our Side.* New York, 1944.

Sobraniye Postanovlenii i Rasporyazhenii Soveta Ministrov Soiuza Sovetskikh Sotsialisticheskikh Respublik (Collection of Decrees and

Ordinances of the Council of Ministers of the USSR). Several vols. Moscow, 1917–.

Sobraniye Zakonov i Rasporyazhenii Raboche-Krest'yanskogo Pravitel'-stva SSSR (Collection of Laws and Ordinances of the Worker-Peasant Government of the USSR). Several vols. Moscow, 1923–1938.

Socialism Victorious. An English translation of the most important speeches delivered at the Seventeenth Congress of the Party in 1934. New York, n.d.

SSSR Strana Sotsialzma (USSR, Land of Socialism). Moscow, 1936.

Sorokin, G., *Sotsialisticheskoye Planirovaniye Narodnogo Khozyaistva SSSR* (Socialist Planning of the Economy of the USSR). Moscow, 1946.

Souvarine, Boris, *Staline: Aperçu historique du bolchévisme.* Paris, 1935.

Sovetskoye Gosudarstvennoye Ustroistvo, Lektsii dlya Rabotnikov Nizogo Sovetskogo Apparata (Soviet State Structure, Readings for the Workers of the Lower Soviet Apparatus). Edited by G. S. Gurvich, F. T. Ivanov, and V. N. Maksimovsky. Moscow, 1930.

Sovetskoye Trudovoye Pravo (Soviet Labor Law). Edited by N. G. Aleksandrov and D. M. Genkin. Moscow, 1946.

The Soviet-Yugoslav Dispute. Text of the published correspondence. London and New York, 1948.

Spiridovich, A. L., *Istoriya Bol'shevizma v Rossii* (History of Bolshevism in Russia). Paris, 1922.

Spykman, Nicholas J., *America's Strategy in World Politics: The United States and the Balance of Power.* New York, 1942.

Iosif Vissarionovich Stalin, Kratkaya Biografiya (Joseph Vissarionovich Stalin, Short Biography). Moscow, 1944.

Stalin, I. V., *Ob Industrializatsii Strany i o Pravom Uklone, Rech' na Plenume TsK VKP(b), 19 Noyabrya 1928 g.* (On the Industrialization of the Country and the Right Deviation, Speech at the Plenum of the Central Committee of the CPSU(b), November 19, 1928). Moscow, 1928.

—— *Ob Oppozitsii: Stat'i i Rechi 1921–1927 gg.* (On the Opposition: Articles and Speeches, 1921–1927). Moscow, 1928.

—— *The October Revolution.* New York, 1934.

—— *O Nedostatkakh Partiinoi Raboty i Merakh Likvidatsii Trot-skistskikh i Inykh Dvurushnikov* (Concerning the Inadequacies of Party Work and Measures for the Liquidation of the Trotskyites and Other Double Dealers). Pamphlet, containing Stalin's speech and concluding remarks at the Plenum of the Central Committee of the CPSU(b), March 3–5, 1937. Moscow, 1937.

—— *O Velikoi Otechestvennoi Voine Sovetskogo Soiuza* (The Great

Patriotic War of the Soviet Union). Fourth edition, Moscow, 1944.

Stalin, I. V., *Problems of Leninism*. Eleventh edition, Moscow, 1941.

—— *Sochineniya* (Collected Works). Several vols. Moscow, 1946–.

Stettinius, Edward R., Jr., *Roosevelt and the Russians: The Yalta Conference*. New York, 1949.

Stuchka, P., *Ucheniye o Gosudarstve i o Konstitutsii RSFSR* (Theory of the State and of the Constitution of the RSFSR). Moscow, 1923.

Supreme Soviet of the USSR, *see* Verkhovnyi Sovet SSSR.

Taracouzio, T. A., *War and Peace in Soviet Diplomacy*. New York, 1940.

Timasheff, Nicholas S., *The Great Retreat*. New York, 1946.

Towster, Julian, *Political Power in the USSR, 1917–1947*. New York, 1948.

Trotsky, Leon, *Defence of Terrorism*. London, 1935.

—— *The First Five Years of the Communist International*. Trans. and edited by John G. Wright. 2 vols. New York, 1945.

—— *Geschichte der Russischen Revolution*. 2 vols. Berlin, 1931.

—— *Kak Vooruzhalas' Revoliutsiya* (How the Revolution was Armed). 3 vols. Moscow, 1923–1925.

—— *K Sotsializmu ili k Kapitalizmu?* (Toward Socialism or Capitalism?). Moscow-Leningrad, 1925.

—— *Lessons of October*. Trans. by John G. Wright. New York, 1937.

—— *My Life*. New York, 1930.

—— *Novyi Kurs* (New Course). Moscow, 1924.

—— *On the Suppressed Testament of Lenin*. Pamphlet. Second edition, New York, 1946.

—— *Our Revolution: Essays on Working Class and International Revolution, 1904–1917*. Trans. by Moissaye J. Olgin. New York, 1918.

—— *Permanentnaya Revoliutsiya* (Permanent Revolution). Berlin, 1930.

—— *Problems of the Chinese Revolution*. Trans. by Max Schachtman. New York, 1932.

—— *The Real Situation in Russia*. Trans. by Max Eastman. New York, 1928.

—— *The Revolution Betrayed*. Trans. by Max Eastman. New York, 1945.

—— *Sochineniya* (Collected Works). Vol. XV. Moscow-Leningrad, 1927.

—— *Stalin: An Appraisal of the Man and his Influence*. Edited and trans. by Charles Malamuth. New York, 1941.

—— *The Stalin School of Falsification*. Trans. by John G. Wright. New York, 1937.

478   *Bibliography*

Trudy Pervogo Vsesoiuznogo Soveshchaniya Sel'sko-khozyaistvennykh Kollektivov (Proceedings of the First All-Union Conference of Agricultural Collectives). Moscow, 1925.

United States Relations with China. Department of State, Washington, 1949.

Varga, Eugene, *Two Systems: Socialist Economy and Capitalist Economy.* Trans. by R. Page Arnot. New York, 1939.

Venediktov, A. V., *Gosudarstvennaya Sotsialisticheskaya Sobstvennost'* (The Socialist Property of the State). Moscow-Leningrad, 1948.

Verkhovnyi Sovet SSSR (Supreme Soviet of the USSR). Stenographic reports:

―― *Zasedaniya Verkhovnogo Soveta SSSR (Pervaya Sessiya), 12–19 Marta 1946 g., Stenograficheskii Otchet* (Sessions of the Supreme Soviet of the USSR, First Session, March 12–19, 1946, Stenographic Report). Moscow, 1946.

―― *Zasedaniya Verkhovnogo Soveta SSSR (Vtoraya Sessiya), 15–18 Oktyabrya 1946 g., Stenograficheskii Otchet* (Sessions of the Supreme Soviet of the USSR, Second Session, October 15–18, 1946, Stenographic Report). Moscow, 1946.

Vernadsky, George, *A History of Russia.* New Haven, 1933.

Vneshnyaya Politika Sovetskogo Soiuza v Period Otechestvennoi Voiny (The Foreign Policy of the Soviet Union in the Period of the Patriotic War). 2 vols. Moscow, 1946.

Voznesensky, N., *Voennaya Ekonomika SSSR v Period Otechestvennoi Voiny* (The War Economy of the USSR in the Period of the Patriotic War). Moscow, 1948.

Vsesoiuznaya Kommunisticheskaya Partiya (b) (All-Union Communist Party (Bolsheviks)), present name of the Communist Party of the Soviet Union; formerly a wing of the Rossiiskaya Sotsial-demokraticheskaya Rabochaya Partiya (Russian Social Democratic Labor Party); and later called Rossiiskaya Kommunisticheskaya Partiya (b) (Russian Communist Party (Bolsheviks)). Directives, summary notes, resolutions, and stenographic reports of congresses and conferences, as follows:

DIRECTIVES

―― *Direktivy VKP (b) i Postanovleniya Sovetskogo Pravitel'stva o Narodnom Obrazovanii za 1917–1947 gg.* (Directives of the All-Union Communist Party (Bolsheviks) and the Decrees of the Soviet Government on Popular Education, 1917–1947.) 2 vols. Moscow-Leningrad, 1947.

―― *Direktivy VKP(b) po Khozyaistvennym Voprosam* (Directives of the CPSU(b) on Economic Questions). Edited by M. Savel'ev and A. Poskrebishev. Moscow, 1931.

SUMMARY NOTES

—— *Protokoly Tsentral'nogo Komiteta RSDRP, Avgust 1917–Fevral' 1918* (Protocols of the Central Committee of the Russian Social Democratic Labor Party, August 1917–February 1918). Moscow, 1929.

RESOLUTIONS

—— *Rossiiskaya Kommunisticheskaya Partiya (Bolshevikov) v Rezoliutsiyakh Eë S'ezdov i Konferentsii 1898–1922 gg.* (The Russian Communist Party (Bolsheviks) in the Resolutions of its Congresses and Conferences, 1898–1922). Moscow, 1923.

—— *VKP(b) v Rezoliutsiyakh Eë S'ezdov i Konferentsii 1898–1926* (The CPSU(b) in the Resolutions of its Congresses and Conferences, 1898–1926). Third edition, Moscow, 1927.

—— *VKP (b) v Rezoliutsiyakh i Resheniyakh S'ezdov, Konferentsii i Plenumov TsK* (The CPSU(b) in the Resolutions and Decisions of Congresses, Conferences, and Plenums of the Central Committee). Fourth edition. Vol. I (1898–1924), Moscow, 1932. Vol. II (1924–1933), Moscow, 1933.

—— *VKP(b) v Rezoliutsiyakh i Resheniyakh S'ezdov, Konferentsii i Plenumov TsK (1898–1939)* (The CPSU(b) in the Resolutions and Decisions of Congresses, Conferences, and Plenums of the Central Committee [1898–1939]). Sixth edition. Vol. I (1898–1925), Moscow, 1940. Vol. II (1925–1939), Moscow, 1941.

CONGRESSES

—— *Protokoly Shestogo S'ezda RSDRP(b)* (Protocols of the Sixth Congress of the Russian Social Democratic Labor Party (Bolsheviks)). Held in Petrograd, August 8–16, 1917. Moscow, 1934.

—— *Protokoly VIII S'ezda RKP(b)* (Protocols of the Eighth Congress of the Russian Communist Party (Bolsheviks)). Held in Moscow, March 18–23, 1919. Moscow, 1933.

—— *Protokoly Devyatogo S'ezda RKP(b)* (Protocols of the Ninth Congress of the RKP(b)). Held in Moscow, March 29–April 4, 1920. Moscow, 1934.

—— *Protokoly Desyatogo S'ezda RKP(b)* (Protocols of the Tenth Congress of the RKP(b)). Held in Moscow, March 8–16, 1921. Moscow, 1921.

—— *Odinadtsatyi S'ezd RKP(b)*, *Stenograficheskii Otchet* (Eleventh Congress of the RKP(b), Stenographic Report). Held in Moscow, March 27–April 2, 1922. Moscow, 1936.

—— *Dvenadtsatyi S'ezd RKP(b)*, *Stenograficheskii Otchet* (Twelfth Congress of the RKP(b) Stenographic Report). Held in Moscow, April 17–25, 1923. Moscow, 1923.

—— *Trinadtsatyi S'ezd RKP(b)*, *Stenograficheskii Otchet* (Thirteenth Congress of the RKP(b), Stenographic Report). Held in Moscow, May 23–31, 1924. Moscow, 1924.

—— *XIV S'ezd VKP (b)*, *Stenograficheskii Otchet* (Fourteenth Congress of the All-Union Communist Party (Bolsheviks), Stenographic Report). Held in Moscow, December 18–31, 1925. Moscow-Leningrad, 1926.

—— *XV S'ezd VKP(b)*, *Stenograficheskii Otchet* (Fifteenth Congress of the CPSU(b), Stenographic Report). Held in Moscow, December 2–19, 1927. Moscow-Leningrad, 1928.

—— *XVI S'ezd VKP(b)*, *Stenograficheskii Otchet* (Sixteenth Congress of the CPSU(b), Stenographic Report). Held in Moscow, June 26–July 13, 1930. Second edition, Moscow-Leningrad, 1931.

—— *XVII S'ezd VKP(b)*, *Stenograficheskii Otchet* (Seventeenth Congress of the CPSU(b), Stenographic Report). Held in Moscow, January 26–February 10, 1934. Moscow, 1934.

—— *XVIII S'ezd VKP(b)*, *Stenograficheskii Otchet* (Eighteenth Congress of the CPSU(b), Stenographic Report). Held in Moscow, March 10–21, 1939. Moscow, 1939.

CONFERENCES

—— *XIV Konferentsiya RKP(b)*, *Stenograficheskii Otchet* (Fourteenth Conference of the Russian Communist Party (Bolsheviks), Stenographic Report). Held in Moscow, April 27–29, 1925. Moscow-Leningrad, 1925.

—— *XV Konferentsiya VKP(b)*, *Stenograficheskii Otchet* (Fifteenth Conference of the All-Union Communist Party (Bolsheviks), Stenographic Report). Held in Moscow, October 26–November 3, 1926. Moscow, 1927.

—— *XVI Konferentsiya VKP(b)*, *Stenograficheskii Otchet* (Sixteenth Conference of the CPSU (b), Stenographic Report). Held in Moscow, April 23–29, 1929. Moscow-Leningrad, 1929.

Walter, Gérard, *Histoire du parti communiste français*. Paris, 1948.

Webb, Sidney and Beatrice, *Soviet Communism: A New Civilization?* 2 vols. New York, 1936.

White, D. Fedotoff, *The Growth of the Red Army*. Princeton, 1944.

Wolfe, Bertram D., *Three Who Made a Revolution*. New York, 1948.

Yakhontoff, Victor A., *The Chinese Soviets*. New York, 1934.
Yal'tsev, P., *Malen'kie P'esy* (Short Plays). Moscow-Leningrad, 1937.
Yugow, A., *Russia's Economic Front for War and Peace*. New York, 1942.
Yvon, L., *L'U.R.S.S. telle qu'elle est*. Paris, 1938.
Zetkin, Clara, *Erinnerungen an Lenin*. Vienna and Berlin, 1929.
Zhdanov, A. A., *Izmeneniya v Ustave VKP(b), Doklad na XVIII S'ezde VKP(b)* (Changes in the Statute of the All-Union Communist Party (Bolsheviks), Report to the Eighteenth Congress of the All-Union Communist Party (Bolsheviks)). Moscow, 1939.
Zinoviev, G., *Probleme der deutschen Revolution*. Hamburg, 1923.

JOURNALS AND NEWSPAPERS

American Political Science Review:
Moore, Barrington, Jr., "The Influence of Ideas on Policies as Shown in the Collectivization of Agriculture in Russia." August 1947.
Nemzer, Louis, "The Kremlin's Professional Staff: The 'Apparatus' of the Central Committee, Communist Party of the Soviet Union." March 1950.
American Sociological Review:
Mandel, William, "Democratic Aspects of Soviet Government Today." June 1944.
Moore, Barrington, Jr., "The Communist Party of the Soviet Union: 1928–1944." June 1944.
Annals of the American Academy of Political and Social Science:
Neumann, Franz L., "Soviet Policy in Germany." May 1949.
Bol'shevik. Theoretical organ of the Central Committee of the CPSU(b):
"Beseda tovarishcha Stalina s . . . Gospodinom Roy Govardom" (Comrade Stalin's Interview with . . . Roy Howard). No. 6, March 15, 1936.
Kaganovich, L., "O vnutripartiinoi rabote i otdelakh rukovodyashchikh partorganov" (Concerning Internal Party Work and the Sections of Leading Party Organs). No. 21, November 15, 1934.
Karavaev, A., "O dal'neishem ukreplenii sel'skokhozyaistvennoi arteli" (On the Further Strengthening of the Agricultural Artel). No. 8, April 30, 1948.
Khmelevsky, K., "O nekotorykh voprosakh raboty apparata partiinykh komitetov—Iz praktiki raboty Molotovskogo obkoma

VKP(b)" (On Certain Questions of the Work of the Apparatus of Party Committees—From the Practices of the Work of the Molotov *Oblast'* Committee of the CPSU(b). No. 23, December 15, 1948.

Khrushchev, N., "Bol'sheviki Ukrainy v bor'be za vosstanovleniye i razvitiye khozyaistva i kul'tury USSR—Iz otchetnogo doklada na XVI s'ezde KP(b)U 25 yanvarya 1948 g." (The Bolsheviks in the Ukraine in the Struggle for the Restoration and Development of the Economy and Culture of the Ukrainian Soviet Socialist Republic—From the Report to the Sixteenth Congress of the Communist Party (Bolsheviks) of the Ukraine, January 25, 1949). No. 3, February 15, 1949.

Kovalev, S., "Intelligentsiya v sovetskom gosudarstve" (The Intelligentsia in the Soviet Government). No. 2, January 1946.

"Nekotorye itogi vyborov partiinykh organov, po materialam otdela rukovodyashchikh partorganov TsK VKP(b)" (Some Results of the Elections of Party Organs, from Materials of the Section on Leading Party Organs of the Central Committee of the CPSU(b). No. 10, May 15, 1937.

"Otvet I. V. Stalina na otkrytoye pis'mo g. Uollesa" (Reply of I. V. Stalin to the Open Letter of Mr. Wallace). No. 10, May 30, 1948.

"Peredovaya—rezhim ekonomii—metod sotsialisticheskogo khozyaistvovaniya" (Editorial Introduction—The Regime of Economics—A Method of Socialist Management). Nos. 23–24, December 1946.

Shatalin, N., "Doklad mandatnoi kommissii XVIII vsesoiuznoi konferentsii VKP(b)" (Report of the Mandate Commission at the Eighteenth All-Union Conference of the CPSU(b)). Nos. 3–4, February 1941.

Zhdanov, A. A., "Doklad na plenume TsK VKP(b) 26 fevralya 1937 goda" (Speech at the Plenum of the Central Committee of the CPSU(b), February 26, 1937). Nos. 5–6, March 15, 1937.

The Communist International:

Text of radio message to Communist leaders in Munich. No. 1, May 1, 1919.

"Letter from Comrade Béla Khun to Comrade Lenin." No. 2, June 1, 1919.

Foreign Affairs:

Historicus, "Stalin on Revolution." January 1949.

Revai, Josef, "On the Character of Our People's Democracy," as translated from the journal *Tarsadalmi Szemle,* March–April, 1949. October 1949.

Information Bulletin. Publication of the Embassy of the USSR, Washington, D. C.

International Affairs:

    Atkinson, George W., "The Sino-Soviet Treaty of Friendship and Alliance." July 1947.

    Warriner, Doreen, "Economic Changes in Eastern Europe since the War." April 1949.

Izvestiya Sovetov Deputatov Trudyashchikhsya SSSR (News of the Soviets of Toilers' Deputies of the USSR). Daily newspaper.

Izvestiya TsK VKP(b) (News of the Central Committee of the CPSU(b)). Organ of the Party Central Committee.

Journal of Economic History:

    Gerschenkron, Alexander, "The Rate of Industrial Growth in Russia Since 1885." Supplement VII, 1947.

Kommunisticheskii Internatsional:

    "Teoretischeskie vyvody tov. Bukharina i politicheskii vyvod Kommunisticheskogo Internatsionala" (The Theoretical Conclusions of Comrade Bukharin and the Political Conclusion of the Communist International). Nos. 34–35, August 31, 1929.

Mitteilungsblatt (*Linke Opposition der KPD*). No. 3, February 1, 1927. Later known as *Fahne des Kommunismus.*

New Times. English-language edition of *Novoye Vremya,* weekly journal published by *Trud:*

    Perevertailo, A., "People's Republic Established in China." No. 41, October 5, 1949.

Partiinoye Stroitel'stvo (Party Construction). A publication of the Central Committee of the CPSU(b):

    Kaganovich, L., "Ob apparate TsK VKP(b)" (On the Apparatus of the Central Committee of the CPSU(b)). No. 2, February 1930.

    Nazarov, P., "Otchetnost'—osnova demokraticheskogo tsentralizma" (Responsibility—the Basis of Democratic Centralism). No. 9, May 1, 1938.

    "Obzor predlozhenii k tezisam doklada tov. Zhdanova na XVIII s'ezde VKP(b)" (Survey of the Proposals Concerning the Theses of Comrade Zhdanov's Speech for the Eighteenth Congress of the CPSU(b)). No. 5, March 1939.

    "O nekotorykh meropriyatiyakh v svyazi s itogami vyborov rukovodyashchikh partiinykh organov" (Concerning Certain Measures in Connection with the Results of the Elections of Leading Party Organs). Nos. 19–20, October 1938.

    "Protokoly partiinykh sobranii i zasedanii" (Protocols of Party Meetings and Sessions). No. 21, November 1940.

    Rodionov, M., "Otchety i vybory v pervichnykh partorganizatsiyakh Gor'kovskoi oblasti" (Reports and Elections in the Primary Party Organizations of the Gorky *Oblast'*). Nos. 5–6, March 1940.

    "Vazhnyi istochnik partiinoi informatsii" (Important Source of Party Information). Nos. 23–24, December 1940.

Planovoye Khozyaistvo (Planned Economy). Political-economic journal of the *Gosplan* (State Planning Commission):

Leont'ev, A., "K voprosam politicheskoi ekonomii sotsializma" (On Questions of the Political Economy of Socialism). No. 6, 1947.

Political Science Quarterly:

Curtiss, John S., and Alex Inkeles, "Marxism in the USSR—The Recent Revival." September 1946.

Pravda (Truth). Organ of the Central Committee and the Moscow Committee of the CPSU(b).

Professional'nye Soiuzy (Trade Unions). Organ of the All-Union Central Council of Trade Unions:

Amelin, K., "Posle otchetno-vybornykh sobranii nizovykh proforganizatsii" (After the Election Meetings of the Lower Trade-Union Organizations). No. 6, June 1947.

Amitin, I., "Uluchshit' okhranu truda v ugol'noi promyshlennosti" (Improve the Safeguarding of Labor in the Coal Industry). No. 6, June 1947.

Dneprovoi, I., "Pochemu s'ezd priznal rabotu TsK profsoiuza neudovletvoritel'noi" (Why the Congress Declared the Work of the Union Central Committee Unsatisfactory). No. 9, September 1947.

Gaisenok, N., "Voprosy okhrany truda v kollektivnom dogovore" (Questions of Safeguarding Labor in the Collective Agreement). No. 2, February 1947.

Il'in, P., "O normirovanii truda i organizatsii zarabotnoi platy" (On Setting the Rates of Labor and the Organization of Wages). No. 1, January 1947.

Kachnova, N., "O nekotorykh voprosakh rukovodstva fabkomami" (On Certain Questions Connected with the Leadership of the Factory Committees). Nos. 9–10, September–October 1946.

Kuznetsov, Al., "Kollektivnyi dogovor v deistvii" (The Collective Agreement in Practice). No. 12, December 1947.

Kuznetsov, V. V., "O zakliuchenii kollektivnykh dogovorov na 1947 god" (On the Conclusion of Collective Agreements for 1947). No. 2, February 1947.

Moskalenko, G., "Pravovye voprosy kollektivnogo dogovora" (Legal Questions Concerning the Collective Agreement). No. 8, August 1947.

——— "Rol' profsoiuzov v regulirovanii uslovii truda rabochikh i sluzhashchikh" (The Role of the Unions in the Regulation of the Conditions of Labor of Workers and Salaried Employees). No. 4, April 1947.

"Na s'ezdakh profsoiuzov" (At the Trade-Union Congresses). No. 6, June 1947.

Pavlik, V., "Uroki vypolneniya odnogo koldogovora" (Lessons from the Execution of a Collective Agreement). No. 12, December 1947.

"Peredovaya—Ukrepit' organizatsionnuiu rabotu profsoiuzov" (Editorial—Strengthen the Organizational Work of the Trade Unions). No. 8, August 1947.

"Postanovleniya XVI Plenuma VTsSPS" (Resolutions of the Sixteenth Plenum of the AUCCTU). No. 5, May 1947.

"Zabotlivo vyrashchivat' profsoiuznye kadry" (Cultivate Trade-Union Cadres with Care). No. 9, September 1947.

Quarterly Journal of Economics:
Erlich, Alexander, "Preobrazhenski and the Economics of Soviet Industrialization." No. 1, February 1950.

Russian Information and Review. Publication of the Information Department of the Russian Trade Delegation, London.

Sovetskoye Gosudarstvo i Pravo (Soviet State and Law):
Borisov, V., "Mestnye organy gosudarstvennoi vlasti v SSSR" (Local Organs of State Power in the USSR). No. 12, 1947.

Sovetskoye Stroitel'stvo (Soviet Construction). A publication of the Central Executive Committee of the USSR:
Il'insky, I., "Predely uprochneniya apparata" (The Limits to Simplifying the Apparatus). Nos. 5–6, May–June 1928.

"K perevybornoi kampanii sovetov" (On the Election Campaign in the Soviets). No. 11, November 1928.

Rivkin, O., "Uchastiye mass v rabote sovetov, po materialam obsledovaniya TsKK RKI" (The Participation of the Masses in the Work of the Soviets, Based on Materials of the Investigation of the Central Control Commission and the Workers' and Peasants' Inspection). No. 12, December 1928.

Sputnik Agitatora (The Agitator's Guidebook). Journal of the Central Committee and the Moscow Committee of the CPSU(b).

Trud (Labor). Daily organ of the All-Union Central Council of Trade Unions.

Voprosy Ekonomiki (Economic Questions). A weekly publication of the Institute of Economics, Academy of Sciences of the USSR:
Gertsovich, G., "Vosstanovleniye mirnoi ekonomiki v sovetskoi zone okkupatsii Germanii" (The Restoration of a Peace Economy in the Soviet Zone of Occupation in Germany). No. 1, 1948.

Vladimirov, P., "Za rentabel'nuyu rabotu predpriyatii" (Toward the Profitable Operation of a Plant). No. 8, 1948.

World Politics:
Leites, Nathan, and David Nelson Rowe, "Choice in China." April 1949.

Index

Academicians, 280, 281

Accountability, electoral: in government and soviets, 42, 275; in Party, 67–68, 139, 249, 261; in trade unions, 328–329

Adler, Friedrich, 127

Aggression and mass discontent: Party methods of channeling, 75–76, 118, 146, 174, 229, 234–235, 293–295, 329, 397, 403; and Soviet expansionism, 396–397

Agriculture: output under War Communism, 91; changes under NEP, 93–95; proposals for reorganization, 100–101, 103–104, 110–111; 1939 figures on scientific personnel, 280; system of authority, 289. *See also* Collective farms, Collectivization, Coöperatives, Peasants, Property

Agronomists, 280

All-Russian Central Executive Committee, 21

All-Russian Peasants' Union, 25

All-Union Central Council of Trade Unions, 181, 320, 328. *See also* Trade unions

Anarchists, 122, 127

Andreev, A. A., 340

Artists, 226–227, 280

Authoritarianism, *see* Authority, Communist Party, Leadership, Masses, Opposition, Status, Terror

Authority:
general features: in prerevolutionary theory, 40–45; system attacked by Party opposition, 93, 152–153, 171–172; factional conflicts over system, 101–102; problems of allocation, 286–290; in

agriculture, 289; in government offices, 289–290
process of centralization: effect of chronic crises, 117–118, 141, 142–143; general principles governing, 138; and bureaucratic competition, 295–296; in Party, 60, 63, 65–66, 141–142, 144, 152, 155, 264–269; in local soviets, 129–130, 136–137, 272–273; in industry, 166, 168–169, 300–302, 309, 313, 314–315, 316; in collective farms, 334–340; in trade unions, 327–331
See also Accountability, Aggression, Bolshevism, Clique, Communist Party, Policy, Responsibility

Bakunin, M. A., 29

Balance of power: general characteristics, 189–190, 351–352, 376, 400–401, 408; and Soviet foreign policy, 203–208, 350, 351, 353, 362–366, 370–371, 376–379, 382–384; structural demands of, 351–352, 390–391, 408–409; postwar polarization of, 370–371, 373, 400–401; and revolutionary aims, 404–405. *See also* Foreign policy

Banking, Soviet, 44, 305

Barmine, Alexander, 267

Bogdanov, A. A., 80

Bolshevik Center, 80

Bolshevism: origins of, 19–29; prerevolutionary goals, 29–32; goals reformulated after 1905, 33–34; problem of doctrinal consistency, 33, 35–36, 357–358, 387–389, 414; and doctrinal concessions, 35, 416–417; continuity in method of